CHIEF JUSTICE
The Judicial World of
Charles Doe

CHIEF JUSTICE

The Judicial World of
Charles Doe

John Phillip Reid

HARVARD UNIVERSITY PRESS

Cambridge, Massachusetts

1967

FOR MY FATHER

CONTENTS

CONTENTS

PART FOUR

THE CONSTITUTIONAL THEORIST

PART FIVE

THE LEGAL PHILOSOPHER

PART SIX

THE CHIEF JUSTICE

ILLUSTRATIONS

When David Cross of Manchester expressed the intention to praise Charles Doe in a speech, Doe said:

> "That will not do. No credit should be given to any living man, especially to a judge, for anything that he has done; wait until he is dead and then, in balancing the good and the bad, what is proved to be valuable and what injurious, speak of him as his life on the whole has proved to have been."

2 *Publications of the Southern New Hampshire Bar Association* 91 (1896).

PART ONE

THE WORLD

Chapter One

A RACE OF YANKEES

Ancestors

LAW, one school of jurisprudence maintains, is found in the changing needs of progressing society. Law is precedent and presence tempered by consideration for tomorrow. It is history as well as justice, experience as well as reason; and the judge who expounds it is speaking from the past as well as interpreting the present for the future. In any appreciation of his work, his ancestors are as important as his contemporaries, his father as immediate as his children. He is a product of his environment and an expression of his world.

Charles Cogswell Doe of New Hampshire was such a judge. Associate justice of the Supreme Judicial Court from 1859 to 1874 and chief justice of the Supreme Court from 1876 to 1896, he sought law from the traditions and circumstances of the society in which he lived. Doe was a Yankee, and his world was a Yankee world. By the time of Yorktown the New England Yankee was more than the forerunner of future English immigrants; he was the descendant of American pioneers. More than four generations of separation, hardship, and Indian wars had made him as different from the English as were his fellow English-speaking peoples, the Irish and the Scots. His laws, his customs, and his political institutions had their roots in the British Isles but were conditioned by the American experience.

The name of Doe appears in southern New Hampshire records from the beginning. Nicholas Doe was the first. Where he came from and how he got to New Hampshire no one can say. We know only that he was of English stock, probably from London, and that he owned land at Sagamore Creek in lower Portsmouth as early as 1663. From a legal document, a will he witnessed, we learn he was a freeman at least by November 15, 1666. Sometime before 1668 he married Martha Thomas.[1] Statutes required him to obtain her parents' consent, for it was a crime to "seeke to draw away ye affections of yong maydens." Dancing at the wedding was forbidden, and the statute books controlled many aspects of life, prescribing among other things the manner of dress. But though courts were active, there were no lawyers, and these prohibitions were probably enforced by religious sanctions, if at all.

Shortly after his marriage Nicholas Doe decided to leave Portsmouth. There were not many places in New Hampshire he could go. The two other settlements were Exeter and Dover, which together formed the frontier. Dover was the province's oldest town. On the west it straddled Great Bay, a saltwater estuary joined to the Atlantic by the Piscataqua. To the east it stretched from the Lamprey River, which marked the boundary with Exeter, to the Salmon Falls River, which marked the boundary with Maine and on the banks of which Charles Doe would live for most of his life. The land Nicholas Doe selected lay near the Lamprey, in a section of the Oyster River district of Dover known as Lubberland. He was not a pioneer in the classic mold. He did not have to tame the land. He purchased a purlieu of over forty acres, with a house which stood on a small rise overlooking Great Bay and a cleared meadow.[2]

It was not long before Nicholas Doe was recognized in the new community as a man of affairs. At the June terms for 1679 and 1680 he served as a grand juror. And on June 6, 1682, he became constable "for ye towne of Dover." The duties of his office consisted largely of enforcing laws based upon the Mosaic code — laws too detailed and too rigid to be applied literally except on at least one occasion. During December 1662 the constables of Dover and Hampton were ordered to fasten three Quaker women "to a cart's tail, and drawing the cart through your several towns, to whip them upon their naked backs not exceeding ten stripes apiece on each of them in each town, and so convey them from Constable to Constable till they are out of this jurisdiction, as you will answer at your peril." It may be that the refusal of

Massachusetts authorities to continue the punishment on their side of the line taught New Hampshire a lesson about the harshness of executed law. Within the lifetime of Nicholas Doe's son a complete reversal occurred, and one of his successors as constable was a Quaker.[3]

It would not be until Charles Doe's tenure as chief justice during the second half of the nineteenth century that New Hampshire would officially extend such tolerance to Catholics. The delay was due not merely to religious prejudices. In the wielding of the Yankee nation no force had been more influential than fear of the Catholic enemy in French Quebec. The danger was Indian, but the power was papist. The confrontation in this marchland of empire might have been less serious had it not been for the rivalry between France and Great Britain. Governor Andros of New England, carrying out the policies of the mother country in 1688, conducted a raid on a French settlement in Maine where the Indians were civilized and Catholic. With the aid of Quebec they retaliated with a series of holy wars, and the resulting conflict matched the Protestant-Catholic struggles of Europe for intensity. Dover, Oyster River, and Lubberland were attacked time and time again. The climax came on July 17, 1694, with the "Great Raid" on Oyster River. Of the twelve fortified garrisons in the settlement, five were overwhelmed. Nicholas Doe's two sons, John and Sampson, along with twelve other men, were able to herd their families into canoes and flee into Great Bay before the enemy moved on to Lubberland. Ninety-four persons were either killed or captured at Oyster River that day, and the destruction was complete.

Of course the settlers could rebuild. But the experience left a legacy of hatred and suspicion which history found hard to erase. For a generation New Hampshire was an armed camp, on guard night and day for the savage foe. Behind the tales of heroism and suffering lay an undying animosity toward the faith of the enemy. An old prejudice was revived: fear of the Indian was transformed into fear of Rome. The "Jesuit menace" became a fact of life. It was not the Indian but his priests that were cursed. These were the men who served the bidding of the Pope and as agents of the anti-Christ, had brought pestilence and plague to the land of God's elect. In battle without mercy, from which no age or sex was spared, kind deeds and generous acts were forgotten. Truth was exaggerated and grew into legend, so that even today there are some elements of the Catholic community of New Hampshire who accept the tradition that the first mass celebrated in the province was offered at the scene of slaughter in thanksgiving for the raid on Oyster River. What matters if this has the ring of a fireside story told to the children of a bitter nation to harden them against the ancestral foe? The important point is that a priest was there and that perhaps the Jesuits had ordained the massacre.[4]

It was in this manner and out of this background that antipapism developed into one of the distinguishing traits of the Yankee character. It sank its roots deep into the national consciousness and came to color both politics and law. After the fall of New France, New Hampshire people were shocked when the government of Great Britain passed the Quebec Act, extending religious liberty to Catholics, as a gesture of reconciliation. They who had borne for so long the hardships of war on behalf of the mother country felt betrayed. The Quebec Act was a major reason why New Hampshire supported Massachusetts during the years before 1776 and so willingly followed her down the path of rebellion and independence. Almost as significant was the effect these memories had on law. Even before the Indian wars began, there had been anti-Catholic legislation. Afterward Catholics could enter New Hampshire only at their peril. With the advent of the Revolution, when France became an ally and Britain the enemy, there was new insight and a lessening of fear. The pull of history was strong, however, and a century of suspicion could not be eradicated. When it came time to write a constitution, the citizens of New Hampshire inserted a clause which barred from public office any person not of "the Protestant religion."

That clause would still be in the constitution in 1868, when Charles Doe was an associate justice. His court was asked to interpret its meaning, and the majority had no doubt that it meant exactly what it said. Positions of public trust, they decided, could be filled only by "those who *are* of the Protestant religion." Judge Doe dissented. It was wrong, he contended, to treat the Protestant test in the New Hampshire constitution as part of church-state relationship traditional to England and the

European Continent. True, before independence New Hampshire had had a religious qualification test borrowed from the Act of Settlement. But the word "Protestant" as used in the constitution was to be interpreted as understood in 1783, the year the constitution was adopted. It was a question for history: "a historical fact to be determined by historical evidence, of which the court takes judicial notice." [5]

Doe sought his answer by looking at the experiences and traditions of the people of New Hampshire. When they enacted the qualification, they had tried to protect their government from a particular danger. Their history demonstrated that danger: the French papists of Quebec were the ancient enemies, and it was the Catholics whom the founding fathers had had in mind when they made religion a qualification for office. They endorsed no religious creed or dogma. Their constitution created, not a state church, but merely a privileged status. With this in mind, and considering the historical heritage of the drafters, the only fair interpretation, Charles Doe argued, was that the constitution did not refer to those of "the Protestant religion," as the majority held, but was intended solely to remove the danger of Catholic public officials. "In the duty of interpretation," he wrote, "we cannot overrule the well-known historic object of the test, which was not to attach disqualifications to any theological belief, but to incapacitate the supposed disloyalty of those who acknowledge the supremacy of the sovereign pontiff." [6]

The implications did not trouble Judge Doe. Admittedly it was absurd to say that "Protestant," as used in the bill of rights, meant "Jew," "pagan," and "atheist" as well as "Congregationalist." Yet such was its constitutional meaning. "The historical fact is, that the religion of Protestants, as a legal test, is the religion of non-Catholics," he argued; "the Protestant test is an anti-Catholic test and nothing else." [7]

As Judge Doe made clear in his opinion, the constitutional prohibition had long been a dead letter against Catholics. He would have been the last to enforce it. But because he also wanted to make sure that it would not be enforced against others, he reached back into the history, the traditions, and the experiences of his ancestors to give it the narrowest construction possible. That his associates found Doe's definition of "Protestant" a semantic argument too sophisticated to adopt was not an indication of their prejudice, for two decades earlier the judge who wrote the majority opinion had stood with United States Supreme Court Justice Levi Woodbury when he returned from Washington to preside over a constitutional convention hoping to expunge the "Protestant" test. The Native American Party of Know-Nothings was making its bid for power and these judges sought to keep Know-Nothingism from spreading to New Hampshire. They failed and in part blamed the Catholics, who, knowing the test was not in actual force, had not voted for the proposed amendment in the expected numbers. By the time the next convention was called, Catholics, somewhat forewarned by Doe's dissent, knew better, and the constitution was amended.

All this, of course, belonged to an era which Nicholas Doe could not have comprehended. He died in 1691, three years before the "Great Raid" on Oyster River. Of the three children surviving him, the second, a son with the biblical name of Sampson, had married a woman with the Puritan name of Temperance. They had three children, the third of whom, Nicholas, was Charles Doe's great-grandfather. We know little of Sampson or of the second Nicholas Doe. Again, what we can discover comes from legal records. From these we learn that in March 1709 Sampson purchased a large tract of land from a man named Richard Waldron. Eventually to be known as Doe's Neck, it extended into Great Bay between the Lamprey River and a small creek and was claimed by both Dover and Exeter. For a time Sampson Doe settled the controversy to his own satisfaction by regarding himself a citizen of Dover. He attended the town meetings, where public offices were filled. The field drivers, or haywards, were elected by direct vote, as was the hog reeve, who enforced the statute prohibiting swine from running at large between April and October unless yoked and ringed. As late as 1880 Charles Doe would be dealing with the duties of the office of fence viewer, but in 1711 Sampson Doe was more concerned with the lott layer.[8]

In a colony without lawyers the people of New Hampshire had included among their elected officials men assigned to settle disputes of specialized types. The lott layers determined the limits of private property — a prosaic task, but one which stabilized a society with no available method of describing land grants more definite than metes and bounds. In 1711 Sampson Doe asked the lott layers of Dover to set the lines of Doe's Neck. His neighbor Abraham Bennick claimed that some of the land Doe was cultivating belonged to him and that the town of Dover, when it had granted the property to Doe's grantor, had included a tract owned by Bennick's grandfather. Thirty-five months after Doe had filed his request Bennick gave his bond to stand by the award of arbitrators. Six days later the award was announced.[9] It was a simple, practical procedure, yet one on which many lawyers might frown. Undoubtedly the lott layers, or arbitrators, looked at the official records, but as laymen they must by necessity have arrived at their decisions partly on terms of equity rather than by rules of law. As yet there could be few customs upon which to rely. In the new world legal memory was too short to have empaneled an assize of the countryside to answer an inquiry as to what land Bennick's grandfather had owned. Charles Doe would have admired the procedure — he was to spend his judicial career fighting for informality in law. Many critics thought his innovations reminiscent of early New Hampshire and out of tune with the complex requirements of the nineteenth century. He reintroduced the use of referees in matters of this type, although he never would have permitted them to delay their decision for three years.

In 1716, following the death of his first wife, Sampson Doe married a widow, Mary Ayers. Under the laws of the colony he was supposed to take an oath that he had no designs on the property of her former husband; that he promised to receive her naked and destitute and to clothe her in his own clothes. This procedure is an example of the Puritan effort to codify the perfect society only to find the code too idealized to enforce. For not only did Mary come with her clothes, but both she and Sampson served as administrators of her husband's estate. In fact, she brought a good deal of wealth to Doe's Neck. Her father and grandfather had been substantial men. As late as 1723 she was selling some of her grandfather's property.[10]

Such records furnish the best index we have of the sophistication of Colonial law and legal institutions — probate procedures far enough advanced that administration of estates was a regular practice and land records so stable that granddaughters could enjoy inheritances. Stability of institutions and reliability of records were probably the most important legal facts in the lives of the Does during the remaining decades of the colonial era. For land — the development of property and speculation through investment — became their major interest. After Doe's Neck was annexed to the village of Newmarket, newly created from the eastern part of ancient Exeter, Sampson and his sons turned to that town for purposes of investment. Before long their speculations took them further afield. Royal governors had begun to grant whole townships in the wilderness to proprietors, and the Doe family received a generous share. Sampson's oldest son was a proprietor of Canterbury, while Nicholas, the great-grandfather of Judge Doe, was a proprietor of Chatham. They reaped the profits of an expanding market. The fourth generation of Yankees was coming of age, and land in the older towns of Portsmouth, Dover, and Exeter was scarce. Parents faced the question of how to provide for their children. Unlike England, the new world had no professional military, no established clergy to absorb the younger sons. Unlike the New England of a century later, the colony contained no Manchesters or Nashuas, with their great textile mills to provide jobs for unmarried daughters, and Boston offered few opportunities for training clerks in her merchant houses. Undeveloped lands held the solution. Fathers petitioned for grants or bought claims from men like the Does, and whole families moved north to start life anew. The development of New Hampshire was a commercial enterprise which the Doe family turned to advantage.[11]

This pattern of speculation lasted for three generations. The second Nicholas Doe bought and sold lands in Exeter and Epping and as far away as Gilmanton. Though he had not been at Louisburg, as had his older brother, or participated in the other great battles of his day, Crown Point and Quebec, he was not deterred from coveting the spoils of victory. During the French and Indian War he and his son Joseph were enrolled in the militia. They saw no action; nevertheless, they and several others joined in a petition for a township "anywhere," as a reward for "having endured the blunt & hardships of the late war."[12]

Joseph was Nicholas' third child. He too became a speculator, and on a scale even larger than had his father and grandfather. Even so, real estate seems to have been only a secondary interest for him. In legal documents Joseph Doe signed himself as "yeoman," "joiner," or "trader," and he probably devoted most of his time to managing the Doe gristmill in Newmarket. When he was sixty-nine, Nicholas gave Joseph the family home. This deed of transfer seems to have been Nicholas Doe's retirement plan. In return for the house, Joseph agreed to let the old man stay on, with all rights and privileges of ownership, for the annual rental of one peppercorn. A generation earlier Sampson Doe had made the somewhat similar arrangement of leasing property from his sons.[13] But where Sampson may have sought to take real property out of his estate, thus favoring his children over their stepmother, Nicholas was probably providing for his old age. It became common practice for New Hampshire farmers, as late as Charles Doe's tenure as chief justice, to hand over their farms to younger men in return for room and board.

It must be admitted that we can only guess at Sampson and Nicholas Doe's intentions. Their deeds do not seem to be the work of lawyers. One has a feeling that they hoped their schemes would work and trusted their sons to carry them out. Beyond that, they could not be sure. How, for example, would a court enforce an agreement that Nicholas was not the owner of his house but that he possessed all the rights and privileges of ownership? To say that a lawyer would not have left rights this vague is to argue that the economy of Newmarket had now reached a level at which lawyers were needed. In the days of the first Nicholas men could still deal with their neighbors without trained counsel. When the people of New Hampshire wanted legal advice, they went to those physicians and schoolmasters who conducted a law business on the side. Since most affairs were probably settled by custom, such assistance may have been adequate for the times.

The first lawyer to open a practice on the Oyster River was a second-generation Irishman named John Sullivan. He arrived in Durham in 1764 and within two years had the populace up in arms. Sullivan was ambitious, and where no law suits existed, he was accused of inventing them. During February 1766 he was attacked in the town of Nottingham. In June a small mob fired into his house. They planned to "rob him of many Writs & Notes of hand which he then had in his possession." Later the same month 133 citizens petitioned the General Court charging that "he with a View of making his Fortune, out of the Ruin of the poor harmless People, taking of them Unreasonable Fees from such as were not able to Command Cash enough to pay their publick Tax, or to provide Bread for their Families, he under pretence of having such Knowledge in the Law, set himself up to the highest bidder, for to plead a Case before a Justice." [14]

If at first Sullivan did not enhance the reputation of the bar, he later redeemed himself and gave the profession a boost toward respectability. He used his talents to rouse the people against England and became a revolutionary leader. It was he as much as any man who decided to attack Fort William and Mary in Portsmouth Harbor. The actual facts are lost in history and in the claims and counterclaims of the descendants of those who were there or said they were there. Yet legend gives Sullivan's law student, Alexander Scammell, credit for hauling down the king's colors, and New Hampshire came to believe that America's first overt act against the mother country was committed by a lawyer.[15] True or not, it helped the legal reputation.

The impending conflict bore hard on the people of Newmarket. Each man had to decide where he stood. Although the town voted to send thirty men to aid Massachusetts, there was wavering. In January 1776 Newmarket joined neighboring towns to protest formation of a rebel government. Such a move was premature, they asserted, and "an open Declaration of Independency, which we can by no means Countenance until we Shall know the Sentiments of the British Nation in General." [16] Years later Chief Justice Doe used these arguments to strengthen the liberties guaranteed by state constitution. The people, he would say, were protesting the lack of restraints on the proposed government, and to satisfy their objections, provisions in the bill of rights were intended to be applied absolutely.[17]

By July 1776 sentiment had shifted. Joseph Doe signed the loyalty oath, promising with 163 others, including nine members of the Doe family, "at the Risque of our lives and Fortunes, with arms, [to] oppose the Hostile Proceedings of the British Fleets and armies, against the United American Colonies." Of thirty-eight men who refused to sign, some were tories and had to post bonds guaranteeing their good behavior; a few were placed under house arrest, while others had their property confiscated and were driven out of town. Judge Doe later called these measures oppressive and said that, while constitutional, they were not "law" in the true sense. But his grandfather, Joseph Doe, must have been a party to them since he worked for the New Hampshire Committee of Safety and was elected a selectman. It was while in that office that he performed the act which symbolized the end of the colonial period for New Hampshire and the Doe family. In 1782 he posted the notice calling all voters to gather at the meeting house "To take into Consideration the Plan of Government proposed by the Convention of this State, by their Resolution of the 21st of August last to be laid before the People — and Take such order thereon as the Meeting may think proper." [18] The constitution which they adopted Charles Doe would remold.

Chapter Two

ROUT OF THE DOE-FACES
Father

IF a judge is a product of his environment, his father is an expression of that environment. Charles Doe's ancestors, English immigrants and founders of the Yankee nationality, had created the ethnic, religious, cultural, and governmental world in which he was to live. It was his father's generation that created his economic and political world.

Joseph Doe, the son of the Newmarket selectman and father of Charles Doe, was born in 1776, the first year of independence. The New Hampshire in which he grew to manhood was beset by hard times. The prosperity upon which his father had built the family fortune was now a memory. Small, impoverished fishing shacks stood along the Lamprey River where three decades before twenty-one ships had been launched during a single year. The repressive economic measures enacted by Lord North's parliament had extracted a heavy toll, from which victory at Yorktown brought no relief. Without markets factories closed, wages decreased, and the area reverted to an agricultural economy. A depreciated paper currency made credit nearly worthless. To prevent judgments against debtors, petitions sent by town meetings to the state government demanded that the inferior courts be closed and that the activities of lawyers be restricted; even that the five counties of New Hampshire be limited to two lawyers each. Several times mobs surrounded courthouses where judges were holding debtor sessions, and on one occasion armed men threatened the legislature sitting in neighboring Exeter.[1]

How seriously the Doe family was affected we cannot now determine. As speculators they may have suffered the discomforts of the debtor class. One of the few available measures of financial position in postrevolutionary New England is the church pew, which was assigned partly by the occupant's age, partly by his ancestry, and partly by his wealth. The closer to the front, the more expensive the pew. In 1792, when the elder Joseph Doe was fifty-five, Newmarket built a new meeting house. He was witness to the deed and member of the committee to select a preacher. Yet of the fifty-four pews on the ground floor, he "bid off" only the twenty-seventh, halfway up the main aisle. When he died in 1817, the pew was worth $20. His entire estate was valued at $6,005. The fact that this is almost four times what his father left is meaningless, since Nicholas had given away most of his real property in anticipation of death, while Joseph did not even make a will. He had six heirs, five of whom had left New Hampshire. Under the procedure followed at the time, an Exeter lawyer was appointed their agent. Joseph Doe, Jr., was named administrator, and a committee of four disinterested men was appointed to divide the property.[2]

When only twenty-six, the younger Joseph was elected constable of Newmarket. He served in that post, as well as sometimes being tax collector, for seven years. He was then probably a farmer, for he called himself "yeoman" or "husbandman"; only later did he describe himself as "gentleman." But there seems little doubt he always had his eye on business opportunities. It was he who refounded the Doe fortune on so solid a basis that his son Charles — one of six heirs — was able to devote a lifetime to public service without financial worry. Joseph did so by anticipating New Hampshire's economic future.

As early as 1811 New Hampshire was able to boast of a romantic past. The decaying wharves of Portsmouth and the rotting shipyards of Newmarket might hold a nostalgia to which the state would always cling, but the water power of the inland rivers pointed to the destiny from which it could not escape. The base of economic power was transferred from graceful Georgian mansions lining Piscataqua docks to unpretentious offices astride dingy brick factories. Such writers as Thomas Bailey Aldrich would one day find the mystique of New Hampshire in the old town by the sea, but Joseph Doe sought its raison d'être in the new world of manufacturing. During 1811 he moved to the industrial town of Somersworth.

Although he had business interests in Dover and in Strafford County, Joseph Doe's primary reason for moving to Somersworth was his marriage to Mary Bodwell Ricker. Her father was a sea captain who had made a fortune so comfortable that he retired young and in 1796 built a handsome home on Quamphegan Hill in Somersworth, just a few rods from the bridge that led to South Berwick in the Maine district of Massachusetts. In this house Charles Doe was to spend most of his years.

In 1821 Joseph Doe was elected Somersworth's representative to the lower house of New Hampshire's General Court. The political world into which he stepped was divided between the heirs of the Federalist tradition and their enemies. The Federal Party had seized control of New Hampshire during the early days of the republic, after forcing the constitution on an unhappy electorate. First John Sullivan of Durham and later John Taylor Gilman of Exeter sat in the chief executive's chair as representatives of the shipping and mercantile classes. They favored a strong judiciary, Hamilton's protective system, and hard money. It was not until 1805, after Gilman had served eleven consecutive one-year terms, that the Republicans elected a governor. Resentment against the embargo and certain Republican judicial appointments gave new life to the Federalists, and in 1809 they recaptured the governorship under the leadership of Jeremiah Smith, a man more famed as a jurist than as a politician. But their hour had already struck. During the very year that Jeremiah Smith and his retinue rode triumphantly into Concord to seize the reigns of power, a frail indigent cripple of twenty-one limped into town, alone and unnoticed, to become editor of the *New Hampshire Patriot*. His name was Isaac Hill.

The story of the battles and triumphs of the first Republican (later the Democratic) Party in New Hampshire can be told through the battles and triumphs of Isaac Hill. It was he who dominated the politics of Joseph Doe's era and created the political world in which Charles Doe later lived. Crude, ambitious, patriotic, and dictatorial, Hill kept the Republicans together during their darkest hours. A keen political observer, he knew that

Jeffersonian republicanism could never become dominant in commercial New Hampshire. A ruthless demagogue, he drove his party to the brink of destruction until he forced it to embrace its ultimate destiny — Jacksonian democracy.

Isaac Hill built his power partly on reaction. While Joseph Doe and his political allies pushed New Hampshire into the industrial age, Isaac Hill asked who would reap the profits. Not yet Whigs and surely not conservatives, the Federalists were champions of government by gentry while Hill spoke for agrarian democracy. Their program was to promote business and to wed the state to economic progress. Hill's was more emotional and more politically astute. He constructed his machine on four major issues: the War of 1812, the organization of the judiciary, the democratization of Dartmouth College, and the disestablishment of the Congregational Church.

The war was his favorite theme. In his first editorial he flung the charge of disloyalty at the Federalists. "Their's is the cause of Great Britain," he wrote, "their's is the cause of our enemy." The Hartford Convention, the suspicion that Portsmouth merchants encouraged British ships blockading the coast, and the anglomania of the legal profession did more to win Republican votes than any other issue. The Federalists could not have been more inept. In his message for 1816 Governor Gilman totaled up the cost of war and asked, "What have we gained?" He was New Hampshire's last Federalist governor.[3]

The year 1816 ushered in a new era. The Republican governor, William Plumer, asked for reform of the judiciary, of Dartmouth College, and of the religious laws. "Reform" was a misnomer as applied to the judiciary. Despite the fact that the constitution provided that judicial tenure be during good behavior, the courts were not free of politics during the nineteenth century; whenever a party swept its opponents from the executive and legislative branches of government, the winners "reformed" the judiciary by "legislating" out the old court and creating a new one. Plumer and Hill removed the Federalists from the New Hampshire court in 1816 to assure themselves of a favorable verdict in the *Dartmouth College Case*. The legislature had amended the college charter by empowering the governor to appoint enough additional trustees to give control to the state, and the old trustees had appealed to the judiciary for protection. No other litigation in American history so sharply drew the legal issues posed by democracy. The Federalists worried lest the rights of private property be abridged, the Republicans were concerned for the rights of the people. Dartmouth, said Plumer, existed for the benefit of the public. It might be proper in a monarchy to secure the public against tyranny by entrusting education to private corporations immune from state interference, but in a republic the people could trust education to no one but themselves. There is no doubt which side was more popular. When Chief Justice John Marshall reversed the decision of the Republican-appointed New Hampshire court and returned Dartmouth to the nonpublic trustees, the rights of property triumphed over the cause of abstract democracy; but in the process many new voters joined the Republican ranks.

The Federalists had to defend Dartmouth College against the state government; that case had involved a question of principle, which their lawyers would never have permitted them to abandon. But they blundered when they defended the Congregational establishment, making themselves the champions of what was rather than what should be. By a statute passed in 1791 the voters of each town were authorized to collect taxes for support of the local "ministry." [4] While in theory the money raised might go to any clergyman whose people were in the majority, by intent and practice the benefits were limited to those of the orthodox faith. As one contemporary put it, "In several instances these worthy preachers of the gospel actually prosecuted for their *tythes* with an overbearing insolence that any Irish Catholic priest might have envied, and recovered heavy sums in the courts of law." [5] They were aided by the Federalist judiciary. In one litigation a citizen of Plymouth, who had joined the Episcopal Church in neighboring Holderness, refused to pay the assessment to support the local Congregational minister, whereupon the town of Plymouth brought suit. Judge Jeremiah Smith charged the jury to find the defendant innocent if his conversion to Episcopalism was bona fide — that is, if he had joined a new church because he could not conscientiously worship as a Congregationalist — but to find for the town if he had become an Episcopalian from a personal dislike of the Congregational minister or because of a tiff with the local society. When the jurors asked for more instructions, Isaac Hill ridiculed the law. "The jury," he wrote, "undertook the task of deciding what was this man's conscience, and they could not agree." [6]

The number of members of other minority faiths and those who attended no church was rapidly increasing. Isaac Hill and William Plumer made their cause the cause of Republicanism. In 1819 tolerance was the chief election issue, and the Federalists were soundly beaten. The religion tax was repealed and Congregationalism disestablished. The following year the Federalists foolishly campaigned on a platform of reestablishment; the Republicans won by an overwhelming majority. As George Barstow noted in the closing sentence of his history of New Hampshire, "it was not religion which was abolished, but the power of the Congregational order." [7] So too was the power of the Federal Party. It remained for such men of property as Joseph Doe to pick up the pieces.

When Joseph Doe was elected to the lower house of the General Court in 1821, he began with a clean slate. He had no Federalist record. It was the era of good feelings. "New Hampshire," Isaac Hill boasted in 1822, "has waded through the trial of political warfare, and is now perhaps more decidedly republican than any other state in the union." [8] During Joseph Doe's first three years in the General Court little happened to prove Hill wrong. But in New Hampshire politics strange bedfellows seldom remain together for long. The heirs of the Federal tradition were merely biding their time. No longer trapped into unpopular causes, they had a new set of leaders, among the most articulate of whom was Joseph Doe. It was he who set into motion the controversy which irrevocably divided the old Republican Party when toward the end of the 1824 term he rose and moved that the General Court proceed to the election of a United States senator. [9]

Joseph Doe's nominee was Jeremiah Mason, who had been the dominant figure of the memorable Rockingham County bar when it included Daniel Webster, Ichabod Bartlett, George Sullivan, and Levi Woodbury. A Federalist and an avowed enemy of Isaac Hill, Mason had been elected to the Senate once before, during the brief Indian summer of power the Federalists had enjoyed as a result of Mr. Madison's war. In 1817, aware that his beliefs were no longer representative of New Hampshire's electorate, he had resigned. Though Mason loved the practice of law and disliked politics, he now yielded to the pleas of Daniel Webster and again was a candidate.[10]

The manager of Mason's candidacy was Nathaniel A. Haven, a Rockingham County lawyer and the editor of a Portsmouth newspaper. He should have won, for this was a presidential election year and Mason had the endorsement of John Quincy Adams, who enjoyed the overwhelming support of the New Hampshire legislature. Hill, by backing William Crawford, was temporarily out of favor. Yet, even though he was unable to name his own choice for senator, Hill knew how to block the man he did not want. When the House of Representatives voted for Mason, the Senate, controlled by Hill, substituted a series of alternate candidates. After almost three weeks of stalemate a bargain was apparently struck. The Mason managers agreed to one more ballot, and the Hill forces agreed to vote on the question of concurring with the House. No other name was to be offered; it would be a yes or no vote on Jeremiah Mason. While Hill gambled on keeping the Senate in line, Haven gambled on the pro-Adams sentiment and to each senator assigned one of his most trusted lieutenants. Joseph Doe was told to deliver the most important senator of all, Nehemiah Eastman of Farmington.

Eastman's was the swing vote upon which both sides counted. A small-town lawyer with a legendary capacity for diligence, he was ambitious to be a congressman. Two years earlier he had been a candidate, but not receiving the nomination of the official caucus, he had lost the general election.[11] Now, in 1824, with Haven and Hill seeking his vote, Eastman enjoyed the endorsement of all factions. In June he was nominated for Congress, in October he was elected, and in December each side came to collect its just debt. That Nehemiah Eastman served but one term in Congress and then disappeared from public life may be due to the fact that he could pay but one.

With Eastman on their side, Mason's people were confident of seven votes — just enough for victory, as Doe told Eastman on the morning of the final ballot. But when the tally sheets were counted, the vote was six to six, and Mason was defeated.[12]

Joseph and Mary Bodwell Ricker Doe, parents of Charles Doe, photographed during the 1850's.

The Doe homestead, Rollinsford, New Hampshire, as it appeared during the first decade of this century. Built in the 1790's by Charles Doe's maternal grandfather, it was the Judge's home from early childhood until his death in 1896.

Charles Doe, around 1863, when he was Associate Justice of the Supreme Judicial Court and was 33 years old.

Edith Haven, age 23, as she appeared about 1863, shortly before her marriage to Charles Doe.

Haven and Doe wanted to fix the blame. Under questioning seven senators maintained that they had voted for Mason. One of these was Eastman — so Doe said. He claimed to have told Eastman that some friends doubted whether Eastman had supported Mason. "I stated this to Mr. Eastman," Doe wrote, "and requested him to give me a certificate of his vote that I might shew it to those who had talked on the subject. After some conversation he signed the certificate and gave it to me, but requested that it might be returned to him after I had shewn it, which I promised to do." Doe further claimed to have shown the certificate to Haven, Mason, Franklin Pierce, and several others before returning it to Eastman.[13]

Eastman told a different story. There had been a certificate — he admitted that much — but when Doe asked him to sign it, he had dashed it to the floor with the exclamation, "I will certify nothing, and I consider your proposition an insult." Doe thereupon apologized and worried about extricating himself from an embarrassing situation. "I shall feel like a fool," he said, "to go and tell Mr. Mason and his friends that you have opposed his election throughout." [14]

It is easier to believe Eastman. True, Doe and Haven obtained certificates from the six senators who did vote for Mason, and Doe undoubtedly asked Eastman for his. But as Eastman himself pointed out, how could anyone think he would give so incriminating a document to "an inveterate foe"? [15] If Doe really possessed it (and it should be recalled that, along with the six other certificates, this was documentary proof that Mason had received a majorty of the votes in the Senate), and if Doe did return it as he said, he was a man of surprising political honor and a rather stupid politician. It seems more likely that when Eastman refused to certify, Doe and Haven went ahead and invented the certificate to dramatize his perfidy and blame it on Isaac Hill.

The trouble was that they were playing Isaac Hill's own game. Hill reprinted everything Doe and Haven wrote. He publicized their charges but refused to debate details. Instead, Hill raised general issues. Doe and Haven, Hill claimed, were forming a new party, and their effort to elect Mason was but the first step in their plot. He even had a name for their party — the "Doe-faces." [16]

It is hard today to appreciate the antipathy toward party government which existed in New Hampshire during that era, when political organizations were thought of as disruptive evils, not as responsible auxiliaries of the state. The excesses of political partisanship during the War of 1812 were still remembered, and when Hill said Haven, Mason, and Doe were reviving party strife, his warnings fell on responsive ears. But New Hampshire had never seen a political boss, and when Haven warned that Hill would soon be the "State's Director," the voters were not alarmed. The election of 1825 was a rout for the Doe-faces. Haven, Mason, and Doe were not reelected. "The *certificate managers* in the House," Hill gloated, "are *hors de combat*, having lost their leaders, *Haven, Mason, Doe*, etc. etc., and not one of the *certificate signers* of the Senate, who were so strenuously supported by the federal party will be elected." [17] Doe's bungling of the Eastman affair gave Isaac Hill the leverage he needed to spring back from the Crawford fiasco. When the opposition subsequently regrouped and finally coalesced into the Whig party, it remained a minority voice in New Hampshire. The political world Charles Doe was to enter in 1852 was formed during the election of 1825. The Democratic party which he joined received its political program from Andrew Jackson, but its power came from the machine built by Isaac Hill out of the wreckage of Mason's candidacy.

If Joseph Doe felt nostalgia for the General Court during 1825, he did not suffer long. In 1826 Somersworth's representation in the lower house was increased from one to two, and he was reelected. When he read the statewide election results, he probably looked forward to the opening of the June session with more than the usual anticipation: for the first time Isaac Hill had also been elected to the House of Representatives. In the personal confrontation that resulted, Doe became the chief spokesman in the state for the business community.

His opponents may have tried to silence him. Hill, the avowed enemy of banking, was appointed to the Committee on Banks, while Joseph Doe was appointed to the comparatively minor Committee on Claims. Doe should have been on Hill's committee. He had been a director of the Strafford Bank in Dover, from 1810 to 1819.[18] His first speech as a legislator had been to notify the House that he intended to introduce a bill to renew and extend its charter.[19] During earlier sessions he had belonged to a small group of experts to whom special banking questions were referred, and he had taken an active part in the struggle to incorporate banks in the newer sections of the state.[20]

Isaac Hill had many reasons to dislike banks. Most bankers were Federalists; Doe, Haven, and Mason had been associated with banks; the speculators, merchants, and manufacturers who supported the administration of John Quincy Adams depended on banks for credit. During the 1825 session, at which Joseph Doe was not present, thirteen banks had petitioned for incorporation, and consideration had been postponed until the following year.[21] Now, in 1826, Isaac Hill read the report of the Committee of Banks recommending a further postponement of the petitions. Doe objected and moved that an exception be made for the Somersworth Bank. The House voted to reject Hill's report and to consider the petition of the Somersworth Bank.[22]

Hill's tactics were to amend the bill to death. Doe objected, but the House supported Hill.[23] After four days of these preliminaries Doe called up the bill as amended, asking that the House give special consideration to the Somersworth Bank, which was located in Great Falls, a growing community whose citizens might have to take their business across the river into Maine if they did not get a bank. Dover had two banks, he argued, both successful; yet the mills of Great Falls had a larger daily expenditure than did Dover's manufacturing concerns. Association with a Dover bank had convinced him that there was room for another bank in the area.[24]

The date — June 29, 1826 — marks the climax of Joseph Doe's years in the legislature. A freshman member of the House that summer was Daniel Christie, the representative from Dover. In 1850, when Charles Doe was studying law in his office, Christie entertained his students with descriptions of Joseph Doe's running debate with Isaac Hill.[25] It was onesided, for Hill had no facility for extemporaneous speaking. He did not dare deliver an address unless he could recite it verbatim from manuscript. A few years later, while he was a United States senator, Hill was scorned unmercifully by Webster, Clay, and Calhoun for reading his speeches. It was a day of great orators, and they said he detracted from the Senate's dignity.[26] It is doubtful, however, if they tormented him more than did Joseph Doe. Hill would read his remarks, and Doe would rise and make an oral reply. Everyone would wait for Hill, but he never answered. Instead he would go home, write out his rejoinder, come back the next day, and read it in his dull, flat monotone. Again Doe would give an offhand reply. At times he was cruel. After Hill had finished one especially long and closely reasoned attack on banks in general and the Somersworth Bank in particular, Doe's sarcasm was biting. "Mr. Doe," the *Patriot* reported, "said he did not rise to contend with the gentlemen from Concord on the question before the House — he had no written speech — had not prepared one — was not able to write one — and did not wish for one on the present occasion." [27]

Joseph Doe easily humiliated Isaac Hill, but Hill had the votes to beat him. The Somersworth Bank was not chartered in 1826, nor was it chartered during 1827 and 1828, Doe's final two terms as a representative. He continued to speak for banking interests, often with success. He managed to get charters enacted for banks as far away as Lebanon, but in his very last week as a member of the House, when he tried to call up the Somersworth Bank bill, he was defeated 99 to 90.[28]

By this time Isaac Hill had a firm grip on the state government. He was even able to defeat a motion praising the Adams administration. In the election of 1828 Hill was momentarily set back by a rally of the pro-Adams forces. Hill supported Andrew Jackson, and New Hampshire voted for John Quincy Adams. But with Jackson's victory federal patronage came under his control, and the fate of New Hampshire was sealed. For a quarter of a century it remained the most Jacksonian state in the Union. There was no place in the new order for Joseph Doe. While the movement to reelect Adams was at its peak, Isaac Hill had singled out Doe as its most active leader and had warned Republicans of his treachery.[29] With Jackson's triumph the heart went out of Doe's will to fight; he was never again active in politics. In January 1829 the Pro-Adams governor, about to leave office himself, appointed Joseph Doe a justice of the peace and quorum.[30] It was an honor with few duties, a mark of respect tendered to those who had made themselves eminent in the

service of the state. It was all the tangible evidence Joseph Doe
had to show for seven terms in the House of Representatives.

A casual observer of political New Hampshire during the years
when Joseph Doe was in the General Court might say that he
had accomplished little; that the turmoil had been nothing more
than a battle over personalities. Such a view would be only
superficial. Joseph Doe had witnessed an unstable New Hampshire during his youth, and what he saw had left a lasting impression. While he was a boy, mobs had attacked the courts and
the legislature and had challenged public and private credit.
When John Sullivan ended the threat with force rather than
concessions, the business community had taken heart, and eventually the state prospered. It was a lesson men such as Joseph Doe
were not likely to forget. Isaac Hill had lived during those same
years, but he had learned a different lesson. He had observed the
same events, but he remembered when New Hampshire citizens
were sent to jail for debt and for not supporting an established
church. The very men whom Joseph Doe admired for restoring
the confidence of New Hampshire's financial interests and for
preserving constitutional order Isaac Hill mistrusted for not supporting their nation in time of war and for repudiating the democratic process by using the courts to preserve the privileges of
Dartmouth College.

These two traditions shaped the political world of Charles Doe.
One — the tradition of Isaac Hill — created the party organization which later carried him to the Supreme Court. The other —
the tradition of his father — defined the forces of moderation
which became his constitutional principles. When Joseph Doe attempted in the 1828 caucuses of Strafford County to stem the
tide of Jacksonianism, he was supporting the last stand in New
Hampshire on behalf of government by gentry. With the triumph
of Jacksonian democracy politics belonged to the people. But
loyal as they became to Jackson's program, the voters of New
Hampshire never consented to an elective judiciary. It was
through the judges that the conservative property interests,
which Isaac Hill had defeated in 1828, retained a voice in the affairs of the state.

For Joseph Doe there remained only the role of minority leader,
a role he had no desire to fill. Perhaps he was happy to be mov-

ing to Derry, beyond the reach of his friends in Somersworth who might have insisted that he continue to serve. He had much to be grateful for. He had been in the General Court during America's most splendid legislative era. In Washington such giants as Clay, Webster, Benton, Holmes, and Calhoun had graced the senate chamber as it had never been graced before and has never been graced since. In Concord he had been the compeer of Mason, Woodbury, Bartlett, Haven, and Hill.[31] It had been a charmed circle in which to walk. It had its frustrations, its disappointments, and its defeats. But it had also been exciting and at times rewarding. From it he gained the conviction that the democratic process could survive only if wedded to the rights of property and to the protection of commerce. This was the political legacy he passed on to his youngest son.

+ *Chapter Three* +

THE BARBARIC COURSE
Education

DURING the nineteenth century most states in the American Union had partisans who extolled their physical or economic predominance or lauded their traditions and institutions. Not so New Hampshire. Since there were no productive natural resources to proclaim, a fierce climate with which to contend, and few material advantages to enjoy, her champions gasconaded her native sons, asserting that these incarcerating influences had somehow managed to produce a superior breed of men. Their claims were challenged by Ralph Waldo Emerson who, looking down upon proslavery New Hampshire with an abolitionist's contempt, sneered in his "Ode to Channing":

> The God who made New Hampshire
> Taunted its lofty peaks with little men.

But Ellery Channing, a fellow abolitionist and a fellow resident of Concord, Massachusetts, did not agree. To Channing there was something remarkable about New Hampshire people. Daniel Webster proved this, Channing thought: "he could not have been produced in Massachusetts." To Frank B. Sanborn, another Concord resident, he said, "There is something native and original in the character of those New Hampshire people, which you never see in Massachusetts; why is it, Mr. Sanborn? Do you think living among those mountains, in that fresh, wild scenery, with so much hunting, has anything to do with it? The Massachusetts people have something narrow and small about them, —

not the generous native strength of the New Hampshire people." [1]

Sanborn was a native of Exeter and all too willing to agree with Channing and disagree with Emerson. Reflecting some years later upon what Channing had said, Sanborn concluded that it was in the legal profession that one found proof that the rugged hill country of New Hampshire did indeed produce a unique specimen of man. That "character" of which Channing had spoken, Sanborn thought, "Webster had something of it; so had Dudley, of Raymond, and Plumer, of Epping, and Doe, of Rollinsford." [2]

Sanborn could not have chosen a more felicitous group to prove his point. During the very decade in which he had been born, within a fifty-mile radius of his Exeter birthplace, three of the great names of American law had begun their lives beneath the shadow of those White Mountains Channing so ardently admired. In 1826 Christopher Columbus Langdell, the founder of modern legal education, was born in the hamlet of New Boston. Five years later, just across the state line in a section of Massachusetts that had once been claimed by New Hampshire, James Bradley Thayer, master of the law of evidence, first saw the light of day. Between these two events, both geographically and chronologically, was born America's greatest adjudicatory reformer, Charles Cogswell Doe. And if it is true that heritage and environment are the factors which mold a man's character, then Ellery Channing's granite hills must be given their due for making these men what they eventually became.

Charles Cogswell Doe, the fourth son and youngest of the six children of Joseph and Mary Bodwell Ricker Doe, was born in Derry, New Hampshire, on April 11, 1830. Joseph Doe had moved to Derry in 1828 after acquiring the farm of Captain John Derby. In local circles it was considered a model farm, containing the latest scientific advancements. It is not known what plans Joseph Doe originally had, but within a few years he discovered that he was not equal to the challenge. He had developed cataracts and feared he was going blind. His oldest son had already left home to try his hand in the business world of New York City. Joseph Doe saw little hope of making the farm pay. He sold the property and moved his family back to the Ricker homestead, on the banks of the Salmon Falls River. For some men it might have

been a forced sale, but Joseph Doe retained the family shrewd-
ness for real-estate dealings. After dividing into several parcels
the land he had purchased for $6,000, he disposed of it for just
under double that amount. By 1836 he had sold all his holdings;
the family had probably already returned to Somersworth, since
papers on the Derby house itself were passed in 1835.[3]

As a result Charles Doe had no memories of living in Derry
among the pertinacious descendants of the Scotch-Irish settlers.
As one man has observed, "It makes no difference where we were
babies, for then, wherever our residence may be, our only home
is our mother's arms; the great question is, where were we boys?"[4]
Charles Doe was a boy, not in Derry where the first American
potato had been grown and the first American linen had been
manufactured, but in the Salmon Falls section of Somersworth,
where back-country loggers still arrived in winter with their ox
teams, dragging loads of oak knees and logs of rockmaple to the
small landings on the Piscataqua. He spent his childhood and
youth in a world made for a boy, in the countryside known as
the river uplands, where a boy could roam to his heart's content
among patches of sweet-fern, bayberry bushes, and small white
pines. From the top of Otis Hill near his house Charles Doe
could see the snow-capped White Mountains far to the north. Directly below were the two villages of Somersworth — Salmon
Falls just behind a bend in the river and Great Falls further up —
with their brick mills and small frame houses painted either red
or yellow since the discovery that ocher found in the neighboring
fields made a durable paint. Turning south he could see the
steeples of Portsmouth and the masts of ships in the harbor.[5]
There another Yankee boy was just beginning his life. He would
immortalize childhood in southern New Hampshire during the
last century in the minor American classic, *The Story of a Bad
Boy*. But the adventures Thomas Bailey Aldrich would recall
would not be Doe's — a boy's life in sophisticated Portsmouth
was different from a boy's life in rustic Somersworth. With his
theatricals and visits to the Atheneum, Aldrich, the future poet
and editor, could let his imagination loose in a greater, wider
world. Charles Doe, on the other hand, was a farmer's son who
lived in a farmer's world. Once he almost missed the big social
event of the year, the Fourth of July celebration, because he had

to hoe beans and was told to wait until the dew had evaporated, since otherwise they might rust.

Charles Doe dearly loved his father. He admired his uneducated common sense and steadfast integrity, claiming in later years that he had been the greatest influence on his young life. He had less to say concerning his mother; all that is known for certain is that she directed his religious training, not very successfully. While in Newmarket Joseph Doe had been a Congregationalist, but after moving to Somersworth he apparently no longer attended services. His wife, who had been a gay, almost wild young girl, went to the other extreme. The neighboring town of South Berwick, across the Salmon Falls River in Maine, had been one of the original centers of the Baptist faith in northern New England. Its parish was famous for erratic exorbitance, staging schisms one year and conducting old-style revivals the next. Mary Doe was converted during a revival, such as the one held in the winter of 1837, when 400 persons were proselyted and 77 were baptized in the icy river.[6] Winter immersion was a characteristic of the sect which she joined, as were the "hell-and-damnation sermons" which Charles Doe always recalled with distaste. He told his children that he had had to suffer through some senseless tirades, and that was why he did not require them to attend church. But he was neither an atheist nor an agnostic. While practicing law in Dover, he became a Unitarian and later explained that he no longer attended services only because he needed Sunday for mental and physical relaxation. Nevertheless, because he did not go to church and was famous for his liberalism, the rumor got abroad that he was a freethinker. This story probably induced a committee of women from South Berwick's Universalist church to come to him for financial aid.

"Judge Doe," one of them is supposed to have said, "I believe you do not believe in Hell; we Universalists do not."

"Oh, you are mistaken," Doe replied. "If there is anything I feel sure of, it is that there is a Hell, and nothing is more certain than that we are punished for our sins." The committee left. Doe, amused, related the story with relish to his friends.[7]

Charles Doe began his formal schooling at Berwick Academy, one of the oldest academic institutions in the state of Maine and the pride of South Berwick. In nineteenth-century New England, an academy was the symbol of a rural community's cultural maturity, a mark of quality which set it apart from less advanced towns. It was a short walk from the Doe house to the academy building, with its white belfry and rows of Lombardy poplars, yet in many ways it was a walk into a different era and a different world. Unlike Great Falls and Salmon Falls, the villages of neighboring Somersworth, South Berwick had not been built around, nor had it surrendered its dignity to, brick cotton factories, unpainted boarding houses, or the wooden hovels of mill hands. Fine houses built by sea captains, merchants, and most particularly lawyers, graced each section of the town. Speaking of South Berwick as Charles Doe knew it as a student, Sarah Orne Jewett would write, "The old order of things was fast passing away, but this was a moment when hope for the future seemed very bright, and pride in the past was more assured." [8] Here indeed was a disappearing way of New England life — a remote provincial life which, with the aid of trust funds and small husbanded inheritances, lingered a few seasons after the dissolution of the West Indian trade before being swallowed in the new civilization of smoke and steam. In the congregation of the old First Parish there were over twenty college graduates, a distinction few towns of larger population could claim and one which South Berwick itself might never enjoy again. They made the tiny village a special place and gave it its most splendid hour. So much so that Miss Jewett, looking back from 1894 to those older days felt safe when she remarked, "In the early years of the fifth decade of this century, perhaps in 1842 or 1843, the influence of the academy and the level of intelligence in the society of the town were, perhaps, at their height." [9]

These were the last two years that Charles Doe studied at Berwick Academy, and Miss Jewett could not have chosen a more apt date to fix its vertex. It was at this time that the school began to decline. The reputation of a New England academy during the nineteenth century rested on its headmaster. Under the preceptorship of J. D. Berry the Academy had enrolled over 100 pupils the year that Charles Doe first attended. When Berry departed for greener pastures, most students left as well. In 1843 there were only seven scholars in all classes. That Charles was still there may have been due to his age, since he would have had to leave home to enter another academy. By the beginning of the January term in 1844 he was almost fourteen, and Joseph Doe decided it was time to send him to Exeter.

"Exeter," Christopher Columbus Langdell would write, "was for me the dawn of the intellectual life." [10] To Langdell, who came from the grubby hamlet of New Boston and from the sweat shops of Manchester, Phillips Exeter was truly an awakening. For Charles Doe it proved little different than Berwick Academy. It had its attractions nonetheless. The town was more sedate, more charming, and more intellectual than South Berwick, and like its academy, was to maintain its position for a longer time. It was then, as it is now, one of the finest specimens of rural New Hampshire life.

It was here, on February 19, 1844, that the thirteen-year-old Charles Doe arrived to sign the school's *Record,* pluckily putting down his age as fourteen. Of those who started the same term, over half were former students from Berwick Academy.[11] The rudimentary entrance requirements were only slightly more formal than when Daniel Webster had been told to read aloud the passage from Luke describing the betrayal of Jesus by Judas and the denial by Peter. When Webster concluded, Benjamin Abbott, the principal, pronounced the verdict, "Young man you are qualified to enter this institution." [12]

Abbott had been a great headmaster, and it was his administration of fifty years which separated Phillips Exeter from the other academies of northern New England. He had built a loyal corps of alumni, a rare accomplishment in those days; raised money from sources outside the town, an even rarer achievement; and set the tone of excellence when he scolded a student who had referred to Exeter as a "schoolhouse." "Remember," Abbott admonished, "that in the future it is not a 'schoolhouse' but an academy." [13]

He was retired now, and it was probably for this reason that Charles Doe remained at Exeter for only about half a year. The new principal, Gideon L. Soule, was an uninspiring instructor, who kept a perceptible distance between himself and his pupils.[14] He had the misfortune to be in the shadow of a great schoolmaster. Soule accepted standards as he found them and, lacking Abbott's personality, monotonously put generations of schoolboys through routine tasks. What humor he had seems to have been unintentional. "The Academy," he would tell entering students, "has no rules — until they are broken. But there is one rule I wish to make: whoever crosses the threshold of a billiard saloon, crosses the threshold of the Academy for the last time." [15]

When he totaled up the cost, Joseph Doe may have decided that Exeter was not worth the expense. Tuition was only $12 a year, but since there were no dormitories, the boys had to live in private houses, where room and board came to about $4 a week. Living was cheaper at Phillips Academy in Andover, Massachusetts, where tuition, was $6 a term and board 75 cents a week. Moreover, Andover had an outstanding headmaster. Whether for financial reasons or because of Soule, by the opening of the next academic year Charles Doe had left Exeter and was enrolled at Andover Hill. [16]

In Samuel Harvey Taylor, headmaster of Andover, Charles Doe met a man to remember. By the sheer force of an astonishing will, he drove generations of Yankee boys through their tasks, always predicating his actions on his unswerving belief that, no matter the command, youth should be taught to obey. One of those rare men toward whom people are unable to assume indifference, his virile nature aroused strong likes and dislikes, and his students either loved and obeyed him as a preterhuman personage or detested and obeyed him as an unmitigated despot. He was a remarkable pedagogue in an era when education was making great strides under many memorable men, and the day was near at hand when parents spoke of sending their sons, not to Andover, but to Doctor Taylor.

Even without Taylor the Academy had much to offer the fifteen-year-old boy who for the first time was seeing life beyond the restraints of the Piscataqua region. Andover had a more urban atmosphere and in some respects a more cosmopolitan tradition than did the comparatively provincial and rustic academies at South Berwick and Exeter. Here for the first time Doe came into contact with unaffected sophistication combined with a highly developed intellectual existence which could not have failed to broaden his social outlook and widen his cultural appreciation. For within the narrow confines of a dogmatically ordained horizon, dominated by the Theological Seminary which guided the destiny of the institution, Andover and its educators practiced not simply the science of pedagogy, but the art of scholarship, which they viewed as a way of life, rather than a mere profession. Of the three secondary schools Charles Doe attended, Andover did most to advance his development because Andover had the most to offer.

Unfortunately the area of competence was very narrow. Taylor may have been a great instructor, but he was interested only in Greek and Latin, and other subjects were neglected. A tyrant in the classroom, he employed a system which rewarded rote rather than imagination; Charles Doe suffered from this, since he was a senior and Taylor taught only the seniors. As a result Charles did not enjoy his year at Andover, and undoubtedly some of the bitterness he later expressed against the Dartmouth College faculty had roots in his experiences under Doctor Taylor. Yet he did gain a fine classical training, which served him well at both Harvard and Dartmouth. And in meeting Samuel Harvey Taylor, the fifteen-year-old Charles encountered at first hand the old Puritan breed which had been so common as church deacons and social arbiters during the days of his ancestors. Taylor's severity, his accuracy, his disdain of frivolity and hatred of evil, his confidence in the revealed word of God, and, above all, his absolute trust in his own infallibility were qualities of the old Puritan code which was swiftly disintegrating before the irresistible effervescences and the secular attitudes which were to characterize Doe's world.

The new order replacing the Puritan way of life in New England was nowhere more in evidence than at the college in which Charles Doe enrolled as a freshman during the autumn of 1845. At this time Harvard was not nearly as radical as it would become — the insular Doctor Taylor of Andover still approved of it. He grew to detest it under Eliot, forbidding his boys to attend when it ceased to stress Latin and Greek. Charles Doe, on the other hand, keenly supported Eliot's reforms and because of Eliot sent his own sons to Harvard rather than to Dartmouth. What made Harvard different in 1845 was that it had been captured by the Unitarians. All this amounted to, however, was that the sermons heard in chapel were a bit more liberal, for the curriculum remained as classical as ever.

Doe must have been discouraged when he saw the catalogue. The only subject besides Latin, Greek, and mathematics offered during the first term was an unpromising series of lectures called "Means of Preserving Health." During the second term, however, he could take chemistry under John White Webster. Five years later, while Doe was studying law in Dover, Webster was the defendant in the most celebrated murder trial in American history, *Commonwealth* v. *Webster*.[17] Chief Justice Shaw's charge to the jury in that case is a legal classic, still studied in today's law schools and one which Charles Doe frequently cited. Having taken classes from Webster would have made Harvard memorable for any nineteenth-century lawyer. In fact, the aspect about Harvard which must have struck Doe was the number of remarkable men on the faculty in comparison to the other schools he had attended. There were Edward T. Channing, Henry Wadsworth Longfellow, Louis Agassiz, Asa Gray, and in Greek classes Evangelinus Apostolides Sophocles (though George Hoar thought Sophocles, despite his splendid name, uninspiring[18]). Joseph H. Choate, another future giant of the bar, recalled with pleasure the Reverend Frank Francis, who was said by students to be unable to stop praying once he got started. "Oh Lord," he once invoked, "we pray Thee make the intemperate temperate, the insincere sincere, and the industrious dustrious." [19]

Not as pleasant as Harvard's prayers was Harvard's hazing, conducted during the first few weeks of the school year with a paragon of adroitness and sometimes under circumstances amounting to cruelty. Three years before Charles Doe arrived, a boy had died as a result of hazing, but this memory did not dampen the spirits of the victim's classmates. They pounced with enthusiasm upon what appeared to be a likely rube from provincial Somersworth. What they did to him has not been recorded, but it certainly aroused Doe's wrath. He was especially angered at one upperclassman. Since to attack him openly would have been social suicide, one night he and another freshman pulled up a loose stump in the Yard — a safe thing to do since there were no lights — and threw it through the boy's window. The panes, the sash, the frame, and all were shattered and smashed. Years later, while chief justice of New Hampshire, Doe, passing through the Yard with one of his daughters, stopped to check the window. He ran his hand over the sash and was uncharacteristically gleeful when he found a small crack in the frame, sure it was a relic of his escapade.

There is no record of the reason for Charles Doe's leaving Harvard College after only one year. It might have been the expenses, which totaled about $194 a year, not counting fuel, washing, and furniture. Or it might have been the Unitarian influence, which could hardly have pleased his mother, or the unsettled state of the college administration. In the summer of Charles' enrolment, Josiah Quincy had surprised everyone by ending a sixteen-year reign and resigning as president. In his place the Corporation elected Edward Everett, who had just returned from England after serving a term as American ambassador to the Court of St. James's. He was unable to cope with the students, who mocked his British airs by wearing bluetail coats to chapel; not knowing how to discipline them, he had to satisfy himself by complaining in faculty meetings. When Everett told the boys that young gentlemen did not blow their noses — in England they used handkerchiefs — the next day at chapel they waved their handkerchiefs at him. It was good fun, but Harvard was headed for a period of decline.[20] Matters were in sounder hands at Dartmouth, where costs were cheaper and the orthodoxy of old New Hampshire was still maintained without compromise.

Then again, it is possible that Doe was expelled from Harvard. Perhaps the window-breaking episode had gotten him into trouble. A decade later Oliver Wendell Holmes was fined for the same act, and President Felton told Holmes's father, "In every other case known to me, breaking windows has been punished by dismission from College, when detected."[21] In the letter he sent President Everett withdrawing his son, Joseph Doe implies that Charles had been asked to leave Harvard. "In compliance with your rules and my Son Charles Promise," the elder Doe wrote. "I would inform you that. He left Cambridge And will go to Hanover. With my consent."[22] Whatever the reason, at the end of his freshman term in college, for the fourth time in as many years, Charles Doe changed schools.

In several respects the Dartmouth which Charles Doe first saw was reminiscent of New Hampshire's former days. It was the last stronghold of Congregationalism. After Chief Justice Marshall in the *Dartmouth College Case* had reinstated the old trustees, the clergy, by holding the purse strings, gained control of the college and were supported by the faculty whose salaries they paid. "Let not one inch be yielded so long as it can be maintained," one professor pleaded. "The interests of liberty, of truth, and of the soul are concerned in this issue." [23] During the years Charles Doe attended Dartmouth, there was no danger that even half an inch would be yielded. The clergy of New Hampshire had planted Nathan Lord securely in the president's chair; he was, indeed, one of their own.

The scion of South Berwick's leading family, Nathan Lord was perhaps the reason Charles Doe was sent to Dartmouth. Armed with an intellect as brilliant as it was narrow, he was more conservative than the most rigid of the old-school precisians. To him any deviation from the teachings of the early New England fathers was heresy. Once he had adopted a tenet, he lost not a moment expounding it, and by the time Charles Doe arrived in Hanover, many of Lord's notions were famous and controversial. His entire philosophy of life was grounded upon his belief in the literal accuracy and inerrancy of the Bible. "All we can know in theology," he used to say, "is contained in the Bible." And this must have made him a well-versed man in his own estimation, because he knew it almost by heart. Someone once stole the copy from his desk in the bare, cold college chapel, and without batting an eye he repeated with perfect aplomb the entire Psalm 119. Everyone agreed that Nathan Lord recited prayers well, despite the fact he occasionally lost his voice, once for a whole year. Some of the boys even liked to hear him pray, and he impressed people with the grasp of his thought, the strength of his faith, and the compelling power of his urgency. [24]

To Charles Doe, however, President Lord must have seemed dreadfully like Andover's Samuel Taylor. Their uncompromising attitudes and their rigid dogmatism had a profound effect on Doe, leaving him with a distaste for incarcerating strictness and an aversion toward the educational system they represented. He attended five of the best secondary and undergraduate schools in New England, only to find them a dreary progression of uninspired pedagogy. In later years he was one of the many products of the old system who vocally supported President Eliot's at-

tempt to reform what Doe called "the barbaric classical course." [25]
When he said "barbaric course," Doe was choosing his words with
restraint; at other times he used stronger language. He was bitter concerning his education, and for a man who was so willing
to forgive his enemies and always refused to pursue a quarrel,
his bitterness is startlingly uncharacteristic. The extent of it is
revealed by a letter he wrote in 1886, when he was fifty-six and
serving his tenth year as chief justice, to Fletcher Ladd, the son
of a former associate justice, who with another student had committed some infraction of the Dartmouth rules, as a result of
which the faculty had voted to graduate both without degrees.
When Doe heard the news, all the stored-up resentment his in-
quisitive nature had felt during three frustrating years under
Lord came to the surface, and he wrote Ladd one of the strangest
letters of advice a disgraced youth has ever received. Doe congratulated him on being graduated without a degree, "but *summa
cum laude,* as they say at Cambridge." Then he wrote:

Pardon a suggestion from an old man who admires your equanimity
& pluck. If the trustees do not overrule the faculty (as it is to be presumed they will not) you will have an opportunity to render the
world an important service by demonstrating, in a striking manner,
the worthlessness of college degrees. The common ignorant estimation of them is a cause of much evil, & a superstition that ought to be
exploded. I am sure that a majority of graduates would have been
better off if that majority had not gone to college.

You start now with the greatest applause from all candid minds
who are informed of the circumstances of the completion of your college course, but under a cloud in the belief of others, not candid, or
not informed.

I cannot resist the impulse to urge you (& by "you" I mean both of
you) to hold fast forever to that imperturbable coolness, self-control &
courage with which you met this petty persecution. Scarcely anything
is more fatal to success than the habit of emotional agitation. Never
mention or refer to your expulsions. Carry yourselves as if there were
no Dartmouth College. Civility may require you to answer questions
on the subject; but I should answer them most briefly. Show by your
demeanor that it is the future & not the past you are thinking of. Express no regret, no resentment. Display no memory of the tyrants
from whose dominion you are happily delivered. In contrast with
their childish spite, exhibit the silent good-natured magnanimity of
men too elevated & too large to stoop to wrangle with anyone, or to
embitter your own lives by bearing grudges against those who used

you ill. You know theoretically that it is the way to heap coals of fire on an enemy's head. Are you capable of holding out to the end on that high plane?

There is no more power in the faculty of Dartmouth College to harm you than there is in the same number of yellow dogs, yelping in the streets of Constantinople.

The only way in which your missions can receive damage from the D.D.'s, LL.D.'s, Th.D.'s, A.M.'s & the rest of the Hanoverian alphabet, is by your recognizing the existence of the personal quarrel they have attempted to fasten upon you. You will be sorely tempted, through a sense of righteous indignation, to remember & take notice of them & their detestable conduct. If you are equal to the emergency, you will not waste a moment upon them except in philosophically considering their illustrations of the creating power of circumstances.

If farmers, merchants, lawyers & express men had been put in the place of the faculty, last Jan'y, they would not have disgraced themselves, the college & the state by the despicable squabble.

The faculty are disqualified for their duties, by being nothing more than men of books. But if they were not men of books they would be disqualified.

Persons qualified by book-knowledge, temper & practical skill, for teaching & managing the students of a non-catholic college in this free country, are exceedingly scarce. Where one hundred are needed not more than one can be found.

To be vexed with the unfitness of the Dartmouth Faculty is to be displeased with the order of nature. If your lives should fall under the influences that have made them what they are, you would probably be as unfit as they are for their work.

The position of a mere priest or teacher of books is narrow & belittling. It is extremely difficult for the largest & most liberal & just man, remaining long in that position, to become a competent leader of students. One of the most injurious influences of the place comes from the exercise of great power, developing excessive conceit, egotism, sensitiveness, an exaggerated & ridiculous idea of one's comparative value & consequence in the world, an inability to understand & practice the doctrine of equal rights, & all the qualities that make despotism vexatious & odious.

For a quarter of a century, I have had occasion to observe & feel the enormous danger to which you expose a man's character, by entrusting him with power over the persons & the rights of other men. There is nothing in the business or surroundings of a college professor to guard him against the danger. These Hanover gentlemen, like other spoiled children, are the mere products of their environment. They are so ignorant as to suppose the graduate's degree is of some value. By work that will show them their mistake, you can do much to correct a very prevalent and very mischievous error. For public usefulness in that direction, they have given you a peculiar opportunity, of which, I judge from your reputations, you will be likely to avail yourselves.

Ys truly
C. DOE [26]

If reaction to the "barbaric course" explains the bitterness of this remarkable letter, it may also explain another inconsistency concerning Judge Doe. For he, a man who literally killed himself with hard unremitting labor during his professional life, used to claim that he was "an idler" who did not work while at Dartmouth.[27] He told one friend that he had not only failed to study all of the prescribed textbooks, but that he did not even own some of them.[28] Joshua Hall of Dover, who was two classes below him, felt that Doe meant to imply that he had had an easy time of it at Hanover compared with his later work in law.[29] Another writer has suggested that Doe may have been referring to his remarkable ability to absorb knowledge when he called his college days the most facile of his life.[30] Actually Doe probably meant exactly what he said. He did little work in college because the "barbaric course" did not inspire him to exert more effort than he had to. One quip, however, was surely made in jest. Speaking of his classmate Clinton W. Stanley, later one of his associate justices, Doe said, "Stanley and I competed for the foot of the class, and I beat Stanley." [31] In truth Doe did quite well in his studies, for he was elected to Phi Beta Kappa.[32]

Though Dartmouth offered little in the way of intellectual stimulation, it was an important influence on the development of Charles Doe. There his personality took shape. At Exeter, Andover, and Harvard he seems to have made no lasting friendships. At Dartmouth, on the other hand, he struck up an intimacy with several boys, who remained close to him for the remainder of his life. Two of these, Stanley and Lewis W. Clarke, later served under him on the New Hampshire Supreme Court. One jocund class historian attempted to pinpoint the moment Doe ceased being a shy farm boy and began to show signs of egregiousness. In the autumn of 1848 the Northern Railroad was opened from Franklin to Lebanon Center, and since Daniel Webster was to be the orator of the day, some students decided to attend. Finding the depot yard crowded with 4,000 spectators, Doe and some classmates made their way to the platform and sat on the edge, their legs dangling over the side. When Webster, wearing a pair of cowhide boots, walked behind them, it was whispered, "Now is a good chance to come into contact with Mr. Webster." Several, including Doe, turned and put their hands on his boots. The class historian reports that prior to this incident neither Doe nor Stanley had shown any marked ability. "After that evening both these men seemed to come out with more power," he wrote. "This was a turning point in their history. The class have always attributed the change to that contact with Webster's boots. Several other members of the class touched the same boots, but the infection did not take." [33]

There is little doubt that Charles Doe enjoyed Dartmouth. He remained loyal to the college, despite the fact that he sent his sons to Eliot's Harvard. In 1859 he returned for his tenth reunion, and in 1873 he accepted an honorary degree. Apparently he even had some fondness for Lord. Through his life he remembered, and perhaps even acted on, advice Lord used to give to the students: "Go out into the world, Young Gentlemen, & turn the world upside down: for then the world will be right side up." [34]

Yet Dartmouth's "barbaric course" contributed little to his intellectual growth and may even have held him back. He was a man of genius, but his genius was displayed only professionally. He did not possess the curiosity that marks an educated man. He read only one novel in his life and seems to have been unaware of the movements in literature which were taking place in his century. He was an astute historian, but not a student of history. He read history only when it bore on a legal problem which he was researching.[35] Indeed, he was not in the habit of reading unless it served a pragmatic purpose.

Of course we cannot blame Dartmouth for Doe's inclinations; but Dartmouth did not help. The outstanding feature of the curriculum was its insularism, as can be seen by considering theology, the one subject in which Nathan Lord hoped to spark any interest among his boys. If any time and place was ripe for doing so, it was New Hampshire during the 1840s. Transcendentalism was in full swing; a community of Shakers was established on the road between Somersworth and Hanover; believers in spiritualism were numerous; abolitionists, vegetarians, and non-resistants were clamoring to have their views incorporated into doctrine.[36] During the very decade Charles Doe was attending the cold, bare Baptist church at South Berwick, up in the village of Tilton, New Hampshire, Mary Baker's doctor was dabbling in mesmerism and attempting mental suggestion to relieve her hysteria. While Mrs. Eddy was to go to one extreme, Charles Doe reacted to his training in the opposite direction. But the theological debates then in progress were not permitted to confuse the minds of President Lord's pupils. New England college students during the 1840s might be familiar with the names of Emerson and Parker, but no one told them of Pusey or Newman.[37] Theodore Parker in Boston and John Henry Newman at Oxford were in the vanguard of movements which might have interested Doe as a lawyer. Parker the transcendentalist pleaded for reason in religion, just as Doe would plead for it in law. Newman the medievalist would use legalist arguments drawn from history to reform religious institutions, just as Doe would draw arguments from history to reform judicial institutions. Doe's genius was such that he might have been excited by their imagination. As it turned out, theology would always be nothing more to him than the "hell and damnation" sermons that a growing boy had been forced to suffer on long, cold Sunday mornings in a small Maine town.

Chapter Four

JOE DOE — EDUCATED
At the Bar

BY the time Charles Doe was graduated from Dartmouth, the public image of the New Hampshire bar had somewhat improved since 1766, when a mob threatened to run Durham's first lawyer out of town. Of course the Yankees were not entirely convinced. When William Plumer announced his intention to become an attorney, his father objected and bought him a farm in the hope of dissuading him. But Plumer persisted, and his father had to acquiesce. "Go then, William, if you must," he said; "it is a bad company you are going into — the lawyers; but I can trust you, even there. They may not be so bad after all. There are dishonest farmers, and even dishonest Christians; why not then, honest lawyers?" [1]

The elder Plumer was more magnanimous than most New England Yankees during the nineteenth century. "He seems to be a gentleman practicing law, and not a mere lawyer," Richard H. Dana said of Franklin Dexter, confident that people understood what he meant.[2] And Chief Justice Joel Parker of New Hampshire, Charles Doe's instructor at Harvard Law School, wrote:

> They'll tell you a lawyer but seeks for the pelf,
> And for that will out-Herod the Devil himself.[3]

The bar suffered from a bad press in every respect but one — the glamor of the profession. Trial lawyers were the colorful figures of the day, their exploits a chief topic of conversation. From their ranks the state selected its leaders. There was a comradeship among them which other men envied. Charles Doe always addressed fellow attorneys as "brother," beginning his letters "Brother Ladd" or "Brother Marston." To join the legal ranks was the ambition of many a New Hampshire youth. The law was the surest, sometimes the only, way to fame and to participation in a world larger and greater than that of their native villages. Their elders might know better, but to the boys of New Hampshire lawyers were often heroes.

Charles Cogswell Doe never doubted that he would be a lawyer. His father was the most decisive force pointing him to the law. Joseph Doe, who had wanted to be an attorney, dabbled in legal matters, acting as executor of small estates, counseling neighbors who sought his advice, and mischievously performing minor tasks which in a later age would be the exclusive monopoly of the bar. His closest associates in the legislature — Haven and Mason — had been lawyers, as were several of his best friends. He made no secret of envying them their profession, and they in turn honored his untrained abilities, for along with the townspeople of Somersworth they called him "Squire Doe," an appellation usually reserved for a venerable old advocate.[4] When it came time for his youngest son to embark on the career he had coveted, Joseph Doe made certain that he received the best possible training. He took him to Dover and apprenticed him in the office of an old political ally.

Immediately after his graduation from Dartmouth in 1849 Charles Doe began his professional education in the Dover office of Daniel Miltmore Christie. It has been said that Christie was the founder of a school of legal study and dialectics. Surely of all the New Hampshire lawyers who trained students, none was more successful than he. At one time three of the six judges on the state's highest court were former pupils of his, and this was no average bench but one which Professor Joseph H. Beale would note as being especially "strong." [5]

Charles Doe told his children that next to his own father Daniel Christie exerted the greatest influence on his life. He may have been referring to Christie as an example of personal integrity and professional dedication — it is hard to imagine what Christie could have contributed to his intellectual growth. Christie stood for everything Doe later sought to expunge from the law;

Doe in time came to stand for all the reforms Christie despised. To Christie law was not the customs of a people, but the science of a trained profession. His legal philosophy has been summed up by one of Doe's fellow students who observed that "*stare decisis* was his motto." [6] This contrasted with Doe's belief that some precedents are but "a frivolous formality." Doe distrusted English authorities; Christie on the other hand was "bred to the common law." He was, as one Dover attorney put it, "the greatest living expositor among us of the Common Law of England." [7] Equity, a recent innovation in New Hampshire courts, seemed to him nothing more than law without precedents, a legal system without discipline. Nor did he look favorably on codes of procedure, which, in his opinion, degraded the study of law from an art to a trade, introducing simplified tools which any inerudite and unskilled attorney could wield. Had he lived to see them, Doe's adjective reforms would have appalled Christie.

Christie's caution was proverbial. When his advice was sought, he never gave an immediate answer, no matter how rudimentary the problem; instead, the question was written down and the client was told to call again. Charles Doe's cynical suggestion that Christie hoped that advice given after careful examination would be valued more highly than if tendered off-handedly on the spur of the moment is probably unfair, for Christie was only carrying to extremes the axiom that no haphazard answer should be offered on any point of law. His mind functioned differently from Doe's, whose mental powers were amazing. This may explain why Doe was impatient where the slow and probing Christie was patient. When he was on the Supreme Court, Doe pushed his colleagues along, telling them to steer away from the "crooked coast line" and to "put out to sea." He did not learn such methods from Christie. "It is a great feat of ship-building to construct a yacht to sail as near to the wind as possible," Doe once remarked. "Mr. Christie did not train his students in that kind of skill. His rule was to run no avoidable risk." [8]

Christie's caution bothered clients but did not hurt his practice. Between 1823, the year he came to Dover, and 1870, the year he retired, he was engaged in nearly every important jury trial in the county. Nor was he less active in appellate work. During Charles Doe's second year in his office, for example,

Christie was connected with fifteen of the twenty cases on the December law-term docket. His office was a place of serious, unremitting labor, in which no student dared to relax even to read a newspaper — in later years Doe did not recall ever seeing one there. Christie usually arrived soon after breakfast and worked until ten at night unless summoned elsewhere on business. Week in, week out, he pored over books and notes in the poorly lit office and breathed the vitiated air of the dingy courtroom without slacking his pace. Indeed, it is said that more than once he was in poor health when he began a trial term but recovered rapidly while being subjected to what other men found the strain of forensic contests.[9]

Perhaps Doe acquired his diligence here. Christie surely demanded a good deal of effort from his clerks. But just what Doe did when not assisting Christie or copying writs is hard to say. He read fewer textbooks than most law students; by his own count he did not study more than three or four, in addition to Kent's *Commentaries* — "But these books," another pupil recalls, "he made his own" [10] — an indication that he depended on Christie for practical instruction. But Christie had little time to spare, and most learning was done by observation. It is said that Christie "was a man saturated with legal learning; and a large amount of valuable matter gradually oozed out from him, and exercised a fertilizing influence upon the young men around him." [11] In other words, he expounded on details relating to daily problems and let his apprentices fit the pieces into the big picture. Though such a procedure now seems careless, it obtained excellent results. During the years Doe was in his office, Christie trained a future congressman, a future court reporter, a future Harvard law professor, and a future state chief justice.

Joshua Hall, who came from Dartmouth to Christie's office with Charles Doe, relates that Doe was a "quiet young man" and that the lawyer instantly took his measure. Ever afterward, Hall says, "Mr. Christie always treated Judge Doe with deference and spoke of him in terms of strong commendation." [12] It may be that the mentor of Chief Justice Ira Perley and Senator John Parker Hale realized that he now had his finest pupil on hand. Before long Christie paid Doe the highest compliment possible when he was stopped on the street and asked whether his new student would make a successful lawyer. "Do you know Joe Doe?" Christie replied. "Well Charles is Joe Doe — educated." [13]

After Charles Doe had completed about three years' study with Christie, it was decided to broaden his legal education with the spice of more formal stuff, and he was enrolled at Harvard Law School, then called the Dane Law School. Though the leading law school in the nation, it was at the lowest ebb of its existence. Joseph Story had long since departed, and it was still twenty years before Eliot was to sweep the place clean with reform. There were no examinations, attendance at lectures was voluntary, subjects were elective, and the residence requirement for a degree was determined by how much law the entering student had read, not how much he was able to recollect. The curriculum was designed for two years, one half given each alternative year, so that each student had to trust to chance whether he commenced at the beginning of the course or was plunged into the middle. In 1853, the year Doe arrived, the first term of the second year was being offered. On the strength of his training in Christie's office Professor Theophilus Parsons put him in the senior class, the top of three groups into which the student body was divided. Doe was able to elect such advanced courses as Bailments, Real Property, Equity, Admiralty, and Bankruptcy.[14]

Parsons, the nominal head of the school, divided most of the instruction with Judge Joel Parker. It is difficult to name two other men with equal opportunity to influence the American legal profession during the second half of the last century. Through their classrooms passed many of the greatest practitioners at the bar. They were privileged to mold a generation of lawmakers, a generation of legislators, and a generation of judges. During Charles Doe's year alone there were two future senators, two future governors, and two future ambassadors, one to France, the other to Great Britain; not to mention future members of the judiciary in Delaware, Indiana, Maryland, and other jurisdictions. Yet, when compared to Christie, it cannot be said that Parsons and Parker left their stamp on those they taught. Christie in his small way founded a school of advocates; they were the teachers of boys who became famous men.

Still, if we were to seek influence through emulation, it seems that Charles Doe learned more at Harvard, especially from the liberal Parker, than he did in Dover from the conservative Christie. Not that anyone who attended Parker's classes thought him liberal. He was a ponderous teacher, who laid out exact assignments in the text and followed them faithfully. Students considered the more charming, quickwitted Parsons a better instructor. Parsons, whose treatise on contracts is said to have had the largest sale of any law book published before the twentieth century, owed his position quite as much to his engaging personality as to his legal ability.[15] He may have made an impression on Doe, for his dislike for the technical side of law, especially certain aspects of pleading and property, was in time echoed by Doe. The difference between them was that Parsons was more the legal litterateur, while Doe was more the common lawyer. Doe agreed that outmoded technicalities which stifled justice should be reformed, but he eventually rejected the solution of legislative codes, preferring to keep the old teachings while sweeping away the cobwebs.

Joel Parker's students viewed him as "the deep repository of all legal knowledge," [16] yet complained that he was precise and involved, almost to the point of obscurity. "If a single step of his logic was lost by the listener, farewell to all hope of following to the conclusion." [17] Even Joseph Choate found him so tremendously profound that he failed to derive benefit from his lectures.[18] What Charles Doe thought of Parker as a teacher we cannot say, but he surely found him interesting as a man. For Parker had been in the House of Representatives in 1826, the year that Joseph Doe debated Isaac Hill on the subject of banking, and later had served ten years as chief justice of New Hampshire. It was during his time as a judge that he set a pattern Charles Doe found useful during his own career; it was demonstrated in his most famous decision, *Britton* v. *Turner*, which his admirers called "a consummate masterpiece of judicial reasoning." [19]

Britton v. *Turner* is one New Hampshire opinion which nearly every first-year law student must still read. The plaintiff had contracted to do a specific job at an agreed price, to be paid upon satisfactory completion. After laboring for some time, he unjustly refused to finish the work and sued to recover the value of what had been done. Parker rejected what is still the majority rule — that recovery can be had only if the plaintiff's breach is "not wilful or deliberate." According to the theory, performance of the whole labor is a condition precedent on which the right to recovery depends and that since the contract is entire, there can be no apportionment. These were, said Parker, technical arguments which caused an injustice, for they meant that the plaintiff would have been better off had he never entered on the performance at all. Rejecting every precedent, Parker held that the plantiff was entitled to recover on a *quantum meruit* the value of the benefit which the defendant had received, deducting damages resulting from the breach.[20]

The decision, with its assumption that there are degrees of breaches, was criticized outside New Hampshire for undermining the inviolability of contracts. In New Hampshire, however, lawyers agreed with Parker's reasoning that the old rule of no recovery without complete satisfaction gave the employer an opportunity to defraud the laborer by driving him from his service near the close of his term, while *quantum meruit* gave neither party an inducement to breach the contract unjustly. For Charles Doe this was to be the importance of *Britton* v. *Turner:* that the bar did accept it; the ruling did become good law. In the name of both reason and justice Joel Parker had successfully rejected precedent, as Judge Doe was to do in many revolutionary decisions. Doe made reason and justice the cornerstones of his jurisprudence and carried to extremes the argument that unreasonable and unjust precedents have no binding authority and that the court may take the initiative in substituting moral judgments for technical rules. He was attacked by lawyers for abandoning the old guideposts, but in *Britton* v. *Turner* he had a precedent for deviating from rules which do not meet the test of justice. The legal philosophy Judge Parker expounded in this one case is the legal philosophy Judge Doe made dominant in New Hampshire law.

To receive his degree Charles Doe had to remain at the Law School for two terms of twenty weeks each, with a vacation of six weeks in between. But after completing only the first term, he returned to Dover in January 1854 and began to practice law. He had been working hard for the Democrats, and it may be that they had promised that once he was established, the party would appoint him solicitor of Strafford County.

Despite Doe's short stay, his studies at Cambridge were an important influence on his life and upon his later attempts, in the pages of the New Hampshire Reports, to reconcile the changing conditions of his world with established legal doctrine. For he had been introduced to the Harvard Law School tradition, founded by Joseph Story, which viewed the law in terms of public policy and social ends and studied jurisprudence as man's greatest system of philosophy. At the Dover law office of Daniel Christie he had received a bread-and-butter training in the fundamentals of practice, which would make him a successful lawyer; at the Harvard Law School he obtained the start of a broad foundation in legal theory which would help make him a great judge.

Charles Doe had no trouble gaining admittance to the bar. There were no requirements except that the candidate be twenty-one. As he said years later, "age and good moral character were the only necessary qualifications. Legal knowledge and skill were not required." [21] Nor did Doe have any difficulty selecting a place to practice. Dover was the largest town and the county seat, and since he was to be solicitor of Strafford County, it was the logical spot to pick.

By the end of the decade Dover had a population of 8,186. Back in Nicholas Doe's day it had been a farming community. Later it was a center of lumbering. Joseph Doe's generation compensated for the depletion of the forests by turning it into a mill town — drab, ugly, and monotonous. Later, with the arrival of the railroad, it became a junction and the hub of its own little world.[22]

The railroads were important to Charles Doe. The Boston & Maine arrived in Dover in 1841, and with it came the era of modern law. The law of torts became a significant and profitable branch of legal activity for lawyers; so too, though less lucrative, did public-utility law, the law of eminent domain, and administrative law. The railroad also spelled the end of the old way of practicing law: the circuit riders, the drunken evenings, and the wild banquets for which lawyers in New Hampshire had been famous. With faster transportation, legal practice became more businesslike because lawyers had less free time on their hands. Still, the tradition of "law week" * continued. Into town came lawyers, judges, suitors, witnesses, and the spectators who found jury trials an entertaining pastime. Attorneys led a privileged life during that week. Special tables were set aside for them at which the food, as one oldtimer later recalled, was often spiced "by sally of wit and clever repartee." During evenings the homes of local lawyers and the parlors of hotels were merry places. The feeling of fraternal regard was at its height. Mock trials, squibs, stories, and rousing songs enlivened the hours, for in those days few bothered to prepare for the next day in court.

We may imagine that Charles Doe passed up the horseplay during law week of February 1855. As Strafford's chief prosecuting officer he was responsible for, among other matters, conducting a first-degree murder trial. As might be expected, the local Democratic press had lauded his appointment as county solicitor, telling the public to expect great things. "Mr. Doe is a young man of eminent abilities, and admirably qualified to discharge the duties of the office satisfactorily to all concerned. His appointment, as we learn, is spoken of very highly, and the talent which is well-known he possesses as a lawyer, will be of vast service to the county." [23] You could never guess from this that Doe was only twenty-four and had never argued a case in court.

The attorney general, John Sullivan, had arrived in town to conduct the state's case. But Doe had prepared it and was expected to make the opening statement to the jury. He must have faced an ordeal. Difficult as it was to start a legal career in a celebrated murder trial sure to attract a large crowd, worst for Doe was his extreme diffidence. His legs quivered and his hands broke out in a sweat whenever he faced an audience. This was why he had become a stump speaker for the Democrats; "to harden himself, so that he could address a jury without having his knees knock together." [24] In this, his first professional effort, he seems to have succeeded. At least the Democratic newspaper,

---

* The days during which the Court of Common Pleas (and later the Supreme Judicial Court) sat in a county seat as a court of first instance was known to lawyers as "Trial Term" and to the general public as "law week." The days during which the full bench of the Superior Court (later the Supreme Judicial Court) sat in a county seat to hear appeals was known respectively as "Law Term" and "court week."

which may have been uneasy about its young prodigy, thought he had done rather well. "The case," the Dover *Gazette* boasted, "was opened on Wednesday afternoon on the part of the State by Mr. Solicitor Doe; this was his first appearance before a jury; the first in a series of brilliant exhibitions which we confidently believe are in reserve for one who has the natural qualities and untiring industry possessed by Mr. Doe. His statements were marked by that perfect propriety, clearness of thought, and elegance of diction, which marks a well constituted and well disciplined legal mind. Mr. Doe evidently made a favorable impression upon the sasembled [sic] crowd." [25]

The story Doe outlined to the jury was not sensational. It started one evening in February 1854, when the victim, William Maxwell, had left Salmon Falls with a mixed party of young people and had gone to a dance in Dover. New Hampshire law had come a long way since the era when Nicholas Doe had not been permitted to dance with his bride, and the descendants of the Puritans could now have a rare time. After midnight Maxwell and his friends started a pub crawl down Central Avenue, visiting such Dover establishments as the Central Saloon, Freeman's, and Twombly's. Tiring of this they sleighed to Great Falls where they enjoyed more drinks at Hodge's Hotel. Hodge, apparently disapproving of fornication, refused to rent them rooms. Following a heated argument during which Maxwell told off Hodge, the crowd went to another, more obliging hotel. Some time later Maxwell returned with a playmate named Moses Lovering and, banging loudly on the door, ordered Hodge to stable his horse. After exchanging heated words from an upstairs window, Hodge came downstairs clutching a cudgel. What happened next was the issue of the trial. Maxwell's friend, Moses Lovering, was the pivot of Doe's case. His story, upon which Doe based his indictment, was that as soon as the door opened, Hodge began clubbing Maxwell. Lovering said he had offered to take Maxwell away, but Hodge had turned on him and driven him into the cab. Then Hodge struck the horses and they galloped off, carrying Lovering back to the other hotel, where he decided to sleep it off. When he returned to Hodge's the next morning, he found Maxwell fatally beaten.

After Doe rested his case, the defense presented a different picture, contending that the accused, despite his anger, never hit Maxwell — not even once. Instead, since all he wanted was to stop the noise, he had used the cudgel to drive away the horses. As he had hoped, Maxwell and Lovering had chased them down the street, waving their arms in a drunken frenzy and shouting curses back at him. The implication was that the two had later quarreled and that Lovering was the one who should have been on trial. Thirteen neighbors took the stand and testified to Lovering's disreputable character. Finally it was explained why the body had been discovered at Hodge's: Maxwell had not only returned to the hotel early the next morning, but had been admitted by the now friendly Hodge. After finding a glass of gin "not bad stuff," he had climbed the stairs, locked himself in a bedroom, and died. There were witnesses who swore to this.

Hodge's counsel, Ichabod Goodwin Jordan, who had rounded up these obliging witnesses, was a second-rate attorney who scraped by on a meager practice in Great Falls. His one asset as an advocate lay in the fact that he was a bully. The demeanor of opposing counsel toward one another during those days was brusque and rude, sometimes even rough, and Jordan was a master of the technique. Exchanges of asperities between attorneys was the accepted custom. It was an evil which Charles Doe later successfully reformed, and he started to do so here, in his first case. Professor Jeremiah Smith recalled in 1897:

The senior counsel for the defense was a man (now almost entirely forgotten) who had gained distinction in what may be called the blackguarding method of trying cases. Better men had essayed to fight him with his own weapons, and failed for the very reason that they *were* better men. It did not seem to have occurred to the bar that there was any way of meeting him except by descending to his level and attempting to pay him back by his own coin. This man began the Hodge trial in his accustomed way, intending, no doubt, to stir up and confuse the young junior counsel for the state. To the intense surprise of the spectators, the new solicitor ignored the existence of the senior counsel for the defense. He did not seem to hear any of his irrelevant remarks, but went on putting questions and addressing the court just as if those remarks had never been made. The consequence was that, ere, the end of the long trial, the counsel for the defense had 'flattened out' as never before.[26]

Jordan was not "flattened out" quite enough, however. One juror, dissatisfied with the state's case, insisted on voting for acquittal even though the other eleven stood for conviction. As a result, the jury was hung and Charles Doe neither won nor lost his first case.

Hodge may be considered to have won. He was reindicted by Doe, but when the second trial was about to commence, Doe had to request a postponement. Lovering was missing; "without negligence on the part of the State," as the *Gazette* assured the public. The following year Hodge offered to change his plea from not guilty of first-degree murder to guilty of manslaughter. The attorney general consented, saying that another trial would have been too expensive. Doe agreed.

Aside from this one murder trial, the prosecutions Charles Doe handled as solicitor of Strafford County were mostly peccadilloes — breaking and entering, assault, and violation of the liquor-licensing law. The liquor statute proved to be Doe's undoing. As the facts in the *Hodge Case* show, saloons were common in New Hampshire during the 1850s. Even more common were the reformers. They had wanted to stamp out the whiskey trade as early as the 1820s, but Isaac Hill lined up the Democrats on the other side. Over the years the temperance group sought alliances with one opposition party after another. By the time Charles Doe was studying law, the party constituted a key section of the Whig-Abolitionist-Know-Nothing fusion. The Whigs, the Know-Nothings, and especially the Abolitionists were willing to support regulatory laws in return for temperance votes. The Democrats strenuously opposed such legislation, blocking its passage for a number of sessions; when it was finally enacted in 1855, they refused to obey it. With half the population opposed, enforcement became a political issue. Most violators were Democrats, and Democratic jurors would not return convictions. The proponents of temperance blamed the county solicitors, all of whom were Democrats.

The year 1855 was one of political revolution in New Hampshire. For the first time since Isaac Hill had led it to power, the Democracy was a minority party, and the opposition coveted the spoils of victory. All through the summer the legislature addressed out of office hundreds of Democrats. Failure to enforce the licensing statute was used as an excuse against the solicitors of Grafton, Sullivan, and Belknap Counties. But for some reason — perhaps because Daniel Christie was on the judiciary committee, protecting him — Doe was spared. During the next session, however, the axe fell. Every Democrat who held an important nonjudicial office was removed within three short weeks. Doe's friends were able to muster little support in his defense. When the resolution to address the governor for his removal was offered, only four of twelve senators voted against it, while in the house it was passed by 138 to 117. After serving less than two years of a six-year term, Doe was removed from office. For the record he was charged with neglecting his duty. Though everyone knew this to be nothing but political evulgation, Doe resented the accusation. His claim that he had diligently enforced all laws, no matter how distasteful he might find some of them, is borne out by the record. The docket of the Court of Common Pleas shows several convictions for licensing violations; while there were many acquittals, at least Doe did not hesitate to seek indictments. Nor is there any evidence that he tried to enforce the statute out of existence by making it more unpopular than it was. He persuaded several defendants to plead guilty, proving that at least their lawyers were convinced he meant business.[27]

By being addressed out of office Charles Doe lost little except prestige. The solicitor's salary was only $40 a year, hardly adequate for the amount of time required by the job. Now Doe could devote all his attention to private practice, which he conducted in partnership with Charles W. Woodman of Dover. It was not usual to adopt a firm name at that time, but they were known as Woodman & Doe.[28] History reveals little concerning Woodman. On the strength of his record he would seem to have been quite successful. He had been appointed county solicitor at the age of thirty,[29] judge of probate at thirty-seven,[30] and circuit justice at forty-four.[31] That he had respectable clients is shown by the fact that, along with Christie, he was a director of the Strafford Bank.[32] But apparently his legal ability was not highly thought of by his fellow lawyers. He is seldom mentioned by legal writers, and in correspondence now extant Doe never refers to him. Governor Charles H. Bell, in his sketches of the bar — a source which is usually quite laudatory and never critical — says Woodman was "not brilliant" but "sensible," hardly a compliment; that he was noted for his honesty, a quality attributed to those in the profession about whom there is little to say; and that he was considered "an excellent 'all round' lawyer," which probably means that there was nothing at which he excelled.[33]

Law practice in nineteenth-century New Hampshire was undoubtedly fun, but it was also routine and often picayune. Daniel Webster cynically called his first office a shop "for the manufacture of justice writs." [34] It was Charles Doe who ended the male monopoly and admitted women to the bar. Until then, many a New Hampshire female pined for the glamorous life of a lawyer and one sent Joel Parker a poem entitled "Vision."

> I'd be a lawyer, gifted with power,
>   Clients to draw to my little retreat;
> I'd pore over Blackstone for many an hour,
>   With pleas and rejoinders fill many a sheet.
> I'd win every cause, and would eloquence shower, —
>   Convince judge and jury, with arguments neat.
> I'd be a lawyer, gifted with power,
>   Clients to draw to my little retreat.

To set the record straight, Parker replied with a rather sorry sample of New Hampshire legal doggerel which he dubbed "Reality."

> Oh! I am a lawyer, and live in a den
>   Called an office — a snug and a quiet retreat:
> It is sixteen feet one way, the other but ten,
>   And the temperature's not far above "fever heat."
> I watch there for clients, but that's all a hum, —
> Like sprites from the vasty deep called they don't come.[35]

Despite the bad poetry, Parker had a point. Clients were not breaking down the doors of New Hampshire law offices during the nineteenth century. Everyone was agreed that there were too many lawyers; the public for one reason, the bar for another. When Doe joined Woodman, nine other attorneys were practicing in Dover, a rough ratio of 1 to every 750 citizens, counting women and children.[36] Many, of course, were not of the first rank, but even Daniel Christie, who managed to keep busy all the time, was able to collect only paltry fees. Portsmouth's best lawyer, Jeremiah Mason, had moved to Boston to make more money. "The Boston people pay well for professional services," he told Governor Plumer's son. "It is a bad trait in their character, and I rather encourage them in it. Your father and I did business enough in our day to make us rich; but, in New Hampshire, much is done for a little money."[37] John Lord Hayes, a friend of Doe's, claimed that his father charged $20 for professional services which in 1886 would have commanded $1,000.[38] This figure was undoubtedly a gross exaggeration, but even had Hayes set it at a quarter of the amount, he would have proved his point. The sum of $20 was a good fee for a New Hampshire lawyer. In a novel depicting nineteenth-century New Hampshire practice, published in 1913 and with the protagonist based on Mason Tappan, who was attorney general while Doe was chief justice, a local attorney receives a retaining fee by mail from a New Yorker. "Twenty dollars for a retaining fee!" he remarks. "Gosh! That's an awful lot to know about law."[39]

It would be idle to speculate on Charles Doe's earnings. When he died he was well off, but it is not known how much of his wealth was inherited from his father and his father-in-law and how much was made from investments. But on the whole he can be called a successful practitioner. Between April 1854, when he was admitted to the bar, and September 1859, when he was appointed to the bench, his name is entered as counsel in 223 separate actions filed in Strafford County. His first case argued at the law term is interesting. His clients had been convicted and sentenced for arson, the indictment charging that they "with force and arms feloniously and unlawfully did set fire, burn and consume a certain building of Stephen S. Chick and George W. Wendell, called a store." The statute, however, made arson a crime only if committed "willfully and maliciously." Doe probably received great pleasure in tripping up his Know-Nothing successor in the county solicitorship, the man for whom he had been removed from office, by pointing out that neither "unlawfully" nor "feloniously" conveyed the idea of willfulness or malice. The court agreed, and his motion for arrest of judgment was granted. Later, as chief justice, Doe refused to dismiss an indictment for this same error, calling it a frivolous technicality.[40]

Doe's most notable civil litigation was *The Kingman Case,* in which he served as junior counsel first to Ira Perley and, after Perley was appointed chief justice, to John Sullivan Wells, the Democratic gubernatorial candidate. "Few civil controversies," Professor Smith has written, "have ever excited greater public interest in Strafford county." [41] This was not due to any challenging or intriguing issues of law, but rather because the facts had the makings of a scandal.

Seven days before John Kingman died, he had executed, without consideration, two bonds of $12,000, one to each of his sons. These bonds were the only substantial claims against the estate, which in its entirety was worth little more than $25,000. The other heir at law was Kingman's second wife, the boys' stepmother. She was Doe's client. The bonds, as legal debts outstanding and not subject to rules regulating distribution, were an obvious attempt to deprive her of her statutory share to his estate. Her stepsons took no chances. One brother challenged the validity of the other's bond. They agreed to submit the dispute to three referees and prayed the Probate Court to issue a rule of reference. Since both bonds were alike, the contest was a sham, intended to establish validity at a hearing from which the stepmother was excluded. Doe excepted to the prayer, alleging it was collusive and fraudulent, since the rule of reference was designed solely to effect and destroy the rights of a third party. The probate judge agreed and denied the prayer on the grounds that the brothers could have only their own claims referred, and to refer them would cause an injustice to their stepmother. On appeal the Superior Court gave the statute on reference the narrowest possible construction and held that the Probate Court had no discretion in the matter. Petitioners, it said, had an absolute right of reference. Doe's client was out of luck.[42]

The case contains an amazing series of technicalities. The bonds themselves were technical gimmicks, with which to avoid the spirit of the law. So too was the scheme to have referees rule on their validity at a hearing from which interested third parties would be excluded. Here is a truly remarkable example of the technical approach to legal science which Charles Doe ended in

New Hampshire. By the time of Doe's death in 1896, no lawyer in the state dared to attempt such an action. Yet back in the 1850s it was not only tried, it worked. Charles Doe was severely criticized for his radical reforms. When judging him, it is important to keep in mind decisions such as the one in the *Kingman Case*. The law he wrote for New Hampshire may have been less predictable, but it was more just.

We know even less of Doe's trial work than of his appellate. His years at the bar remain a mystery save for Jeremiah Smith's assurance that he tried cases "with success against such opponents as Daniel M. Christie, and John P. Hale." [43] Indeed, it is said that in one trial Christie paid Doe the tribute of ranking him with other former students, Senator John Parker Hale and Chief Justice Perley.[44]

"I was asked yesterday," Joshua Hall said at the memorial session of the court held to honor Doe in 1896, "by one of the younger members of the bar, if Judge Doe as a young man gave proof of the remarkable powers of mind that distinguished him in later life. I shall say in answer, not fully, but from the first he showed that tireless application, that discriminating judgment, and that remarkable power of thoroughly analyzing every legal proposition he encountered in the books, or in his daily business, which brought him his great fame in later years." [45]

Chapter Five

SWALLOWING HIMSELF
Politics[1]

In this age of uninterest in political platforms and of apathy toward party loyalties, it is impossible to recapture the atmosphere of New Hampshire politics from the 1840s to the 1870s. No other state was more politically minded; no other state so tightly organized. Holding the year's earliest elections, it was the country's political barometer for issues, causes, and personalities. Vast sums of money were poured into local contests, and the major parties sent their leading orators to speak in rural hamlets and crossroad towns from the Upper Coös to the Piscataqua. Elections for the legislature, for Congress, and for the presidency were held at different times, and since state offices were filled annually, campaigning was a year-round affair.

Politics in nineteenth-century New Hampshire has been called an "intermittent fever"; "no one infected with it was ever long without it." [2] The open ballot prevailed, and the voters, far from reluctant to display their party allegiance, were proudly partisan. When they hired help, they gave preference to laborers who voted their way. The average citizen with a minor civil litigation retained lawyers belonging to his party. And his lawyers sought a jury of party members. Each town had at least two newspapers, as for example Dover, where the *Gazette* was Democratic and the *Enquirer* was first Whig and then Republican. No Democrat read the *Enquirer*, no Whig read the *Gazette*. In larger towns each party had its own hotel. In Dover the Democrats stayed only at the American House and Republicans only at the New Hampshire Hotel. In smaller towns there were Democratic and Republican stores. The merchant who voted your ticket received your trade. Political loyalty was an aspect of life, and though men might change parties, they did so with the same feelings with which they might change their religion or their wives.

This was the political world which Charles Doe entered in 1852. It was essential for an ambitious young lawyer to be active in politics. Doe had the further reason of hoping to overcome extreme bashfulness through stump speaking. While there is no reason to doubt his statement that he used political gatherings to harden himself so that he would be able to address juries without his knees knocking together, it may be noted that Doe was busy in Democratic campaigns for more than a year and a half before his first jury trial. Perhaps he meant to say that he did not begin stump speaking in earnest until he had experienced stage fright before a jury. In any event, stump speaking helped Doe overcome the problem. He told a student that it "did him a world of good in the confidence he gained thereby, and the ability to think and express himself on his feet." [3]

To understand the Democratic Party of New Hampshire which Charles Doe joined in 1852, at the age of twenty-one, it is necessary to go back to 1828, the year of Joseph Doe's last term in the General Court, the year when Jacksonian democracy was sweeping the United States and New Hampshire was caught in the tide. Joseph Doe had helped to rally the forces of the right for one last struggle against the new order. Under the banner of John Quincy Adams they had carried the state, but with Jackson's triumph in the nation the power and the glory had passed to Isaac Hill. With it he forged a new party; a party that ruled supreme in New Hampshire for the next twenty-five years. The organized right collapsed.

In election after election the machine Hill built delivered New Hampshire into the Democratic fold. An example occurred in 1840, when New Hampshire was the only state in the northeast to reject William Henry Harrison, giving Martin Van Buren four-fifths of the aggregate majority he received in the two free states that voted for him. Even Daniel Webster could not win his native state for the Whigs. New Hampshire became known as the "South Carolina of the North": a New England state of proslavery sentiments, ruled by that breed of antebellum politicians who proudly boasted that they were "northern men with southern principles."

In large part what attracted Doe to the Democratic Party was its stand for unity in a nation headed for division, in which all other parties were sectional. The Democrats stood for the Constitution; and the Constitution was the most important item in Charles Doe's political and legal philosophy. By treating slavery as a property matter to be handled on the state level, the Constitution provided the only peaceful solution to the agitation stirring the country during the 1850s.

This does not mean that by joining the Democrats Charles Doe approved of slavery — far from it. He had learned to hate slavery at about the time that he entered politics. When on a visit to his brother Thomas in Danville, Virginia, he had been invited to dinner by his brother's neighbors. In that Virginia house the children ate at a table set apart from the grownups and were waited on by the children of the slaves who served the main table. Charles Doe was revolted by the sight. Perhaps it was his New England background, perhaps the Puritan sense of social balance inherited from his Yankee ancestors which caused him to feel distaste. The effect of this rather insignificant incident was enough to make him passionately antislavery. But the sentiment was still an emotion, and for Charles Doe emotion was no guide. He could sympathize with the aims of the reformers, but rationally he was at home in the Democratic Party. The Democrats of New Hampshire did not approve of the Fugitive Slave Act, but they were prepared to enforce it. In 1851 they had reconvened the state convention and had rejected their original gubernatorial candidate when it was discovered that he had written a letter in which he stated he could not in good conscience support that act. "All admit that the Constitution requires the surrender of fugitive slaves," the Party's leading organ had explained. "It matters not that we do not like it — there are many laws that we dislike, but that affords no excuse for opposing its execution." [4]

What Charles Doe did not realize was that the Democratic Party was walking on political quicksand. It was still the organization into which Jackson and Hill had breathed life, but its soul belonged to the South and it was losing contact with the

New Hampshire spirit. No one more clearly appreciated this than did Doe's cousin-by-marriage, John Parker Hale. Few would suggest that Hale spoke for the conscience of New Hampshire. Half Yankee and half Irish, he was a handsome, eloquent, and colorful man who had been a successful though unspectacular politician until Texas applied for admission to the Union. The Dover *Gazette* seemed to speak for the New Hampshire Democracy in 1843 when it stated, "The admission of Texas into the Union would be a public disgrace and disgrace us in the eyes of all the civilized world." But in 1844, with the election of James K. Polk, the South gained control of the Party, and compromise was no longer Democratic policy. New Hampshire was the first state to fall into line. Hale, who was then a congressman, misread the signs and made the mistake of proposing that Texas be admitted as two states, one free and one slave. It was a harmless enough suggestion and seemed to fit New Hampshire thought. The Exeter *News-Letter,* a key party voice in Hale's congressional district, said, "We do not perceive then that there is any issue, upon any matter of principle, between Mr. Hale and the Democratic party, so far as Texas is concerned." But party leaders feared that he had antagonized the South. By its next issue the *News-Letter* had received the word and demanded that Hale be replaced. Anti-Texas Democrats were purged throughout his district, and the party dropped Hale as its candidate. He was, in turn, adopted by the political forces opposing the spread of slavery. Southern reaction had furnished them a candidate to run against the regular Democratic and Whig nominees. Four elections were held that year; each was a stalemate. Decision was postponed until 1846, and the free-soil movement was born in New Hampshire.[5]

In 1846 Hale withdrew from the congressional election and ran for the state legislature. The Whigs, the Independent Democrats, and the Free-Soilers rallied to his banner. In the greatest campaign in New Hampshire history he and Franklin Pierce fought the battle in each city and hamlet in the state. The great political machine Isaac Hill had so patiently constructed floundered on the Texas issue. The opposition carried New Hampshire. A Whig was elected governor, and in June the General Court named John Parker Hale the new United States senator. It was ironic that

New Hampshire, the most proslavery state in the North, sent the first free-soil senator to Washington. In the "Hale Storm" of 1846, the seeds of Democratic destruction were sown. A decade later the Republicans reaped the harvest.

In the meantime, however, the Democrats under the leadership of Franklin Pierce regained the ascendancy. When Pierce was elected President in 1852, he carried the state by a wide margin. Hale was removed as United States senator and in his place the General Court elected Charles Atherton, one of the best-known proslavery politicians in the North.

In 1853 the Democrats were again triumphant, and Charles Doe was given his first political office as the assistant clerk of the state Senate. At about the same time his neighbors in Rollinsford * chose him as a delegate to the annual party convention. He took no part in the proceedings, but it is safe to surmise that he voted for the resolution calling on the national government to recognize "the equal rights of all the States under the Constitution, and the power to establish for themselves, without hinderance or molestation from the people of other States, such domestic institutions as they may deem best for the promotion of their interests and happiness." [6]

The Democrats won again in 1854, and Doe's services were once more rewarded. In May the governor appointed him a justice of the peace, in June he was elected one of the two clerks of the state senate,[7] and in October he was made solicitor of Strafford County. He was clearly marked for promotion. The trouble was that the Democratic party had no future. This was the last statewide election it won for eighteen years.

The cause of Democratic disintegration in 1855 was the Nebraska bill. When the party's national leadership adopted "popular sovereignty," thousands of New Hampshire voters deserted and shifted their allegiance to the Know-Nothings. As a result victory that year went to a coalition, each member of which received a share of the spoils. The Know-Nothings got the governorship. James Bell, a Whig, and John Parker Hale, a Free-Soiler, were elected to the United States Senate. The proponents

---

* In 1849 the town of Somersworth was divided. The new village of Great Falls kept the name Somersworth. The old village of Salmon Falls was incorporated as Rollinsford.

of temperance received a statute regulating the sale of liquor. And the anti-Nebraska Democrats had the satisfaction of seeing Franklin Pierce repudiated by his native state.[8]

Charles Doe seems to have accepted the Nebraska Act without reservation. He regretted the repeal of the Missouri Compromise, but this was not enough to persuade him to join those abandoning the Party. Perhaps the jobs he had received the year of the Nebraska Act kept him loyal, but this appears unlikely. In truth, he had nowhere to go. The Whigs were finished as a political organization, and the Free-Soilers were destined to remain a sectional group. As for the Know-Nothings, he wanted no part of their bigoted political program. He detested them, and when the Democrats of Concord asked him if he would speak in their city during the presidential campaign of 1856, Doe replied that he would be "glad to act in any capacity to aid in wiping out the disgrace that rowdyism is bringing to my native state." [9]

Doe worked hard for the Democrats that year. As early as September he had to beg off from addressing a meeting because, he said, he was "engaged to speak that day and every other day next week except Friday." [10] Perhaps Doe many years later was referring to this election when he told a friend that he had spoken in every schoolhouse in Strafford County. At first his speeches had been "disconnected talks," [11] but by the fall of 1856 he had developed into one of the chief Democratic orators in the state.

The cause was forlorn. The appearance of the Republican Party gave voters a clearcut alternative, and many decisively left the Democrats. Though the election was close, when the ballots were counted Fremont had beaten Buchanan. For the first time since the days of John Quincy Adams, New Hampshire cast her electoral votes against the Democratic candidate.

During 1857 and 1858, with no control of the state government, the only patronage left to the Democrats was dispensed from Washington. There were not many available offices, but Charles Doe thought that he had earned one of the choicest. Early in 1858, when he heard rumors that John H. George was planning to resign as United States district attorney for New Hampshire, Doe wrote George to ask for the job. "I should be gratified to see you remain; but if a change is to take place I am so selfish as to desire the place, & so vain as to think I should inflict no lasting injury on the State or party." [12] An important political plum, it was the one from which John Parker Hale had launched his career. Whether Charles Doe received serious consideration is not known. Less than a year after he had been rejected, he became a Republican.

The reason for Charles Doe's conversion to Republicanism was the same one that had first led him to join the Democratic fold — the Union. It had been obvious for some time, at least from New Hampshire's vantage point, that the Democracy was no longer a national party. Policy was dictated by its southern wing. Buchanan's insistence that the North accept Kansas' proslavery Lecompton Constitution, a repudiation of the Nebraska Act's provision of popular sovereignty, was proof on that score. In 1852 Doe had believed that the South wanted to preserve the Union; by 1858 he felt differently. His brother Thomas inadvertently helped to open his eyes. On another visit with him, Charles came to see the southern attitude in a new light. "He now realized what the answer was to his own speech about the danger of breaking up the Union, an answer which his former Republican opponents had failed to make. It was this: 'There is no Union now. The old Union is gone. Nothing remains but a shell ready to fall to pieces at any moment.' " [13]

In later years Doe cited the *Dred Scott Case* as the cause of his tergiversation. "Taney's decision," he wrote in a confidential letter, "was the worst in American history. The inevitable adoption of it by the Democratic party drove me out of that party." [14] In an odd twist of perspective, he saw this product of Jeffersonian constitutionalism as a triumph for extreme federalism. "I am as strongly anti-federal as you or anybody else," he explained to a Democratic friend; "& when Taney's dicta in the Dred Scott Case made local slavery a federal institution, & crushed State Rights under the heel of the slaveholder, establishing a theory that the Dem party were inevitably to maintain, I left the party, because I regarded his theory as the most infernal piece of Federalism that had ever been invented." [15] Doe now believed that "nothing would be effectual short of complete surrender to the demands of the extreme Southern leaders," and that *Dred Scott* outlined "the terms upon which they would insist." The Democratic Party which Charles Doe abandoned was now a sectional organization. [16]

The first newspaper to note Doe's departure from the Democratic ranks was Portsmouth's *New Hampshire Gazette.* It referred to him as "Another Lawyer Lost" and set the theme for future attacks by observing, "He never thought of leaving the Democratic party while it was strong enough to keep him in office." It named five other "disciples of the green bag" who had been proselytized, implying what everyone already knew — that lawyers were not to be trusted.[17] This attack brought a gleeful response from the Republicans. "Reflect on the subject for a moment," the Portsmouth *Journal* editorialized. "John Sullivan, N. B. Bryant, J. E. Sargent, Samuel Herbert, George Williams and Charles Doe. Have the Democracy of New Hampshire six other such men to spare."[18]

The amount of newspaper print devoted to Charles Doe's conversion to Republicanism is simply amazing. Of the thousands who bolted the Democratic Party during the 1850s few caused such excitement as he. Certainly no one else in Strafford County was so violently attacked by his former cohorts. Hardly a week passed in which he was not vilified by a Democratic writer.

The reason for the fuss is puzzling. Doe's place in the councils of the party certainly did not warrant such furor, since he was neither an office holder nor a candidate. There is not even evidence that the Democrats planned to nominate him for any office in the near future, save for a hint that he had enjoyed some backing for Congress.[19] A Republican newspaper in Concord furnished a clue when it commented that Doe had been one of the ablest Democrats in Strafford County and "by far the best speaker they had in the eastern part of the state."[20] Much the same point was made by a Portsmouth editor who wrote, "When Mr. Doe supported the Democrats he was regarded by our friends as altogether the most able opponent in that part of the state."[21] Whatever the explanation, Doe could take satisfaction from the summary of his old enemy, the Dover *Enquirer*: "It is fair to infer that the fruit of Mr. Doe is of the best kind, or else there would not be so much ado about his abandonment of his associates."[22]

Once Doe was safely in their camp, the Republicans wasted no time announcing "that he will immediately take the stump and give reasons for the faith which is in him."[23] When the editor of the *Gazette* read this, he invited Strafford County to see the fun.

We learn from the Enquirer, and other sources, that our quondam political friend, Charles Doe, Esq., is about to take the stump for the Republican party, and to illustrate the phenomenon of swallowing one's self — that is — to eat one's own words; to repudiate one's own sentiment; and abandon positions held for years; to charge upon himself either ignorance or duplicity, one or the other of which his present course fastens upon him — it is the Doe of 1859 v. the Doe of 1858.[24]

The Republicans were probably delighted: it was unprecedented for the *Gazette* to advertise opposition rallies. The party's Central Committee assigned to Doe the heaviest schedule of any stump speaker in the southern part of New Hampshire, committing him to more than seventeen addresses in twenty-three days.[25] Doe was billed as chief speaker on each occasion, except when he appeared on the same platform with Congressman Gilman Marston. He was then twenty-eight years old.

In those days Charles Doe did not write out his speeches. He prepared them with great care, to be sure, using topics or head notes from which he would get his main thought and sequence of ideas, but to the audience his delivery seemed extemporaneous. While he found this method best suited to his talent, it is doubtful if he could have written his speeches even if he had wished, since he spoke on the average for two and a half hours. Often he exhibited newspaper clippings to illustrate a point. Years after Doe died, one of his former law students was shown a volume of addresses by well-known politicians of the 1850s which Doe had had bound. Within the volume were loose, narrow sheets on which topics for a speech were written, along with many of the newspaper cuttings which Doe read and upon which he commented. On the inside cover he had written, "Upon the following authorities I founded stump speeches during the canvass for the State Election March 1859."[26]

Doe made his debut as a Republican stump orator in Farmington, just a few miles north of Dover, on February 11. It was perhaps a mark of confidence that he was chosen to open the campaign there. While not a large town, Farmington was politically significant, since its voting strength was evenly divided between the two parties. Traditionally it leaned toward the Democrats, but the Republicans hoped to carry it in 1859 and assigned some of their best men to speak there. Doe led the way.

The previous year Doe had told a Farmington rally that slavery was not a legitimate issue but a political smokescreen behind which Republicans hid their Know-Nothing program. Now he had to reverse his stand. To the delight of Republicans and the surprise of Democrats he adopted the theme of the *Gazette*'s editorial that he would "swallow himself." It was the Democrats who had done the swallowing, he asserted. They had swallowed slavery by endorsing *Dred Scott*.[27] It was now a Democratic principle that the Constitution guaranteed to slave owners the right to take their property into previously free territories. We are told by a Republican that "he deprecated strongly the practice of sticking to a party that had nothing left but a name."[28] He had remained with the Democratic ship as long as there was a single timber or a single plank to which to cling, but now that the very last splinter had gone down, overwhelmed in the black pool of slavery, he would stand by a name no longer. "Let them call me what they will."[29]

Doe could be pleased, especially when he read the Democratic newspapers. "If the Republicans are satisfied with the effort of their new crony," the *Gazette* reported, "and feel their capital has been well invested, truly they are thankful for the smallest favors. Surely the Democrats have nothing to fear from such weak and shallow effects come from where they may."[30]

The following night Doe opened the Republican campaign in Dover, before an audience which had long known him as a rabid Democrat. It was a cold, bitter evening, that twelfth of February, yet an overflow crowd was on hand. Once again Doe quoted the *Gazette*'s remarks that he would "swallow himself." The *Enquirer* thought his performance hilarious. "Taking this for his text," it reported, "he proceeded to show *who* had performed this feat of legerdemain, and *what* had been swallowed."[31] Doe divided his remarks into two parts, "Who has swallowed anything?" and "What's been swallowed?" It was the Democrats who "had done all the swallowing and swallowed themselves." As at Farmington, he attacked the Buchanan wing of the party. Reading an old party platform, he pointed out that the Democrats had staked their political future on popular sovereignty. He had accepted popular sovereignty, but through *Dred Scott* and acts of President Buchanan the Democrats had repudiated it. This was "bad democracy and bad law." [32]

Doe had a fine time with the word "swallow." The Republican press reported, "There were two emphatic and sarcastic sentences which were cutely drawn out at the end of every argument, viz: 'Who's been swallowed now?' and speaking of popular sovereignty (and the Dred Scott decision?) — his 'P-E-R-fectly free!' brought down the house repeatedly, which completely abashed the few Democrats present." [33]

The editor of the *Gazette* was not abashed. He felt sorry for Doe. "The performer continually paced the deck and appeared in a great agony. The cold damp sweat of a dying politician appeared to stand upon his brow, wrung as it were by the conscious ignominy of his position, and the full conviction that he had not the shadow of a foundation for the poor and feeble effect he was about to make." [34] Concord's *Independent Democrat* called the meeting "one of the best ever held in Dover." [35] The *Gazette* called it "A feat in political gymnastics." [36]

In truth, there was much goodnatured humor in the campaign. Although the outcome was always in doubt, there were no local issues and little bitterness. Charles Doe's treason aroused the only strong animosities in the southern part of the state, and admittedly the Democratic press was hard on him. But even the *Gazette* did not forget that New Hampshire likes its politics to have light moments, and often Doe came in for tongue-in-cheek kidding. When the *Enquirer* printed a letter praising a "masterly three hour speech" delivered by Doe, the *Gazette* suggested that Doe had written the letter.[37] When Doe spoke at Barnstead, the *Gazette* sent a correspondent to keep a drollish eye on him. Concord's Republican newspaper, *The Independent Democrat*, also had a representative there, and between them they give a fair idea of how some political rallies were reported in nineteenth-century New Hampshire.

Doe spoke at Barnstead on the afternoon of February 17, the Thursday following his triumph in Dover. He shared the platform with a lawyer named J. H. Ela. Although they were the only speakers billed, the *Gazette* reported that they were preceded by a man named Moore, "a sort of two-legged portable rum-cask from Concord, and, as we are informed, pretty well filled up to the bung." He uttered a few inaudible words and then "vamoosed"; when last seen he was "sitting half erect in an old sleigh with no horse attached to it, crying out as loud as he could, 'hooray for Gilmun's Mutton; go lang, dang ye, old hoss!'" The Republican reporter failed to mention Mr. Moore.

An excellent crowd had turned out. *The Independent Democrat* estimated three to four hundred "ladies and gentlemen present." The *Gazette* counted "about 75 Republicans (all there is left in Barnstead) and about 100 Democrats who were there to see the monkeys dance." "Brudder Ela" spoke first. *The Independent Democrat* found him persuasive. The *Gazette* thought he had nothing to say. "On the whole we are inclined to think that Ela is rather a harmless sort of man, and would not set the world on fire if he knew there was a negro in it in danger of being burned." The second speaker was more interesting. He was "The last renegade whom 'the Democratic party have gone off and left' standing out in the wet up to his eyes in Black Republican mire, THE VERY FINE LAD THAT CHARLEZE DOE." *The Independent Democrat* found Doe's address "one of the ablest and most unanswerable arguments against sham Democracy ever listened to in this state" and said it was "received throughout with frequent and hearty cheers."

By now Doe was a bit weary of the "swallowing" act. He used it, for it was expected, but on the whole he concentrated on documentation. Going back to the Democratic state conventions of 1847, 1848, and 1849, he quoted their platforms to show how the party had backtracked on slavery. Although he had swallowed these changes when he joined the party in 1852, he now said they were "too much right about face for him." His central theme was that the *Dred Scott* case had turned slavery into a national institution, making a fraud of popular sovereignty and a mockery of the compromise of 1850. "Taken as a whole," *The Independent Democrat* summed up, "no abler speech has been delivered in this state." The *Gazette* found it about as anticipated. After all, the "performer was the veritable, astute, decapitated, and metamorphosed Charles Doe." [38]

That night Doe and Ela stayed in Barnstead and went to a

Democratic meeting held during the evening. The *Gazette* says, "It was a different, more glorious, and important event" than the Republican rally. "Ela, Doe and Co., were torn limb from limb, disintegrated and demolished, and their fragments hung up by the wayside, a warning and terror to all evil-doers of a like kin and kindred." Doe probably attended because Daniel Marcy, the Democratic congressional candidate, was the chief speaker. Just as the *Gazette* had found nothing of value in Doe's address, so *The Independent Democrat* found nothing of value in Marcy's. It reported that he "said he was not a public speaker, but a *common man!* The announcement produced a sensation." Marcy asserted he was honest, just, and upright, and as for those who doubted him and wanted to find out for themselves, he would gladly pay their expenses to his hometown of Portsmouth — or so *The Independent Democrat* said. What substance there was in Marcy's speech is not recorded. The *Gazette*, which should have paid closer attention, was too busy watching its Republican friends.

Ela and Doe were there, and sat writhing and twisting, the Doe looking a great deal softer than usual. He seemed to be humming over something like the following. —

> "O that I were a geese
> All forlorn, all forlorn.
> I could eat my grass in peace
> And accumulate much grease
> Eatin' corn, eatin' corn."

It was a colorful campaign, with banners, torchlight parades, and marching bands. Yet the election was probably the quietest of the decade. "We saw no one intoxicated, heard of no brawls or quarrelings, or even of high words at the ballot box," one Manchester paper complained. "The police had nothing to do. The streets seemed still as upon the Sabbath." [39] Isaac Hill's old newspaper summed up the results when it reported, "The black republicans have again swept the board, but by a greatly reduced majority." [40]

The contest had been very close. Doe, however, could be of good cheer, since the Republicans did well in the areas where he had spoken. They were victorious in both Dover and Rollinsford, even carrying his ward for the first time. He could be especially proud of Farmington, where the Republicans won by thirty-one votes, the highest plurality they had ever received. One Farmington Republican wrote that they had been so confident they had sent "five good Republicans down to Newcastle to vote; and they carried that town by just that majority, and elected a Republican Representative." They were reciting what they felt to be a parody on Lord Byron's "Greece." " 'Tis Farmington, but Democratic Farmington no more." [41]

The outcome had important repercussions nationally: for the first time no Democrat from New England sat in either house of congress.[42] Perhaps the best comments came from the leading newspapers of each party. The election, reported *The Independent Democrat*, proved "that New Hampshire is still true to the Republican faith of the fathers — true to Liberty, and true to herself." [43] *The Union Democrat* replied, "There is no doubt that the state of New Hampshire is going to decay." [44]

Six months after the election and eight months after Doe had changed parties, his career as a politician came to an end. In September the Republican governor appointed him associate justice of the Supreme Judicial Court. How far would he have gone had he remained in politics? Some of his friends thought that he was not cut out for the rough and tumble of a campaign and that he would have detested it. But such judgments were made after many years on the bench had changed his temperament, his outlook, and his interests. As the election of 1859 showed, Doe could stand up and slug it out with the best of them. Indeed, he nearly accomplished the rarest feat possible in New Hampshire politics — he almost made a newspaper editor eat his words. Doe met the *Gazette* on its own terms and enjoyed his most successful moments when he accepted its dare by showing who had swallowed what.

Perhaps the only man qualified to offer a guess was Joshua Hall, who knew Doe well both in the 1850s and four decades later, at the height of his judicial fame. Hall understood the requirements of New Hampshire political life. He occupied many offices, including United States district attorney, the post Doe had vainly sought in 1858, and later he was a congressman. Speaking of Doe, Hall said, "Had he given his life to politics he would have been a leader in public affairs. He might have been regarded as a politician for a time, but not for long, for he was too great and sagacious for such a position, and he would have taken his appropriate place among the statesmen of his time." [45]

The events of 1859 were to remain with Charles Doe throughout his life and handicapped his judicial work. The accusation that he had sold out his party for political office was to follow him no matter where he went. His greatness as a judge could not wipe away the Democrats' legacy of suspicion. The fact was always there that, unlike his father who was denied any part in public life when he abandoned the dynamic Democracy of Isaac Hill in 1828, Charles Doe was rewarded with a secure place in the ascendancy by abandoning the decrepit Democracy of Franklin Pierce in 1859. There can be little doubt, however, that Doe himself was satisfied that he had been right and that his belief that compromise with the South was no longer possible was borne out by subsequent events. He proved this two years later, just before the firing on Fort Sumter. When his brother Thomas wrote him from Virginia imploring him to work for peace, Charles Doe refused, replying that it was now too late. The sooner the conflict came, the better. It was inevitable, and it was best to have it at once and have it over.[46]

PART TWO

THE JUDGE

Chapter Six

ENTIRELY ACCORDING
TO DOE
Trial Judge

THE leaders of the Republican Party in 1859 had to be astute jugglers when balancing the interests of opposing factions. It caused no concern when they appointed Charles Doe to the honorary office of "justice of the peace and quorum throughout the state." [1] But to name him to a more significant position required delicate manipulation. No matter how well he had served the Republican cause, what counted were the spoils owed to former Democrats. To give him a post which the Whigs or Know-Nothings thought belonged to them might alienate many and satisfy few. That despite these complications the Republican Party could reward the twenty-nine-year-old Charles Doe, is the full test of his service.

During the first week of August, Ira Perley announced his resignation as chief justice of the Supreme Judicial Court. He was a Whig-Republican, and the old Whig press began the game known as "newspaper nominations." [2] The Dover *Enquirer* demanded the seat for southern New Hampshire — which had no judge — and suggested a Whig war horse, Mayor Thomas E. Sawyer. [3] A Democrat-Republican might have little chance, yet that wing of the party insisted that its members be considered. Few names were more frequently mentioned than that of Charles Doe. [4] The editor of the influential Manchester *Mirror* attended a political picnic in Dover during the late summer of 1859 and returned home a Doe supporter, calling him "a formidable candidate." [5]

Doe's hopes remained slim until a few weeks later, when two other judges resigned, giving the governor room for maneuver. He promoted Judge Samuel Dana Bell, of New Hampshire's leading Whig family, to the chief justiceship, and filled one of the vacancies with George Washington Nesmith, a Free-Soil Whig. Two places were left open for former Democrats. Henry Bellows, a middle-aged lawyer from a northern county, got the first appointment. Doe furnished an ideal balance. He was an anti-Lecompton Democrat who lived in a part of the state which had no representative on the bench. His age might have been a drawback in most jurisdictions, but New Hampshire had a tradition of young jurists. Levi Woodbury had been twenty-six when he was made a judge. Doe was three years older. Daniel Christie and Congressman Gilman Marston "strongly recommended his appointment," [6] and their support probably clinched it. On September 20, 1859, Governor Goodwin nominated Charles Doe for the Supreme Judicial Court and he was confirmed by the Executive Council.

The selection of Charles Doe met the expected reception. The Republicans said that they were pleased. More important, the independent newspapers were not displeased. [7] The Democrats, on the other hand, reacted as might have been predicted. Doe, they knew, "was without any qualifications for the position, except a very recent abandonment of the Democratic party." [8] When a Boston editorial called his appointment "a splendid compliment" for so young a man, the Dover *Gazette* set the record straight. "The appointment of Doe was never intended as a 'splendid compliment to his abilities and learning'. It looks to us like the 'stipulated consideration' for the transfer of his body, soul, boots, breeches and all, into the charming embrace of Black Republicanism some six or eight months ago. That's all." [9]

The Democrats were not blindly partisan. Their newspapers had found no fault with Bellows' appointment. But Doe's "was conferred upon him as a reward for party service, in accordance with a bargain by which the judicial ermine was made the consideration for treachery to political friends and principles." [10]

Doe might be a good lawyer, but he had not been at the bar long enough to have earned a judgeship, as had Bellows. Democrats, one editor complained, "see in his youth too much of Young Americanism, and it makes the 'old soldier' decidedly incompatible especially those who were on hand for it themselves." [11]

Charles Doe took these strictures philosophically. A judge, he later said, should be measured by performance, not appointment. During the 1870s John Major Shirley published an article complaining that a United States Supreme Court decision had been made by politically appointed judges. Doe protested. "The two most genuine & unmistakable recruits from political life were Marshall & Taney, the two great men from which it has derived ⅞ of its celebrity," he wrote. The test should not be the reason for a judge's appointment, but who could have been named in his stead? This was especially true of the court Shirley had criticized.

I am strongly inclined to believe that they have not been consciously influenced by politics at all, & that their errors have arisen from a want of time, learning & mental strength. There is no Marshall or Taney among them; but I should like for you to take the dates of their appointment, & say whom you would have appointed. I suppose in two or three instances, you & I think we could have found somebody better; but are you sure that, on the whole, you would have made a better court? I presume I am as much dissatisfied with them, as you are; but I fear I am more successful in finding fault with them, than I should have been in selecting others for their places. I should rather have Thurman than Chase or Swayne. On the other hand, I should not have appointed Clifford; but he has probably made a better judge than I should have put in his place.[12]

Even without Democratic attacks, it might be wondered why Doe sought the judgeship. Its duties were characterized more by peregrination than contemplation. When reporting Doe's appointment, the Great Falls *Advertiser* observed, "The labors of a learned and conscientious Supreme Court Judge are far more arduous and unremitting than those of any other officer in the state." [13] The bench was not divided between appellate and trial courts, and the judges took turns presiding at *nisi prius* trials in each of New Hampshire's ten counties. Even the law term, at which appeals were heard en bloc, was not confined to the state capital but was held at various shire towns, although for this purpose the state was divided into five districts, the appeals of two counties being disposed of at one session.

With his intellectual endowments Doe was prepared to be an appellate judge. But his few years at the bar had given him scant experience for presiding at the trial term. He may have been referring to this when he said, "When I reflect upon the ignorant audacity with which I first approached the duties of a judge of the Supreme Court of New Hampshire, I am appalled." [14] In truth, he had little to worry about. He held his first trial term in Plymouth during December 1859, and the Laconia *Gazette* reported he had been "excellent." [15] His grand-jury charge was well received, and "A gentleman conversant with all the courts of this state, says the Judge made a very favorable impression, presiding with dignity and ruling with promptness." [16]

"Dignity" was a word that would not long be associated with Charles Doe. "Informality" characterized him better. He permitted breaches of court etiquette which would not have been tolerated in most states. Lawyers were allowed to sit while questioning witnesses, while speaking to the jury, and even while addressing the bench — that is, if Doe was on the bench. When he wanted a different view of witnesses or exhibits, Doe tried cases sitting with the lawyers.[17] It was not unknown for him to experiment with trial techniques by rearranging courtroom furniture.[18] Indeed, Doe did not think a courtroom always necessary. He gave audience to counsel and heard petitions wherever he could be found.[19] There were times when his informality bordered on judicial sloppiness. Once a divorce hearing was scheduled for his hotel room. Leaving dinner, he encountered the petitioner and the witnesses, took them to his room, questioned them, and sent them home. Sometime later counsel arrived, apologized for the delay, and requested a postponement because he could not find his client or the witnesses. "I have seen them," said Doe, "and granted the divorce." [20]

At times his casualness appeared studied. He paid no heed to judicial decorum, as is shown by the events of the Sawtelle murder trial. Isaac Sawtelle was the most notorious fratricide in American history, and the courtroom was packed with reporters from all over New England. Tension was high and Doe may have sought to relax the atmosphere. Before calling the court to order on the third day, he took a walk within the bar, talking first to the defense lawyers and to the prosecutors. Then he went to the jury box to shake hands with each juror and to the press table to exchange words with the correspondents. On his way back to the bench, perhaps as an afterthought, he turned to the defendant, saying with a smile, "Good morning, Mr. Sawtelle, I hope you are well today." Sawtelle stumbled to his feet, made a half-bow, and timidly accepted Doe's hand.[21]

That Judge Doe would deign to shake hands with Sawtelle offended Boston editorial writers. "We are not familiar with the court proceedings in New Hampshire," commented the *Journal*, "and therefore we ask if it is customary for judges to shake hands with criminals during a trial." [22] The *Daily Globe* professed to be shocked: "Perhaps this was an extreme Christian charity, but most men would have shrunk from touching that hand until the prisoner's innocence is established — if it ever is." The *Globe* was playing the hypocrite; just a few hours later its reporter shook hands with Sawtelle. "I'm glad *The Globe* is giving me such a fair show," Sawtelle said. "All I want is fairness and I know I shall not be convicted." [23] Regardless of the standards it thought proper for the chief justice of New Hampshire, no Boston newspaper ever passed up a friendly blurb, especially the *Globe*.

Besides relaxing court atmosphere, Doe eliminated many court formalities. One of the first customs he abolished was the practice of the sheriff's escorting the judge from his lodging to the courthouse and back. Formerly the sheriff had carried a drawn sword, but by Doe's day the sword was out of fashion; he thought the whole proceedings should be dropped. One morning Daniel L. Stevens, deputy sheriff of Hillsborough County, called at the Manchester House to escort Doe to the court. "Don't bother with me, Dan," Doe said. "I'll be over in a little while. If folks see us together they'll say, 'What bounty jumper is Dan running in now?' " There was little the sheriff could do. This was the death knell of the custom in New Hampshire, although attempts were made later to revive it.[24]

That Judge Doe could begin without the sheriff was another product of his distaste for formality. He considered the sheriff's proclamation opening and closing each half-day session of court a waste of time. Impressive as it was to listen to the sonorous declamations of "Hear ye, Hear ye," Doe was impatient to get to work. Since he could not abolish the custom, he ignored it by taking "recesses" or "intermissions" rather than adjournments, and the only proclamations were his announcements, "Come back at two" or, "We will take a recess till tomorrow morning." [25] His informality occasionally caught lawyers off guard, especially those from out of state. A Massachusetts attorney named Rice was in the midst of a jury argument in Keene one day when the noon hour was reached. Doe announced in his quiet, rapid manner, "Come in at two," slipped off the bench, and left the courtroom. Rice went on talking, to the amusement of the jury, until the opposing counsel leaned over and asked, "Hadn't you better stop, Brother Rice? The Court has gone." [26]

Judge Doe used much the same tactic to avoid the customary prayer at the opening of each trial term. When possible he ruled a session part of an adjourned term and "the old prayer held over." [27] He could not always do this and was annoyed by clergymen taking up the court's time to lecture to the lawyers. At a trial term in Manchester, when the sheriff asked which minister he wanted, Doe replied that it made no difference provided he was brief. The sheriff approached the Reverend Dr. Buckley, a Methodist, and told him he could best earn the $2 fee by being fast. Buckley had the right idea. "Oh Lord," he prayed, "bless this court and bless these lawyers. Make them feel that life is short, that time is precious and should not be wasted in empty declamation. For Christ's sake. Amen." Doe was delighted. "That's a great prayer. A model prayer," he told Buckley. "It ought to be printed and preserved with the records of the court." [28] This was the only time Doe was known to praise a court formality.

"It has sometimes been thought," Doe's colleague Judge Lewis Clark observed, "that the Chief Justice failed to sustain the dignity of the court properly, on account of his neglect to observe some trifling matter of form, which he regarded as of no consequence." [29] The ostentation, the ceremony, the trappings, the petty little trimmings which Doe found so useless, so unnecessary, were intended for lesser judges — those without his personality or prestige — to add dignity and mien to their presence. Doe tailored things to his own needs. The reverential atmosphere was lost, and trials degenerated to the level of mere hearings. This did not seem to matter while he was presiding, but after his death New Hampshire judges reinstated some formalities, most notably the custom of wearing judicial robes. As another colleague noted many years later, "Of course, one with Judge Doe's alertness and ingenuity of mind did not need a sheriff to keep order. But times have changed." [30]

These innovations were frivolous compared with Doe's major reforms, the first of which was so drastic that it nearly cost him the judgeship. He tried to end the firmly entrenched and time-honored prerogative of New Hampshire lawyers to cross-examine a witness in any manner they chose. Most New Hampshire advocates, including Doe's two teachers, Daniel Christie and Joel Parker, were in the habit of asking whatever questions they pleased and of treating a hostile witness with discourtesy, roughness, and all the disdain, contempt, and sarcasm they could muster. Judge Doe ended all that. "While I was a law student in his office," Judge Robert Pike wrote in 1916, "he told me among many matters of the struggles that he underwent in bringing about the reforms referred to. He had seen in his five years' practice women and children and even men so controlled by the overbearing and coercing manner of some lawyers on cross examination, that in an effort to bring truth to light they brought falsehood in its stead." [31] Doe had begun his campaign of reform while at the bar when in his first trial, the *Hodge* murder case, he refused to stoop to the tactics of the opposing counsel. By example, he and Charles H. Bell, an Exeter attorney of about the same age, tried to persuade their brethren that calm reason would produce surer results than stormy abuse. They had some success, but Doe's real opportunity came with his appointment to the bench. From the beginning he insisted that cases be tried civilly, expeditiously, and upon the merits. He was asking older lawyers to abandon the habits of a lifetime — a hard task for a judge so young and so unpopular with the Democratic members of the bar. But Doe had courage, and to get his way he was willing to gamble his career.

Daniel Christie was one of the first to learn that Doe was serious. In his usual manner Christie was crossexamining a timid witness with unnecessary brusqueness, and the witness seemed unable to express a single thought. Doe suggested that Christie try a milder form of questioning, but the older man went on in the same commanding and demanding way. Doe cut him short, telling him to be more polite if he wished to continue. Doe, fully aware of what was at stake, took a calculated risk. As leader of the southern New Hampshire bar, Christie's reputation was such that, had he defied Doe, there would have been little hope of bringing other lawyers into line. A long silence followed as Christie, uncertain what to do, sat down and shuffled some papers. Then, slowly rising to his feet, he questioned the witness the judge's way. It was Doe's most important triumph in his struggle to reform court procedure. Doe later expressed gratitude to Christie, saying that Christie had yielded only because Doe had been "one of his boys, and was anxious for him to succeed." [32]

Judge Doe clinched his victory over Christie by repeating it with Congressman Gilman Marston. Marston, who had a strong personality and enjoyed breaking witnesses, was shaking his finger in a witness's face at Exeter when Doe told him to be more conciliatory. Marston mumbled to himself and redoubled the abuse. Doe ordered the witness not to answer the questions. Gathering up his papers, Marston stormed from the courtroom, muttering, "What a damned fool!" Accounts differ as to whether Marston returned after the recess. But in time the two again became friends.[33]

It was important for Doe to make peace with Marston. Opposition to his reforms had begun to solidify and attempts were made to break the spirit of the young judge. It is known that he was boycotted in several counties. One term which should have lasted for three weeks was ended in three days. In the Democratic stronghold of Grafton County, Doe once had to adjourn court after only two days. Professor Jeremiah Smith, then practicing at the New Hampshire bar, has described it as "a somewhat stormy season, which would have induced the majority of new judges either to submit to the old regime or resign their office in despair." [34]

It was not merely Doe's insistence on trial reforms which aroused opposition. There was also the animosity of the Democrats, his new-modelling the forms of action (to be discussed in Chapter Seven), and his many unorthodox *nisi prius* rulings, one of the most memorable of which was the *Haverhill School House Case.* Few judges would have dared to act as Doe did in that case. More than an early example of his audacity, it presaged the utter disregard for precedent and the remarkable search for abstract justice which became the hallmarks of his jurisprudence. Moreover, the case was the occasion of his first clash with Alonzo P. Carpenter, the man whose conservative tendencies were destined to challenge all of Doe's premises and bring them into their sharpest focus.

The citizens of Haverhill were a contrary lot. One faction wanted a central school, but the majority preferred not to spend the money. When the town meeting voted to leave matters as they were, the minority in broad daylight demolished the old school. It was a bit of old-fashioned New Hampshire self-help which had long since gone out of style. The majority were in no mood to tolerate it and complained to Carpenter, the county solicitor. His sense of order and respect for the democratic process outraged, Carpenter obtained indictments for riot. The situation was an awkward one: the defendants were respectable citizens, willing to pay for a new school building themselves. They had probably intended to do so all along and just wanted to be rid of the old edifice. It fell to Doe to preside at the trial, over which feelings ran high. After listening to Carpenter's recital of the facts, Doe, without waiting to hear from the respondents, denied the state's motion for trial and announced that he would issue an order calculated to give substantial justice. He referred the case to a referee, directing him to receive testimony from one witness on each "side" and to determine who had taken part in the affair and how the costs of a new school could equitably be appropriated among them. "If the sums so assessed are paid, and the schoolhouse is built, before the next term," he provided, "then this case is not to be brought forward on the docket, but is to be regarded as dismissed." [35]

Judge Doe asked the state and the defendants to agree on a referee, but Carpenter refused; a criminal case had never been referred before, and Carpenter wanted no part of so fantastic a scheme. Doe thereupon went ahead and appointed one himself.

Between terms the referee held a hearing and settled the matter along the lines Doe prescribed. But Carpenter would not accept the solution. When Judge Nesmith arrived to hold the next session of court, the county solicitor accused Doe of an outrageous dereliction of duty and moved that the referee's report be rejected. Nesmith was in an impossible corner. He confessed himself troubled by Doe's unprecedented procedure, admitting he would never have issued such an order. Yet it was a delicate matter to interfere with the decrees of a fellow judge, and Nesmith thought it safer for all concerned if he left the case as he had found it. "I wash my hands of the whole affair," he said.[36]

It is difficult to blame Doe for his action. The defendants had not acted with criminal intent, and the matter was better settled out of court. Yet the criminal docket is not the place for arbitration proceedings, and he had no authority for improvising unique methods merely because he thought the traditional procedure unfair. For the sake of abstract justice he mocked concrete law. It is the business of a judge to administer law, not justice. Unable to tell what he might do next, it is little wonder the bar resisted him.

Judge Doe seems always to have been listening to complaints. Completely indifferent to what was said about him, he not only remained undisturbed by criticism, but even enjoyed courtroom exchanges. Once he interrupted an attorney in the middle of a summation. "You cannot argue that," he warned; "there is no evidence in the case to sustain it." Twice or three times more the lawyer started on the same theme, only to be stopped by Doe. Apparently at a loss, he turned to the jury and said, "I have argued cases in this courtroom before Judge Richardson and before Judge Parker, and. . . ." Here Doe interrupted again. "Proceed, Brother A," he said, "you are in order now."

At the end of a rather lengthy trial term Doe was going over the docket with the Merrimack County bar. It was after the usual hour of adjournment, and one lawyer had protested a ruling with tears. He was followed by another attorney, who underlined his exception to a ruling with a fervent speech of ten minutes. Then the eloquent Mason Tappan joined in the denunciation and ended by saying, "I protest against the action of the court." After listening for about half an hour, Doe quietly told the clerk, "Enter

Colonel Tappan's protest and any other motion or protest he desires to make, and enter them all overruled."

Many years after Doe had referred the criminal charge of riot to a referee in the *Haverhill School House Case,* he was presiding over a murder trial in Portsmouth, and Marston was serving as defense counsel. Following the prosecutor's opening statement, Doe called Marston to the bench.

"You have heard the statement of the solicitor?" Doe asked.

"Yes," Marston replied.

"Can he prove what he says he can?"

"I suppose he can prove some of it."

"Well," Doe wanted to know, "don't you think this is a case to settle?"

Marston was amused. "Settle," he said. "We can't settle, but you might refer it." [37]

Though during his years as a trial judge Charles Doe never tried to refer a murder case, he did try just about everything else. He felt especially free to experiment in criminal matters, since the state could not take appeals. His most famous departure from clear, undisputable precedent has been described by Jeremiah Smith:

Before the passage of the Statute of 1869, making respondents competent to testify in their own behalf, it was very common for counsel representing the accused to complain bitterly of the fact that their client's lips were sealed; and to assert that, if they could only have the privilege of testifying, they could satisfactorily explain all incriminating circumstances. Judge Doe had probably got very tired of hearing this sort of talk in cases where there was no reasonable doubt of guilt. One day, when a lawyer opening for the defense was making these stereotyped assertions, he was suddenly interrupted from the bench. "Mr. ————, you may put your clients on the stand." "What, your Honor?" "You will be permitted to call your clients as witnesses on their own behalf." The learned counsel, gradually recovering from his astonishment, turned, and whispered to his junior: "Well, John, we shall have to put the rascals on, and the result will be a conviction." [38]

Doe is apparently the only judge ever to do this. His ruling is truly astonishing. One of the great legal debates of that era was whether defendants in criminal cases should be permitted to get their own stories on the record, and if so, in what form — as sworn testimony subject to crossexamination, as a deposition, or as an unsworn statement, the probative weight of which would be left to the jury. Chief Justice John Appleton of Maine became one of the famous judicial reformers of the nineteenth century on the strength of his battle to remove the incompetency of respondents. But even he did not think the courts could proceed without legislative authority. As will be seen, the belief that courts can act in matters of this type on their own initiative was one of the outstanding aspects of Charles Doe's jurisprudence. Here he extended the lawmaking power even to trial rulings from which no appeal may be taken.

Doe was forever interfering with criminal prosecutions. "He sometimes investigated the preliminary question whether they ought to be tried; and, if he came to a negative conclusion, practically coerced the state's counsel into entering a *non pros.*, or accepting a plea that the respondent was guilty of a minor offense. If the state's counsel declined to accede to his view, he would sometimes, as a last resort, bluntly refuse to try the case." [39] On the other hand, Doe might insist that an accused person be brought to trial and not be permitted to enter a plea of guilty.

Even after trials had commenced Doe tried to direct their outcome. A notable instance occurred during the prosecution of an uxoricide — a man named Hodgman, indicted for first-degree murder. Just before the proceedings began, Doe went to Charles H. Burns, the defense attorney, and asked him to compromise with a plea of second degree, telling him that the jury was certain to convict. Burns consulted the defendant and his father, but they refused, saying that though the young man had intended to frighten his wife, the gun had gone off accidentally. At the same time Doe advised the attorney general to seek a plea of second-degree murder, saying there was little chance of getting a conviction. Here too he was turned down. Neither side knew of Doe's double game. The case was brought to trial and lasted two weeks. At five o'clock on the morning after the jury had retired to consider the evidence, Burns was walking to the courthouse when he met Doe. The judge told him that the jury had not agreed and suggested that if Hodgman would plead to a minor offense, he would impose a sentence of only five years' imprisonment.

Doe said that, while the defendant had not intended to kill his wife, he was responsible for her death and ought to be punished. He wanted to discharge the jury, but just then the sheriff arrived with news that an agreement had been reached. It was for acquittal. A short time afterward Doe sent Burns a letter for Hodgman, offering the young man advice as to his future course in life.[40]

Lawyers could tolerate these out-of-court maneuvers. What annoyed them was the way Doe took over their cases. In criminal trials he and not the lawyers usually selected the jury.[41] And he frequently examined witnesses — especially in murder trials. If a child was on the stand, Doe might ask all the questions.[42] In one murder trial he cross-examined the key witness for two hours — a "masterful" cross-examination says Judge Pike, who thought himself "fortunate" to hear it.[43] Doe did the same during the *Almy* murder trial in Plymouth. The prosecution's case to an extent depended on the testimony of the victim's mother. Doe, a newspaper reported, "took her in hand interrogating her to the absolute exclusion of counsel from participation — a little eccentricity of the Chief Justice's that may perhaps be strictly according [to] Hoyle, or entirely according to Doe." [44] The fact is that Charles Doe was the dominant figure in his courtroom, and after the first difficult years he always kept the proceedings under control. His trials were known for the strict enforcement of order, both inside and outside the court. One off-beat item on the *Almy* murder case appeared in the Boston *Record*. "Justice Doe's common sense and appreciation of the fitness of things was never more notably displayed than when he announced, after two large panes of glass had been broken by the crowd at the window, that the first person who attempted to gain entrance to the court house by any other means than the door, would be put under arrest; and again when he made the phonograph man, who wanted to sell Almy's sobs after the trial at so much per sob, pack up his machine and big funnel and walk." [45]

The jury knew Doe was in control, and he is said to have had remarkable success with jurors. Jeremiah Smith thought this one reason why the bar acquiesced in his reforms of trial techniques: "the jury were inclined to sympathize with the court, and a lawyer who made himself offensive to the bench was likely to lose the verdict. In one of the stormiest trials over which Judge Doe ever presided, a trial during which he was obliged continually to restrain the counsel on one side; the jury formed the opinion that the judge thought the merits of the case were against the side he was so often constrained to check; and the view undoubtedly exerted great influence upon the verdict, which was against the troublesome counsellors. In fact, the jury drew a wrong inference, for I happen to know that the judge, if himself a juror, would have returned the opposite verdict." [46]

One reason Doe was effective with juries was that he avoided legal idioms. An associate justice relates that during a conference Doe asked another judge, "Did you instruct the jury in the precise language set out in the reserved case?" When his colleague said that he had, Doe replied, "Well, it is all sound law, and would have been admirable for an essay in a law review; but the jury could not have got any idea from it. You do not want to use legal phraseology to the jury. In charging them, you should translate the law into farmers' and mechanics' talk." [47]

In his own instructions, Judge Doe seldom departed from general propositions. He did not attempt to explain exceptions or limitations which might confuse the triers of fact. In one criminal case he told the jury, "Gentlemen, I shouldn't want to convict the prisoner on this evidence, but you can do as you like." [48] Former United States Attorney General Caleb Cushing was shocked when Doe settled a controversy about mental capacity by saying, "I am going to tell the jury that if this man knew what he was about, the transaction will stand; and, if he didn't, it won't." [49]

In one case Doe proved himself too down-to-earth. In a minor litigation, in which plaintiff seemed to have had the better argument, the jury could not agree. Doe, annoyed, after sending for the jurors tried to impress upon them in vigorous terms their duty to arrive at a decision which would end the suit, one way or another, *then and there*. To his surprise the jury returned with a defendant's verdict. When asked why, the foreman explained that Doe had ordered them to end the case *then and there*. Since the defendant was rich, they knew he would appeal a decision against him. The plaintiff, on the other hand, was poor.

He would have to accept the verdict and the case would end *then and there.*[50]

Such misunderstandings were rare, and Doe was satisfied with the way things went in his court. "I have ceased giving charges to the grand jury & to the petit jury," he wrote in 1870. "I merely state the question & the law, omitting the laborious review of the evidence which is burdensome to me & useless to the jury. I find the bar approve my present course on this point. I take no minutes of the evidence of any consequence." [51] A few lawyers not familiar with his retentiveness were upset by his casual air. "Sometimes," a leading advocate observed, "it would seem as though he did not give attention to the testimony as it went to the jury, or in equity cases, but when the trial was through, counsel would see that no point on either side had escaped his observation." [52]

By the end of his first decade as judge Doe claimed to have so abbreviated his duties "that to hold a trial term is now to me the easiest kind of work. The wear & tear — the anxiety & general expenditure of nervous, & all physical & mental power — is much less on the bench than in practice at the bar. I can try half a doz. cases as judge, more easily than I could try one as counsel. The mental anxiety, the enlistment & excitement of the feelings, so exhausting, wearing & prostrating in counsel, do not disturb the court." [53]

Within another decade Doe had completely reversed his attitude. The repetition, the boredom, and the constant strain of adjusting his mental facilities to slow-thinking counsel began to weary him. The tedium was often unbearable. "I have sat trying a case about 13 cents, day after day, costing the county $100 every day," he complained. "I have sat several days, at that expense, trying a case about two or three wormy apples, not worth one cent." [54] Shortly after he was appointed chief justice in 1876, Doe reached the breaking point. "I find I will not be able to try any more jury cases," he is reported to have said. "For example: Just before the jury is drawn the plaintiff's lawyer says to me. 'Your Honor, this is a horse case.' Now in my experience, I have tried every possible form of a 'horse case' and I know what the lawyers are going to say before they begin and I am losing my patience. I find it impossible to wait for what statement they have to make. It's no use." [55] He told his associates that he would have to resign. They begged him not to, but he was insistent. Trial terms with their constant traveling and the long hours spent in drafty, noisy hotels were impairing his health. His habits had changed since the days when he found stimulation in politics and in litigation, and he wanted to lead the life of a scholar.

His colleagues proposed a bargain. If Doe would remain as chief justice, they would take over his trial duties and he could devote full time to legal research and to writing appellate opinions. Doe agreed, and for the last eighteen years of his life he presided over no trials save for an occasional emergency session or first-degree murder prosecution. Since the law required that two judges be present at murder trials, Doe felt it his duty as chief justice to preside. The arrangement was an excellent one. At the height of his powers Doe was free to pursue his studies and to prepare the lengthy decisions for which he became famous. Had he been tied to trial work, many of his great judgments might never have been written. Yet his years on the trial bench were not wasted. He had been at the bar only five years, and the additional experience and knowledge of trial practice which he gained as a *nisi prius* judge proved immeasurably valuable when he reformed the law of civil procedure, evidence, and criminal insanity.

Chapter Seven

NEW-MODELLING THE FORMS
Civil Procedure

THE surgical instruments of a trial lawyer are the rules of pleading, which govern each step in a litigation from the moment the writ is filed to the moment the clerk enters the judgment upon the records. They are the tools of the advocate's trade, and their origin extends back through history to the fusty pages of the Year Books and to the inventiveness of the justiciars of Henry II and Edward I. The attorney who does not use them methodically may lose his cause on the snare of a technicality.

Many laymen, uneducated in legal science, share the notion that law is a labyrinth of petty details, intricate niceties, and unbending technicalities. In truth, law turns more on reason, public policy, and social custom than it does on technicalities. Yet in one respect laymen are right: technicality is the soul of the law, for it is the measure of pleading. Even here, however, rigidity is not absolute but is relaxed or stiffened according to the temper of the times. In perhaps no other jurisdiction was this more clearly demonstrated than in nineteenth-century New Hampshire. Following the Revolutionary War, New Hampshire reacted against the formalism of royal justice. Nonlawyers were appointed to the bench for the very reason that they were not trained in the law. During an age of political democracy it seemed but right that the private affairs of free men be regulated by legal democracy. The ideal jurist was one who used common sense to render offhand, spur-of-the-moment verdicts without regard for what the magistrates of the defeated mother country would have done. Indeed, he was thought wiser and more useful than those with the ability and industry to track down a precedent. "It is our business," the greatest of these judges told juries, "to do justice between the parties, not by any quirks of the law out of Coke or Blackstone, books I never read, and never will, but by common sense and common honesty as between man and man." [1]

For a time the jurisprudence of common sense suited the state. "Justice," Congressman Arthur Livermore wrote, "was never better administered in New Hampshire then when the judges knew little of what we lawyers call law." But what may have been "justice" was not "law"; it was unequal, crude, uncertain, and sometimes unfair, for judgments were often decided by sentiment or politics. Change was inevitable after Joseph Doe and his generation began their effort to reestablish New Hampshire's economic prosperity. Businessmen needed greater predictability in their dealings, and legal democracy was no longer fashionable. In 1802, when Jeremiah Smith was appointed chief justice, he inherited a judicial system which operated without rules, which did not have a rudimentary set of maxims and principles, and which had no published reports or precedents. "With him," said Joel Parker, "there arose a new order of things, and the practice of law was reduced to a practical science." [2]

Jeremiah Smith had only a few years in which to establish his reforms, yet by the time the Republicans removed him from office, New Hampshire practice had turned half cycle. From the loose, chaotic era of democratic common sense, when law was administered without rules, when procedure was informal, and when the only instructions given to juries was to apply justice and equity according to the facts of each litigation, New Hampshire had evolved into a rigid and formalistic era of English common law, where uniform rules often determined the issue and the merits of the case were never reached. Smith taught the New Hampshire bar — especially the generation of Joel Parker and Daniel Christie — that general knowledge "is but another name for general ignorance." Lawyers began to think of law, not in terms of broad principles, but as a set of narrow rules by which actions could be commenced or halted. The remedy, not the right, was the focus of learning. "Indeed," Smith's biographer wrote in 1845, "the matter was carried so far, that the New Hampshire practice has become almost proverbial for its severity." [3] The most important fact in the life of a New Hampshire lawyer when Charles Doe was called to the bar was that Jeremiah Smith had been chief justice.

The common-law rules of pleading which Smith had introduced were in full force. Mastery of technical niceties was the key to success, and the lawyer with the methodical mind of a martinet had an advantage over a more versatile colleague, who combined a grasp of broad fundamentals with a contempt for triviality. "Half the labor of the bar was bestowed upon questions of pleading, and the lawyer who mistook his form of action sometimes lost his case from that cause alone. The merits of the case were often wholly lost sight of and never brought to trial." As one observer expressed it, nothing sharpened the wits of New Hampshire advocates as did the art of special pleading. "Men became so astute and acute that they not infrequently got lost in their own tortuous paths. The practical difficulty with a system of special pleading was that it was really bottomed upon the theory that human affairs were controlled by the rules of logic and capable of being reduced to mathematical propositions, whereas few things are further from the truth. The result was that justice became entangled in the meshes of petty technicalities." [4]

The tyranny of pleading was complete, and at its root lay the forms of action, or writs, the means by which a litigation was commenced and its progress defined. Various writs had such names as "Debt," "Trespass," "Trover," and "Assumpsit." They differed not only in the circumstances with which they were designed to deal, but also in the type of pleading and evidence with which they were proven and the redress which they sought. A person suing a thief could not use the same form of action as a person suing an assailant. He was limited to writs dealing with wrongful conversion and had to choose the one which offered the relief he wanted. Should he desire money damages, he filed an action of trover. If he wished to recover possession of the stolen property, he filed an action of replevin. Once he made his choice, he was bound by it. If he had selected replevin and during the trial discovered that the goods had been injured and were no longer of value, he could not change his action to trover and collect money damages. The technicality of selecting the wrong writ could defeat a plaintiff's valid claim.

Many causes were defaulted because the plaintiff filed the wrong action. Simple as the selection of a proper writ might appear to nonlawyers, it was a decision filled with difficulty. Consider the forms of action which offered remedies for personal injuries. They were "Trespass" and "Trespass on the Case." Trespass was one of the most sharply defined forms of action in New Hampshire and lay for redress, in money damages, for any unlawful injury done the plaintiff by the immediate force or violence of the defendant. It could be used only for a direct and unauthorized interference with land, goods, or person. Thus trespass did not lie against a physician in a suit for malpractice, because the plaintiff had voluntarily submitted himself to the defendant's ministrations. Nor did it lie against a property owner who by lawful use of his land accidentally flooded the plaintiff's land, because the damage was indirect. In such cases the proper writ was trespass on the case, which lay for injury unaccompanied by direct or immediate force or for injury which was the indirect or secondary consequence of the defendant's act.

The New Hampshire case of *Dalton* v. *Favour* illustrates the difficulties. Favour accidentally shot Dalton in the foot, and Dalton sued him by bringing an action of trespass on the case. Favour moved for dismissal. The issue posed was enough to drive a judge to distraction. The court upheld the action on the excuse that, although the shooting had been immediate and direct, it was occasioned by carelessness and negligence. Hence, trespass on the case was the proper writ.[5]

Charles Doe ended all this. "Our time," he believed, "is too much needed for the consideration of subjects of some importance, to be properly occupied with the unnecessary and barren question of pleading." It is doubtful if ever a presiding trial judge in America had less patience with procedural technicalities than Doe. "The idea of a court being so fettered by forms fabricated by a court, that the general principles of the law cannot be administered, is preposterous," he wrote. "The judgment, and any necessary process for carrying it into effect, being directed by the ends of justice, cannot be obstructed by imaginary barriers of form."[6]

Doe's task was to convince his colleagues that forms of action were "imaginary barriers." Most lawyers tended to equate them with law itself — they thought of law in terms of writs. In other words, there were no legal rights except those vindicated by an established form of action; the remedy defined the right. Doe, on the other hand, viewed law in terms of general principles. There is, he said, a "common-law principle of the inviolability of legal right" which "requires specific and adequate remedies, and convenient procedure." He called it "a legal paradox" to say that one has a legal right to something and yet to deprive him of that right by not giving him a remedy with which he can vindicate it. "If the plaintiff has a right," Doe argued, "he must of necessity have a means to vindicate and maintain it, and a remedy if he is injured in the exercise or enjoyment of it; and, indeed, it is a vain thing to imagine a right without a remedy. Want of right and want of remedy are reciprocal." [7]

There was no mistaking Doe's meaning. If the court finds that a plaintiff has a legal right which has been violated, the court must vindicate that right even if it has to devise novel remedies. "The necessity of a plenary remedy for the infringement of a legal right, accepted as a general rule of the common law, authorizes and requires the use of convenient procedure for ascertaining and establishing the right, and obtaining the remedy." Since common-law procedure was devised by courts it is a ritual, not law; an "invaluable ritual" to be sure, but still a ritual. It is nothing more than "the remedial branch of immemorial custom" and has "not been extinguished or exhausted by its inventions; and it does not confine the duty of maintaining rights to ways and means that are defective." What courts can invent, courts can alter. Judge Doe even had a name for the process; he called it "new-modelling the forms." [8]

Charles Doe's first effort at new-modelling was as ingenious as it was simple. The marvel is that other judges had not done it before him. Yet it was he who initially saw the answer to the absurd technicality of English common-law procedure when he ruled that the forms of action are by amendment mutually convertible. He took this course first at the trial term when a defendant moved to dismiss a case on the grounds that an improper writ had been filed. Doe asked what form of action would have been correct. "Very well," he said on receiving the answer. "Let an amendment be filed making it as suggested, and we will go on with the case." [9]

In 1909 Professor Crawford Dawes Hening of the University of Pennsylvania wrote a sketch of Charles Doe for an eight-volume series entitled *Great American Lawyers*. Even at that late date Hening was amazed by Doe's boldness.

> Upon this question Judge Doe exhibited a disregard of precedents and a judicial audacity which has been rarely paralleled. Lord Mansfield's plan of obtaining special verdicts from juries of merchants and then proceeding to pronounce the custom of merchants thereon, though directly opposite to what the jury had found the custom to be, will always be regarded as one of the most radical, most audacious acts of a common-law judge. Scarcely less striking was Judge Doe's novel announcement that the differences between various forms of action were in reality not substantial, but only formal. If a plaintiff had selected a trespass writ when the remedy to which he was historically entitled was administered through the mechanism of what was called a trover writ, justice demanded, so Judge Doe contended, that he should be permitted by amendment to cure the informality without losing his position in court or the security for his possible judgment. This conception of common-law writs was Judge Doe's masterpiece of procedural invention.[10]

At first Judge Doe's associates were unwilling to accept so radical an innovation. As late as 1873 they overruled him, holding that amendment of a declaration changing the form of action is not allowable.[11] It was not until 1879, after Doe had been on the bench for twenty years and as chief justice was in complete control, that his reform was adopted. In *Stebbins* v. *Lancashire Ins. Co.* the court ruled that an amendment may be made at any stage of the proceedings to prevent injustice and that the form of action may be changed by amendment.[12] It was more than what Doe called it — a "judicial restoration of the true principles of the common law" [13] — it was a judicial revolution, carried out as Doe insisted it could and must be, without the aid of a statute.[14] By establishing the tenet that writs are not substantive but merely formal, Doe cut the jugular vein which sustained most of the technicalities traditionally associated with common-law pleading. He clinched his victory when he held that the justice of an amendment changing the form of action is a question of fact determinable at the trial term; that is, it is within the discretion of the lower court and cannot be overturned on appeal.[15]

Once *Stebbins* became precedent, the floodgates were opened and Doe had considerable leeway. With the principle that writs are convertible by amendment as his base, he quickly extended the power of amendment to other situations where technicalities might otherwise defeat valid actions. He ruled that counts in contract and torts may be joined in a declaration on a single cause;[16] that an amendment may cure a defect of form, but that even without an amendment the defect may be disregarded;[17] that parties may be joined or substituted by amendment;[18] that a declaration against a surviving partner as endorser of a note may be amended by the addition of a count against him as individual endorser;[19] that an amendment changing the form of action may be made after a plaintiff's verdict has been entered without a new trial when the verdict could not have been affected by the amendment if it had been made before the suit;[20] and that in a suit seasonably brought, where the writ has been abated because it contained no declaration, the declaration may be amended after the time when a new action for the same cause would be barred by the statute of limitations;[21] finally he arrived at his ultimate goal and held that in some cases it is not even necessary to amend a writ but that if a party is entitled to relief on a writ of error, *certiorari, mandamus, audita querela,* or prohibition, it is not necessary to decide which he should use.[22]

Merrill v. *Perkins* illustrates the extent of Doe's departure from tradition. In that case he held that, since an objection to the form of action might have been obviated at the trial by an amendment adding a new count, or since it could be made after the verdict as it would not disturb the verdict, it is not even necessary after the verdict "to enquire whether case, or trespass, is the right form of action." This was how Doe settled questions such as the one in *Dalton* v. *Favour.* He said it was of no consequence whether Favour shot Dalton "immediately" or "indirectly." Speaking of *Merrill*, Professors Richard H. Field and Benjamin Kaplan have observed, "This would have been unthinkable at strict common law: an amendment changing the form of action from case to trespass, or *vice versa*, was not permitted; and joinder of counts in trespass and case was also improper." [23]

Judge Doe lost no time extending *Stebbins*. That same year, in the landmark case of *Metcalf* v. *Gilmore*, he held that pleadings at law and pleadings in equity are by amendment mutually convertible. Again he is said to have presaged the reform by rulings at *nisi prius*. "The story goes," Professor Hening reports, "that a defendant demurred to a declaration at law because the facts averred showed the only remedy to be in equity. Judge Doe asked the defendant's counsel if his only objection was that the proceeding should have been a bill in equity, and, receiving an affirmative reply, said: 'Very well then, Mr. Clerk, you may just write "bill in equity" on the back of that writ, and now, gentlemen, we will proceed with the hearing.'" [24]

Doe's ruling that a new process is not needed to bring into court a party already there or one who, having been previously notified, is bound to be there, was a decisive blow against technicality, delay, and injustice. But its impact was even greater. From one point of view the decision was the most remarkable of his career, for he accomplished what Lord Mansfield unsuccessfully attempted: he achieved by judicial fiat what every other common-law jurisdiction, including England's, accomplished only by statutory reform — he successfully merged law and equity.

As a result of Doe's leadership, it was settled in New Hampshire, long before it was common practice elsewhere, that any declaration at law may be amended into a bill in equity; that a bill in equity may be amended into a form of action at common law; that a bill in equity is a good declaration in a writ; that a bill in equity may be joined to a declaration at law; and that the two may be filed together in an original action. [25]

There is little in the modern practice codes, drafted by twentieth-century experts, which Doe did not anticipate. In his court the merits of a case never took second place to procedural questions. He paved the way for the simple complaint used in most jurisdictions today when he permitted unrelated counts to be joined in a declaration on a single cause of action and held it immaterial whether a transaction "came under the technical appellation of payment, accord and satisfaction, or release, or under no particular head usually found in the books." [26] In other pioneering decisions he allowed judgments in severalty through a liberal method of joinder;[27] he made justice and convenience, not technical rules, the test for joinder and discovery;[28] he held that damages may be recouped "to avoid a useless multiplication of suits and that a sound rule of set-off cannot be constructed upon the mere form of action;[29] he permitted set-off by amending an action in assumpsit with a bill in equity;[30] and he ruled that a claimant might interplead even though the overwhelming weight of decisional authority, both before and after, has allowed only the stockholder to do so.[31]

Hardly a year went by in which Doe did not disturb legal purists with some unorthodox pronouncement. In 1885, for example, he said that if a trial judge learns that the jury has made a mistake as to law, he may recall the jury and recommit the case for a second verdict whether the lawyers have left town or not, whether the jurors have or have not separated, and whether the first verdict has or has not been recorded.[32] Perhaps Doe's most influential procedural opinion — the one most frequently cited in other jurisdictions — was *Lisbon v. Lyman,* the case that is the leading authority for the then radical principle that when an error has happened in a trial, the party prejudiced has no right to a new trial if the error can be otherwise corrected; and when it cannot be corrected except by a new trial, it is the correction of the error, not the new trial, to which he is entitled.[33]

The extent to which Charles Doe revolutionized the procedure of New Hampshire can best be appreciated by considering two paragraphs, one written by Chief Justice Smith in 1808, the other written by Chief Justice Doe in 1890. These two paragraphs epitomize the extreme poles of thought — although it must be admitted that Doe was more extreme as a reformer than was Smith as a traditionalist. Smith was concerned with form. Correct, proper form was his despair, as well as his joy.

The declaration is incorrect, the service is bad, the plea would be bad on error, it would not be cured by verdict, the replication is bad, the rejoinder is incorrect, the causes of demurrer are many of them absurd, and even the joinder in the demurrer might itself be demurred to, if such thing were allowed. It is painful to peruse such a collection of blunders — and this remark applies to our pleadings in general. I do not think that many causes are lost in our courts for want of good speaking at the bar, at least for not speaking enough; but, for want of good and orderly pleading, many a just cause or just defence has been overthrown in judgment. When there is no good pleading there can be no correct knowledge of the law, though there may be much speaking, and even much eloquence. Our pleadings, when not incorrect in substance, are slovenly in the extreme. Most of our pleadings are too bad for criticism.[34]

Obviously Smith thought it proper that "a just cause or just defence" be lost for procedural reasons. The fact that his imagination would concoct the idea that a joinder in a demurrer might itself be demurred to offers us the key to his professional mind. To him, the fault lay with the inexpert pleader and not with the system of pleading, and until there is "good pleading there can be no correct knowledge of the law." Doe, on the other hand, thought pleading unrelated to "law." In his opinion, Smith talked nonsense. The ideal system is not one in which every man is a perfect pleader, but one in which the rules of pleading — even the forms of action — can be ignored.

The statement that a *mandamus* can be granted, or a bill in equity can be maintained, when there is no other adequate remedy, may be understood in a sense at variance with New Hampshire law. There would be adequate remedies if a *mandamus* were unknown in England, and chancery had never been invented as a separate jurisdiction. "*Mandamus*", "trespass", and other names of ancient forms of action, are used here as references to the character of rights asserted, wrongs complained of, or remedies sought, in particular cases, but with no recognition of the forms as tests or limitations of rights or remedies. When, as in this petition, with due precision and brevity, a plaintiff asserts a legal right and an infringement of it, and asks appropriate relief, his case is decided on the facts proved, without a waste of time in consideration of a form of action. It may be said that there is no form of action, or that the only one is a party's application for a judgment, and his averment of a ground on which he is entitled to it. Such terms as *assumpsit, certiorari,* and *mandamus,* when used to measure and define causes of action, may present an obsolete doctrine of procedure and an inaccurate view of rights.[35]

There can be no mistaking Doe. Had a New Hampshire lawyer been bold enough to venture it, Doe would have accepted a petition similar to the complaints authorized by today's procedure codes, especially the Federal Rules of Civil Procedure. As he said, "The question of form of action is not considered when it is of no practical consequence and time spent upon it would be wasted." [36] Much study, effort, expertise, and propagandizing were devoted to the formulation and adoption of the Federal Rules during the 1930s. They were the product of hard work and of many men, and reformed the law of pleading throughout the United States. Yet it is safe to say that they contained few improvements or innovations which Charles Doe had not introduced into New Hampshire practice by the time of his death in 1896.

In a sense the Federal Rules of Civil Procedure, late as they were, are the vindication of Charles Doe's vision; their universal acceptance today proves the soundness of his reforms. Yet there is irony here, because in the perspective of history the Federal Rules and Doe's reforms do not belong to the same tradition. Though the Federal Rules, like Doe's reforms, emanated from the court, they were drafted by a committee appointed under legislative authority — an authority Doe did not seek and which he insisted he did not need. If anything, the Federal Rules belong to the tradition of the nineteenth-century practice codes, such as the Field Code of New York or the English Judicature Acts. It was opposition to codes which made Doe's reforms popular with the New Hampshire bar. New Hampshire may be the only state in the Union which has not experienced a campaign for procedural codification. Doe was given the credit for this. It was said that he "saved" New Hampshire from the fate of becoming a code state. Because of Doe, said Professor Smith, the New Hampshire court "did not feel constrained to sit with folded hands, waiting for the legislature to enact a poorly-drawn code." Because of Doe, echoed Attorney General Samuel C. Eastman, "New Hampshire practice now has all the flexibility of the code practice without the rigidity of the hampering statutes. It is all controlled by the court, and all debate as to the meaning of a statute is avoided." [37] To appreciate what this meant to New Hampshire lawyers one need only realize that in 1897 — the year in which Smith and Eastman wrote — the New York code of procedure had 3441 sections. While New York lawyers labored to master the intricacies of that "reform" and appealed many practice questions, New Hampshire lawyers enjoyed the least complicated system of pleading in the common-law world and no other jurisdiction saw so few procedural questions appealed. There was no New Hampshire lawyer that year who lost his action on a technicality rather than on the merits.

This, Roscoe Pound thought, was Charles Doe's great contribution to legal history: he proved that codification was not the only method of reform. "Indeed," Pound wrote, "Doe's achievements in procedure are a striking testimony to what a masterful personality, joined with sound legal instincts and thorough knowledge of the traditional legal materials, may do in the way of practical law reform by judicial decision alone, without the aid of legislation." Others have made the same point. "His special genius," it has recently been said of Doe, "lay in the fact that New Hampshire through him was able to accomplish judicially what other jurisdictions had to achieve by a multiplicity of procedure and practice codes." [38]

During the generation following Doe's death this fact was keenly appreciated, and Doe's accomplishments became an argument for rejecting legislative codes. In 1912 the Committee on Reform of Judicial Procedure to the Virginia Bar Association reported New York's William Hornblower, an outspoken opponent of codes, as saying, "Under the principles of the common law and by rules of court, Judge Doe worked out his radical reforms in the procedure of New Hampshire, and the power to regulate details of practice should be restored to the courts where it originally resided." [39] The next year the Georgia bar was told: "An illustrious exponent in this field of endeavor was Chief Justice Doe, of New Hampshire. It appears that no judge in any of the States has been more active than he in simplifying court procedure, and in expediting litigation, so that to-day court procedure in New Hampshire is perhaps, more simplified, and on a better working basis than any other State in the Union. Due largely to the efforts of Chief Justice Doe. A case can probably be brought more readily to a final hearing and decision with less delay and obstruction from technicalities in New Hampshire, than in any other State. Illustrating the tremendous power that a strong man can exert, when his energies are applied in a given direction." [40]

The implication was that there was no need for legislation, that Doe's reforms proved that courts could do a better job. The proof lay in a comparison of New Hampshire's simple procedure with New York's, which was said to be worse than in the common-law days. Perhaps in no other respect was Doe's judicial career more influential. In him the anticodifiers found an effective but negative argument. Doe was used by the forces of reaction. No other state court accomplished what New Hampshire's did because no other state had a judge of Doe's genius and audacity. They did not even need a Doe for judges with less originality and boldness had his example to follow; but there were none who did. Every major reform in the twentieth century has come from the legislature or from committees adapting the Federal Rules to local needs. Outside of New Hampshire Doe's work was so forgotten by 1949 that Arthur T. Vanderbilt doubted whether a judge could be trusted to reform procedure.[41] "The great name in the history of reform in American procedure is David Dudley Field," [42] Vanderbilt wrote. Field was the author of New York's abortive, intractable, and adipose practice code. Because of his method, Field's failure has been more honored than Doe's success.

Chief among the many reasons why Doe's reforms did not serve as a model elsewhere is the fact that few judges shared Doe's legal philosophy. He believed every plaintiff had a right to the easiest and cheapest remedy which justice and convenience could devise and that not only did the court have the power to invent the best procedure possible but it had no authority to withhold relief because of a technicality sanctioned by precedent. While many legal scholars have expressed the same theory, a rare judge will act on it — it is simply too contrary to the training of a lawyer. Rules which Charles Doe saw as technicalities other judges accepted as rights vested in the defendant, which only the legislature could take away.

Another aspect of Charles Doe's jurisprudence which most judges did not share was his notion that many legal issues traditionally treated as substantive law should be questions of fact, to be determined in each case by the demands of justice. Any judge who wished to accept Doe's procedural reforms would also have had to accept this theory. It was the secret to Doe's success. By saying that the law requires the trial court to devise the most convenient procedure, and that what kind of procedure is convenient is properly a question of fact,[43] Doe barred appeals. As a result, his reforms did not breed a new set of technicalities to take the place of the old, as have most codes, including the Federal Rules. In another jurisdiction Doe's reforms would have been refined, minutized, and complicated by constant interpretation and reinterpretation. In New Hampshire, where their application is a question of fact within the discretion of the trial judge, such processes did not happen. It was by making the justice of a procedural ruling a question of fact that Doe guaranteed the purity of his reforms and gave to them what Chief Justice Frank N. Parsons later called their "spirit." The spirit of Doe's reforms, Parsons said, did not lie in the fact that they were made by the court rather than the legislature. "It is rather that the rule does not govern, it only guides. It may be waivered at any time when necessary for the prevention of injustice." [44]

There were, of course, drawbacks to Doe's reforms. While he never went so far as to endorse pleading *ore tenus*, he came close to it in practice. This could be unfair to defendants; an unfairness which Doe mitigated by permitting liberal continuances to defendants caught off guard by novel rulings.[45] Professor Hening has complained that he "permitted a greater laxity in dispensing with written pleadings than was required to render elastic the rigidity of the common law pleading." [46] In truth, the trouble was that Doe did not go far enough. Though he suggested that he would have liked to have done so, he did not substitute the simple complaint for the forms of action. Knowing they could amend at any time, lawyers became careless. The plaintiff was allowed to proceed on almost any possible ground and a case might be well along in trial before the real matter in controversy was developed.[47] Pretrial conferences were necessary, and so, too, was occasional discipline. Doe himself did not want the bar to ignore the writs. "At the present time," he wrote in 1889, "when the plaintiff has a legal and just cause of action, and the sufficiency of the declaration is contested, the question of remedy is disposed of by amendment, and not by disregarding the distinctions between common law forms of action." [48]

In this ruling lay perhaps the most remarkable feature of Doe's reforms. He freed litigants from the technicalities of the common-law writs, yet unlike the codes, he did not break the law's continuity. By maintaining the historical name and meaning of every writ, he preserved the link with the past so vital to any legal system. This may be why he was willing to dismiss an occasional case where the wrong action had been brought[49] — yet even then he usually permitted the party to return to the trial term and amend his pleading.[50]

By 1892 the wheel had fully turned since the days when Jeremiah Smith had set out to teach New Hampshire lawyers the art of pleading. In that year the president of the Southern New Hampshire Bar Association expressed doubt whether there was an attorney then in practice whom Smith would call "a respectable special pleader." [51] In many ways New Hampshire had returned to the loose standards of the pre-Smith, common-sense era. "Pleadings!" one judge is reported to have exclaimed when a point of adjective law was challenged, "This court has not paid the slightest attention to the pleadings, in any case, in the past ten years." [52] This statement could as easily have been made by the common-sense judge who nearly a century earlier had told Jeremiah Mason that he would not entertain a demurrer. "Let me advise you, young man, not to come here with your newfangled law," he had warned. "You must try your case as others do, by the court and jury." [53]

The encomium of the common-sense jurists was written by Chief Justice Jeremiah Smith when he said, "There are now two lawyers on the bench, but I think they are by no means the best of the four." [54] The encomium of Chief Justice Smith was written by Judge Doe when he said, "Chief Justice Smith found the law of New Hampshire in practice and administration a chaos, and left it comparatively an organized and scientific system." [55] The encomium of Judge Doe was written by Smith's son, Harvard Professor Jeremiah Smith, who said of Doe's reforms, "The result is a flexibility of remedies in New Hampshire not surpassed by any of the so-called 'Code States'; and, further, the absolute certainty that cases will be decided on their merits and that justice will not be 'strangled in the net of form.' " [56]

By mentioning "the net of form," Professor Smith put his finger on the crux of the problem. "If the world should be pleased to speak of me after I am dead," his father had written, "let them say, he was a judge who never permitted justice to be strangled in the nets of forms." [57] But it was the fate of the elder Smith to be remembered as the weaver of the nets which almost strangled New Hampshire justice — the nets Charles Doe cut away. Every judge wants to be remembered as a jurist who disregards the nets of form and does not sacrifice justice to technicality. The crux is in the definition of "technicality," and Judge Smith's misfortune was to come from the same jurisdiction as Charles Doe. Doe's definition of procedural technicalities made almost every other judge in American history appear narrow and small. Yet if the emphasis is taken off the "net of forms" and placed on precedent, if the rights of defendants are placed above the abstraction of justice, other judges make Doe appear reckless and irrational.

It may be that Charles Doe's distaste for the "net of forms" drove him too far, that in reaction to Smith's legacy of special pleading he veered too much in the opposite direction, that he came too close to reinstating the loose procedure of the common-sense era. But the fact remains that of all his major reforms "new-modelling" was the only one completely accepted by the New Hampshire bar — the procedural revolution he wrought was not opposed by New Hampshire lawyers. They fought most of his other innovations, sometimes bitterly, but they were grateful for the new-modelled forms. As Judge Clark said on Doe's death, "Whatever views may have been entertained of these changes, as they occurred, they are permanent. The old system will never be restored." [58] "The verdict of the bar," added the attorney general, "is that this reform has been a successful one." [59]

In essence Charles Doe had established in New Hampshire the principle that there was no longer a distinction between "law" and "right." A few months before his death he wrote to the newest member of the supreme court to explain what this meant. "The court," he said, "is nearly unanimous, as a general rule, for doing what ought to be done in matters of procedure (& in many other matters), if there is no clear & distinct legislative prohibition." [60] The judge to whom he wrote understood Doe. Years later he became chief justice and told the New Hampshire bar, "As long as our procedure remains what justice requires, the only improvement will come from a better knowledge of what justice is." [61]

Chapter Eight

THE LABYRINTH
OF AUTHORITY
The Law of Evidence and Criminal
Insanity

TRIAL duties were a nuisance for Charles Doe. Yet we may
wonder whether his new-modelling of the forms would have been
successful without the dual perspective which these duties provided. It was not merely that he could introduce procedural innovations at the trial term and sustain them on appeal. More to
the point, he could watch law in action, study its weaknesses and
defects in day-to-day court business, and couple this practical
experience with the broader vision permitted a policymaking
appellate judge. After all, Doe had been at the bar for only five
years. Had he been confined to an appellate court, his docility
for procedure might have been stunted and his reforms more
discriminate. The same is true of his reforms in evidence. Here
was a second area of law where the duties of a trial judge furnished Doe with the perception upon which successful appellate
innovation depends.

John Henry Wigmore, the man whose name has dominated the
law of evidence during our century, considered Charles Doe and
James Bradley Thayer the leading nineteenth-century reformers
of the American law of evidence. To them he dedicated his monu-
mental treatise, *Wigmore on Evidence.* It is more than coincidence that their biographers, writing in the same volume of *Great*

American Lawyers, use the metaphor "jungle" to describe the law of evidence as it was before Doe and Thayer began their work. Writing of Thayer, James Parker Hall called evidence "a legal jungle where mere unsophisticated intelligence might fail to find the track of a single clear idea." Crawford Dawes Hening, in his sketch of Doe, referred to evidence as a "tangled jungle of ideas represented by the phrases '*prima facie* evidence', 'presumption of fact', 'presumption of law', and 'burden of proof.' " Doe, he claimed, was the pioneer who "let in the light." [1]

In contrast to his piecemeal new-modelling of procedure, Doe approached the reform of evidence with a broad theory more characteristic of the appellate than of the trial judge. Here for the first time we find him supplementing stark rational analysis with the sweep of legal generalizations. Envisioning the common law as a unitary whole, Doe blamed its fragmentation not on substantive doctrines pulling one against the other, but on misapplication of the fundamental rules of evidence. At the heart of the problem he saw the failure of courts to draw a clear distinction between law and fact. The practice of turning law into fact, Doe believed, "introduces arbitrary rules and disorganizing exceptions into the scientific system of the law, overwhelms that reason which is the life of it and changes the law into a chaotic collection of fragmentary and incoherent regulations, to be mastered only by sheer force of a rare and marvellous memory." [2]

Doe knew that expansion of the area of fact and complementary contraction of the area of law bears heavily on defendants in tort cases. After all, many of the rules of law to which he objected were designed to counter the prejudices of juries; if left to themselves, jurors might hold railroads and other corporate defendants liable for every act. This circumstance was immaterial to Doe. Wrong done in the decision of factual questions, he insisted, cannot "be legally prevented or rectified by a judicial alteration of the law." [3] To any criticism that he was extending liability, Judge Doe would have replied that he was restoring to the jury its proper functions.

As will be discussed in subsequent chapters, Doe carried the law-fact dichotomy to extremes, using it as a pretext for reforms more substantive than adjective. But it was in the area of evidence that his ideas had their initial impact. Legal presumptions were his first target; for what is a legal presumption but a question of fact mistakenly held to be a matter of law? "Among the various ways in which the province of the jury has been encroached upon," Doe argued, "the use of legal presumptions as substitutes for evidence, is one of the most conspicuous." [4]

State v. *Hodge,* the first of Judge Doe's decisions to attract attention outside New Hampshire, sums up his teaching about legal presumptions. He was questioning one of the oldest rules in the common law — that the unexplained and exclusive possession of recently stolen goods raises a presumption that the possessor is the thief. "It is useless to call such a presumption a presumption of law," Doe said. "Call it what we may, it is a presumption of fact." Whether a defendant had possession of stolen goods, and "whether his possession, if any he had, was recent enough, or exclusive enough, or unexplained enough, to raise a presumption of guilt, — were questions of fact for the jury." [5]

Common-law judges, Doe thought, delude themselves if they believe there can be unmixed legal presumptions. No matter how much fact they change into law, there are still factual issues to be resolved. To say that recent and exclusive possession of stolen property creates an unmixed legal presumption of guilt implies that the issues of recentness and exclusiveness are to be determined by legal formulas. Surely the question of recentness is one of fact under the circumstances; why not, then, be candid and admit that the entire matter properly belongs to the triers of fact?

By undermining the strength of legal presumptions Judge Doe opened an avenue for reforming the law governing burden of proof. Ordinarily a plaintiff who avers a fact necessary to sustain his case has the burden of proving that fact; he must first persuade the court of the truth of the allegation. If he does, and if the defendant counters with evidence which makes the issue doubtful, the plaintiff has the burden of coming forward with additional facts which will satisfy the jury that he has proved his case by a preponderance of the evidence. Many rules governing proof had grown up over the years, creating exceptions to the general principle that the plaintiff must sustain the burden. Doe reformed many of these by rephrasing the burden-of-proof issue in terms of questions of fact or of presumptions. His most telling success with this approach was scored against the rule which shifts the burden of proof whenever the facts to be proven are peculiarly within the knowledge of the defendant. This rule, traditionally viewed as an exception to the general principle that the plaintiff must sustain his case, was considered sensible: if the defendant possesses all the evidence, the plaintiff is helpless unless the burden is shifted. Doe, however, held a different view. The rule does more than shift the burden of proof; it creates a legal presumption by converting fact into law. That a party has produced all the evidence in his power and his opponent does not produce evidence easily obtained, "the slight evidence produced by the former, and the circumstantial evidence of nonproduction by the latter, may be, as a matter of fact, very strong proof against the latter." But, Doe concluded, "this belongs to the weight of evidence for the consideration of the tribunal trying the fact, and does not affect the burden of proof to be fixed by a court of law." [6]

Charles Doe was so committed to the law-fact theory that he made only one concession — and it can hardly be called a concession. Admitting that "obvious impracticality on one side, contrasted with obvious feasibility on the other," might "authorize the invention of an exception to release a litigant from his duty of proving the essential facts of his case," Doe showed himself willing to make the entire law of evidence a question of fact by saying that "the existence of such impracticability and feasibility, is a question chiefly of fact." [7]

This was letting theory have its head with a vengeance; yet with little hesitation the court adopted Doe's ideas. His reforms of the rules of evidence came to be accepted as completely as his new-modelling of the forms. The fact-law distinction reshaped New Hampshire legal theory and in time was recognized as the hallmark of that state's jurisprudence. Outside of New Hampshire it made less headway and has frequently been misunderstood. In another area of evidence, however, Doe exerted a decided influence upon American law. His decisions helped to establish the doctrine that the best evidence should always be admissible.

Doe's most important pronouncement dealing with the admissibility of evidence was *Darling* v. *Westmoreland*. Both Dean John

Henry Wigmore and Professor Edmund M. Morgan have called it a "classic." [8] The plaintiff claimed that while crossing a bridge his horse had been frightened by a pile of lumber belonging to the defendant; as a result, the horse had reared and backed off the bridge. The defense contended that the horse was vicious and unsafe. To counter this allegation the plaintiff offered to show that another horse, owned by a man named Fletcher, had been frightened by the same pile of lumber. The lower court rejected the offer on the grounds that it was collateral evidence. The plaintiff appealed and Doe, speaking for a unanimous court, set aside the verdict.

That a court should accept the best evidence available, Doe argued, "is the fundamental principle upon which all rules of evidence are framed." [9] The rule prohibiting the trial of collateral issues merely excludes what is irrelevant. "It is a rule of reason and not an arbitrary or technical one, and it does not exclude all experimental knowledge." [10] At that time "collateral" meant "immaterial," not "remotely probable" or "indirectly connected." As Wigmore points out, Doe "incisively exposed the fallacy of this ambiguous usage." [11] Doe believed that judges had been mistaken when they held that evidence, such as the fright of Fletcher's horse, was offered to show that Darling's horse was probably frightened in the same manner. In fact, it was offered to prove the "terrifying quality of the pile." The capacity of the lumber to frighten the plaintiff's horse was an issue involving "the secondary question of its capacity to frighten other horses." [12]

Darling v. *Westmoreland*, Wigmore has claimed, "utterly discredited" the earlier precedents "as an obstacle to the investigation of truth." [13] It is possible that Wigmore could have gone further and given Doe credit for showing him the potential scope of the best-evidence rule. When Doe heard that Wigmore planned to write a treatise on evidence to replace the hopelessly inadequate study by Professor Simon Greenleaf, long the only authority available to lawyers, Doe sent him a letter warning of the pitfalls. He knew that Wigmore, a law teacher, had had little trial experience, and he was afraid he might rely too much on the abstract theories which had guided American courts during the Greenleaf era. Doe wanted Wigmore to abandon the idea that the burden of proving competency is on the party offering evidence. Doe thought it was for the party objecting to prove its inadmissibility.

If you read the reports of trials in the London Daily Times, or are otherwise acquainted with English practice, you have knowledge, which Greenleaf did not have, which the American Bar & Bench do not have, of the variety & amount of evidence that is constantly admitted in England without objection, though excluded or not offered in this country. . . . There are more than ten times as many objections made to evidence in the trial of a case in Mass. or N.H. as would be made in the trial of the same case in London. Undoubtedly a great deal of evidence is introduced in Eng. without objection, which is not understood to be strictly competent. Their practice in that respect is much more liberal than ours. If I were writing a book on evidence I should make special investigation of the question whether English decisions apply the rules of evidence with the same strictness as American, & I should investigate the proportion of Eng. & Am. reported decisions of questions of evidence. Justice is certainly delayed & defeated in this country by objections to evidence, & by the exclusion of evidence, that is admitted in Eng. without objection.[14]

And the practical difference is very great. Doe, of course, had an answer for the difficult problem of how to determine if evidence is collateral or remote. Whether an issue is collateral and whether evidence is too remote, he held, should be a question of fact and not a rule of law.[15]

As with questions of fact, Judge Doe did not confine his discussion of the best-evidence rule to exposing past errors but also gave body to theory through practical application. It was on this point that his colleagues rebelled. When Doe tried to admit the opinions of witnesses who were not qualified experts on specialized subjects, he found himself in dissent, as occurred in the famous cases of *Boardman* v. *Woodman* and *State* v. *Pike,* in which the majority upheld lower-court rulings which had excluded from evidence the opinions of nonexpert witnesses on the question of mental capacity. *Boardman* was a probate appeal involving the validity of a will; in *Pike* insanity was raised as a defense to a murder indictment. Doe's colleagues were willing to permit nonexperts to describe the appearance and conduct of the person said to be insane. But the majority would not allow them to testify that they believed the testator in *Boardman* lacked mental capacity or that the defendant in *Pike* was irresponsible, because it was for the jury to say what inferences should be drawn from the facts described.

Doe pointed to the inconsistency of permitting witnesses to a will, even though nonexpert and with no previous association with the testator, to give their opinions of his capacity, while holding incompetent similar testimony from servants, acquaintances, neighbors, and friends, who have had many more opportunities for observation. What value was the testimony of subscribing witnesses except as to the testator's capacity? The same was true in criminal cases where opinions of the influence of alcohol were admitted but opinions of insanity were rejected.[16] "The opinion of an unprofessional witness," Doe argued, "is competent, not because he can give no description of the appearance which might indicate sanity or insanity, but because, ordinarily, he cannot give an adequate description of them. The law, always demanding the best evidence, receives his opinion because his description of symptoms alone is not the best." [17]

A common thread of thought runs through Judge Doe's decisions on the rules of evidence. There is, first of all, the general theory that the law is a unified whole, not to be fragmentized by what he called "the labyrinth of authority." [18] This is supplemented by the argument that the jury, as the trier of fact, should hear testimony unencumbered by presumptions, exceptions, or instructions regarding special burdens of proof. The best example of his thought is also the most controversial — the New Hampshire doctrine for criminal insanity. Herein is an instance of Doe's remarkable originality. Conventional legal patterns have always placed criminal insanity under the heading of criminal law or medical jurisprudence; Doe reassigned it to the law of evidence. Of course the doctrine has penal and medical overtones. But its formulation is intertwined with rules governing presumptions, burden of proof, and nonexpert-opinion evidence.

When Judge Doe turned his attention to criminal insanity, the law was dominated by the M'Naghten rules — a test of rationality the jury must apply when deciding whether a respondent was insane at the time he committed an otherwise criminal act. The M'Naghten rules provide that "to establish a defence on the ground of insanity, it must be clearly proved that, at the time of the committing of the act, the party accused was labouring under such a defect of reason, from disease of the mind, as not to know the nature and quality of the act he was doing; or, if he did know it, that he did not know what he was doing was wrong." [19] In some American states the M'Naghten rules have been supplemented by the "irresistible impulse" test, which provides that if at the time of the alleged crime the defendant knew the nature and quality of his act and knew it to be wrong, he might nevertheless be not guilty by reason of insanity if he suffered from a mental disease which so overwhelmed his conscience and judgment that he was rendered incapable of resisting an impulse which led to the commission of the act.[20] These tests, the M'Naghten rules, supplemented in a few American states by the "irresistible impulse" additive, have remained the criteria for criminal insanity in most common-law jurisdictions down to the present day. Doe was the first to challenge them, and he is still the only judge who has seriously questioned the legal as distinguished from the medical foundations upon which they rest.

It was on the issue of criminal insanity that Judge Doe's theories concerning the law of evidence converged to form a unified doctrine. At the center is his antipathy toward legal presumptions. On first glance the M'Naghten rules appear to be substantive law, and as such they have been treated by nearly every commentator. Doe preferred to look upon them as a presumption of law which presumes that a man is sane unless he proves he does not meet a certain standard of rationality. One objection to this presumption is that it places the burden of persuasion upon the defendant, a presumption rectified only in part by the added presumption that the defendant is sane. In murder cases this additional presumption is necessary when the jury is told that there is a presumption of malice. Malice implies rationality, and rationality, under M'Naghten, implies sanity. Thus, from Doe's point of view, the law of criminal insanity, as expounded by the courts of the nineteenth century, presented a sorry picture of presumption thrown upon presumption. Not only were the rules defining insanity a presumption, but on top of them were piled the presumption of malice and the presumption of sanity.[21]

Basic to Doe's analysis was the distinction between law and fact. By sanctioning one test for insanity and excluding proof not related to it, and by instructing the jury to ignore all symptoms of mental disease which do not bear on the knowledge of wrong-fulness, the M'Naghten rules treat as a matter of law what Doe considered a question of fact. Here he was on controversial grounds: no other authority has agreed with him that the defini-tion of criminal responsibility is a question of fact. Like the definition of causation, of self-defense, and of crime itself, it seems clearly a matter of law. But Doe thought that he had history on his side. In former times, when the jury's role was not firmly settled, English judges had ignored the demarcation be-tween law and fact. They had given to juries their opinions as to current medical dogmas, and as a result of repetition these opin-ions had hardened into legal formulas. By 1843, when the M'Naghten rules were devised, what had been fact was erroneously thought to be law. The judges who decided *M'Naghten's Case* adopted the latest psychiatric notions, converting contem-porary medicine into petrified legal doctrine. "Whether the old or new medical theories are correct," Doe argued, "is a question of fact for the jury; it is not the business of the court to know whether any of them are correct." [22]

Doe laid the foundation for the New Hampshire doctrine of criminal insanity in *Boardman* v. *Woodman*. Not a criminal case, to be sure, it was nevertheless essential to his theory, since it helped to establish the premise that a uniform approach could serve both civil and criminal law. "Your doctrine," he explained to a correspondent, "is, not that the common-law prescribes a test of any disease, physical or mental, but that an act caused by mental disease is not a crime, a contract or a will." [23] In *Boardman* Doe pleaded with his colleagues to restore reason and unity to the law by abandoning the delusion test for capacity to make a valid will — a test repudiated by medical science. "That cannot be a fact in law, which is not a fact in science," Doe argued; "that cannot be health in law, which is disease in fact. And it is unfortunate that courts should maintain a contest with science and the laws of nature, upon a fact which is within the province of science and outside the domain of our law." [24]

Doe was in dissent in *Boardman*: the court was not ready for so radical an innovation. But within four years there occurred a remarkable reversal. In 1869 Josiah L. Pike, indicted for first-degree murder, pleaded not guilty by reason of insanity. At his trial Chief Justice Ira Perley presided, with Doe as assistant judge. During the evenings between court sessions Doe argued and Perley listened. The older man was persuaded to instruct the jury that the definition of criminal insanity and the issue whether the defendant suffered from insanity are questions of fact. When Pike appealed his conviction, Doe wrote the opinion for a unanimous court sustaining Perley's charge. In *State* v. *Pike* Doe's dissent in *Boardman* became law, and the New Hampshire doctrine was born.

During 1871 another respondent, indicted for first-degree murder, pleaded criminal insanity as a defense. In this case Doe presided and was able to instruct the jury in his own words. On appeal Judge Ladd wrote the decision, again for a unanimous court. Ladd's opinion, *State* v. *Jones,* together with Doe's in *State* v. *Pike* form the basis for an approach to criminal insanity which has worked successfully in New Hampshire for nearly a century. Instead of telling the jury that the defendant must have known the alleged criminal act was wrong when he committed it, as do the M'Naghten rules, the New Hampshire doctrine tells the jury to weigh rationality along with the other evidence offered to prove or disprove sanity. As Doe told the jury in the *Jones* case:

If the defendant killed his wife in a manner that would be criminal and unlawful if the defendant were sane, the verdict should be "not guilty by reason of insanity," if the killing was the offspring or product of mental disease in the defendant. Neither delusion, nor knowledge of right and wrong, nor design or cunning in planning and executing the killing and escaping or avoiding detection, nor ability to recognize acquaintances, or to labor, or transact business, or manage affairs, is, as a matter of law, a test of mental disease; but all symptoms and all tests of mental disease are purely matters of fact, to be determined by the jury.

Admittedly there is inconsistency in Doe's charge. In describing the criminal act as "the offspring or product of mental disease" he implied that the jury, in order to exculpate the defendant, must find that the disease caused the act. But there can be little doubt Doe intended causation — both its definition and its necessity — to be a question of fact. He made this clear in *Boardman,* and it is significant that he ended his charge in *Jones* with the instruction, "Whether an act may be produced by partial insanity when no connection can be discovered between the act and the disease, is a question of fact." [25]

The ambiguity has led many writers to call the New Hampshire doctrine the "product test." Some have even read into the word "product" an implication of intent, concluding that the New Hampshire doctrine calls for "a specific mode of causality, namely, the total destruction of the actor's capacity for self-control, the nonconcurrence of his will." [26] To claim as much is to misread Doe, in that the statement ignores the theories about the law of evidence from which the doctrine evolved, turning it into a test of volition, which is farthest from Judge Doe's intention.

Another unfortunate development has been the tendency to misinterpret the New Hampshire doctrine as a formulation grounded on medical theory rather than on the distinction between law and fact. Here too Doe contributed to the confusion. While he was struggling with his dissent in *Boardman*, he began a correspondence with Doctor Isaac Ray, then the leading American authority on forensic psychiatry. When it was published in 1953, this correspondence lent substance to the charge that the New Hampshire doctrine is a medical and not a legal formulation. The following year this contention was reinforced when the District of Columbia Circuit announced a new approach to criminal insanity — the *Durham* test — which, the court claimed, "is not unlike" the New Hampshire doctrine. "It is simply that an accused is not criminally responsible if his unlawful act was the product of his mental disease or mental defect." [27]

The similarity between the *Durham* rule and the New Hampshire doctrine is superficial, since *Durham* is a medical test. The jury must accept the expert testimony of alienists, and if psychiatric opinion changes overnight, a person convicted as a result of the obsolete opinion may be entitled to another trial at which the jury cannot "arbitrarily reject" the new opinion. Shifts in medical theory and even in medical nomenclature may determine the conduct of trials and the fate of defendants.[28]

Judge Doe would have been shocked. It is difficult to conceive of a test for criminal insanity more unlike what he had in mind. Although both the New Hampshire doctrine and the *Durham* rule have the merit of insuring that the best evidence will be admitted, the New Hampshire doctrine makes that evidence a question of fact, while *Durham* makes it a matter of law. Yet the New Hampshire doctrine has been inseparately associated with *Durham*. Commentators, neglecting Doe's theories on the law of evidence, have accepted the *Durham* dictum that it "is not unlike" the New Hampshire doctrine. When criticizing and rejecting *Durham*, courts have assumed that they are also criticizing and rejecting Doe's doctrine. In the extensive debate which has followed the announcement of *Durham* the New Hampshire doctrine has been blamed for all the faults to which *Durham* is heir.[29]

Such has been the fate of Judge Doe's most famous decision. If there is any case for which he is currently known, it is *State* v. *Pike*, and if there is any legal theory with which his name is connected, it is the New Hampshire doctrine for criminal insanity. Yet it has been misunderstood and misinterpreted ever since it was first laid down. Judges who served in jurisdictions where the terms "presumptions," "burden of proof," and "question of fact" are not so sharply defined as they are in New Hampshire have missed the law-of-evidence foundation upon which Doe built his doctrine. Doe waited twenty years for proof that the New Hampshire doctrine was based on an erroneous theory of law; instead he saw judges and writers reject it on the mistaken argument that it was the result of medical fantasy. It was with a sense of frustration that in 1889 he wrote to the editor of the *Medico-Legal Journal* asking why lawyers had ignored the common-law questions which he had raised in *Pike*.

How long will it be before the candid minds of the profession will demand a satisfactory answer to these questions? Such minds are not swayed by the superficial or general allusions, or mere assertion. They insist upon argument solid, thorough and profound, going to the bottom of the subject, free from cavil and sophistry, shunning no difficulty and misrepresenting no position of an adversary. I merely suggest in the course of your writing on the subject, an appeal perhaps in the interrogative form, to the candor of the legal profession, for an explanation of the fact that twenty years have passed without any material answer being made to the N.H. argument on the common-law question.[30]

Doe's challenge has remained unanswered. As a result of the *Durham* rule the misinterpretation of the New Hampshire doctrine as a medical test has been compounded. The theory of evidence upon which it rests is ignored by American courts overzealous in their desire to shield the law from psychiatric radicalism.

The New Hampshire doctrine of criminal insanity devises no test, but rejects all tests; creates no presumptions, but rejects all presumptions; it is not so much a rule of law as an affirmation that there are no rules of law to determine legal responsibility. It is not an isolated principle of criminal law, but a universal principle applicable as well on the civil side. It may not consider fully the problems of ends, needs, and public policy, but it is the only pronouncement on insanity which considers the problem of legal function — the correct function of the judge and of the jury, of the determiner of law and the decider of facts. It may be that Judge Doe failed to take into account the practical, utilitarian value of a jury of laymen confronted with the language of psychiatry, but he did take into account the value and validity of an old presumption of law which, from a mistaken assumption of fact, had grown into *stare decisis*. It may be that Judge Doe accentuated the prejudices and intolerance of the jury, but he did so by eliminating the narrowness and reaction of the judge. It may be that Judge Doe gave to the jury a vague question of fact, but he offered it in place of dubious rules of law.

Chapter Nine

A PRIVATE CONJECTURE

Rules of Construction[1]

THE doggedness with which Charles Doe pushed his theories concerning the law of evidence did not abate once he had reformed the tests governing the definition of criminal insanity. The inbred distrust for rules which had motivated him when writing *State* v. *Pike* remained throughout his judicial career. Once he had completed his reform of the law of evidence, Doe turned his attention to rules governing the construction or interpretation of instruments such as statutes, wills, deeds, and contracts.

When he began his work, the construction of instruments was governed largely by legal formulations. Rules of law decided issues which might reasonably have been determined as questions of fact. Again Doe made use of his historical theory that opinions given to juries as gratuitous expressions during the era before courts drew a clear distinction between law and fact had, with constant repetition, hardened into doctrine, as a result of which the reason of the common law had been forgotten. This legal ossification, abetted by "defects in the remedial branch of the common law," accounted for most rules of construction.[2] Because of these rules the common law was unreasonably inflexible, turning on technicalities which "result quite as often in defeating as in promoting" the intention of the person who had drafted the instrument being construed. The more Doe surveyed the labyrinth of authority, the more he rebelled, finally concluding that only one absolute can be laid down — "No technical rules of construction applicable to all cases can be established. The intention in each case is determined by the evidence bearing on the case." [3]

Judge Doe's jurisprudential tenet that the common law is a unified whole also affected his approach to the rules of construction. Since law is a unit, held together by a few general principles, there is no justification for treating various instruments differently. A corporate charter, for example, should be interpreted as is any other grant, statutory, contractual, or testamentary. If lawyers insist on rules, the only rule necessary "is, that a grantor intends, if he is able, to convey those rights and powers without which the grant would be of no effect, or the means reasonably necessary for the enjoyment of the granted property or right, the exercise of the granted power, and the accomplishment of the object of the grant." [4]

In construing statutes Judge Doe refused to be sidetracked by disputes over the meaning of language. The task, to him, was to find the intent and to carry it out. If competent evidence shows that a statutory proviso or clause, "taken in its strict, literal sense, would not express, but would defeat, the legislative will, it is to be construed with such liberality as will execute the proved design of the law-making power." [5] After all, "if evidence establishes the fact that the literal sense is not the true sense, a literal construction would be an alteration of the law." [6] The one concession Doe made toward distinguishing constitutional and statutory provisions from other instruments was to acknowledge that their meaning "is often shown by the nature of the danger which was apprehended, and against which the legal barrier was supposed to be necessary" — that is, by "the public history of the time." [7] By this method he determined the meaning of the word "Protestant" in the religious-qualification clause of the New Hampshire constitution: he employed history to ascertain the danger against which his Yankee ancestors had sought to guard. Once the evil the legislators or constitution makers wished to remedy is known, their intent can be ascertained in the same manner as the intent of private documents, such as wills and contracts. "There is less use of history in the construction of a contract or will," Doe wrote. "When we get beyond historical evidence of the mischief, how do you draw a line between the construction of a statute or constitution, and the construction of a will or contract?" [8]

Doe answered that no such line can be drawn. The principle he stated in a testamentary case was the principle he used to solve every problem of construction from the Constitution to a simple agreement: "The interpretation of the will is the ascertainment of the testator's intention; and the question of intention is ordinarily determined as a question of fact, by the natural weight of competent evidence, and not by artificial rules of interpretation." [9] As he put it in its most succinct form, "the testator's intention, proved by competent evidence, is his will." [10] He called this rule the doctrine of general intent. Its jurisprudential aim was to do away with rules and to restore reason to the law of construction. The working tool Doe employed to get around these rules was the argument that intention is a question of fact.

The only rule Doe formulated for solving the factual question was to say that no rules can be laid down. He even treated as a presumption of fact rather than a presumption of law the presumption that a legislature does not intend a statute to operate retroactively.[11] A "preponderance of probability" was what he looked for.[12] "The whole instrument," Doe wrote of a deed, "is to be read, and applied to the subject-matter, to ascertain the primary and leading purpose of the parties; and an ambiguous word or phrase is to be construed, as it reasonably may be, as best to promote and accomplish that purpose." [13]

Judge Doe apparently thought it relatively easy to ascertain intent. At least he never declared an instrument void for vagueness. On the contrary, he wrote the leading American opinion repudiating the rule that when a grantor of land reserves an uncertain, undefined or undescribed right, he can have no recovery at law. The theory is that the court cannot enforce the grant unless its exact limitations are spelled out in the deed. Precedents supporting such rules, Doe argued, turn remedial defects into substantive law.[14] He preferred to recast them as construction problems, even if they must then be solved subjectively. Thus, when a testator left money to the "Bible Society" and no organization of that name was in existence, Doe held there was "no patent ambiguity" making the factual issue incapable of solution. "The question is not by what name any Bible society was known to others, but which one of several Bible societies was intended by the testator." To find the answer Doe turned to objective evidence, such as the fact that a collection to benefit one particular society was taken regularly in the testator's church, and to subjective evidence, such as the fact that only that society had been known to the testator.[15]

Candidly Doe admitted that some of his results were "very doubtful"; he realized that when applying his doctrine of general intent, the court is as likely to disagree on a question of fact as on a matter of law.[16] Yet he denied substituting "a private and unauthorized conjecture" in place of a certain and predictable outcome.[17] One reason for abandoning rules of construction is that they make law arbitrary by freezing it within preconceived patterns unrelated to the facts of the cases they are to resolve. Thus Doe was careful to maintain that the alternative he offered to these rules is not a different form of arbitrariness founded on personal judgment. "The evidence of intention," he admitted, "may include various inherent probabilities and the probative force of many circumstances, as well as the literal sense of the words used." This is not to say that the trier of fact has a green light to ascertain intention by a private conjecture. "When the meaning is found by giving due weight to everything that legally tends to prove it, it is not a matter of discretion whether it shall be adopted or rejected." [18]

There would be more than a touch of naivete in Doe's suggestion that judges are able to apply subjective tests objectively were it not that he was speaking relatively. From his point of view it was he, not the advocates of fixed rules of construction, who provided more certain and predictable results. Rules make law uncertain, since it is not possible to predict which of many and often contradictory rules a judge will elect to follow. But when choice is limited to finding intention according to the dictates of reason and justice, the outcome can be prophesied with greater certainty. Even if it should prove a private conjecture, it will be a private conjecture reasonably foreseen.

The practical impact of Doe's reforms can be measured by the law of wills. In rural New Hampshire only the meaning of testaments was questioned often enough to furnish an opportunity for rebuilding in one specialized area the law of construction. In the result lies an indication of what Doe might have done with non-testamentary issues of construction had the economy of nineteenth-century New Hampshire given him the chance. Here, too, can be seen the full implications of his quarrel with rules which confine inquiry to the etymological and grammatical arrangement of phrases to which professional usage and English precedent have given fixed, technical meanings. His purpose was to loosen the rigidity of words and to substitute reason in place of syntactic absolutes.

Doe conceded that when a word appears to be used in a peculiar sense, its apparent meaning is its legal meaning. "But," he insisted, "there is no legal presumption that all testators and contracting parties are lawyers, or that their understanding and use of language is peculiar." [19] Wills written by a layman should be construed according to "the vocabulary of ordinary life," or by finding "the popular significance of his language." [20] Lawyers are at a disadvantage "because they are more familiar with legal phraseology than with the terms in which the mass of their neighbors express themselves on legal subjects." [21] To anyone arguing that courts lack power to change long-established rules for reading instruments describing title to property, Chief Justice Doe replied that the legislature never "made the effect of a devise depend upon the legal education of the devisor or his scrivener." [22]

One case may be cited as typical. In *Sanborn* v. *Sanborn* Doe held that a life estate, expressly devised, is not enlarged into a fee simple or full title by a *habendum* to the life tenant "and his heirs." By correct legal form the property should have been left to the tenant for life. His heirs, since they were to receive the fee after his death, should have been designated as remaindermen, and not called "heirs." Doe decided that what counted was the testator's intent, not his choice of words. "In common speech, the whole of a homestead at a future day is not a 'remainder' of it, and expectants who will never have the possession, use, or income unless they outlive a life tenant, are not 'remainder-men,' but 'heirs'." [23]

While *Sanborn* v. *Sanborn* is a bold departure from legal formalism, it is hardly startling. By the standards of reason and

justice it makes common sense. Judges who cannot bring themselves to take the same position may nevertheless admire Doe's
consistency and originality. Yet when he applied the same reasoning to words of limitation, defining property interests, he seemed
to be going too far. A grantor who wishes to convey the full title
in land to a person must grant it to that person "and his heirs."
The words "and his heirs" are the words of limitation which
create the fee; no other words of perpetuity may be substituted
in their place. "A grant to a man to have and to hold forever, or
to have and to hold to him and to his assigns forever, will convey
only an estate for life." [24] Most judges, including some of Doe's
colleagues, saw no way to alter the fact that words of limitation
are a requirement of substantive law.[25] Doe may be the first to
have treated them as a rule of construction. If the grantor intends
to create a fee simple, he argued, the omission of words of limitation is immaterial; the intent, not the words, will be enforced.

Words of limitation, Judge Doe contended, are an anachronism
left over from the days when the law of feudal England favored
a man's heirs and frowned upon the sale of family property. In
commercial New Hampshire, if the law has any policy, it should
be toward free alienation; a rule which makes it impossible to sell
land unless certain prescribed words are used is out of place. In
Smith v. *Furbish* the grantor conveyed real property by deed to
the grantee, "his heirs and assigns forever," clearly creating a fee
simple. In the same deed, however, he reserved to himself a part
of the premises, and this reservation did not include the words
of limitation — "his heirs and assigns forever." The grantee
claimed that failure to use the redundancy meant that the grantor
had reserved a life estate only and not full title. Doe rejected the
argument. "The question whether a general devise of a described
tract of land, or of 'all and singular my lands, messuages, and
tenements', was intended to give all the testator's title, or to dis-
pose of only a life estate, and leave him intestate as to the remainder, is determined as a question of fact, upon an impartial
consideration of all competent evidence by balancing probabilities, and not by technical rules." [26]

Judge Doe's most dramatic — and questionable — application
of the doctrine of general intent is *Edgerly* v. *Barker.* In that
case he tried to eliminate those aspects of the rule against per-

petuities which often defeat the intentions of testators. A perpetuity, in this sense, is any limitation upon the power to sell or
use property. To prevent the "dead hand" of past generations
from tying up society's wealth, the common law has devised the
rule that a grant, testamentary or otherwise, is invalid unless the
interest which is being conveyed will vest in the grantee not
later than twenty-one years after the death of a person or persons
living at the time that the interest is created. For example, if a
testator leaves property to his nephew for his life, with the remainder to the nephew's children after the last child becomes
thirty years of age, the grant is invalid because there is a possibility that the remainder may not vest until twenty-one years after
the nephew's death. The rule against perpetuities cancels the devise, and the property passes to the testator's heirs at law as
though no will had been written.

In *Edgerly* v. *Barker* the testator left his property in trust to his
son and daughter for their lives, with the remainder to their
children "when the youngest of said children shall arrive at the
age of forty years." As Doe read the will, the remainder was not
to vest until the youngest grandchild became forty years old — a
contingency which violated the rule against perpetuities. The
son and daughter petitioned to have the will declared invalid,
praying that the court award them the entire estate as the heirs
at law. Although the specific fact pattern had never been decided
in New Hampshire, precedent both in America and England
supported their claim.

Perhaps Doe should have followed precedent, as he could have
done without violating the doctrine of general intent, since the
issue of the testator's intention can be separated from the issue
whether the intention violates the rule against perpetuities. The
testator had intended to create a trust for the life of his children
and to vest the remainder in his grandchildren after the youngest
had become forty years old. This intent, under the rule against
perpetuities, could not be enforced. The fault lay with the testator, not the law.

In *Edgerly* Doe added a fresh dimension to the doctrine of
general intent. The ascertainment of intention, he said, is not
limited to expressed provisions in the will. True, the testator did
not intend that his grandchildren take the property until the

youngest is forty years old. But what of his implied intention that they eventually are to own the property? The rule against perpetuities, by voiding the will, ignores this unexpressed but perhaps primary intention. In this sense the rule against perpetuities is a rule of construction which conflicts with the doctrine of intent. Why not eliminate the conflict by enforcing both the rule against perpetuities and the doctrine of general intent? "The law determines not what will he would have made if he had known that the last nineteen of the forty years were too remote, but what will he did make in ignorance of this flaw in his appointment of time. His intent that the grandchildren shall not have the remainder till the youngest arrives at the age of forty years is modified by his intent that they shall have it, and that the will shall have effect as far as possible." [27]

Thus Doe found that the testator's primary intent was to make a gift to his grandchildren, the intent that the gift not take effect until the youngest became forty years old — the intention which violated the rule against perpetuities — being secondary. Since a secondary intention should not defeat a primary intention, but a primary intention is to be executed as near as possible to the testator's instructions, Doe held that the contingency could be reduced by judicial construction to the maximum valid period. In other words, the remainder would vest in the grandchildren when the youngest became twenty-one years old. The finding of fact upon which he based this decision was the common-sense conclusion that the testator wanted the remainder to vest sooner rather than not at all. "The devise," Doe wrote, "is effective *cy pres,** in pursuance of his implied intent to divide according to common reason, throw out what is against the law, and let the rest stand. This legal intent, correctly inferred as a fact, is a part of the will, not less operative or less important than it would be if set forth in express terms in the writing. A refusal to execute it would be an alteration of the will, and a violation of common-law principle and statutory right." [28] With this in mind Doe defined the doctrine of general intent as "a rule of approximation that makes the least sacrifice of a testator's declared intention concerning realty and personalty (or a mixed fund of realty and personalty), rejecting no more of his will than the law makes

* As near as possible.

it necessary to reject, and preferring 'the greater part,' and the 'weightiest' intent, when the greater and the less cannot both be carried into effect." [29]

By formulating the doctrine of general intent and applying it in *Edgerly* v. *Barker* Charles Doe was making the kind of law to which he dedicated his career — not a rule, but a measure of approximation which sets the guideposts of policy while leaving the law free to pursue justice through reason. Professor John Chipman Gray, speaking for the opposition, bemoaned Doe's sacrifice of the rule against perpetuities, a rule "concatenated with almost mathematical precision." [30] Gray represented a school of jurisprudents for whom law is analytically scientific; with this school Charles Doe had no dealings. "It would," Doe admitted, "be very convenient and useful if the question of intention could always be truly determined by the mere application of well defined formulas, in the same way that a carpenter ascertains the exact length of a board by applying the foot rule." [31] But convenience and usefulness are not purchased at the price of unreasonable rules. "The argument for the judicial enforcement of formulas judicially enacted is, the convenience of a mechanical method of construction, free from the fault of uncertainty. The argument against it is, the certainty with which it would frequently sacrifice the legal rights of parties to the convenience of the courts." [32]

Professor Gray might have replied that "legal rights" are not sacrificed by such rules as the rule against perpetuities, since these rules as established by precedent are the true source of legal rights. By ignoring rules, it is Doe who sacrifices rights. To this contention Doe might have answered that the harsh application of rules is unreasonable, and reason is the life of law.

If the very numerous rules of construction to be found in the books are regarded simply as inferences of fact of more or less importance, and if they are not given an undue authoritative effect on account of their antiquity of statement over other equally important rules or evidentiary facts, which on account of their indefinite variety and subtility never have been and probably never will be expressed in dogmatic formulas, the work of constructing written instruments and ascertaining the true intent and purpose of parties will be less exposed to the just criticism of intelligent laymen, and less involved in mystery and doubt.[33]

Thus in the legal world of Charles Doe, "dogmatic formulas" had to yield to the ideal of legal unity and legal simplicity. "Contracts, wills, and statutes," he said, "are the makers' intentions, proved by competent evidence," [34] and eventually the New Hampshire bar agreed with him and with all he implied. When the time came to decide *Edgerly* v. *Barker* he had built a body of precedent and had assured himself a unanimous court as he struck down the harshness but not the substance of the rules against perpetuities, making a vital area of law more conformable to reason. Today other jurisdictions are struggling with this problem, which Doe solved in 1891. It is ironic that some are hailed as pacesetters because they have appointed study commissions and have enacted legislation to accomplish results which the New Hampshire Supreme Court effortlessly brought about by applying Doe's principles. His example of judicial surgery may still be too radical for other states.[35]

Edgerly v. *Barker* is the climactic product of Charles Doe's life-long effort to eliminate disorganizing exceptions and restore reason to the law through the medium of rules of construction. It is the vindication of his theories on "justice," "reason," and "approximation." With a sense of pride he once boasted, "There is probably no jurisdiction in which a legislative purpose is carried into effect by a more liberal mode of construction than that which prevails in this state." But even more important than results, he reminded New Hampshire lawyers, is the principle which brings about results — the principle that "the most liberal construction is nothing more than the ascertainment of that purpose from competent evidence." [36]

In this state, the intent duly proved and the statutory rights of the testator and devisee are not defeated by a spirit of favoritism that sets aside the conclusion reached by a performance of the judicial duty of weighing legal proofs and balancing probabilities. The rejection of such a conclusion as a private and unauthorized conjecture exhibits in a clear light the mode of construction in which the acknowledged meaning of written instruments is overridden by arbitrary rules. Among the most instructive decisions are those in which the employment of this method in the accomplishment of this result is accompanied by a confession of wrong. Authorities of this class, . . . and others based on the same theory — that testamentary or contractual intent found by weighing competent evidence in the balance of probability, is legally overthrown by unwritten rules of construction, — affirm the soundness of opposite results in a jurisdiction where intent, so found, prevails over those rules.[37]

Chapter Ten

EXPERIENCE OR REASON
A Theory of Torts[1]

THE years during which Charles Doe was a member of the New Hampshire judiciary mark the emergence of torts as a disciplined branch of common law. Since a tort — a personal injury for which redress may be obtained in the courts — arises from the relationship of men in society and not from a private agreement, as does an action in contracts, the law of civilized nations contains no more important area. By determining the portion of loss to be reallocated from the victim to the wrongdoer, torts adjusts much of the damage citizens accidentally inflict upon one another by their commercial or private activities and thereby serves to prevent friction or extralegal remedies. Yet when Charles Doe studied law, there were no ready answers to such fundamental questions as "What is a wrong?" "Who is a wrongdoer?" and "What wrongs will the law redress?" There was not even a textbook for him to read: the first American treatise on torts was not published until 1859, the year of his appointment to the bench, and more than a decade later Oliver Wendell Holmes still doubted whether torts could be "a proper subject for a law book." [2] But by 1895, just five months before Charles Doe died, all had changed; in that year Sir Frederick Pollock was quoted as saying that "there is really a law of torts, not merely a number of rules about various kinds of Torts, — that there is a true, living branch of the common law, and not a collection of heterogeneous instances." [3] Though Mr. Holmes has received most of the credit for awakening the bar to the need for a theory of torts and for developing the main lines along which that theory was first formulated, others were working in the vineyard, notably Charles Doe; his determination to bring rationality to the chaotic patterns of tort liability is one of his most significant contributions to American law.

During the 1870s many legal scholars felt the need for a theory of torts or, as Holmes put it, "to discover whether there is any common ground at the bottom of all liability in tort."[4] The difficulty lay in the fact that tort liability had not as yet acquired a generic significance. Torts being incidental to remedies, the law of personal wrong was viewed as a system of writs rather than of principles. For centuries, as Holmes said, "each of the recognized torts had its special history, its own precedents, and no one dreamed, so far as I know, that the different cases of liability were, or ought to be, governed by the same principles throughout."[5]

Holmes and Doe belonged to the first generation to feel the need for a theory of torts. Previously the writ system had served as a substitute, but when Doe began to new-model the forms in New Hampshire and reformers in other jurisdictions were enacting procedure codes, this rickety scaffolding was no longer available.[6]

During the year 1873 Holmes completed work on his pioneering article, "The Theory of Torts." Arguing that the law's concern is not with the sins of men but with their actions, Holmes criticized Austin's thesis that tort liability depends on fault alone.[7] When the article was still in proofs, Holmes sent a copy to Doe. Apparently Doe reacted against Holmes's theory. While acknowledging the possibility of nonfault liability for accident, Doe thought that it should be severely limited. In the same year Holmes's article was published, Doe wrote *Brown* v. *Collins,* the leading American precedent restricting liability to circumstances from which fault can be imputed.

The moment was opportune. *Rylands* v. *Fletcher,* the chief judicial pronouncement with which Doe had to contend, was only five years old and still a novelty in the minds of lawyers. Under *Rylands* a man, regardless of whether he acted without fault, is liable for injuries caused to his neighbors by things he has lawfully brought upon his land and which subsequently escape.[8] "This," Doe wrote, "is going back a long way for a standard of legal rights, and adopting an arbitrary test of responsibility that confounds all degrees of danger, pays no heed to the essential elements of actual fault, puts a clog upon natural and reasonably necessary uses of matter, and tends to embarrass and obstruct much of the work which seems to be man's duty carefully to do." [9]

He elaborated his view in *Brown* v. *Collins*, which has the earmarks of a test case. The defendant had been driving along a street in the town of Tilton when his horses, frightened by a passing train, bolted, left the road, and damaged a stone post which stood on the plaintiff's land. The facts, according to the court reporter, "were agreed upon for the purpose of raising the question of the right of the plaintiff to recover in this action." Doe wanted to come to grips with *Rylands*, and it seems likely that he persuaded counsel in this minor litigation to give him the opportunity. "We take the case," he wrote, "as one where, without actual fault in the defendant, his horses broke from his control, ran away with him, went upon the plaintiff's land, and did damage there, against the will, intent, and desire of the defendant." [10] The issue could not have been drawn more clearly: can a defendant who acted lawfully be held liable for damage resulting from an inevitable accident not his fault? The *Rylands* decision held that under special circumstances he could. Judge Doe's answer was that he could not.

By ignoring the elements of fault, Doe argued, the *Rylands* doctrine is too sweeping in its sociological implications. It forces the law to hold an owner of real property liable for all damages resulting to a neighbor from anything done on his own land and makes answerable those who, while improving their own land for their own benefit according to their own best skill and diligence, do not foresee the injury the improvement may produce to unwittingly damage their neighbors. To avoid this result, crippling to commerce, Doe stated what he considered a better ground for tort liability.

When a defendant erroneously supposed, without any fault of either party, that he had a right to do what he did, and his act, done in the assertion of his supposed right, turns out to have been an interference with the plaintiff's property, he is generally held to have assumed the risk of maintaining the right which he asserted, and the responsibility of the natural consequences of his voluntary act. But when there was no fault on his part, and the damage was not caused by his voluntary and intended act; or by an act of which he knew, or ought to have known, the damage would be a necessary, probable, or natural consequence; or by an act which he knew, or ought to have known, to be unlawful, — we understand the general rule to be, that he is not liable.[11]

Thus, *Brown* v. *Collins* holds, if an act which accidentally produces harm is lawful and proper — that is, one both reasonably necessary and which the defendant might perform by the use of proper and safe means — and if the plaintiff's injury is caused by such an act performed with due care and proper precautions, the defendant is not liable. Applying this rule to the facts, Doe concluded that the defendant, whose horses had been frightened and had caused damage through no fault of his own, was not liable "unless everyone is liable for all damage done by superior force overpowering him, and using him or his property as an instrument of violence." [12] In terms of evidence, this means not only that a defendant in a tort action may plead inevitable accident as a defense, but that the plaintiff has the burden of proving fault.

Doe knew that the *Rylands* judges had not intended to create blanket liability for inevitable accident but had sought to limit *Rylands* as a special exception to the general requirement of fault for liability in accidents. Lord Cairns made this clear in the appellate decision when he emphasized "non-natural use" as the distinction upon which the exception turned. If the defendant's use of his property is "natural," a plaintiff must prove fault to recover damages for an accidental injury. If the defendant's use is "non-natural," the *Rylands* exception applies and the defendant may be liable for the consequences regardless of fault. A "non-natural use," Lord Cairns explained, is a use "for the purpose of introducing into the close that which in its natural condition was not in or upon it." [13]

"It is impossible," Doe argued, "that legal principle can throw so serious an obstacle in the way of progress and improvement." To create an exception to the defense of inevitable accident — an exception which depends upon whether the activity is a natural or nonnatural use of the land — would impede social enterprise by penalizing acts of commerce conducted in a lawful, skillful, and careful manner. Perhaps Judge Doe read too much into Lord Cairns's "non-natural," but since the *Rylands* case had involved damage caused by water escaping from an industrial reservoir, Doe felt justified when he criticized the exception on the grounds that it placed a crushing tort liability on nineteenth-century business. Few New England manufacturers made "natural" use of property; in one degree or another they disturbed "the original order of creation" and tried to control elements in a manner not known during the "primitive condition of mankind." *Rylands* would have made them responsible for all the consequences of their actions, even those performed both lawfully and carefully.[14]

A great deal has been written concerning the economic and social reasons Judge Doe gave for rejecting Lord Cairns's "non-natural" rule. A favorite hypothesis has held that he developed the distinction between liability for accidents regardless of fault and liability imposed only where there is failure to use reasonable care or skill in order to make this distinction the ounce of legal difference by which courts sanction the social objectives of industrial development. But this objective was at most a secondary consideration. His primary aim was to establish the rule that an inevitable accident, without actual fault in either party, "is not a cause of action."[15]

The question Doe did not have an opportunity to answer in *Brown* v. *Collins* concerned the definition of fault. He got his chance a year later, in *The Androscoggin River Case*. The plaintiff owned lands along the banks of a river; the defendants were incorporated to regulate water levels for commercial needs, most particularly for lumbermen running logs downstream. The plaintiff sought damages for injury to his land resulting from flooding caused when the defendants released water from their upstream dams. The plaintiff agreed that the defendants had acted lawfully and had "used and managed said water in a prudent manner . . . and in the use thereof were careful to do as little damage as possible."[16] Doe held that there could be no recovery.

Fault, Judge Doe ruled, is not established by use, but by the manner of use, reasonable use being a defense to the charge of fault. The defendants were not liable for the lawful use which they made of the water — that is, for holding it back and then releasing it when logs had to be floated — since they had used it reasonably.

As to what constitutes reasonable use, Doe would not say. It is a question of fact, in the determination of which the jury may weigh subjective factors. One of these, the issue of reasonable care, "often depends upon actual knowledge, or reasonable and rightful expectation." Not only is the defendant's "full knowledge of probable consequences" an element to be considered when determining due care, but so is his "knowledge" of any peculiar inability under which the public in general might labor when confronted by the danger which he has created.[17] Doe pointed out, however, that "reasonable expectation of danger," objective or subjective, is but one criterion for determining reasonable care. "Light, air, water, and many natural and artificial agencies, may render a reasonable use of one's own [property] detrimental to others; and many considerations, besides reasonable expectation of damage, may enter into the broad question of reasonable use." [18]

The law of torts was sometimes called the law of wrongs during the latter half of the nineteenth century, yet Doe often approached it in terms of rights. In *Androscoggin* he did not speak of the "flowing" as a wrong committed by the defendant. Rather, he began by establishing the plaintiff's right, as an owner of real estate, not to be injured by a neighbor making an unreasonable use of his land. By way of illustration he explained why the careful and skillful use of fire on one's own land, for a reasonably necessary commercial or domestic purpose, will not form a basis for liability even if the fire spreads to an adjacent estate. Such damage is not subject to legal redress because reasonable use of one's property without fault "is not an invasion of another's right." [19]

As a consequence of approaching liability in terms of "right" rather than "wrong," Doe thought of the defendant as assuming the risk for violating the plaintiff's right. "Taking the risk," Holmes observed in 1899, is "an expression which we never heard used as it now is until within a very few years." [20] Perhaps so, but Doe had used it as understood by Holmes as early as 1860, when he said that if a servant "takes the risks of known defects of machinery, it would seem that he also assumes, to some extent, the risks of known incompetency and insufficiency of fellow-servants." [21] This, the usual meaning of assumption of risk, is an element in the fellow-servant rule — the harshness of which Doe tried to mitigate during his final decade on the bench by making the test subjective, holding that an employee assumes only the risks "apparent to his observation," not those which, "on account of his want of experience, he could not reasonably be expected to apprehend." [22]

What seems significant is that Doe turned the assumption-of-risk concept around, employing it not only as a defense against, but also as a test for, liability. And he did so when approaching the issue of liability in terms of either the plaintiff's or the defendant's right. Thus, in *Brown* v. *Collins* Doe said that a defendant who assumes he has a right to act undertakes the risk of maintaining that right and the responsibility for its natural consequences.[23]

It has been suggested that in *Underhill* v. *Manchester* Doe "anticipated" the risk theory of tort liability.[24] The plaintiff ran a saloon in the city of Manchester, using the front room to sell "spirituous liquors" and the rear for gambling. As Doe laconically described the events, "A bank bill was alleged to be counterfeit, a dispute arose, the dispute grew into an assault, the assault into a riot, in which his property in the saloon was destroyed." Both the sale of liquor and public waging were illegal, yet the plaintiff sued Manchester under the "rioters' statute," which made the city liable for property destruction by mobs. But since the statute barred recovery by one whose illegal or improper conduct had caused the riot, the court held that the city was not liable.

By way of *dictum*, Judge Doe went on to consider whether the plaintiff himself might be liable at common law to innocent third parties whose property had been damaged by the rioters. He admitted that saloon keepers are usually not held responsible for the acts of those whom they have made drunk and that such damage is so remote that it would be difficult to set a limit on the consequences an ordinary person can anticipate. But these are difficulties of fact, not of law, and are no excuse for barring a just claim. Why, Doe asked, should not the keeper of a drinking and gambling house "be regarded as one who negligently sets mechanical forces in operation beyond his power to stop or safely direct, or carelessly puts destructive implements or materials in situations where they are likely to produce mischief"? [25]

This *dictum,* written a year before *Rylands,* contains elements which at first glance seem to anticipate the extrahazardous activity doctrine as much as they do the risk theory of liability. The teetotaler, Doe, however, would have drawn a distinction on the grounds that the excessive sale of spirits is not a reasonably necessary occupation and that an illicit saloon keeper may be guilty of fault by the very nature of his enterprise. "By openly keeping a saloon for such purpose, he invited such company as usually frequent such places, solicited them to gamble, and offered them a stimulus highly promotive of brawls, affrays, riots and all other crimes." [26] The owner assumes the risk and must abide the consequences.

One could argue that Doe, far from anticipating the assumption-of-risk theory of liability, was formulating an assumption-of-risk theory of negligence by defining culpability through finding fault in the assumption of risk. The unreasonable assumption defines the fault which creates the liability. This, however, is not what Doe had in mind. He made it clear that a person who is without fault may still be liable for asserting and acting upon a right, for he has "assumed the risk of maintaining the right which he has asserted, and the responsibility of the natural consequences of his voluntary act." [27] Knowledge of the unreasonableness of the risk takes the happening out of the category of "accident" which requires fault for liability.

Combining the decision in *Brown* v. *Collins* with the assumption-of-risk doctrine, the theory of torts which Charles Doe formulated in 1873 may be summarized: *A person will be liable for damage resulting from an accident for which he is at fault* (the test for "fault" is whether he acted reasonably or as a man of average prudence); *for damage resulting from his intention to inflict an injury not justified or privileged at common law; for damage resulting from unlawful actions; and for damage resulting from the assumption of an unreasonable risk.*

Oliver Wendell Holmes, who began his search for a theory of torts at the same time as Doe, formulated a different concept of liability by dividing the law of torts into three sections. At opposite ends he placed rules "determined by policy without

reference of any kind to morality" — at one end, harms intentionally inflicted; at the other, acts for which, "although his
conduct has been prudent and beneficial to the community," the
actor must answer at his peril when they result in damage.[28] In
the vast center section, Holmes placed acts for which liability
attaches when, as Professor Mark DeWolfe Howe says, "the
defendant's conduct did not satisfy the objective standard established by current morality." Holmes determined this standard
by weighing the risk, not in terms of reasonableness as Doe would
have done, but in terms of danger; that is, "by considering the
degree of danger attending the act or conduct under the known
circumstances." Once experience shows a given act to have the
tendency to cause harm under given circumstances, Holmes
would turn the standard from a question of fact into a rule of law
designed to govern specific cases. Holmes envisioned each section
of his tripartite division of tort law as containing rules which
insure predictability to the solution of liability.[29]

Holmes desired certainty in the law; Judge Doe did not make
certainty an overriding consideration. Then, too, the jurisprudential tenets of these two jurists were strikingly different. Holmes
sought to create a philosophical order which would encourage the
formulation of rules, drawn from the experience of jury verdicts,
to reduce the jury's lawmaking role and replace capriciousness
with stability. Doe, on the other hand, sought to increase the
jury's role by decreasing the lawmaking function of the court,
thereby introducing flexibility, justice, and reasonableness to the
law of tort liability. More significant than the contrasting origins
of their tort theories are the discordant results produced by these
divergent theories as seen in the solutions offered by Holmes and
by Doe to one of the most common liability problems of their
era, accidents at railway crossings. Both were asked to determine
the standard of due care which must be exercised by a person
seeking damages for injury sustained when struck by a train
while driving over railroad tracks at a public junction. Holmes's
answer is in *Baltimore & Ohio* v. *Goodman*; Doe's is in *Huntress*
v. *Boston & Maine*.

In *Goodman* the deceased had been traveling in daylight in a
motor truck over familiar ground; he slowed from ten or twelve
miles an hour to half that speed about forty feet from the

crossing. Although the track ran in a straight line, his view was obstructed by a section house until he was about twenty feet from the rails. The train, approaching at sixty miles an hour, sounded no warning. Probably he could not see it until he was within eleven and one-half feet of the danger point. At his rate of progress, seven to eight feet per second, this gave him only one and one-half seconds to avoid impact. He had, counsel argued, "been led into a trap."

In *Huntress* the plaintiff's wife was traveling in a carriage on a public highway. The train was coming at a speed of thirty-five to forty miles an hour. There was no gate or flagman, but in obedience to the only applicable statute, the railroad had erected warning signs. The track was straight for a mile or more in the direction from which the train was approaching, and there was an unobstructed view "for a long distance." It was a May afternoon, which in New Hampshire meant plenty of light. Both parties agreed that the horse was "kind and gentle" and that the engineer and fireman were not at fault. At the whistling post the signal required by law was given, and the bell was rung constantly from post to crossing. Yet, despite these warnings and the favorable conditions, the plaintiff's wife attempted to cross in front of the train. She was struck and killed.

In both actions counsel for the defendants claimed that the deceaseds were guilty of contributory negligence and therefore could not sue the railroads for fault. A traveler is barred from recovery, the defense argument ran in *Goodman*, if his view is obscured and he fails to stop. "The deceased could have seen the train had she looked," it was argued in *Huntress*. "If she saw it, she could have avoided collision by stopping her horse." Justice Holmes sustained the defense in *Goodman* and held that as a matter of law the deceased had been contributorily negligent.

When a man goes upon a railroad track he knows that he goes to a place where he will be killed if a train comes upon him before he is clear of the track. He knows that he must stop for the train not the train stop for him. In such circumstances it seems to us that if a driver cannot be sure otherwise whether a train is dangerously near he must stop and get out of his vehicle, although obviously he will not often be required to do more than to stop and look. It seems to us that if he relies upon not hearing the train or any signal and takes no further precaution he does so at his own risk. If at the last moment Goodman found himself in an emergency it was his own fault that he did not reduce his speed earlier or come to a stop. It is true that the question of due care very generally is left to the jury. But we are dealing with a standard of conduct, and when the standard is clear it should be laid down once for all by the Courts.[30]

On reading these words, Sir Frederick Pollock expressed surprise that anyone could disagree with them.[31] Doe would have been surprised that anyone could have written them. He doubted whether any standard is as "clear" as Holmes assumed. A rule which freezes legal conduct always overlooks factual issues. A man may well pass in front of a train and not be negligent.

In the full possession and vigorous use of his faculties, without even a momentary absence or preoccupation of mind, with his intelligence alert and diligently applied to the question of waiting for the train to pass, he might act upon an error of judgment in regard the speed of the train and the time that would elapse before its arrival. There is reason to believe a mistake on this point is the cause of many accidents. A large portion of the community have such knowledge of the danger of crossing a street in front of a horse team moving at a moderate gait as is necessary in determining whether safety requires them to wait for the team to pass. But high rates of speed create a degree of danger that is not generally realized by those with no special means of information on the subject. Whether a train is going twenty miles an hour or forty, is a question on which the opinion of but few observers would be considered valuable by a railway expert.

It is, therefore, a question of fact, he continued, whether the particular defendant against whom contributory negligence is alleged could accurately estimate the danger by measuring speed in terms of time, distance, and visible rapid motion. "From the mere fact of great danger," Doe wrote, "it does not necessarily follow that he exposed himself recklessly and consciously. When there is no evidence of insanity, intoxication, or suicidal purpose, and no evidence on the question of his care, except the instinct provided for the preservation of animal life, it may be inferred from this circumstantial proof that, for some reason consistent with ordinary care and freedom from fault on his part, his attempt to cross was due to his inadequate understanding of the risk." [32] As a question of fact, did the deceased, judged by the average, prudent man's ability of measuring speed in terms of time and distance, understand the danger and knowingly assume the risk?

For Justice Holmes, Doe's emphasis on "understanding of the risk" was a conjecture both unscientific and inexact. It was to avoid law by supposition that Holmes urged courts to formulate external standards of conduct, which, reflecting the morality of the community, were to be gathered from experience. But how, Doe might have asked, are they to be gathered? "A judge who has long sat at *nisi prius*," Holmes said, "ought gradually to acquire a fund of experience which enables him to represent the common sense of the community in ordinary instances far better than an average jury." [33] Doe knew better. In *Goodman* Holmes had said that a driver when approaching a railroad crossing should stop and perhaps even get out of his car to look along the track. He had sought a standard drawn from experience, but as Judge Cuthbert Pound remarked, he had come up with "a standard not in accord with the present conduct of the prudent man." [34]

Since Doe believed that rules governing conduct were bound to fail, he had to offer an alternative. Here again he appears in conflict with Holmes, for his answer — that tort issues are questions of fact for the jury — was one Holmes rejected as unsound. How far Doe was to extend this doctrine is shown by his discussion in *Huntress* of the defendant's culpability. The engineer and other employees had not been at fault; everything required by statute had been done. Many, if not most, American courts would have ruled that there could be no recovery as a matter of law. But Doe held that there was an issue of fault for the jury; and he made this issue as wide as all outdoors.

Railway managers may be presumed to have special knowledge of the dangers of their business, and to be aware of the constant peril arising at level crossings from the fact that intelligent and careful people frequently overestimate the safety of attempting to cross in front of trains moving at high speed. The danger thus caused was probably not foreseen when the defendants' road was built. The speed required by public convenience on railways is found to be inconsistent with the public safety at level crossings where there are no gates or watchmen. The expense of watchmen, or gates and watchmen, at all such crossings, would increase the cost of transportation. . . .

But the practical difficulties resulting from the conflict of public interests do not change the legal principles applicable to this case, or affect the plaintiff's cause of action. The knowledge which the defendants may be presumed to have of the fact that persons of ordinary prudence frequently go upon level crossings in front of moving trains, when they would wait for the trains to pass if they had been long employed as railroad managers or trainmen, is a knowledge of a danger caused by high speed, and common misapprehensions and miscalculations. The defendants, presumably aware of this customary danger and its cause, are bound to act upon their superior knowledge, and to take such precautions as men of ordinary prudence would take, under the circumstances, in their situation.[35]

Without the least apology or reservations, Doe was permitting the triers of fact to apply a subjective test to this defendant within the external standard of what the prudent expert, possessing "superior knowledge," would have done. Moreover, by framing the issue in terms of preference between safe crossings and cheap transportation, Judge Doe was asking the jury to set the public policy of the law. To this extent he had rejected Holmes's theory of the jury's function in tort activities. To Holmes the only question with which the jury should concern itself is the conduct of the parties; the standards to be applied to that conduct are for the court to establish. In *Huntress* Doe took a stand for the exact opposite. It is, he insisted, "a question of fact whether a person of ordinary prudence, operating the defendants' road with their knowledge of the dangers of level crossing, would guard against accidents by stationing flagmen there, or slackening the speed of the trains." [36]

In one respect the role of the jury only symbolizes the variance between the tort theories of Holmes and Doe. More basic is the question whether experience or reason should guide the law. Holmes justified the standard he set up in *Goodman* on the grounds that it was sanctioned by experience. Doe would have rejected it — along with most standards — on the grounds that it might prove unreasonable in other fact situations. As we shall see in a future chapter, few judges expected as much from the concept of "reasonableness" as did Doe. He called it a "general principle" [37] and in the law of torts made it the instrument for resolving most factual issues. Thus the issue whether the defendant acted lawfully can be resolved by the question of fact —

whether he acted from reasonable necessity. The issue of fault in cases of inevitable accident can sometimes be resolved by asking whether the defendant acted reasonably. And the issue of assumption of risk can be resolved by the question of whether the defendant acted reasonably when he assumed the risk, knowing the consequences which might result from his act. Indeed, Doe went all the way and defined the tort in terms of "unreasonableness" alone in an action on the case against a railroad for rate discrimination. The question, Doe held, is not discrimination or inequality of service but unreasonableness. "Although reasonableness of service or price may require a reasonable discrimination, it does not tolerate an unreasonable one; and the law does not require a court or jury to waste time in a useless investigation of the question when a proved injurious unreasonableness of service or price was in its intrinsic or in its discriminating quality. The main question is, not whether the unreasonableness was in this or in that, but whether there was unreasonableness, and whether it was injurious to the plaintiff." [38] Again we find Doe framing a question of fact in terms which permit the jury to set public policy.

Judge Doe seized upon the doctrine of "reasonableness" as the unifying factor in the law of torts. Oliver Wendell Holmes also prized "uniformity" in torts, but he took greater pride from the conviction that, in Mark DeWolfe Howe's words, "he had formulated a theory which might increase the law's certainty and, therefore, the law's utility." Above all else Holmes objected to uncertainty, and it was on this point that he offered his most basic challenge to Doe's theory of tort liability. The elements of most torts, Holmes wrote in the 1873 article Doe had read in proofs, "are permanent, and there is no reason why a case should be decided one way to-day, and another way to-morrow. To leave the question to the jury forever, is simply to leave the law uncertain." At the very moment when Holmes's article was being published, Doe was handing down an opinion in which he offered to Holmes a challenge of his own. He was considering whether the concept of "reasonableness" is so vague that courts will find it too difficult to apply. Difficulty, he concluded, is no excuse for tampering with general principles. "If the doctrine of reasonableness is not the doctrine of justice, it is for him who is dissatisfied with it to show its injustice; if it is the doctrine of justice, it is for him to show the grounds of his discontent." [39]

It was partly to show his discontent that Holmes later expanded his article on the theory of torts into *The Common Law*, the book which made him famous. Doe's conclusion upon reading *The Common Law* was that Holmes had failed to prove his case.

PART THREE

THE MAN

Chapter Eleven

A DOSE OF OZONE

The Public Man

As Felix Frankfurter has suggested, few speculations are more risky than diagnosis of motives or genetic explanations of the position taken by judges in their decisions.[1] Speculations, however, are asked of judicial biographers, and the demand is hard to resist. Attempts can be made to explain Charles Doe's tort theory in terms of New Hampshire economic or religious history. It can be argued that the history of a state built on commercial and industrial enterprise compelled him to reject the *Rylands* doctrine. On the other hand, the ultraindividualism of Doe's every-man-for-himself rule — the philosophy of *Brown v. Collins* — could be interpreted as an instance of Puritan traditions, inherited from his ancestors, influencing American law. In Puritanism, Roscoe Pound has written, originated an uncompromising insistence upon individual rights and individual property as the central point of jurisprudence.[2] "Here," he said of the *Rylands-Brown* problem, "we have to choose between the general security, calling for an absolute liability, and the individual life, calling for liability only where there has been fault. It has been suggested plausibly that the difference between the English conception of land as a permanent family acquisition and an American conception of land as an asset or a place to do things and carry on enterprise, in other words, a different ideal or picture of society, has dictated the starting points for reasoning."[3]

These generalities read well, but they abuse the historical method; nor are speculations in the particular more satisfactory. Professor Bohlen analyzed Lord Blackburn's *Rylands* decision in terms of England's dominant class (the landed gentry) as unsympathetic to industry, and Judge Doe's *Brown* decision in terms of New England's dependence on cotton mills. Considering New Hampshire's need to develop industry, Bohlen wrote, it was "not surprising" that Doe rejected liability without fault.[4] In Dean Pound's opinion Bohlen had oversimplified the issues by reducing the economic factor to one of family ownership versus the commercial use of land. Pound believed that *Rylands* was laid down in England because it was a crowded country, where security is an obvious interest, and rejected by Doe because America was sparsely settled. To repudiate Bohlen's theory, Pound pointed out that, far from representing the landed class, Lord Blackburn came to the bench from a commercial practice, while it was Doe who was associated with the gentry and with pastoral land, spending his life on his ancestral acres.[5] Had Pound pursued his facts further, he might have been less confident: Blackburn was by no means a judicial representative of industrial interests, while Joseph Doe, as we have seen, established the Doe fortune on commercial investments, and the Doe homestead — while run as a farm — was located in a region of concentrated manufacturing.

Of course Doe's personality entered into his decisions. It has been suggested that Holmes's search for objectivity in legal standards and his awareness that the days of individualism were almost over resulted from the fact that he was a Boston Brahmin, with an aristocrat's concern for theory rather than for effect. Doe's insistence on questions of fact and on flexibility of judgment norms are attributed by the same argument to his democratic attitudes. If this analysis were to mean the attitudes are manifestations of Holmes's and Doe's contrary personalities, it would contain much truth; but to imply more would be unwarranted. Holmes and Doe came from similar backgrounds. In his little world Doe was as much an aristocrat as Holmes was in his. They shared a common Yankee heritage, their ancestry stretched back to the first settlements of the Puritan commonwealths, and they both grew to manhood in the conformative traditions of New England's middle class — the Church, Harvard College, Harvard Law, and a profession made up of friends, relatives, and fellow Republicans. True, Holmes apprenticed himself to the intellectual elite at an age when Doe was concerned with politics, and this circumstance goes far to explain their differences. But the differences are in personality and interests, not in economic background, educational opportunities, political loyalties, or social connections.

While to attribute this or that decision to Doe's personality would be to return to speculation, it can nevertheless be admitted that his general judicial outlook finds reflection in his general personal outlook. A comparison of Doe's soft and intentionally indecisive solution of tort questions with Holmes's hard, empirical solution indicates how much light is thrown upon them by differences in their personalities. One incident illustrates part of these differences. As previously mentioned, Doe encouraged John Henry Wigmore during the early stages of Wigmore's work on evidence. When his great classic was published eight years after Doe's death, Wigmore made Doe codedicatee — "To the memory of the Public Services and Private Friendship of Two Masters in the Law of Evidence, Charles Doe of New Hampshire, Judge and Reformer, and James Bradley Thayer of Massachusetts, Historian and Teacher." Except for a Harvard reviewer who thought "most of Professor Thayer's pupils would probably place him before Judge Doe in such a dedication," [6] Wigmore's tribute stirred no fuss until 1910, when he published his *Pocket Code of Evidence* and dedicated it to Holmes. Writing Wigmore to thank him for the honor, Holmes went on to criticize Doe as severely as anyone has ever done.

I never quite understood your predilection for Doe. He seemed to me to write long-winded rather second-rate discourses and I thought he did rather an unfair thing when I was a young essayist. I sent him proofs of an article in which I spoke of the gradual working out of a line in the law by the contact of decisions grouped about the two poles of an undeniable antithesis — e.g. — night and day — Almost before my article appeared a decision of his used the notion with no credit given, which in those days I felt. Perhaps my memory is wrong as it was long ago, and I would not do injustice to the dead, but I guess I could find it. But at all events I thought there was not a great deal of brandy in his water.[7]

The article referred to by Holmes is the one on torts (mentioned in the previous chapter). Doe borrowed it while struggling with his own theory of torts. It appeared in Holmes's *American Law Review* for July 1873. The Doe opinion of which Holmes complains is *Stewart* v. *Emerson*, dated June 1872. There can be little doubt that Holmes was right: Doe did pirate his ideas. This is how the material originally appeared:

> The growth of law is very apt to take place in this way: Two widely different cases suggest a general distinction, which is a clear one when stated broadly. But as new cases cluster around the opposite poles, and begin to approach each other, the distinction becomes more difficult to trace; the determinations are made one way or the other on a very slight preponderance of feeling rather than articulate reason; and at least a mathematical line is arrived at by the contact of contrary decisions, which is so far arbitrary that it might equally well have been drawn a little further to the one side or to the other. The distinction between the groups, however, is philosophical. . . .[8]

Holmes had little difficulty recognizing this when he saw *Stewart* v. *Emerson*. Doe's version reads:

> On this subject [fraud], as on many others, it may not be easy to fully describe the dividing line, on one side or the other of which all possible cases must fall (a difficulty from which moral philosophy is by no means free). The whole line may not be judicially promulgated at once, with an exactness and minuteness of detail superior to the fraudulent inventive faculty of all future time.[9]

Nowhere in the opinion does Doe give Holmes the slightest credit; nowhere is there a hint that the idea is anyone's but his own. Why did Doe slight Holmes in this way? Several excuses could be offered, but none are convincing. The discrepancy in time is no justification. True, *Stewart* is dated 1872 and the article 1873. But despite this fact, the opinion was not published until after the article. Moreover, Holmes said he sent Doe "proofs"; he does not say "manuscript." This implies that the article was already in the printed stage and Doe could have assumed that it would be published before his decision. Nor does it seem likely that Doe skimmed through the article and absorbed Holmes's theory without appreciating its originality or noting its source, thus letting it pass into the realm of his own discoveries. This will not wash when we consider Doe's careful, systematic methods of research and compare the similarity of language in the article with that in the opinion. The impression, at least, is strong that Doe took notes directly from the proofs.[10]

Any thought that Doe may have regarded Holmes as too unimportant, too unknown to be worth citation seems out of place in view of his thoughtfulness toward younger men; a thoughtfulness he demonstrated exactly one year later when, in the much more significant case of *Brown v. Collins*, he not only cited the same article but made a point of acknowledging "Mr. Holmes" as author — a gesture he may have regarded as a compliment, since articles were then unsigned. He even went Holmes one better by adding a reference to the twelfth edition of *Kent's Commentaries* which Holmes had edited but had not cited.[11]

While it is possible that Doe did not appreciate the originality of Holmes's thesis, the most plausible explanation for his action — and for Holmes's reaction — lies in the personalities of the two men. In no respect were they more unalike than in their attitudes toward the chase after public acclaim. To Doe it was a toxic, to be avoided like the plague. To Holmes it was a tonic, to be revisited like the fountain of youth. Far from being slighted when not given credit, Doe sought anonymity. A case in point was his refusal to accept credit for the New Hampshire doctrine of criminal insanity. It was his concoction, no one else's: he had formulated it out of his jurisprudential theories, defended it while others were skeptical, and by pertinaciously marking its logical assonance with accepted principles in private law, sold its merits to his colleagues, including the reluctant Chief Justice Perley. If any man believed in or had a greater right to take pride in his work, Charles Doe did here. Yet when Doctor Ray was preparing to praise the New Hampshire doctrine in Mr. Holmes's *American Law Review*, Doe insisted that all credit be given to Perley. "My great point, about which I am very solicitous," he told Ray, "is that you bring in Judge Perley immediately after the extracts from my opinion, and substitute his name for mine whenever it occurs afterwards in your article. . . . It may occur to you to join my name with Perley's. Allow me to protest most decidedly against this."[12]

True, Doe's request was clothed in the argument that the New Hampshire doctrine needed "the authority of such a name and position as Perley's as responsible legal endorser" to win acceptance. But this was part of his strategy to persuade Ray, and had Doe meant nothing more, he would have permitted Ray to couple his name with Perley's. Instead, wanting anonymity, he forbade it. During later years he gave others credit for his procedural reforms and insisted that Judge Ladd was the real author of the insanity doctrine. Even after he was more famous than Perley had ever been, Doe refused to put himself forward. At some time in the 1880s Baron Bramwell published an article justifying the execution of insane criminals, and Sir John C. Buckhill appealed to Clark Bell, editor of the *Medico-Legal Journal*, for a rebuttal. Bell, in turn, appealed to Doe. "In my young days," Doe told Bell, "I adopted a resolution to abstain from everything but the study and administration of the law and to carry the practice to such an extreme as not to use my name, or allow it to be used, in anything outside of my daily occupation, and I have vigorously adhered to this rule of concentration, and think it has been useful." [13]

It was not that Doe was disinterested. He took pains to assure Bell of his full support — "and my ardent interest in your success." "He took a deep interest in the question," Bell later explained. "He corresponded with me freely, but he had an unsurmountable aversion to the use of his name, in any way, in any publication. This embargo he laid upon me most emphatically. He has said to me that after his death he does not care, but during his life he forbade the slightest allusion to his name." [14] Such a man could easily forget that others wanted the limelight.

Holmes was of a different breed. Mark DeWolfe Howe, his biographer, makes clear that one of Holmes's less attractive characteristics was his astonishing thirst for recognition. He craved it so badly that his friends were embarrassed and his critics amused. Others besides Doe suffered the sting of his wrath. James Bradley Thayer (the codedicatee of Wigmore's treatise) was one of several. When Holmes left Thayer's name off the title page of a publication they were to have edited jointly, Thayer wrote, "he is, with all his attractive qualities & his solid merits, wanting sadly in the noblest region of human character, — selfish, vain, thoughtless of others." [15] As one spoilsport put it: "Van Wyck Brooks reports that when Holmes was a small boy his father rewarded every bright saying with a spoonful of jam. In later life the jam had been replaced by his secretary's shout of approval." [16] This judgment is unfair if it implies that Holmes sought praise for praise's sake. The jam proved that the saying had indeed been bright, and it was incentive for another. Holmes put much stock in this kind of incentive; no hypocrite, he valued it for others as well as for himself, and nothing better shows the stark contrast between his attitude and Doe's than their remarks on posthumous praise: Doe thought the decent time for praise was after death; Holmes felt that by then it would come too late.

"No credit," Doe said, "should be given to any living man, especially a judge, for anything that he has done; wait until he is dead and then, in balancing the good and the bad, what is proved to be valuable and what injurious, speak of him as his life on the whole has proved to have been." [17]

"One is almost ashamed," Holmes seems to be replying, "to praise a dead master for what he did in a field where he was acknowledged to be supreme. When his work is finished it is too late for praise to give the encouragement which all need, and of which the successful get too little." [18]

Holmes needed encouragement; Doe did not. But this fact hardly absolves him of blame — he was aware that some men sought it. He told Ray that he could not publicly thank him for his help in formulating the New Hampshire insanity doctrine because it might antagonize lawyers if they knew a psychiatrist had had a hand in it, "although I felt that by omitting to acknowledge the obligation which I felt towards you, I was doing you great injustice." [19] And as we shall see, he unashamedly fed jam to associates by the shovelful. He knew the rules of courtesy and ignored them. But the crux of the matter is that he probably did not know that Holmes needed the encouragement, any more than, had their roles been reversed, Holmes would have known that Doe did not need it. The personality gulf between them was impossible to bridge. It was an encounter between two honest scholars — one of whom was professionally the most modest of men, the other the most vain. Doe simply did not attach importance to his failure to cite Holmes; he never suspected that he had touched a raw nerve. Holmes could not believe the slight unintentional; it was inurbanity too well defined by his personal code of ethics. We can see the reflection in their tort theories. It is not surprising that Holmes, for whom scholarship was a personal achievement, came to believe that judges should formulate precise rules for juries to apply dogmatically; or that Doe, for whom scholarship was a public service, would mistrust the infallibility of the theorists and leave most issues to be settled on their facts.

Another of Doe's public qualities which influenced his judicial work was mental swiftness. "The rapidity with which his mind worked was simply marvellous," [20] Jeremiah Smith says. And considering that Smith was the Harvard compeer of Langdell, Ames, Gray, Beale, and Williston, this is quite a tribute. Yet Smith considered Doe the most gifted of his acquaintances and felt his power of perception especially remarkable. "He had all his faculties at instant command," Smith explained. "He not only possessed unusual legal knowledge, but he had also the power of applying this knowledge to facts, and with lightning-like rapidity. He was never puzzled or confused. He was not only able speedily to arrive at a correct conclusion, but was also able instantly to explain his views in short, crisp sentences, which completely disposed of the matter in hand, and frequently caused everybody to wonder how there could ever have been any doubt about the result." [21]

This faculty, the wonder of the bar, was the characteristic most mentioned by those who spoke at the memorial service following Doe's death and by newspaper obituaries.[22] It had been cited to President Arthur as a reason for promoting Doe to the national court, and it was still being recalled a quarter of a century after his death.[23] Yet at first it had been a handicap, for men distrusted Doe's swiftness and thought him a show-off. As Governor Bell observed, "The quickest perceptive faculties are not understood to be commonly associated with the strongest grasp and broadest range of intellect. We usually attach the idea of ponderous deliberation to great minds, and imagine that they require like the elephant, a long time to turn around and get in motion." [24] When Doe was appointed to the bench, Lemuel Shaw was just completing his thirty years as chief justice of Massachusetts. He had been acknowledged the greatest judge in New England history, and his success made Doe's rapidity suspect. "Judge Shaw's mind moved very slowly," Senator Hoar has explained. "When a case was argued, it took him a good while to get the statement of facts into his mind. It was hard for him to deal readily with unimportant matters, or with things which, to other people, were matters of course. If the simplest motion were made, he had to unlimber the heavy artillery of his mind, go down to the roots of the question, consider the matter in all possible relations, and deal with it as if he were besieging a fortress." [25]

Doe's mental process was the opposite. "No lawyer was too fast for him." [26] As soon as an attorney stated his case, the president of the New Hampshire Bar Association said, Doe "seemed to comprehend the whole situation from beginning to end" [27] as if "by intuition," the attorney general added.[28] Once they appreciated that Doe was not showing off, lawyers took extra pains to be well briefed on the facts and law before appearing in his court.[29] He, on the other hand, tried to readjust his mental processes to the slower pace of the bar.[30] On the whole he failed. His outstanding characteristic as a presiding judge was the way he pushed matters along. "Motion denied," he would say. "Proceed! Proceed!" [31] Even murder trials could not move fast enough for him. "Can't you hurry up this case a little?" he asked the prosecutor during a murder trial held in December. And to the defense he said, "What is to be gained by being here all summer?" To win his good will, both sides reluctantly hustled.[32]

Surprisingly Doe's impatience with the slow pace of trial lawyers did not make him impatient toward lawyers, and here again he differed radically from Shaw, of whom it is said that, because his mind moved so slowly, he was hard on young advocates or on any one else not strong-willed and self-possessed.[33] Doe's colleague Ira Perley was another slow thinker who had a fearsome temper on the bench. But Doe was famed for his patience, especially toward younger attorneys. He could grow irritated with the rate of progress or by arguments he thought a waste of time, yet he was never discourteous or abrupt.[34]

A public quality which helped Doe maintain an equilibrium, especially during the early difficult years, was his sense of humor. "There is plenty of fun in the world," he wrote Gilman Marston, "if one only has an eye for it; & I am coming to the opinion that one of the most desirable talents, — most desirable for pleasure, good digestion, sound sleep, & long life, — is the talent for seeing the funny side of things." [35] After studying the Irish and the Irish question he concluded that "they and it are incapable of solution." [36] Asked whether Massachusetts would adopt the New Hampshire doctrine of criminal insanity, he replied, "Oh no, in Massachusetts they won't condescend to take the law from New Hampshire." [37] When William E. Chandler congratulated him on the way New Hampshire people had urged his appointment to the United States Supreme Court, Doe told Chandler not to be impressed. "Most people," he said, "can be induced to sign anything that is not a promissory note." [38]

A few months later it was Doe's turn to congratulate Chandler, who had just been made secretary of the navy. "Of course everyone in N.H. expects you to give them great employment at the Navy Yard," he wrote. "Your situation must be delightful. You will probably be assassinated by some disappointed crank. So many crazy people get office (in Washington, I mean,) it is no wonder the rest of that class think themselves wronged. Comfort yourself with the reflection that the chance of your irresponsible slayer being hanged is greater than it would have been some years ago. What other comfort is possible for you, I do not see." Doe was asking Chandler — who owned a Concord newspaper, the *New Hampshire Statesman* — to give someone a job in the Portsmouth Navy Yard. He had told another applicant that he had no more influence with Chandler "than with the Czar," but when the man persisted, Doe wrote to Chandler. "I know no reason why he should not be employed. He is an active, working Black Republican of your stripe. He reads your paper, & believes in it as I do not. He believes in the Statesman as he does in his Bible; & I guess he reads it more. Perhaps, if he were questioned by the church, he would admit, *pro forma*, that the Bible is higher authority than the Statesman; but, for the practical purpose of life, I guess the latter, with him, outranks the former." [39]

In 1886 Doe went to Europe with his son Perley and several friends, including Jeremiah Smith. He objected to being addressed as "Judge" while off the bench and asked them particularly to call him "Mister Doe" during the trip. They did, putting emphasis on the "Mister." "Good morning, *Mister* Doe," they would say. On the homeward voyage an American lawyer took no notice of what was going on. "By the way, Mister Doe," he asked, "are you in any way connected with that famous New Hampshire Chief Justice Doe?" "Not near enough to mention," Doe replied.[40]

There were occasions while Doe was presiding in court, Judge Allen tells us, that the sense of the ludicrous so prevailed that Doe was obliged to recess so he could retire to his chamber and have a laugh.[41] It seems odd — even for Doe — but since the story is repeated by another friend, it may be true.[42] He did not mind if the joke was on himself. In 1876, following a two-year absence from the bench, Doe was presiding over a call of the docket when a case of some antiquity was called. With a show of impatience he asked why the matter had not been disposed of earlier. "We did not expect his Honor back so soon," one lawyer replied. Adapting himself to the occasion, Doe ordered the case continued, with the suggestion that he would hold the next term of court.[43]

Some of Doe's best wit was saved for the conference chamber. When the court was considering the validity of a statute regulating applications for reduction of bail, Doe found himself a minority of one. The other judges seemed to think that the old law, with which they had long been familiar, was the constitutional standard. Doe thought it merely "unique." "It could," he argued, "be equalled by a law requiring candidates for the Kelley Cure to be prepared by a course in daily drunkenness." When counsel made an argument concerning legislative intent which seemed "absurd," Doe wrote, "The greater the absurdity, the greater the amount of legislative intent. But I hesitate to take a stand on a distinction of that kind." [44] His associates had to be on guard to keep these gems from popping up in his formal opinions. In *Ricker's Petition*, the decision which admitted women to the New Hampshire bar, Doe is supposed to have written, "Who will be bold enough to say now that in a hundred years hence it will not be true that English courts will not be as much surprised to see a lawyer appear dressed as a lady as they would be now to see him appear dressed as a gentleman." The other judges saw to it that this sentence was deleted before the opinion went to the printer.[45]

Despite his associates' watchful eye, Doe's opinions are spiced with humor. *DeLancey* v. *Insurance Company* is perhaps the best. A superb example of judicial satire, *DeLancey* is a scorching indictment of insurance companies in general and of insurance policies in particular. Though well worth reading for what Doe has to say about nineteenth-century insurance practices, it is too long to be outlined in full. His discussion of the insurance policy being sued on is indicative of the remainder of the opinion. He calls it a "trap" written with a "cultivated ingenuity," which, had it "been exercised in any useful calling, would have merited the strongest commendation." The policy, he says, is not so much a policy to protect the "premium payer" as it is an "act of precaution" intended to guard the company against liability for losses. A "most complicated and elaborate structure," it was filled with covenants, exceptions, stipulations, provisors, rules, regulations, and conditions.

These provisions were of such bulk and character that they would not be understood by men in general, even if subjected to a careful and laborious study: by men in general, they were sure not to be studied at all. The study of them was rendered particularly unattractive, by a profuse intermixture of discourses on subjects in which a premium payer would have no interest. The compound, if read by him, would, unless he were an extraordinary man, be an inexplicable riddle, a mere flood of darkness and confusion. Some of the most material stipulations were concealed in a mass of rubbish, on the back side of the policy and the following page, where few would expect to find anything more than a dull appendix, and where scarcely anyone would think of looking for information as that the company claimed a special exemption from the operation of the general law of the land relating to the only business in which the company professed to be engaged. As if it feared that, notwithstanding these discouraging circumstances, some extremely eccentric person might attempt to examine and understand the meaning of the involved and intricate net in which he was to be entangled, it was printed in such small type, and in lines so long and so crowded, that the perusal of it was made physically difficult, painful, and injurious. Seldom has the art of typography been so successfully diverted from the diffusion of knowledge to the suppression of it. There was ground for the premium payer to argue that the print alone was evidence, competent to be submitted to a jury, of a fraudulent plot.

The company even disavowed the solicitor who sold the policy, saying that he was not its agent but the plaintiff's agent. This was too much for Doe. "But corporations, pretending to act without agents, exhibited the novel phenomena of anomalous and nondescript as well as imaginary beings, with no visible principal or authorized representative; no attribute of personality subject to any law, or bound to any obligation; and no other evidence of a practical, legal, physical, or psychological existence than the collection of premiums and assessments. The increasing number of stipulations and covenants, secreted in the usual manner, not being understood by the premium payer until his property has burned, people were . . . made to formally contract with a phantom that carried on business to the limited extent of absorbing cash received by certain persons who were not its agents." [46]

Some years later, when the insurance lobby appeared certain to defeat a bill pending in the Massachusetts General Court, a member of the House of Representatives began quoting *De-Lancey*. "Before the reading had progressed far the House was convulsed with laughter, and there was no effective opposition to the passage of the bill." [47]

Another decision in which Judge Doe employed the light touch to ridicule formalistic or technical arguments was the *Mink Case*, in which the defendant was accused of killing minks out of season. His defense was that he had shot them in the belief that they menaced his geese. The lower court had held that the shooting was justified only if the minks were a real and not merely an apparent danger to the geese. This was the rule applicable to human attackers, and to show its inappropriateness to animals, Doe discussed the question from the viewpoint of the "rights" of the minks. "For the legal purpose of this case," he wrote, "as between the defendant and the minks, the pond and the island were the pond and island of the defendant; his geese were rightfully there, and the minks were there without right. And there was something to be done; for there was no duty of living with or yielding to intruders who manifested a propensity to eat their co-tenants." The prosecution countered that the defendant had offered no evidence that minks kill geese.

Doe thought this foolish. The issue, he held, was the danger the defendant reasonably believed existed.

He might have entertained, and had good cause to entertain, erroneous ideas of the character of the minks. Their pursuit of the geese, some of whom were young, was a seeming threat, and an overt act calculated to excite a suspicion of hostile designs, and ability to execute them. The evidence against them tended to show what, in a human creature, would be the ordinary symptoms of a felonious spirit regardless of social duty and fatally bent on mischief. And if they never did and never could kill a goose of any age, their reputation might be bad; and their reputed character was one of the circumstances of apparent danger or apparent safety. . . .

The reputation of the minks, their pursuit of the geese, and the alarm and retreat of the latter, may have shown apparent danger, when the real character of the pursuers may have created no actual danger. Mr. Blood, a near neighbor of the defendant, did not know whether minks are accustomed to kill geese or not. The defendant may have been equally uninstructed. And it was not his duty to postpone the defence of his property until, neglecting his usual occupations and incurring expense, he could examine zoological authorities, consult experts, or take the opinion of the country, on the question whether his "half-grown" geese were actually endangered, in life or limb, by the incursion of "one old mink and three young ones," "all about the same size." [48]

Doe was not being humorous for the sake of humor — both *DeLancey* and the *Mink Case* are serious discussions of law. Though the claim of one respected practitioner that they were Doe's best opinions[49] is exaggerated, they would have made the reputation of a lesser judge. *DeLancey* is a masterful treatise on statutory construction as well as a satirical exposé of the contractual technicalities employed by many lawyers. The *Mink Case* is as fine an explanation of the right to defense as can be found anywhere. Even while employing the technique of levity, Doe kept the importance of the issue before the reader.

The claim that the defendant was liable if the geese could have been protected by driving them away from the minks, cannot be sustained.

Requiring the defendant to drive away the minks if he could, is an admission that he had a right to drive them away, and that they had no right to remain on his premises without his consent. But requiring him, if he could not drive them away from the geese, to drive the geese away from them, is a practical denial of his right to keep geese in his own pond or on his own land, if he could only keep them there by killing minks. It amounts to this: it being impracticable to permanently eject the assailants, he must banish the assailed; and the raising of geese being impossible, the raising of minks is compulsory. A freeholder, permitted to fire blank cartridges only to cover the endless retreat of his poultry before these marauders, and obliged to suffer such an enemy to ravage his lands and waters with boldness generated by impunity, is a result of the fact of the reasonable necessity of retreating to the wall before a human assailant into a universal rule of law. This rule practically compels the defendant to bring his poultry to the block prematurely, and to abandon an important branch of agricultural industry. His right of protecting his fowls is merely his right of exterminating them.

Not only is one species of his personal property extinguished, the freedom of rural life restricted, and a profit of husbandry cut off, but he is forced to surrender his domain to hostile occupation, — his rights in real estate are materially impaired. The fee, to be sure, remains in him; but he involuntarily holds it in trust for the use of others, whom he is physically unable to expel, because the only defensive measure that would be effectual is prohibited. . . . His right of compensation is annihilated; and his right of defence, established by the primary law of nature, and guaranteed by the common law and the constitution, is reduced to an aggravating abstraction by the error of giving to vermin the benefit of a test of the reasonable necessity of defensive homicide, founded on the transcendent legal worth of human life.[50]

It was an important point, and Doe was dead serious. He won a tactical victory with his frivolity, since judgment had already been announced against the defendant; but when his colleagues read his opinion, intended as a dissent, they called back the case and reversed the verdict. Since Doe had been unable to win them over in conference, his light yet biting style may have made the difference. The verdict was, however, a strategic defeat, because Senator Hoar used it to prove Doe's unfitness for the federal bench, as will be discussed. In New Hampshire tradition the *Mink Case* is known as the decision which kept Charles Doe off the United States Supreme Court.

The public image Judge Doe presented to his contemporaries fits the pattern of a man who disliked formalities, was modest in the extreme, and maintained a beguiling sense of humor. He was, according to the press, a homespun jurist if measured by personal appearance;[51] that is, he was completely indifferent about his dress. The *Boston Journal* wrote that he wore shabbier clothes than farmhands and factory workers and held court in a suit "that some of the prisoners whom he sentenced would refuse to be hanged in." [52] The coat in which he presided during the 1890s was described as "his shiny prince albert, that is generally turning from a glossy black to yellow, owing to nobody knows how many years' wear." [53]

For cold New Hampshire winters Doe had an ulster, but he seldom wore it except when traveling to Concord or Boston. Usually, especially when he was riding in a sleigh, he was wrapped in a horse blanket with special buckles which fastened tightly over his shoulders. The garb made him an oddity, true enough, but he said that he wore it because it was the warmest garment he could find; he cared not a fig for how it looked. For the same reason he wore a dark-blue cloth cap with flaps pulled down over the ears. No stranger could possibly guess that he was chief justice of New Hampshire.

Doe's apparel became a local legend. Men claimed that in his youth he "gratified his desire for fine clothes by appearing in elegant attire which amounted almost to frippery"; that while at the bar he had kept apace of fashions; that only later, when a judge, did he neglect his appearance.[54] This charge is important because it implies that Doe's eccentricities were affectations. It appears that many New Englanders in the nineteenth century believed this, yet nothing could be further from the truth. In the matter of Doe's clothes, it is a fact that even as a lawyer they were below standard. When he became a Republican, the Democratic press enjoyed poking fun at his dress. In August 1859, for example, the *Gazette* compared him to his friend Daniel Hall, another apostate, whom the Republicans had rewarded with the office of school commissioner. The possibility that Doe might be appointed to the bench was just then being mentioned for the first time, and the *Gazette* thought it might help if Doe improved his attire.

Charley is, speaking after the manner of the world, a pretty tolerably nice young man, though nothing compared to Dan Hall. He don't begin to look so slick, in the first place, and it is doubtful if he has near so fine an appreciation of fashionable etiquette. Daniel looks all the time "fixed up", as pert as a canary, whereas Charley don't even keep the hair combed out of his eyes. Daniel though small in stature, is particularly in "fuss and feathers", albeit he curls his hair and, we presume, "parts it in the middle"; whereas Charley pays apparently but little regard to his toilet, but appears to be of a more meditating and sombre mood — at times looking cast down and dejected, and sometimes getting decidingly "snarled up", an example of which occurred some six months ago, from the effects of which it is supposed he has not yet wholly recovered. The appointment in question will undoubtedly be an effective "straightener". . . .

At all events the aforesaid are a pretty brace and we really do not see how the world could possibly wag without them.[55]

The only item of apparel in which Charles Doe took an interest — aside from the horse blanket, a matter of utility — was his shoes, which were of "unique patterns." Wider and straighter than ordinary shoes or boots, they were long, low, and custom-made. He designed them himself, apparently on some theory of hygiene, and supervised their manufacture by a local cobbler. When he died, his family found a large bag of these odd shoes but little else in his wardrobe. Even so, Doe never troubled to shine them.[56] At night, in his hotel, he exchanged them for what a Boston reporter described as "a pair of old-fashioned cheap leather slippers, such as might be bought on Hanover street, for 25 cents, which clattered on the floor at each step, exposing brown home-knit socks." [57] This story scotched the rumor that he did not wear socks because he thought them unhealthy. New Hampshire people did not seem to mind the fact that their most distinguished jurist cut such a poor figure. They knew he was incorrigible after Chief Justice Bellows' funeral, at which he and the other judges were pall bearers: they wore black kid gloves; he wore blue-and-white mittens.[58]

Outside the state, however, Doe's tastes were not so widely known. Once when he was sitting in the lobby of Boston's Parker House, he was taken for a tramp and ordered out. Only the arrival of Professor Smith saved the management from the embarrassment of having ejected the chief justice of New Hampshire.

The Doe eccentricity which seems to have been most famous was his love for fresh air. "Like all great men, Judge Doe thinks he knows something about the laws of hygiene," the *Boston Globe* reported. "Fresh air is his hobby." [59] Before the start of a trial or law term Doe would write the sheriff to open the court-room windows and keep them open for at least five days.[60] No one objected to this. If Doe could not tolerate the musty smell of stale courtrooms, people were willing to have him purge it with fresh air. The trouble was that he insisted on fresh air during trials even in the coldest weather. "Let the windows be lowered," he would periodically order while presiding at the *Sawtelle* murder trial in Dover during December 1890. It was freezing outside, but this did not matter. A "dose of ozone was administered to the audience," at least every half-hour, and "the wintery wind whistled through the whiskers of the witnesses and reporters." [61]

"Now I like fresh air myself," an out-of-state reporter complained, "but the currents of polar germicide that swept through the building left icicles with me. Verily, I should prefer a light term in Dover's revolving jail to a gust of his honor's international disinfectant. A few cold blasts through the jury room after his honor's charge will doubtless hasten a verdict." [62] The bar was just as unhappy. As the New York *Herald* put it, "Lawyers declare that to attend court in winter, when the Chief Justice presided, was equal to a trip to the Arctic regions." [63] Doe usually wore his horse blanket on the bench and kept his feet in a box of straw. Counsel were permitted to wear overcoats and hats, and sometimes Doe provided blankets and straw for the jury. Reporters were warned to come well prepared, but even then they would complain that their fingers were too numb to take notes.[64]

The most extreme "freezeout," as they were called, occurred at the *Almy* murder trial in Plymouth during a particularly cold November. Since Plymouth is in the White Mountains, it must have been very cold indeed. Doe was annoyed by the large crowd of sensation seekers and ordered the sheriff to remove the windows.[65]

"Remove them?" asked the sheriff.

"Yes," Doe said.

"What shall I do with them?"

"Take them to Holderness," Doe replied, referring to a neighboring town.

Doe did the same at the *Palmer* murder case, tried during February on the seacoast. The windows had been opened, but

Doe still detected "bad air" and ordered them taken out. Gilman Marston, Palmer's attorney, put on an overcoat and later donned a hat. Still he was chilled. Unable to stand the cold, he banged the table with his fist. "I'd rather try this case out of doors than here," he shouted at the bench.

"So would I, Brother Marston!" Doe replied. "So would I!" [66]

Inevitably there were reports of pneumonia. Rumor even attributed the death of a young Dover attorney to Doe's "dose of ozone." True or not, the story gave his critics ammunition with which to attack him. One of the boldest, Concord's *Independent Democrat,* printed an article entitled "The Law of Assault and Battery and of Torture by Over-Heating or Freezing." It was a mock indictment, written in the form of a legal brief, and it cited for authority the "principle" that a person has as much right to be free from freezing air as from bodily assault.

If in severe cold weather a man opens or causes to be opened the doors and windows upon inmates of a room, and thereby subjects them to such a low temperature that they are put in distress, or take cold, or become sick, and are compelled to abstain from labor and pay for nurses and doctors, the wrong doer is liable for full damages for all the injury and loss sustained.

Every citizen, male or female, of good behavior has the right to attend an open court and to remain during a public trial. If any person deliberately overheats or overcools the room to the injury of those in attendance, whether prisoners, officers, jurymen, witnesses, lawyers, or spectators, and damage to health results, that person is liable for the injuries thus occasioned.

A man may endanger his own life by his eccentric habits and not be punished for his wrong doing, but when he undertakes to freeze to death a whole room full of people it is time to call his eccentricities by the right name, and to pursue and punish the torturer of the helpless victims.

A judge has no right to commit suicide or murder even at the trial of a Sawtelle or an Almy.[67]

Many people attributed Doe's own sicknesses to his eccentricity. "Chief Justice Charles Doe is ill at his home in Rollinsford, still suffering from the severe cold contracted during the Sawtelle murder trial," *The Dartmouth* reported four months after the trial ended.[68] In fact, he had been ill before the trial began.[69] He appears to have suffered from chronic bad health, not merely from too much cold air. He had two long illnesses during his first six years on the court, and later he had to stop work for long periods. Insomnia, caused by overwork, was a recurring problem.[70] His colleagues were sympathetic and made every effort to ease his burdens. So too were the newspapers, although they could not resist implying that if he closed the windows he might feel better. Just a year before the *Sawtelle* case he was sick in bed, and the Manchester *Mirror* tried to cheer him by telling him that he was well off — New Hamphire's first woman lawyer had just announced that she was going to apply for admission to the bar. "Chief Justice Doe isn't the man to shirk a duty because it is dangerous," the *Mirror* said, "but when he learns that Mrs. Marilla Ricker, Esq., is taking an active part in the law term at Concord, he will doubtless feel that if he must be sick this winter he caught cold at just the right time. We should prefer to try conclusions with twenty colds than with one Marilla Ricker, especially when as in this instance she is determined to 'practice.'" Mrs. Ricker was from Strafford county and the Dover *Enquirer* came to her defense by saying this "sneer" was made by "a dirty dog of an editor."[71]

Doe may have been something of a hypochondriac; his letters are filled with allusions to his health. "I have been sick and am scarcely able to write. . . . I have been so sick that I do not know the present state of things among the counsel. . . . I am too feeble to write at lengths as I wish to. . . . My health still reduces me to the last economy of time & effort. . . . I staid in bed for a few days in March, & spent most of April & May out of doors, & believe I am as well as ever."[72] He constantly warned friends to take care of themselves. "I hope you will not be confined to your bed or house many days," he told Martston; "but that you will have patience to be confined as long as you ought to be."[73] And to young Wigmore he sent pessimistic advice which appears to be his own medical testament.

The greatest danger of men of your stamp generally is in overwork & a violation of the laws of health of which so few have any knowledge. It is not probable that you will reach the age of fifty with a sound constitution, or any vigor or power of endurance capable of accomplishing anything. You will damage your body in some way so as to make life a burden & probably bring it to an early close. You will be influenced by no caution on the subject. No such man ever heeds any warning but actual disability produced by excessive continuous labor & lack of exercise, sleep & regular hours.[74]

For many years Judge Doe's physician was Theodore Jewett, famed as the hero of Sarah Orne Jewett's novel *A Country Doctor.* He had some strange notions, believing family histories the best guide to cures, since illness is hereditary; nonetheless the judge had faith in him. After Jewett's death none of the younger men satisfied Doe; he got the idea that only an English doctor would do. "I have always desired to go to England," he wrote in 1878, "& almost wish I were ill enough to have an excuse for going now." [75] The excuse came eight years later, when he caught pneumonia in Concord's Eagle Hotel. In England he consulted cardiologists while Jeremiah Smith, who had tuberculosis, saw lung specialists. They received little encouragement. "Well Jerry," Doe said to Smith, "these European doctors don't seem to know much more about medicine than you and I do about law." [76]

After returning from Europe Doe resumed his judicial duties, but he never regained his former vigor.[77] His friends noted that his face had become "pathetic." [78] His heart condition dictated his routine and habits.[79] One morning in Nashua Judge Doe, Judge Clark, and a lawyer were walking toward the court house. "Suddenly without warning," the lawyer recalled, "Judge Doe fell back a step and as he looked upward his face was ashy gray. It was all over in an instance and his breath returned." To avoid seizures such as this, Doe said, he needed fresh air.[80]

Chapter Twelve

WONDER OF THE NEIGHBORHOOD

The Family Man

A few months after Charles Doe was appointed to the Supreme Judicial Court, his father died. The old veteran of the political wars had been inactive for more than thirty years, and it is remarkable that the newspapers could still recall his career. Yet they did, linking him with some of the great names of New Hampshire history — Webster, Hill, Mason, Pierce.[1] It must have given Charles Doe a feeling of pride that his father was remembered, but the death left a void in his life. The old house in Rollinsford was empty now, except for his mother, and the judge decided to move away. While he was in law practice, he had kept rooms in Dover. As a judge he thought it better to live in Portsmouth. Just why, we cannot say. It may have been that Portsmouth had more convenient rail connections to the other shire towns, or he may have preferred the town itself.

The cultural capital of New Hampshire, Portsmouth was a genteel city, proud of its manners, its good taste, and its blue blood. With a population of 11,000, it had three libraries and four newspapers. The years Charles Doe lived there, at the Rockingham Hotel, were the city's Indian summer, an era of gracious living, when seances were in vogue, dancing masters were the social arbiters, and ice-cream parlors were the latest fad. It was the comfortable afternoon of a proud old seaport, described by Thomas Bailey Aldrich when he wrote, "The phantom fleet sailed off one day, and never came back again. The crazy old warehouses are empty, and barnacles and eel-grass cling to the piles of the crumbling wharves, where the sunshine lies lovingly, bringing out the faint spicy odor that haunts the place — the ghost of the old dead West India trade." [2]

That ghost was the legacy of the sea captains. Their mark was on the old town — in the inheritances of its leading citizens and the handsome dwellings which lined every street. Among the finest was the home of the Havens, a three-story federal-style frame building with a New England picket fence in front and a solid board fence along the sides. The head of the family was George Wallis Haven, a Dartmouth graduate who belonged to that class of men who make up for their inactivity in the world of affairs by providing intellectual tidbits to the culture-seeking women of provincial towns. One of Haven's hobbies was lecturing, and he had quite a bit to say. In 1859, for example, he "consented" to speak to the Mercantile Library Association on "Coins"; an address to which members, gentlemen, and ladies were invited free. After the talk had been scheduled, Haven announced that one evening would not give him enough time to tell all he knew about coins. The subject, he said, "occupies two lectures, neither of which is complete without the other." Either his talks were exceptionally good or the Association was starved for entertainment, for Haven got his way. On two separate nights he spoke, and this was but part of his "course of lectures on political economy." [3]

When his daughter Edith was sent home from school for pouring ink on another girl and was told not to return, Haven decided to educate her himself, along with her sisters. He had spent two years in Europe following graduation from college, and he thought himself well versed in modern languages, manners, and morals. He gave his daughters a demanding "bluestocking education," teaching them French and German, guiding them through such books as *The Wealth of Nations*, and seeing to it that they got out into the world by having them join walking clubs. It was Edith Haven whom Charles Doe married in 1865. He was thirty-five years old, and she was eleven years younger.

The daughter of George Wallis Haven was ill prepared to be a housewife. For their first meal she purchased a sixteen-pound roast. From then on the judge did the marketing, at least until they moved back to the old homestead in Rollinsford following the birth of their first son. There Doe's mother managed affairs for a while. She did not have much respect for her daughter-in-law's abilities. "Well, boys," she would say to her grandsons. "If you have a lazy bone in your body it didn't come from your father's side."

Even had the remark been true, which it was not, it would have been beside the point. The true mettle of the younger Mrs. Doe is seen by the spirit with which she accepted her husband's way of life. It is remarkable how a woman of her background could adapt herself so completely to his standards. She put away her silk dresses, locked up her jewelry, and turned her back on fashion. Some thought her more eccentric than him. She went about the neighborhood in clothes just as practical, and often just as shabby. Several times she was mistaken for a gypsy and told to move her wagon elsewhere. Although her father was disgusted, she seemed undisturbed by the radical change in her circumstances. She arranged matters to suit the judge's schedule, invited to dinner only those guests whom he enjoyed, and read magazines and reviews to mark passages which he might wish to see. She loved the old furniture they had inherited along with the house and salvaged many pieces, such as a gateleg table that he had consigned to the dairy barn. Yet she did not protest when he took it into his head to saw the posts off the canopy beds. He thought them useless, and so they had to go.

Edith Doe was no recluse. She spent several weeks each winter visiting friends in Boston. During the summer months she went horseback riding almost daily with Sarah Orne Jewett, sometimes as far as the seashore, and each year she celebrated the strawberry season with a fête which attracted an impressive section of the social and literary aristocracy for miles around. Miss Jewett treasured her company.[4] "We all dined at the Doe's last Wednesday and had such a jolly time," she wrote in January 1872.[5] She found the Doe family one of her best sources for stories, and she received surprising cooperation. Fictional characters drawn by various writers from Charles Doe's reputation as an eccentric caused Mrs. Doe much pain in later years. Some of these were downright cruel. One of the least offensive was especially resented because it was created by the respected Winston Churchill. In the depiction of a boss-controlled New Hampshire judge as a grizzled man, with a great unkempt head and shoulders, who wore a yellow-and-red horse blanket[6] everyone recognized Doe. The suggestion of political corruption was unfair and increased Mrs. Doe's aversion to publicity, a fact which prevented biographical studies during her lifetime. While Miss Jewett was writing, however, Mrs. Doe was not yet bitter. She not only furnished her friend with stories but let her draw them from life. In one tale Miss Jewett leaves us the only description of Mrs. Doe's personality that we have. It is a children's story, in which the author playfully changes the name of "Doe" to "Forne" and calls three brothers Ralph, Perley, and Haven — the names of the oldest Doe boys. The story is a simple one, about a little girl named Jake who lives not far from the Fornes but is at first too shy to join their fun.

Jake is very fond of going down the road about half a mile to a big white house where the Forne boys live, for here one may always have a good time, unless one is an unhappy child, who is always cross and never has a good time anywhere. . . . The Forne boys play out-doors all day in the summer — either in the garden or out on the lawn, under the elm trees; and when our friend Jake and her sister Polly were seen one afternoon wistfully looking in through the fence, the eldest boy, whose name was Ralph, called them in, so he might drive a four-horse team, instead of a span. Afterward they went to the orchard for apples; and after this good time the little girls went down quite often. Sometimes the Fornes' mother would come out and sit on the lawn, under the trees; and Jake thought her so kind. She never acted as if children were in her way and good for nothing, or very much to blame for not being sensible grown people. If you asked Jake, I think she would tell you she would be perfectly willing to live there all the time.[7]

Charles Doe, too, has left us a description of his wife — an indirect description, but even that is more than might be expected. In 1889 he sent John Henry Wigmore advice on marriage which friends took as an embarrassed tribute to Mrs. Doe.

I trust you will be fortunate in your companion. The wives of the present generation of professional men are generally, in one way or another (often in more than one), a heavy burden & incumbrance, —

a drain upon the time, the attention, the comfort, & the mental & financial strength of the unhappy victims. I know more than one able man whose success at the bar has been made impossible by domestic distraction, extravagance, folly & misery. A young woman of education & refinement, content with her lot, & willing & able to be anything but a constant annoyance & inordinate expense to her husband, has become a rare bird. I hope you will both begin right, with sensible notions of expenditure, contentment & harmony, & thus stand some chance of attaining that position of honor & independence to which your talents are entitled. A vulgar notion of display, & an affectation of social rank, are besetting sins, so universal & so ruinous, that an old man fails in his duty when he neglects a fair opportunity to warn every young person who is worthy of a high place in the world. With due labor, you are sure of fulfilling your ambition. Without an economical, unpretending, peaceable, quiet & happy home, the necessary continuous, intense & undisturbed mental application is impossible.[8]

It is clear that Doe regarded the home as an auxiliary of the office, and not the office the support of the home. His career on the court took first place. His wife was content to leave it that way.

The Does had nine children, four boys and five girls. In their household such items as perambulators were superfluous. The youngest child would be placed in a clothes basket, each parent would take a handle, and the other children would trudge behind. They were a strange sight, for all were dressed alike. The girls wore smocks of blue-and-white-checkered cloth, and the boys wore blue denim overalls. Mrs. Doe's relatives complained that the family looked like an orphan asylum. But as with everything else about Judge Doe, style did not matter, and the material was practical — it was so tough that a child could be picked up by the collar — and this is why he insisted upon it. He wanted his daughters to do things their brothers did — to climb trees, to ride astride, and to play lively games. The life their mother had led in Portsmouth was not for them.

Here again we see an aspect of Doe's character which contrasted with Holmes's. Holmes was content never to have had children. "This is not the kind of world I want to bring anyone else into," he explained.[9] Doe could not have understood this attitude. He tried to give his children the best possible life. Although he insisted on living penuriously, he was extremely liberal toward them.[10] He built a gymnasium in the upper story of his barn and turned the hen shed into a billiard room. Thinking the river too windy, he forbade sailboats and canoes, but he let each son have a rowboat of special design. Every child had a horse or pony, sometimes two, and there were always at least three dogs, some sheep, and whatever else might catch their fancy. Miss Jewett sought to capture the spirit of the Doe place for children's eyes when she wrote: "there are so many playthings in the house for rainy weather, and out of doors there are carts, and wheelbarrows, and a tent, and garden tools, and iron spoons to dig in the sand with, and nobody to scold at you, and two tame calves, and a goat, and three good-natured dogs." [11] When one of the boys built a shack on Wells beach, Doe had a carpenter expand it so that all would have a place to stay.

Doe thought the salt air would be beneficial for the children. He was very concerned about their health. When he was still young, the oldest boy, Ralph awoke one night screaming. Dr. Jewett, who was sent for, advised that the boy's shoes and socks be removed to allow him to absorb electricity by walking through the grass. After that they all went barefoot, except in winter, when the electricity was covered by snow.

Judge Doe had the children learn music, not so that they could play instruments, but because he thought it would discipline their minds and muscles. He directed their education from beginning to end. In one of his judicial opinions he described the public-school system as "the foundation of society," [12] but he wanted something better for his children. He hired tutors to educate them at home and he personally selected their textbooks. He would quiz each one, and whenever he encountered a professional educator, he inquired about the latest techniques and methods.[13] He did not always have his way; he favored the new system of teaching writing by sound, but the tutors refused to employ it, and the children learned by alphabet. When one teacher told Doe that his daughter Helen needed competition, he enrolled her at a local private school. She did so well that he sent the two youngest girls there also. His sons, however, remained at home until they were ready for Exeter.

Judge Doe valued physical exercise, but the beauty of the surrounding countryside should have been enough to lure him away from his books. His home, not as large as some others in the neighborhood, was set on the brow of a hill above the Salmon Falls River, overlooking Rollinsford and South Berwick. That area on the river's bend where the alluvium from the mountains joined the salt from the sea was a composite of rural splendor; a panorama of pine woods and rocky fields, of farms half hidden by snow-covered trees, of the frozen river with children sliding, of the two villages with their white frame houses and of the horizon bright with jutting hills. The Doe house might have been an attractive place, but the judge gave little thought to its appearance. "It is," the Boston *Globe* reported, "a *two-story* block house, from which all outward semblance of paint was long ago effaced, if indeed there ever was any." [14] The Boston *Journal* called it "one of the wonders of the vicinity." [15] Every year in early March the windows were taken from their frames; in late November they were put back on the ground floor only. As one contemporary source described it, "In the summer time the window sashes and their panes are out of the window frames altogether, the air, wet, hot, windy or foggy having free play throughout the house. In winter a concession is made on the first floor in having the sashes put in, though they are often raised." [16]

There were many mornings when the Doe girls awoke with snow on their pillows. The children took turns at being the first to get up to start a fire in the kitchen stove. It was often so cold during the winter that the bread froze overnight and had to be thawed before breakfast, and water had to be boiled to unfreeze the drain in the sink. The judge himself was immune to extremes of temperature. In the attic above the kitchen he installed one of the first bathtubs in Strafford county, and he took a cold bath every morning.

Doe's eccentricities were well known. The Boston newspapers made much of them. As the *Journal* said, "The judge was a good deal of a character, and his own townsmen confessed that they didn't understand him." [17] Neither did the Boston reporters, who consequently maligned the entire Doe family. Gossip appearing in the press probably increased the Judge's aversion to publicity and helps to explain some of Mrs. Doe's attitudes. After her husband had died, an artist painted his portrait for presentation to the Supreme Court. Mrs. Doe purchased it and destroyed it, partly, she said, because he would have wanted her to and partly because she could not tolerate the thought of his picture hanging in a public place where it might be an object of ridicule.

Her bitterness obscured her vision. There were hundreds of citizens of New Hampshire who loved Charles Doe as he was and who respected him for his abilities. Even Boston reporters were fond of him. "Chief Justice Doe is all right if his little personal eccentricities do stick out rather prominently," a correspondent wrote in the Boston *Record*. After attending a session of his court, the press always remembered him with "the kindest recollections." [18]

Doe was oblivious to most of this affection. He did not read newspapers, a fact that amazed his acquaintances. He was always asking friends for news, adding that he did not read the papers and was indifferent to what was happening.[19] Some thought it a caprice, others an affectation, still others a "figure of speech." [20] Actually he meant it literally: he did not read newspapers, except for the *Dartmouth,* the *Times* of London (which he took for the law reports), and perhaps the London *Spectator.*[21] There were several reasons for this attitude. One was the editorial makeup of nineteenth-century American newspapers; Doe thought they had nothing to say, and reading them would be a waste of time. Then again, he disliked the brand of personal journalism which had caused him such pain when he was in politics and which still characterized the New Hampshire press. That the most famous jurist in New England made a public fetish of ignoring their wares troubled some newspaper editors, who sought to treat it as his most amusing eccentricity. It proved, however, too much for the Boston *Globe.* After Doe's death the paper tried to quash the legend that somehow he had kept himself informed without reading the *Globe* or other newpapers. "It is barely possible that he may not have read them," it observed, "but he bought them and carried them home, and in the drug store at Salmon Falls, where he supplied himself with current literature while waiting for his evening mail, he often looked at the *Globe* with that expression of interest which plainly told of concentrated attention and evident appreciation." [22] This would have amused Doe had he read it.

He did not have to read newspapers to realize what they were saying about him. His wife, more openly sensitive than he, was upset that they showed greater interest in his eccentricities than in his judicial work. She should have been better prepared; after all, his style of living, which she shared, was bound to intrigue reporters even more than did the open windows in his court room. Why two people who had inherited the wealth of Judge and Mrs. Doe were content to live on the same scale as farmers and millhands was a puzzle made to order for the Boston press.[23] There is little doubt that the Does had money. Some members of the family tried to say that there had never been as much as people thought, and that Doe had been forced to maintain an abject existence to stay on the bench, but the evidence is that he did not have to go to the extremes to which he went. His father had been considered a wealthy man at the time of his death.[24] In 1870, shortly after his mother died, the judge listed his assets at only $22,000.[25] But just four years later, when he was forty-four and had been removed from the court, he turned down several job offers and intended to retire, claiming that he did not need the income. In 1881 his former law partner told President Arthur that Doe was "independent by inheritance," [26] a statement repeated after his death by those who knew him best.[27]

Yet he chose to live like a farmer or a millhand. In fact, considering the standard of living in New Hampshire during the last century, in some respects he lived on an even lower scale. Many a local farmer had a surrey or rig for Sunday use, selected with an eye for comfort if not for style; Doe permitted his family nothing but a democrat wagon with a detachable rear seat. His test was whether a buggy could carry a barrel of flour. If it could not, he thought it impractical and ostentatious. His sense of utility was consistent if eccentric.

Eccentricity therefore became Charles Doe's trademark. "Full of whimsies and sometimes as eccentric as a March Hare," was the way Judge Harold Medina summarized him as late as 1952.[28] Fearful that this bent would scar his reputation, his friends rushed into print just hours after he had died to persuade the world that he should be remembered for greater, better things.[29] They did him a misservice — he wanted no defense, nor did he need one. Years before, Gilman Marston had given up trying to understand Doe's odd tastes. "Doe is demagoguing," Marston concluded, and let it go at that.[30] The others should have done the same.

Instead they concocted all sorts of explanations. He was unpopular with the bar, Hening claimed, and by dressing poorly and living like a peasant he sought "to win the confidence of the people and to make them believe that he was acting as their judicial agent in their behalf."[31] This was silly and would have annoyed Doe had he lived to hear it. Even more ridiculous was the suggestion that his humility was a studied effort at ideal democracy. He had dropped the middle name of Cogswell after he became a judge, and he later dropped his Christian name as well, preferring to sign documents as "C. Doe." This, it was said, "he liked to have interpreted as 'Citizen Doe.'"[32] In the same vein it was claimed that by his simplicity, his parsimony, his disdain for superficies, he was trying to "set an example only too much needed in the prevalent extravagance of these times."[33] In fact Charles Doe cared little for what other people did; surely he did not think they would take him as the pattern for their life.

Doe was better served by those who accepted him as he was and offered no apologies. "Judge Doe had his eccentricities as we all know," one of them wrote. "They neither added to nor detracted from his greatness. They may have given him an ephemeral distinction, but he did not need it. He was great and good over and above his pecularities. They were something of themselves — distinct from the qualities of head and heart that have rendered his name imperishable in the annals of our jurisprudence."[34] They were, said another, "completely overshadowed and become wholly inconsequential in the light of a noble life of consecration to home and to his great profession."[35]

But Charles Doe's eccentricities cannot be dismissed as something to be swept under the rug and forgotten while attention centers on judicial achievements. Professor Smith was the only one to see a connection. The eccentricities of Doe the man, he said, explain many actions of Doe the judge. The dislike of formalities and court ceremonies was a professional extension of

Doe's mode of living, his democratic habits, and his hatred of ostentation.[36] The simplicity of his procedural reforms, the practicality of his evidentiary reforms, and the rationality of his reforms of construction rules, all were reflected in his family life.

Chapter Thirteen

PUDDING AND MILK
The Private Man

THE heritage of the Yankee race was stamped on Charles Doe's high cheekbones. Over the years his hair steadily receded, leaving a thin gray line in the center to meet his forehead, which rose above a pair of large, bushy eyebrows. On the sides the hair was quite thick, covering parts of his ears, and in the back he wore it almost as long as his beard in front. Despite the forehead and eyebrows, his head appeared lengthy, not massive, for it was dominated by a large, accipitrine nose which ended in a round point over his chronically unkempt beard. He was thickset and muscular. If there was a discordant note, it was that he struck the viewer as rather long-bodied, for his legs were shorter than the length usually found on a man five feet, eight inches tall. In sum, his appearance was as shaggy as were the clothes he wore. Despite the humor in his eye, men sensed his reserve. "He might well be taken for a Presbyterian Covenanter, or a Puritan stranded two or three centuries behind his time," an acquaintance wrote. "If frivolity could smile at him, it could not talk with him." [1]

We know of only one intellectual hobby which absorbed Judge Doe's interest — the battle of Waterloo. He collected every account published in English and had a large library on that topic alone. He was addicted to marking marginal notes in these volumes. Several times he scribbled the word "Improbable" beside passages. On one page, where an author blamed Grouchy for failing to apprehend his mission, Doe wrote, "All wrong. He did act intelligently in obeying orders, exactly, with what energy he had." And where in Wellington's memorandum it appears "that the allied British and Netherland army was in line at Quatre Bras," Judge Doe wrote, "Horrible lie." [2]

While in Europe, he visited Waterloo and was able to point out to his companions the stations of all the battalions, both French and British, and he related what each had done during the action. He gathered many battlefield mementos, including a flower which he sent to General Gilman Marston. Hearing of this, the clerk of the Hillsborough county court, a lawyer named Luce, asked Doe if he was interested in reading about Waterloo. Doe replied that he had read everything printed on the subject, but when Luce mentioned *Les Miserables*, Doe confessed that he had never heard of it. Luce gave him a copy, which he read while presiding over a trial. He was so absorbed that he paid scant attention to the proceedings. Every now and then he would be brought back to the business at hand by some lawyer's rapping his desk to register an objection, whereupon Doe would look up, ask the attorneys to review the facts and repeat the objection, make his ruling, and return to the book. [3]

It may be that *Les Miserables* was the only fiction he ever read. At one time he had become interested in the Baconian theory of Shakespeare's plays, and he had perused them thoroughly for proof that Shakespeare had legal training. He discovered passages which he felt only a lawyer could have written, but there is no evidence that he received pleasure from the plays themselves. He was not in the habit of reading unless it served some useful purpose. His education had not introduced him to current literature, and in later years he could not spare the time. Jeremiah Smith says that "he never read for the mere sake of reading; nor did he make use of light literature as a mental rest or recreation. I believe it to be a fact that in his whole life he read only one novel, and not more than three books outside of his special studies." [4] This must be an exaggeration, for surely Doe skimmed through the books of Sarah Orne Jewett, if for no other reason than to see what the Doctor's daughter was doing with herself and how she was portraying the Doe family. But he knew nothing of the other writers of the day, just as he knew nothing of fashion. He was a perfect example of the prosaic lawyer to whom William Wirt referred when he wailed, "To be

buried in law for eight or ten years, without the power of opening a book of taste for a single day! O, horrible! horrible! most
horrible!" [5]

Doe was too stern and his social outlook was too boresome for
him to have understood or appreciated Wirt's jeremiad. At the
very most it would have amused him. Surely he never realized
that there was anything lachrymal about his attitude. He would
have been insulted had anyone suggested that he lacked intellectual curiosity, and he might even have insisted that he
possessed more than most men — which he did, at least in the
narrow and confining area of legal studies.

There is no question that as a jurist Charles Doe was curious,
just as he was strikingly original. Yet it is somewhat paradoxical
that a man who did not have the energy or inclination to open a
book of current fiction and who subscribed to no American newspapers except a college journal would delight in legal study, frequently investigating principles to their foundations and embody-
ing his findings in opinions which were often treatises on the law.
The answer is that Doe loved theory and cared little for beauty.
He also loved work — dull, hard, sustaining, lucubratious work.
When writing an opinion he was indefatigable in research. His
efforts were never confined to lawbooks alone, but led him into
fields few other nineteenth-century judges would have dared
explore. After all, he is the American judicial pioneer in forensic
psychiatry and the first to seek medical advice on the question of
criminal insanity.

Then again, it is only fair to note that Judge Doe was not entirely without an appreciation of nonlegal disciplines. While he
paid no heed to Jefferson's admonition to law students that they
peruse such subjects as natural science, belles-lettres, criticism,
rhetoric, and oratory and read them from dawn until bedtime,
Doe did not ignore the advice of Chief Justice Jeremiah Smith
concerning history. "A judge," Smith said, "should think and
reason as one long accustomed to the judicial decisions of his
predecessors. He should be well versed in the history of the constitution, laws, manners and customs of his own country. The
study of New England antiquities, if we may allow the expression, is a necessary qualification of a New England judge." [6] Doe
was willing to study local history, but always as a lawyer with

some pragmatic purpose in mind, never with the sweeping search of the student. Only a legal problem could command his interest. Yet he was a master of the historical method. When it came to exposing historical fallacies in the law he had what Holmes called "the touch of history." [7]

The best clue to his historical sense is found in his scolding of John Major Shirley, who was writing a history of the *Dartmouth College Case* and sent Doe some prepublication proofs for criticism. Doe's comments were uncompromising. Time and again he called Shirley to task for twisting facts or inserting irrelevant observations to fit preconceived prejudices. He apparently failed to impress Shirley, because years after the book appeared Doe wrote to Frederick Chase, who was working on a two-volume history of Dartmouth, deploring Shirley's lack of discipline. "He may have found some valuable evidence," Doe observed, "but unfortunately, instead of giving us the original evidence which he claimed to have found, he constantly gives his interpretation & his inferences, — which is not according to the modern historical method." Doe wanted Chase to examine Shirley's manuscripts, confident that something of value might be uncovered. "Shirley wrote me that he had made great effort to find Pinckney's view for argument . . . but he could get no clue to Pinckney's papers. Shirley probably left many letters which he rec[eived] on such points." [8]

Judge Doe's interest in legal biography marks him as something of a hypocrite. As a student of history he deplored Shirley's failure to leave personal letters, yet he left none of his own. He insisted on the importance of studying law from the viewpoint of the men who made it, but he did nothing to enlighten us on his own contributions. "I should like to know," he wrote, "what Mason, Smith & Webster really thought of the law of that case, & what Pinckney's argument would have been." [9] Yet he did not consider it important that future generations know what he had thought about his own opinions. While these opinions are replete with citations from Campbell's lives of the chief justices and other biographies,[10] Doe did much to frustrate the efforts of his own biographer. He not only wrapped his personality in anonymity and left an astonishingly small collection of papers, but he often shifted credit for his work to other judges and forbade contemporary writers to praise his accomplishments. To say that Doe's attitude was based on a belief that the judiciary should appear impersonal is no justification since he himself valued primary sources. He lamented the fact that Shirley had not provided that his manuscripts and materials might "fall into the hands of a man of sound & candid historical judgment," and with this in mind he added, "So little of what is called history is free from great errors." [11] Yet Doe did nothing to prevent future errors concerning his own work. His sin was greater than Shirley's, for he was a historymaker, while Shirley was a mere historian.

Perhaps "historian" is too kind a term for Shirley,[12] but it would be no exaggeration to apply it to Doe. He even saw a relationship between history as pursued by historians and history as employed by lawyers. He knew they were opposing interests, but he thought they might be harmonized. He expressed this idea in two letters to a local historian named Bouton, written while he was investigating the abolition of slavery. The first shows that Doe valued the perspective from which historians view evidence, for he asked Bouton, who was not a lawyer, for his thoughts about a legal interpretation. Bouton had examined some of the material uncovered by Doe bearing on the intent of the constitution's drafters, and Doe wondered if it was Bouton's "opinion that the Bill of Rights abolished slavery entirely, at once, or gradually by making free the afterborn." [13] Even more to the point was the second letter in which Doe urged Bouton to "dig up & print" whatever information he could find on how the constitution affected slavery, assuring him that such a tack would be of great help in "judicial construction of that part of the bill of rights in other cases of natural, essential & inherent rights, not committed with the defunct custom of African slavery." [14] Perhaps Judge Doe was asking more of history than history can provide. If we are to criticize him, however, we must do so because he was too much the lawyer rather than because he was not enough the historian.

Historians such as Shirley, Chase, and Bouton added to Doe's wide circle of acquaintances. Some men who did not know him have suggested that Doe invited no intimate association in social life;[15] they were misled by his austerity and by newspaper stories printed at the time of his death.[16] In truth, Doe sought company, and he was esteemed an entertaining conversationalist and a good listener.[17] "Socially Judge Doe was one of the most delightful of men," Professor Smith recalled. "He did not reserve himself for great occasions, but always abounded in good sayings. Few persons have ever spent an hour in his company without carrying away something to remember him by."[18]

Doe welcomed visitors to his house in Rollinsford — but did not want them to stay too long. He tried not to be impolite. "I lost all this afternoon, going to Dover to tender my respects to Stanley who is holding court there," Doe wrote in 1876 while temporarily in retirement. "What a waste of time it is to make a special business of civility & etiquette! But I haven't much to reproach myself with on that score. On the contrary, I am inclined to regard my economy of time an example worthy of being imitated by some who give too much of this fleeting life to the courtesies & amenities cultivated in polished circles. I did really hope however to be able to be civil to Stanley and to have a visit from his wife & himself, for they are very good people."[19]

"Nobody could really know the man unless he was his personal friend," Joshua Hall has said of Doe.[20] The eccentricities proved a barrier for many. Surely Doe's father-in-law never understood him. Mr. Haven was too impressed by his own self-importance to have comprehended Judge Doe's effacement. Haven preserved every item relating to his life, recording events in his diary and journals faithfully and in detail. Matters he thought earthshaking Doe would not have noticed. When the seventh Doe child was born in Rollinsford, the judge did not — as his father-in-law thought he should — send a telegram, to be followed by a long letter giving the particulars. To Haven so important an occasion demanded at least that. Instead Doe mailed a postcard on which he scribbled, "It's a girl. Mother & child doing well. C. Doe." With no idea of date, name, or weight to record in the family Bible, let alone information to put in his journals, Mr. Haven complained to his second wife that their son-in-law was beyond comprehension.

One friend of Mr. Haven's who thought she understood Charles Doe was Sarah Orne Jewett. There were times when she was in and out of the Doe house almost daily. The two were not intimate, yet one Jewett scholar feels that Doe indirectly influenced her work. "Over the callow authoress he cast a spell," it is said. "She came often and noted well his idioms and idiosyncrasies, his diamond-hardness, his unbending sense of truth. From his copious temperament she derived intimations for a dozen gritty portraits and the impetus to seek out other figures of comparable authenticity." [21]

Sarah's father had been Charles Doe's closest friend, and this alone would have drawn Sarah near to the judge. She clung to her father's memory as only a spinster could. Despite her triumphs and honors, her friendships with Whittier and Willa Cather, her conversations with Tennyson and Arnold, and her interviews with DuMaurier and Henry James, there was nothing in which she gloried more than in being the doctor's daughter. "I never feel prouder, or more of the sense of owning or being owned," she explained, "than when some old resident near Berwick meets me and says, 'You're one of the doctor's girls aren't ye?' It makes me feel as though that were really my place in the world." [22] It probably was to Doe.

They were congeneric spirits, she and Doe, but forever poles apart. They could appreciate one another because they lived in worlds separate from other people — she in her world of enthusiasm; he in his world of contemplation. In hers she sought no rest because she was so busy poking her nose into the affairs of other people; in his he was allowed no rest because other people were forever poking their noses into his. The laughing, happy little mind of Sarah Orne Jewett skipped in and out of Doe's world, but they never made contact. She was too vivacious for his world; he too stern for hers. She became excited when she read that the *Mayflower* had sunk on its last voyage carrying a cargo of rice and had to tell everyone about it. "I don't know why I was so *wildly* interested!!" she exclaimed.[23] Doe could not have told her. "When I read the 'Saturday Review' and 'Spectator,'" she wrote, "I find myself calling one politician a Saxon and the next a Norman! Indeed I can pick them out here in Berwick." [24] Doe would not have tried. When Charles Doe took a walk he became lost in thought, oblivious to his surroundings. Sarah Orne Jewett never could. A stroll down South Berwick's Main Street thrilled her, for she found it "neighborly with the hop-toads and with a joyful robin who was sitting on a corner of the barn, and I became very intimate with a great poppy which had made every arrangement to bloom as soon as the sun came up." She even saw a bright little waning moon over the hill. "Really, so much happened in that hour I could have made a book of it." [25] If she had, Judge Doe would never have read it.

Once their minds had almost met. It was during that moment when Sarah, sitting at her little sunlit writing table overlooking her garden and Main Street, had written, "Conformity is the inspiration of much second-rate virtue." [26]

The quality about Judge Doe most highly prized by Miss Jewett, Professor Smith, and his other friends was his kindness of heart. He seems to have been one of the most thoughtful of men.[27] His charity, they admitted, was sometimes eccentric, especially on the bench, for he "recognized the frailty of human nature, its trials and temptations, and often mitigated the rigors of the law accordingly." [28] He was reluctant to see the bad in anyone and preferred to blame crime on hereditary or environment rather than to find the source of human cruelty in a man's free will.[29] Trying to talk the meanness out of a friend he wrote, "I have not a scintilla of unkind feeling towards any human being. By long drill in the official duty of having no personal illwill, I have attained a very happy frame of mind based upon a development of the blessed spirit of the Society of Friends." A few days later he added, "The Quaker is my ideal man. Albeit I was not a Quaker by nature; but I have become one by habit & usage — the long habit of trying to do that duty of my office which requires a frame of mind constantly calm, impartial & just. A better school is impossible." [30]

Judge Doe's neighbors could always depend upon his philanthropy. He never permitted his acts of charity to become known, though he seems to have been remarkably generous.[31] One which he could not hide was the distribution to the needy of surplus food grown in his gardens — mostly apples. Often he had so many that he would pile them in front of his house and invite everyone to take what he needed. When he heard children returning from school, he would go out to urge them to help themselves. He wanted to see if they would conform to a pattern. Not one to type people, in this instance he was pleased to find types. The French-Canadian boys were generally polite, or so he said, the Irish boys would sass him, and the Yankee boys would pelt him with the apples. He would run into the house, highly amused, to tell the family. The types were a bit too pat, and one suspects that the boys were doing what Doe had hoped. It was a favorite local pastime during the late nineteenth century to evaluate New Hampshire's nationalities in terms of politeness and honesty. Mrs. Doe believed the French Canadians the most polite of people, though not always the most honest; the Irish honest, though not always courteous; the Yankees often neither polite nor honest. This seems to have been the common view. Irish servants were preferred on the theory that, though they knew little of housekeeping and would not learn, they could be trusted.[32] And politicians believed that while they could purchase the votes of Yankees and occasionally of French Canadians, Irish votes were seldom for sale.[33]

Judge Doe's thoughtfulness especially manifested itself toward young lawyers. He made a practice of encouraging new members of the bar and of easing their first experiences in court. Men marked this characteristic during his lifetime and recalled it with gratitude long after his death. Most of his kindnesses were of an unofficial nature. When he learned that a student had lost his preceptor, Judge Doe sent a prominent member of the bar to volunteer his assistance in any way that might be needed. On another occasion a student who had been studying law for two years and nine months wrote to Doe requesting admission to practice, asking that the requirement of three years of study be waived because his mother, who had worked hard to pay for his education, was about to die and before she passed away he wanted her to know that he was a lawyer; Judge Doe saw to it that the boy was admitted.[34]

We catch a glimpse of Charles Doe's interest in young lawyers by his concern for his law students, the most memorable of whom was Robert G. Pike of Dover. In 1878 Pike, a surveyor, was working on the road in front of the Doe house. Since Pike's sister was then tutoring the children, the Judge went out to meet him. Impressed by Pike's intelligence and native abilities, Doe told him that he was looking for men of his caliber for the New Hampshire bar and invited him to study law in his office. Pike accepted and vindicated Doe's judgment by succeeding to his seat on the high bench and eventually becoming chief justice of the Superior Court.

Pike has left us the only description we have of Doe as a law teacher. Since Doe was not in practice and therefore could not set his students to drafting writs and performing practical tasks, his instruction must have taken general lines, with a great deal of reading followed by discussion of broad principles. According to Pike, it had a moral tone.

It was a delight to labor in his study under the inspiration of his presence. Whenever I asked him questions about principles, that seemed to me obscure, he would instantly lay aside his work and give such illuminating answers that the subjects would stand out clear without a question or a doubt remaining. These answers or explanations would be lectures, in effect, upon the principles of law involved. And often he would rest from his work at hand and give a talk on some important subject most helpful to a student who in time would practice law. I recall that one talk was on "Honesty," — as a necessary asset of every lawyer. Another was on "Tact," and its importance to a lawyer if he would succeed. All of these talks made reference to different lawyers in the state and received force as their conduct illustrated the points he desired to bring out.[35]

Another young man who revered Doe as a mentor was John Henry Wigmore. The two were destined never to meet, but for a number of years they worked closely in a manner akin to the present-day judge-law clerk relationship. New Hampshire law libraries during the nineteenth century were not up to the standards requried by a scholar of Doe's ken, and for many years he went to Boston to pursue his research. As his health began to decline, however, the wearisome trainride and distractions of the city became too much, and he sought assistance. Wigmore, who had just opened an office in the winter of 1887, was recommended. Judge Doe was pleased by the results, although Wigmore was not sure why. "I cast my results in the form of judicial opinions," he wrote; "and being much flattered by the task given me, I expected to be able to recognize my handiwork in the published opinions. But — I frankly admit that I never could find any resemblance at all between what I sent and what he turned out. Master mind that he was, my stuff was simply raw material to him, and he used it, or cast it out as he found fit. I had simply been a searcher to him, and he made his own use of it in his own way." [36]

Doe had no fault to find. In his generous manner he took pains to flatter Wigmore by heaping on large doses of encouragement. "My curiosity asks your age, education & date of admission to the bar," he wrote. "I am utterly unable to understand how your work can be done by anyone but a lawyer of long experience & extensive practice in this kind of labor." [37]

Unless, by some strange accident, you happened to be familiar with the subjects, or were aided by somebody, who was familiar with them, or have a facility for handling books & finding things beyond what I can conceive of, you must have spent a great deal of time with intense application. How any young man could do what you have done, in the time, without special previous knowledge of the subjects, is something I can't understand. And if you were an old or middle aged man, the marvel would be very great. The only unsatisfactory thing is the evident inadequacy of your charges. What they should be, I cannot [?] guess. Enclosed is draft for $50, which cannot be enough. For future work, I must insist that you charge what you think your work is worth, remembering that I appreciate the value of all time spent in search that shows what cannot be found. You cannot be more annoyed by the fear of charging too much, than I am by the fear of your charging too little. When I get any idea of what the enclosed ought to be, I will make up the deficiency.[38]

Judge Doe found it difficult to criticize. Even when he caught Wigmore in an error, he tried not to give offense and even took the blame himself. "You have just given me a bad fright," he wrote in 1889, referring to Wigmore's interpretation that a New York decision had denied the right of jury trial to a city. "On looking at the case, it seems you or I greatly overstated the matter. It might be inferred that the court would have denied the right if the question had been raised. But your statement is too strong & would be misleading. Perhaps the error is one of mine which you did not correct. I merely mention it as a caution against haste." [39]

It is evident that Judge Doe was a student of human nature. "I used to think he could read one's character as quickly as anyone I ever knew," Pike has written. "A look into the face, — a few inquiries, with answers given, and the measure of the man was taken." [40] Once when a chronic beggar asked Doe to "lend" him five dollars and Doe did so, a friend expostulated, pointing out that Doe would never again see the money. "If he had simply asked for it, I would have refused this time, sure," Doe explained, "but putting it in the form of a request for a loan, I am pretty secure from any more attacks from that quarter until he has repaid me." [41]

The "Quaker ideal," which he sought to imitate, led Judge Doe to consciously strive for a tolerant attitude, especially on such political issues as states' rights. "Every year of my life makes me vastly more charitable towards others, & vastly less certain of my own infallibility, in such matters, than I was when I was admitted to the Bar; & I suppose that is the common experience." [42] He tried to apply this lesson to his judicial work, bending over backward to see both sides of every question. He was especially ready to pardon human failings, as is illustrated by his concluding remarks in *Hale* v. *Everett,* a particularly nasty litigation, originally an intraparish squabble over religious doctrine, which had erupted into a bitter struggle for control of church property — the typical sort of fraternal friction which brings out the worst in everybody. Doe had been a member of the parish and knew the people involved. He believed that the plaintiffs, shocked by their opponents' heresy, had been carried away by their overzealousness, while the defendants had displayed an unnatural restraint, probably to win public favor. His knowledge of human nature was never better displayed than in this *dictum.*

Notwithstanding the unfavorable light in which all the evidence, admissible and inadmissible, presents the plaintiffs, they should be judged leniently, in consideration of the intemperate and blinding excitement with which human nature, engaged in any strife, is apt to be transported. Misrepresentations and distortions of facts, insinuations and calumnies poured out upon the victims, are what everybody expects the persecuting party to be guilty of. To that party, many of the best men have generally belonged. And we ought not hastily to conclude that the plaintiffs are less respectable than the defendants. The scrupulously frank and fair, the singularly meek, gentle, and forebearing manner in which the evidence shows the defendants have carried themselves, under circumstances of extreme provocation, from the beginning of this controversy till now, may be due, in some measure, to peculiar and temporary influences. It is not improbable that there is something transient in the situation of the parties, that depresses the plaintiffs below, and exalts the defendants above, the real level of their characters.[43]

What makes this especially noteworthy is that the plaintiffs had won the case and Doe was dissenting on behalf of the defendants.

With his grasp of human nature Judge Doe had a sure touch when it came to handling men. It was an immeasurably valuable facility when he presided at court conferences as chief justice, and, as we shall see, it helped him carry many reforms over the opposition of reluctant associates. One incident from private life shows his astuteness. It will be recalled that General Gilman Marston stormed out of court after Doe told him that if he did not question a witness politely, he could not question him at all. Doe and Marston were close friends, Marston regularly taking the train from Exeter to Portsmouth on Sundays just to call on Doe. He had been a key support in Doe's appointment to the bench and was doubly peeved at Doe's treatment of him. After Marston did not return to continue the trial, Doe recessed court and stepped out into the hall. There he saw Marston pacing nervously up and down, chewing a cigar, and muttering to himself. Doe walked over, laid his hand on Marston's shoulder and asked, "General, are you coming over to see me Sunday?" "Not by a damned sight," Marston snapped. Doe laughed and took his leave. The matter became less amusing as the weeks went by and Marston not only refused to speak to him but gave indications that he might support the opposition that was being organized against Doe's procedural reforms. Doe knew he had to end the quarrel if he wished to keep a friend and avoid developing a dangerous antagonist. So one Monday evening he went to Marston's house where, when holding trial session in Exeter, he often ate. He was fond of the pudding and milk the General's housekeeper served for dessert. He timed his arrival perfectly and when the housekeeper opened the door she said that Marston was just finishing supper. "Mary," Doe asked, "are we having pudding and milk tonight?"

She said they were and Doe walked into the dining room. He greeted Marston, but the General did not look up. Doe pulled out a chair and sat down. "General," he said, "please pass the pudding and milk."

Marston shoved the dish across the table. They ate in complete silence, the only sounds coming from the kitchen, where the housekeeper was busy, and from the irritated General as he noisily ate his pudding and milk. After he had finished, the puzzled, angry, but completely defeated Marston, got up and went into his sitting room. Doe followed him, closing the door. How long before Marston spoke we do not know, but it hardly matters, for Doe had won the day.

"How is it that you made up with the judge?" a local lawyer later asked.

Marston had a better question. "How in thunder can you keep mad with a man who walks into your house, uninvited, and asks you to pass the pudding and milk?" [44]

Chapter Fourteen

A POLITICAL FOOTBALL
Nonjudicial Activities

THE American people have set the standards for their ideal judge: he is honest, tolerant, temperate, sagacious — and free from partisan politics. Charles Doe had most of these attributes. His dress may not have fit the judicial image, but as his friends said, his strength of mind and heart made up the deficiency. Yet in one respect he missed the ideal: he could not divorce himself from politics, and his contemporaries knew it.

Doe tried to be neutral, and by the standards of the time he was. He never dragged the bench into partisan politics. Yet there were pressures that were hard to resist. For one thing, politics intruded itself upon the court — not, to be sure, on the court's decisionmaking process, but rather by jeopardizing the tenure of judges and by using judicial personnel as election issues. Furthermore, Charles Doe was not always the abstract scholar he liked to think himself. Try as he might, he could not remain aloof; when matters were not proceeding as he thought they should, he could not resist offering advice and even direction.

The raid on Harpers Ferry occurred a month after Doe's appointment, and as a result he was back in politics almost from the moment he became a judge. It could not have been otherwise. New Hampshire being the most pro-Southern of the Northern states, the specter of civil war cut deeply into its conscience. Even the Republican Party was divided.[1] Some elements, including old Whigs, were moving toward abolition,[2] but John Parker Hale still spoke for the majority when he assured the United States Senate that the federal government had no more power to strike at Southern slavery than to deal with Russian serfs or English laborers.[3] This was the slogan of the Democrats — that slavery was legally if not morally right.[4] In New Hampshire, loyal to the traditions of constitutional legalism, it was an argument bound to give pause.

As soon as Lincoln made clear his intention to pursue a full-scale war, the position of the Republican Party in New Hampshire began to deteriorate. Throughout the conflict no state would be more loyal or more active on the Union's behalf, but the boldness of its stand belied the dissension within its ranks. Perhaps Charles Doe sensed more danger in Democratic resurgence than existed, but he was alarmed enough to take an active hand in Republican affairs. "Is there anything that can be done in this state to forward any of your interests," he asked Senator Hale; "if there is I will gladly do anything." [5]

The war gave the Democrats a new lease on life. For the next decade elections were close. The Republicans always won — but not by much. Though the Democracy did not recover the strength it had possessed in the days before its ranks were torn apart by the Nebraska bill and the *Dred Scott* decision, it won back enough apostates to fight the Republicans on equal terms. But there was never any likelihood of Charles Doe's returning to the Democratic fold. The party had written him off with its abusive criticism. Moreover, the Civil War made him a Republican body and soul. His allegiance was unshakable. Democrats he called "the rebels," "the opposition," "the enemy," and "those rogues." Republicans were "our folks." Sending a friend in Washington a proposed bill for congressional enactment, he warned that it "should be kept out of the enemy's hands." [6] Still, he was not blindly partisan. He was a Republican, he thought, because he endorsed the principles of the party. "I do not propose to attempt to resist an ocean tide, nor to meddle with public affairs in any way," he explained, "further than to vote in favor of making a dollar worth 100 cents, reducing public expenses, putting honest men into office if such can be found willing to endure the miseries of public life, against the public support of sectarian schools, & against handing over the government to unrepentant rebels. Those are some of the main points of the Republican creed, as I understand it, & therefore I am enthusiastically Republican." [7]

While always disclaiming interest in public affairs, Doe managed to let party leaders know his opinions on important events and questions.[8] Not the "power behind many thrones" as some thought,[9] he was nonetheless influential. Crawford Dawes Hening, who tried to discover just how influential, had to admit that Doe had successfully covered his tracks. "He had great genius for political intrigue and, though no bill of particulars concerning his political activities can be furnished, politicians speak mysteriously of 'his wonderfully active and original mind in matters of large public concern,' and of 'his instrumentality in several matters of the first order which were discussed during his time.'" [10] Contemporaries knew that Doe provided Republican newspapers with unsigned articles and gave generously to the party treasury.[11] This was expected. Less well known was his willingness to do more. At times he even took an active part in campaigns, as shown by a letter he wrote the chairman of the Republican state committee in 1868. "I send by express a quantity of [Governor] Walter Harriman's speeches on the negro question and a slip on impeachment. We are using these with capital effect in this part of the State, sending them around to every store and house. Please send them to different towns for distribution and charge the expense to me. This is a part of my contribution to the cause." [12]

This letter seems an exception to the rule. Doe usually did not participate as directly as this. Most of his politicking — at least what we know of — was related to the court. For example, he often lent his influence to legislation bearing on jurisdiction, as when he supported a bill transferring divorce cases to the trial term.[13] He also had much to say about appointments. There is a tradition that Doe prevented the appointment of Edgar Aldrich to the attorney generalship. During the waning days of the Arthur administration he tried to persuade the infirm Judge Clark to resign as judge of the federal district court rather than risk having the appointment fall to Cleveland.[14] This incident is revealing, for Doe took an opposite track with his own court. There were no Democratic judges, and he thought there should be. The bench would never be free of politics while its personnel came from Republican ranks alone. There were men in both parties who felt the same, but Doe was their most articulate spokesman. "It is substantially the universal sentiment of both parties," he optimistically wrote a Democrat in 1870, "that both parties ought to be on the Bench. After years of fighting my own party and very many of yours too, on this point, I am certainly very near success." [15]

Doe was wrong when he called the sentiment "universal." There were Republicans dead set against any change. "While the responsibility is upon us as the governing power," one Republican lawyer argued, "let us bear it without seeking to divide or evade it. When we pass into the minority, let others do the same." [16] Plenty of Democrats, scenting victory, would have been happy to leave matters as they were. But Doe persuaded Governor Onslow Stearns of the need for reform. Over the heads of several candidates with strong political backing, Stearns selected Harry Hibbard to be the first Democratic judge appointed by a Republican administration. Hibbard was a war horse of his party, yet his chief support came from Doe who had been pressuring him to take the job. The appointment, which was a highwater mark of Doe's influence, came to naught. Despite Doe's urging, reinforced by Republican editorials praising the selection and a promise of salary increase, Hibbard refused to serve.[17] William Spencer Ladd, another Democrat, was named in his place. Three years later the Republicans appointed a second Democrat, thus establishing the policy of drawing members of the judiciary from both parties. What remained was to see if this would remove the bench from politics.

Some hoped that it would, that the presence of their own men as judges would give the Democrats pause before they overturned the court.[18] Doe was more realistic — he knew that if the Democrats won control of the state they would remove him from the bench.[19] One of his arguments to Hibbard had been that when this occurred, "your party must not only retain you, but they must make you Chief Justice." [20]

Doe did not expect to be "addressed" out of office as rudely as when he had been ousted as solicitor of Strafford County in 1856. The legislature was more polite toward the judiciary. It did not draw up individual indictments charging each judge with incompetence or corruption. Instead it handled the justices painlessly and collectively, by "legislating" them out of office. The structure of the court, not the membership, was attacked. Usually the party out of power trumped up issues (such as delays in justice) and campaigned on a promise to change the judicial system. If it won the election, it would, in the name of reform, create a new court. In this way it legislated out the old judges and appointed its own men to the new places.[21]

In 1874 politics ran true to this pattern. The Democrats, promising judicial reform, captured the state government for the first time since 1854. There were attacks on Chief Justice Sargent and Judge Doe as political appointees who owed their jobs not to their abilities but to corrupt bargains. On the whole, however, personalities were laid aside. The Democrats had a program for reform: the personnel of the trial court should be separated from that of the appellate court, they claimed, and judicial opinions should be *seriatim*. On this excuse they legislated out the Supreme Judicial Court and created the Superior Court of Judicature. Some of the old judges were retained, but not Sargent and Doe. Thus in the summer of 1874 Charles Doe went into forced retirement.

Political attacks on Judge Doe did not stem from spite alone. True, some Democrats were still kicking the dead horse of his betrayal in 1859, but the main idea may have been to remove a potential candidate. A few Republicans had seen the handwriting of defeat on the wall before the election of 1874, and to avoid disaster "earnest appeals" had been made to Doe to run for governor.[22] He would have nothing to do with the idea, but that did not matter. Just the mention of his name allowed the Democrats to say that he had violated judicial neutrality. Two years later he refused to run for Congress, even when he was told that he was the only man who could beat the Democratic incumbent. "The whole business of politics is to me unutterably detestable," he wrote William E. Chandler. "And I shall always be greatly indebted to you or anyone else who does anything to keep me out of it."[23]

Doe might have been more convincing had he really kept himself out of it. While he wanted Chandler to leave him alone, he did not leave Chandler alone. Chandler was using his newspapers to promote the presidential ambitions of James G. Blaine before the national convention of 1876, and Doe advised him to tone down his editorials. Scandals in Washington, Doe warned, had introduced uneasiness, discontent, and mutiny "in our ranks, and the tendency to independent voting or staying at home on election day." People were growing tired of "machine" politics. "If Conkling, Morton & Cameron don't know that the nomination of Conkling or Morton or any man of their stripe, would elect a Dem president, it is high time they did know it." [24] A party "that allows itself to be put on the defensive is doomed." [25]

As a result, Doe sided with the reformers and, despite an admiration for James G. Blaine, favored the nomination of Benjamin Bristow, the man who had exposed the "Whiskey Ring".[26] It was a pragmatic choice, as he explained to a Blaine supporter. "However much inclined you may be to the fault of excessive confidence in the triumph of the right; & however much I may be inclined to the opposite fault; I suppose we agree in the imminence of the danger of the gov't going into rebel hands, & the necessity of our nominating the man most likely to be elected." [27]

Doe wanted New Hampshire to send an unpledged delegation to the convention, but when he was asked if he would lead it or serve as a member, he refused. Though pressure was brought to bear, he would not even let them use his name. One man asked what he would do if elected anyway. "I said, if the [state] convention, knowing that I refused to be run, & that I was as averse to going as a man could be, should find it necessary to send me, — if that was the only way an impartial & unpledged delegate could be got, — I should go, — that the only condition on which I would go was, that no other perfectly unpledged, unbiased & impartial man could be elected; & that I had no fear of being conscripted on such conditions; that the convention would certainly agree with me that I should be excused; & that there could be no necessity for my going." [28]

When the Republicans nominated Rutherford B. Hayes, Doe was "profoundly satisfied." [29] He supported Hayes's policy of derequisition and even anticipated it. "Wouldn't it be well," he wrote early in 1876, "for our folks to introduce, in the House and Senate, a bill or resolution for amnesty to all rebels except

Jeff Davis, & press it with vigor, as a centennial measure demanding immediate attention." [30] But he did not want the Republicans to abandon the emotional appeal of the Civil War as a campaign issue. "The hottest fire ought at once to be opened on Tilden's record in war & peace, to prevent independent, & reform voters being caught with the Dem cry of reform." [31]

That year the Republicans of New Hampshire had a cry of their own — "the Senate steal." In the election of 1875 the Republicans had won the House of Representatives, but the Senate stood at five Republicans to five Democrats, with two contested seats. For the second year in a row neither gubernatorial candidate had carried the majority of popular votes, and the election was thrown into the legislature. With Republicans outnumbering Democrats in the House, a Republican governor was certain to be chosen. The only obstacle to complete Republican control of the government was the margin of doubt in the Senate. To get these two senators for their party, the outgoing Democratic governor and his executive council had taken it upon themselves to canvass the contested returns. By throwing out 3,771 ballots cast for the Republican Natt Head on the grounds that his lawful name was Nathaniel Head, and by disallowing 46 votes cast for the Prohibition candidate because he had not resided in New Hampshire the mandatory seven years, they declared the Democratic candidates elected.

The Republicans were up in arms. There was no precedent for what had been done; indeed, what precedents there were sanctioned neither the jurisdiction assumed by the governor nor the principle that improper ballots were not to be counted in the total of votes cast. Asked for his advice, Charles Doe told Republican leaders that only a convention of both the House and the Senate could ascertain and fill vacancies.[32] When the five Republican senators refused to sit with the seven Democrats and temporarily set up a "rump" Senate, they may have been acting on Doe's suggestion.[33] At least the party chieftains thought he was in favor of stiff action. "I called on Doe yesterday," the chairman of the Republican central committee wrote a colleague. "He is all right in sentiment, agrees with us on all the legal questions, and is in favor of maintaining our rights at every hazard, even coolly contemplates a double-headed State government." [34]

It seems likely that, although he refused to take a public part in the controversy, Doe directed the legal strategy from behind the scenes. Whatever he did, it certainly pleased the Republicans. "Doe is a trump," one wrote. "He has done a big thing." [35]

The Republican House of Representatives asked the Superior Court of Judicature to rule on the legality of the senatorial elections. The justices, despite recent precedent to the contrary,[36] and with the Republican member Isaac W. Smith concurring, ducked the issue by holding that the principle of separation of powers put the matter outside their jurisdiction.[37] This decision sealed the fate of the Democratic court. Running on the slogan of "the stolen senate" and promising to legislate out of office the "corrupt" judges, the Republican handily won the election of 1876.

While he had more to gain than anyone else, Charles Doe's voice was one of the few raised against legislating the Democratic court out of office. "In the language of Jeff Davis," he wrote to one Republican newspaper publisher, "'I have no view of the future which makes it desirable for me' to suppress an unpopular opinion; & thinking, as I do, from my own knowledge of them, that the present judges are perfectly honest men, I do not hesitate to say so." Doe admitted that many would disagree. "But I have learned that the fact that one man's conclusion on a legal question appears absurd to another man, is not generally to be taken as evidence that either of them is dishonest." He compared the "Senate steal" to *Dred Scott*, which he still called an "infernal outrage." "And I take precisely the same view of the decision of the N.H. court in the Senate case. [Judges] Cushing, Ladd & Smith made a terrible blunder; but they are as honest as Taney was; & Taney, in making a diabolical decision, was as honest as St. Paul; and according to Paul's own account, he was as honest before his conversion as he was afterwards." It may be that Doe even believed the hand of vengeance could be stayed. "I am glad," he concluded, "to know that the Republican party is the party of personal liberty & toleration; & that it is quite in accordance with Republican discipline for me to think that a court of justice ought not to be a political football." [38]

Doe was indulging in wishful thinking. The victorious Republicans were not to be placated. The court was still a political football. Doe urged the chairman of the party not to give in, and he underlined the point by insisting that he would not serve on a new court.[39] To others he emphasized his argument in the same way. "The courts, I suppose, will be overturned again," he said in one letter; "but I hope they will leave me alone. Some of the work I like, but a great deal of it, after 15 years of drudgery, became exceedingly irksome. There are a variety of circumstances that would make the work very disagreeable to me, under any system likely to be adopted." [40] He was referring to the fact that the Republicans intended to reunite trial and appellate duties under one court; he did not want to return to circuit riding or to presiding at *nisi prius* terms.

When told that his refusal to be a delegate to the Republican national convention had hurt his chances of being appointed chief justice, Doe expressed gratification. "If the kind compliance of the [state] convention with my wish, & my declination, has created such hard feelings as a reason for my not going back to the Bench, I shall be fortunate indeed." [41] But once the Democratic Superior Court of Judicature was legislated out and the new Supreme Court created, no man but Charles Doe was thought of for the chief justiceship. Remembering the bitterness of his early years on the bench, Doe could not at first be convinced that the bar wanted him.[42] Told there were "peculiar & irresistible reasons" for his acceptance, Doe wrote: "I don't believe there will be any such reasons, & unless there are such reasons affecting the public interest & plainly making it my duty to sacrifice my own comfort & my strong inclinations, I shall not go back." [43]

But back he went, and as he himself explained, it was Jeremiah Smith who persuaded him of the duty to "sacrifice" his comfort and to become chief justice. "I was then on the invalid list, and completely out of practice," Professor Smith recalled.

Hence Judge Doe came to me, as to one who was a disinterested witness, and put me through a very searching cross-examination as to the real reasons for the apparent desire that he should fill the office. He was willing to accept only in case he could be satisfied that he was really the first choice of the better element at the bar. . . . He distinctly remembered the days when he was *persona non grata* in certain sections, and it was difficult to persuade him that a very different sentiment towards him now prevailed. I called his attention to the fact that some of the bar leaders who formerly opposed him had now passed away; that others no longer occupied their former commanding position; and that still others (including some of the worthiest) had come to understand him better and now fully appreciated his services. But what I think made more impression upon him was my insistence upon the fact, that a new generation had come upon the stage during the seventeen years which had elapsed since his first appointment, and that the best of these younger lawyers were his warm friends and enthusiastic admirers. I remember asking him if he thought that a combination could now be successfully made to break up one of his terms in the county of A, if Mr. X should oppose it; or in the county of B, if Mr. Y should oppose it; X and Y being men who in 1859 were unfledged law students or inconspicuous juniors, but who in 1876 stood in the front rank and were among his hearty friends.[44]

This clinched it, and after two years in retirement Doe returned to the New Hampshire judiciary, now as chief justice. Jeremiah Smith had been right: the old animosity was gone. It recurred to embitter Charles Doe's final years, but for about a decade he experienced almost universal popularity. The realization that he did not want the honor of heading the court had sobered even the Democratic editorial writers, and they greeted his appointment with soft complaints which amounted to near-approval. It was to be a happy period for him. He turned his back on politics and gave himself to judicial work. The only occasion when we see him showing any interest in the affairs of state was when he informally offered advice to the constitutional convention of 1889 — the convention which passed a prohibition amendment which Doe, in a reversal of his former beliefs, supported. Characteristically he did not do so with the zeal of a reformer; rather, he seemed more interested in the political considerations. The Democrats were financed by liquor and railroad interests, and prohibition was to him a matter of party warfare.[45]

Charles Doe was pleased that he was no longer playing an active role. He remained loyal to the party which had appointed him, and to anyone who asked he admitted that he was a "political recruit on the N.H. Bench." But he had "outgrown politics," he said. "I know that the Bench is the place most calculated to knock politics out of a man, that is, out of his judicial judgment; &, I flatter myself, it has had that effect upon my mind."[46]

Chapter Fifteen

THE NEW HAMPSHIRE
METHOD

The Court Leader[1]

A CHIEF justice exercises few powers. He is the court's presiding officer and little more. Yet he has the job of making his colleagues work together harmoniously and efficiently. The measure of his success is the cooperation he receives and the dissension he prevents. By this standard Charles Doe was a great chief justice. The New Hampshire Supreme Court over which he presided from 1876 to 1896 sheltered extreme shades of opinion, was burdened with some rather fainéant members, and became the target of unusually severe criticism. Yet it knew no periods of rancor, nor were there any outward signs of discord. This effect was only part of Doe's accomplishment. He did more than provide astute management; he gave his court remarkable leadership. He dominated that bench as few benches have been dominated in American legal history, and he forced his more conservative colleagues to swallow radical innovations about which they were far from enthusiastic.

Professor Hening, who interviewed several of Doe's associates, wrote that the chief justice looked upon each decision as a joint effort; that his correspondence with other members of his court probably consumed thousands of reams of paper, for he was constantly suggesting analogies, authorities, and lines of argument.[2] An example of this was his work in *State* v. *Gerry*.[3] He had assigned the job of drafting the opinion to Judge Carpenter. "It is his case," Doe wrote. Yet the notes which he himself circulated as helpful suggestions and informal "views" were in actuality a full-length opinion, which included headnotes.[4] Professor Leon Henderson has said that "By sheer weight of ability, learning and personality he dominated the Court."[5] Henderson might have also cited Doe's indefatigable drive and his insatiable insistence on settling every question to his own satisfaction. He literally flooded his colleagues with material which they could not ignore. By being the first to get his ideas on paper he guaranteed himself a fair hearing. The associate assigned to write the opinion would not encounter Doe's views as arguments contending with his own, but as a preliminary draft which could save him time and effort. Moreover, Doe painstakingly wrote in an unusually legible style.

This point may seem unimportant, but it cannot be overlooked when seeking the explanation for Doe's remarkable management of his court. He did everything possible to ease the burden on his colleagues. Speaking of Doe's manuscripts, Judge Isaac Smith recalled, "Every word was as legible as if in print, while there was absolute accuracy in the use of italics, quotation marks, and in punctuation. This was characteristic of the thoroughness with which all his work was done."[6] Doe left little for the others to do, and he certainly gave them no excuse for not reading what he had to say. He laboriously copied passages from New Hampshire statutes and cases which they could easily have looked up. In fact, when quoting a case Doe would not only give the volume and page of the citation, but at times might add that it came from the "middle of the page."[7] He even evaluated his own work in terms of usefulness. Across one nine-page memorandum he wrote, "Not to be read nisi anybody's appetite is not satisfied with the other papers."[8]

The extant manuscripts show that Doe did not spare himself for the printed page; he worked as hard to produce the polished phrase and the concise statement which he knew would not get beyond chambers as he did when preparing a decision for the official reports. Able to coin judicial slogans with the ease of the professional huckster, Doe was especially apt at creating a favorable climate for his ideas. One of his favorite expressions, "the New Hampshire method," he used to dispel the doubts and soothe the fears of hesitant colleagues. "But I suspect that, instead of paddling a little way near the shore for the purpose of this case, & starting on a voyage likely to be as crooked as the coast line between Portsmouth & Brazil, the New Hampshire method requires us to put out to sea, & take a straight course — at least much straighter than is laid down on the maps." [9] The "New Hampshire method" is the way he summed up his legal philosophy in chambers; he apparently never used the expression in his published opinions. It implied, as will be shown, a dislike for precedent and reliance on "justice" and "reason." As he wrote in one memorandum when discussing the use of House journals for discovering legislative intent, "The inconsistency & contradiction in the latest decisions of the highest federal court, & the unsatisfactory condition of the mass of authority, are such that it is apparently dangerous to go beyond an 'if' unless we take time to lay out a highway of reason according to the N.H. method." [10]

Doe was telling his colleagues that the best way to travel down the "highway of reason according to the N.H. method" was not only to discard but even to forget old maps. He urged them to call a spade a spade, to admit they were striking out in new directions, and not to dilute their decisions with false analogies or weaken their arguments by resting on inept authorities. "Purposes that are not practical need not be considered," he wrote in one court memorandum; "& the administration of justice gains nothing in accuracy or strength, or in the estimation of mankind, when a court pretends to deceive itself by distinctions & refinements that are merely verbal & therefore fictitious, or phrases that are purely metaphorical." [11] Doe constantly reiterated his philosophy in this manner. By using techniques of salesmanship which were in advance of his time he kept his colleagues aware, at least subconsciously, that theirs was a reform court.

Doe's technique of salesmanship was in marked contrast with that of Justice Holmes. Doe employed what might be called the "soft sell," while Holmes used the "hard sell." Holmes sometimes phrased his draft opinions in a manner calculated to annoy, expecting "the boys" to cut "one of the genitals . . . in the form of some expression that they think too free." [12] By sending up a red herring they were sure to shoot down, Holmes might "retain what he had all along intended." [13] Doe's tactics were different. He constantly expressed doubt concerning his own work, asking "was there an answer to this" or "can this stand up," thus placing the other judges on the defensive. He did not dangle "genitals" to divert their attention; instead, if he thought an idea too bitter for them to swallow, Doe covered it with a sugar coating, as when he persuaded the court to adopt his "burden of proof" theories by giving them the respectability of an honorable lineage in legal history. He used the soft sell to weaken the confidence of others. "He was," Hening wrote, "known to prevent dissents sometimes by the device of first agreeing with the dissenter and suggesting that the latter write a dissenting opinion in which he would agree to concur. A few days later Judge Doe would hunt up his companion and guide him to the anxious seat by suggesting new doubts and difficulties besetting the path of dissent and now apparently for the first time troubling his own mind. Finally after much struggling and wrestling he would effect their joint conversion." [14]

Doe tried to make criticism as painless as possible. His approach and tact, his interest and concern, can be gathered from a letter he wrote to a junior, Isaac N. Blodgett, in 1886. Blodgett had been assigned the *Hoitt Will Case*[15] and Doe was commenting on a draft Blodgett had sent him. The letter is worth quoting, for nothing else available is so revealing of his approach to opinion writing and the manner in which he handled his associates. It shows us how he labored over every word that went into an opinion, even when he was not its author; explains his theory that the court should aim the level of its writing at "the infants of the profession," the "dullest lawyers"; restates his belief in the apodictic summation at the end of a decision, an art in which he had few peers; and bares, almost embarrassingly, his technique of the "soft sell," combining criticism and a degree of flattery which he himself would have resented.

You have put it in the best form I can conceive of. You have a faculty for putting an argument in a condensed, clear, strong, judicial & most admirable form; & you ought to cultivate it assiduously. It is a rare talent of the highest rank, and capable of boundless development & expansion.

Your first sentence may seem inconsistent, in one particular, & in respect to one word, to the average reader. In the 2nd line the word "sound" will carry to many minds the idea of universal, & unlimited soundness of law as well as fact, including the ultimate result that a "sound" position is right, & the will should be disallowed. The clear headed lawyer would so understand it until he had read more of the opinion. When he got further on, he would see what you mean; but he would misunderstand your first 3 lines until his misunderstanding was corrected by reading further. And many who are not clearheaded (the majority) would be more or less confused.

I don't think you make quite allowances enough for the dullness of the ordinary mind of the profession; at least you don't allow so much on that score as I do. Much of my work is sharply criticized, by the brighter class, as being too rudimentary, & too much of a primer for a low grade of readers; but I doubt whether that complaint is made by the lower half of the profession.

To write a legal opinion which the dullest lawyer can easily understand at the first reading, & which no one will complain of as being too much adapted to infants, is no easy task. On many subjects, it is impossible to make the infants of the profession fully and clearly understand what we mean.

But when, by labor we can make everyone understand at first glance without revision of their first impression, & at the same time leave the opinion all right for such a man as Jerry Smith, it is best to make an effort in that direction, — the majority being, in facility of apprehension, a long way from Jerry.

Wouldn't something of that kind, at the end of the opinion, give the dullest reader a very clear, sharp & well-defined idea, which he might retain, in favor of the result you reach, although he could not retain in his mind the various steps of the legal argument on the construction of the act of 1822? And even for the brightest reader, wouldn't it give, in the last sentence, a short & simple idea of the fallacy of the def's specious argument about carrying the testator's intention into effect? & won't that idea be knocked further into the reader's head, & stay there longer in a well-defined shape, if it is vigorously presented in the very last line?

I bore you so long with this talk about words, not because you need it (I don't know anyone who needs it less), but by way of suggesting a general method of working an important opinion over & over again (especially its most important & effective passages). Nobody but Carpenter does it, & he sadly lacks your facility in vigorous & graceful composition.

It will not take many such opinions as yours in this case to put you at the head of the N.H. law writers; & when I find anybody capable of maintaining our standard among the foremost and highest, I can't help trying to help him even in the most trifling verbal matters of composition, whether he considers me officious & impertinent or not.

Your opinion was universally spoken of, by court & bar, as one of the best, if not the best, that has been heard in a long time. What tells the most is an opinion in the book, carefully studied by a few of the leaders of the bar who finish reading it with the remark "That is a masterly work of law & of art." Its popular & general value is fixed by the estimate put upon it by a very few of those who are admitted to be the best judges of such work; & their unqualified admiration is not won without hard work & a great deal of it. In your rapid ascent I bid you God-speed.[16]

Doe meant what he said — on another occasion he called Blodgett "one of the best law writers I know of." [17] Still, there was method in his praise. Only two or three other judges were dominated by Doe to the extent that he dominated Blodgett.

It must be obvious that Doe put no stock in the theory that a judicial opinion is the product and sole responsibility of the judge to whom it is assigned. He certainly had no truck with the notion which prevails today among some United States Supreme Court justices that they speak as individuals and owe it to their admirers to file concurring opinions whenever they disagree with the slightest aspect of the "official" pronouncement. To Doe, the author of an opinion spoke for the entire court. A colleague who thought a point needed clarification was expected to prepare a memorandum for the "author" to insert, with or without editing the language. He was not to fracture the opinion simply to show the world what ideas had originated with him. As Attorney General Eastman said, "Many of the opinions bearing the name of some other judge must have emanated in a large degree from the pen of the Chief Justice." [18] Indeed, others have suggested that he wrote many of the decisions credited to colleagues, partly because he did not want his own name to appear too often.[19] A student of Doe would not be hard pressed to name at least half a dozen. Eastman, who undoubtedly had inside information, suggested that one was *State* v. *Sanders*.[20] "Were it not for the astonishing fact recorded at the end of the opinion that 'Doe, C.J., does not sit,' no one would hesitate to say that every word emanated from the mind of [Doe]." [21] Jeremiah Smith, who sat with Doe on the court, describes an episode characteristic of the Doe manner:

It was not the least of Judge Doe's merits in the consultation room that he had not that excessive pride of opinion which handicaps so many men. Before the statute of 1874, the judges were accustomed to sit at the law term in cases where their own trial term decisions came up for revision. Some rulings made by Judge Doe upon a certain trial in Coös county were subsequently overruled at the law term. The opinion was read by Judge Nesmith, and he commented with unusual severity on the mistakes made at the trial. Mr. William Burns, the counsel whose exceptions were thus triumphantly sustained, hurried up to the bench and borrowed the manuscript of Judge Nesmith to gloat over at his leisure. What was his astonishment at finding that every word of the opinion was in the well-known handwriting of Judge Doe! [22]

What Smith does not make clear is that Judge Doe continued to write opinions anonymously even after passage of the statute of 1874 and that he did so in cases in which, under that statute, he was not supposed to participate. Perhaps such behavior was not completely ethical. Surely some lawyers would have been disturbed had they known their appeals were settled by a judge not present during their oral argument. Some of Doe's associates had qualms, even if he did not. Judge Chase was especially touchy about authorship, and he resisted Doe's attempts to force manuscripts on him. Chase had been assigned to write the opinion for an appeal in which it is recorded that "Doe, C.J., did not sit." Doe prepared an opinion of his own and sent it to Chase along with a letter accusing his colleague of being overly sensitive. He should not, Doe said, treat opinion writing as if it were literature designed to bring credit to the individual. That was neither "the judicial view nor the judicial tradition" in New Hampshire. Rather, an opinion is like "a resolution passed in town meeting," and the writer is merely an announcer.

You are the only judge, with whom I have been associated, abnormally & excessively squamish abot using other folks' ideas. When I came to the bench, & long afterwards, there was no hesitation in adopting anybody's ideas or language. Judge [Samuel Dana] Bell frequently mentioned the necessity of the practice. He said we were one body; the spokesman in each spoke not for himself but for the court, & was understood to say what he was told to say; his opinion was understood to be in form & substance, language & ideas — what the majority voted it should be, like a resolution passed in town meeting. The notion that an opn is the work of the man who reads it, is a recent & a very unfortunate growth. In this state, you are the only judge, except Jerry Smith, who has manifested any serious reluctance on this score. If you knew what has happened in my time, to my personal knowledge, in carrying Judge Bell's theory into effect, you would feel bound by precedent to regard as inappropriate, uncalled for & out of place, what you have once or twice written me as your feeling on this subject. I can understand how a sensitive person would feel on this point, if he regarded his reported opns as so many books on other subjects, published under his name as their author. But that is not the judicial view nor the judicial tradition in regard to the opns of the ct, wh are & are regarded as the opns of the ct & not of the judge who is directed by his associates to announce them.[23]

This, then, was Doe's approach to opinion writing. A self-effacing man in a profession of egotists, he nevertheless managed to dominate his colleagues in their deliberations. Without Doe they might have been a good court; with him they were a splendid one. To his acknowledged judicial courage, brilliance, and originality he added fantastic industry, infinite patience, and a remarkable ability for dealing with men to keep them moving down the path of justice according to "the New Hampshire method." To the legends of Doe as a trial judge and to his famous far-reaching opinions must be added his work in chambers when we total up his contributions to the law; they show that a great opinion writer does more than merely write his own opinions. "No case, large or small, escaped his eye. He was a great demolisher of legal fictions, but no greater fictions were ever invented in the dark ages than the one often appearing in the New Hampshire Reports — 'Doe, C.J., did not sit.' "[24]

This does not imply that Chief Justice Doe always got his way. He lost few arguments with his colleagues, but he did lose some. He had often been in dissent during his years as an associate judge. Some of his best work — such as the New Hampshire criminal insanity doctrine — grew out of intracourt battles. After 1876 the others seldom forced him into dissent. Nevertheless, they did not accept all his ideas. The bare record of a case gives no hint of the passionate disagreements which preceded its resolution. On at least one occasion Doe, barred from participation, had to suffer defeat in silence.

The action involved a petition for abatement of taxes filed by the Winnipiseogee Lake Cotton and Woolen Manufacturing Company against the town of Gilford. The issue was simple: what property interest subject to taxation did the plaintiffs own by their use of Lake Winnipesaukee* as a reservoir to provide power for their textile plant? The plaintiff's dam stood on an inlet called Long Bay at the head of the Winnipesaukee River, a tributary of the Merrimack. Since the Merrimack was the main artery of industrial New Hampshire, along which lay the mill towns of Franklin, Concord, Manchester, and Nashua (as well as Lowell, Lawrence, and Haverhill in Massachusetts), this dam, by regulating water levels, was of vital concern to most factories in the state.

The matter had been before the court on several occasions. In 1887, for example, while Doe was in Europe, Judge Carpenter had ruled that water power, or rights in a reservoir of water, are an interest in the land upon and by which they are created and are taxable in the town where the land is situated.[25] But just what constituted that "interest" in terms of rights and duties was still in controversy. Until it could be determined, a tax assessment acceptable to both sides was remote. After disposing of two preliminaries appealed in 1889 and 1891,[26] Chief Justice Doe decided to join Associate Justice Clark at the September 1892 trial term and to preside over what everyone hoped would be the final hearing on the matter. An unusual step for him, it shows the importance he attached to the question.

Following the conclusion of the trial, at which evidence of ownership was submitted by both parties, Doe and Clark ruled that under the original act of incorporation passed in 1831 the plaintiffs had not acquired, nor had the state parted with, "the title to the basin of Long Bay (which is a public water), or an indefeasible right to change the natural level of the water in the bay." The most granted by the charter (and a subsequent amending act passed in 1846 authorizing capital expansion) was "a perpetual right to a reasonable use of the lake as a reservoir and source of a reasonably uniform stream, for the improvement of the Winnepesseogee and Merrimack rivers." This construction of the legislature's intent, they said, was a possible basis of owner-

---

* For the remainder of this chapter the name of New Hampshire's largest lake is spelled four ways: 1) "Winnipiseogee," as it is spelled in the plaintiff's corporate charter; 2) "Winnepesseogee," as Doe spelled it in his manuscript opinion in the lower court; 3) "Winnipisseogee," as Doe spelled it in the intercourt memorandum and once in the opinion; and 4) when it does not appear in a quote it is spelled by today's usage — "Winnipesaukee."

ship for purposes of tax appraisal, but what it meant in terms of property interests held by the plaintiffs as against the state was another question.

If, by the true construction, the right above described was not granted, if the grant is revocable without compensation, or if, on any ground, the state, by the exercise of any other power than eminent domain, can stop the plaintiffs' reasonable use of the lake as a reservoir, or prevent their making reasonable changes in its natural level, the value of the plaintiffs' property is less than we have found it to be, and there should be another hearing. While the wrong that would be done by depriving the plaintiffs and the Winnepesseogee and Merrimack valley of the benefit of the improvement made by the plaintiffs, would be so apparent and so great as to afford a degree of moral assurance that it would not be done, the legal right of the state to do it would effect the value of the plaintiffs' water power and mill property in Gilford, as well as the value of all property benefited by the improvement in N.H. and Mass.[27]

The implications did not seem to worry the plaintiffs' attorneys. When the defendants appealed, the plaintiffs declared themselves "willing to accept the conclusions of the presiding justices upon the law" and moved "that decrees be entered accordingly." [28] But the reference to "moral assurance" balancing "the legal right of the state" showed that some matter troubled Judge Doe. Regardless of what the plaintiffs thought, Doe believed that the decision he and Clark had written threatened their interests.

Judge Doe knew that he himself had created the difficulties. Just three years before, in *Concord Manufacturing Co. v. Robertson,* he had laid down the rule that New Hampshire's great ponds and lakes belong to the people and are held by the state in trust for their common benefit. As will be shown, this case was the most extreme instance of Judge Doe's tendency to legislate. It established a doctrine of vast importance to lake-studded New Hampshire, which the chief justice used to strip littoral land owners of exclusive control over ponds which they had stocked, cleared, and maintained and which they had long believed their private property. This was probably all he had intended — to preserve New Hampshire's lakes and piscaries in common for all the people and to keep them from falling into the hands of a privileged few, as he believed had happened in England.[29]

It was apparently not until he began considering the *Gilford* case that the full implications of the doctrine dawned on Chief Justice Doe. In fact, it seems likely that for this reason he sat on the trial below — to help lay a proper factual foundation for the decision he wanted. Doe now realized what *Robertson,* carried to extremes, could mean. If ponds of over ten acres were held by the state in trust for the people, what right had private corporations to make them into reservoirs and raise and lower water levels whenever they pleased? If they had no definable property interest in these waters which could be protected in court, then New Hampshire's industrial enterprises would depend on the grace of the legislature for their power — a situation the chief justice (who based his constitutional tenets on a social-compact theory limiting the role of government and protecting the equality of property) would have deplored.

Doe and Clark had been aware of their dilemma. They also knew that on appeal the parties might ask the law term to settle the question of ownership. If that happened, the state should be heard, and so they ordered copies of their opinion sent to the governor and attorney general. The chief justice either did not trust the attorney general to act or lacked confidence in his ability to appreciate the problem, because a few weeks later Doe prepared an amicus brief for the government to submit. It is a remarkable document: the chief justice of the state was writing an argument to be used before his own court by a potential party in a litigation upon which he would be barred from sitting, since he had presided at the trial below. Whether Doe intended telling his colleagues the origin of the state's brief, had the attorney general submitted it, will never be known.

The manuscript is no mere collection of notes, arguments, or suggestions — it is a formal brief in every respect. Upon receiving it, all the attorney general had to do was sign his name at the end. Doe cited authorities in full, provided liberal quotations from cases, and referred to his own decisions in the third person. He did not even leave it to the attorney general to determine the state's interest, but decided for him what type of appearance to enter and upon what statutes to rely. From this introduction Doe went on to fill thirty-seven large sheets of paper in his meticulous clear handwriting, doctored with interlineations, alterations, and marginal notes.

The question the attorney general was supposed to worry might be settled in the state's absence related to the lower-court decision by Doe and Clark that the acts of 1831 and 1846 granted the plaintiffs a reasonable use of Lake Winnipesaukee as a reservoir. In *Robertson* it had been held that alienation of the title of the soil beneath a great pond or lake was "not an executive function." "It was," Doe stated in the brief, "assumed that the legislature have the power, but the question has not been settled or considered by the court." Adoption of his lower-court opinion that the legislature had made a limited grant would imply that it also had power to convey title in fee. Moreover, he went on, "If one of those rights can be alienated without a trial of this question, & without a decision of it in favor of the grantee, all of them can be given away, the state's title to the soil can be rendered worthless, & the entire beneficial interest of the public in inalienable trust property can be extinguished. There is no distinction but a verbal one between a conveyance of land, & a conveyance of all the rights in the land that can be useful to its owner." [30]

Judge Doe wanted the attorney general to argue that he and Clark had been wrong; that a careful reading of the plaintiffs' charters showed that nothing had been conveyed "but authority to do, as a corporate body, what they could have done as unincorporated partners . . . by exercising their private rights as landowners, without overflowing highways, or invading public rights or public property. No section, line or word of either act can be construed as a conveyance of land or an interest in land, or as evidence that such a conveyance was thought of." [31] This, Doe knew, placed the problem back where it had been at the start — what was the nature of the property interest which the plaintiffs owned (and the defendant taxed) by virtue of their right to use Lake Winnipesaukee as a reservoir and to raise and lower water levels?

Seeking the answer, Chief Justice Doe considered and rejected various solutions. He demolished, for example, the previously accepted rule, even though he had concurred when Chief Justice

Bellows laid it down in 1871. Calling it "the erroneous doctrine of an incidental private reservoir easement in public waters," Doe found that it did not stand up under examination. In *Robertson* he had suggested that a governmental grant of abutting land conveys no title to soil under a great pond even if the land entirely surrounds the pond. In a later case, he had said that a private owner of all the littoral property could not acquire title to the bed of a pond by prescription.[32] These pronouncements cut the ground from under Bellows' easement doctrine, even though Bellows had been careful to say that the easement did not depend upon prescription but was an incident to the land. Doe saw no way around the views he had expressed in *Robertson*, and in the amicus brief he had the attorney general deny the "soundness" of Bellows' easement theory and assert that it "must be regarded as overruled."

After thirty-eight pages Judge Doe had not only eliminated most possibilities but overruled the one theory of ownership that (at least for purposes of taxation) had been accepted in the past. He was quite discouraged. He had unqualified faith in the common law's ability to settle every problem without legislation, but now it was letting him down. This was doubly bad, for not only would the legislature have to straighten out the problem, a solution Doe intensely disliked, but it might pass a statute of an especially undesirable kind. As likely as not, some politicians would take advantage of the embarrassment in which mill operators would find themselves once the court held that they owned no interest in their reservoirs and would seek to win votes by making them pay exorbitant rates for privileges which, before *Robertson*, nobody had doubted belong to them. Judge Doe's constitutional tenets and ideas on government were involved in a question of this sort. There can be no doubt that he would have annuled any statute, no matter how popular, which tried to capitalize on the mill owners' predicament. But on what grounds?

Suddenly and unexpectedly Doe saw the answer. With high spirits and buoyant enthusiasm he broke off the amicus brief. The thirty-ninth page of the manuscript which contains the brief is written in the form of a note, dated on the morning of November 23, 1893. The chief justice had apparently passed a restless night, but now the concern and worry are over. A great load was lifted from his shoulders and he describes to himself the sheer joy of having found a solution:

The foregoing [i.e. the first 38 pages] was written with the idea that if it were presented to the court & the parties, as suggestions made in behalf of the state, & extended & applied by further suggestions according to the views entertained by the writer when the foregoing was written, the result might be that there would be judgment by agreement. The mischiefs of that result were apparent. Great interests would be left on no legal footing. Demagogues would be tempted to endeavor to induce the legislature to levy black mail on the great numbers of people who use ponds of more than 10 acres as reservoirs. But I saw no way of avoiding that result. After long & severe cogitation, a new light dawns. Judge Bellows was right. Everybody & everything is right. The law is equitable & wise, & clear as the sun, although I didn't apprehend it till after sunrise this morning. This change of view changes my whole plan. I will send this to Chase instead of the gentleman for whom it was written, changing the conclusion, & completing it according to the new light.[33]

Nowhere else can the reason for Judge Doe's judicial greatness be more clearly seen than in this note written during the early hours of a November morning. His insatiable quest for the proper solution to every legal issue is shown by the immense labor he poured into the first thirty-eight pages of the manuscript. His unselfish devotion to scholarship is shown by the fact that he intended his untiring research to be presented to the world as the work of the attorney general and in no way to add to his fame or credit. His love for the common law, something he stated on many occasions, is shown by the excitement with which he discovers that once again the answer to a difficult problem is to be found among its "wise" principles. And his belief that justice and reasonableness are the foundations of all true law is shown by the satisfaction he expresses now that the matter at hand can be settled in a manner equitable to all parties.

The "new light" dawned upon Chief Justice Doe while he was rereading his decision in the *Robertson* case. There was, as Bellows had said, an "established right of abutters to a reasonable private use of public waters." But Bellows' theory that the right was founded on an easement incidental to the land did not express the reason of the law. For the true explanation of the right, Doe turned to what he regarded the source of unwritten law — the usages and conditions of progressing society. As he expressed it, the right had been sanctioned by the "experience of more than 250 years." [34]

The private use of a large pond as a reservoir for manufacturing purposes by building a dam & opening & shutting gates at the outlet, differs materially from other rights of using the same pond which are incidents of abutting lands. But the difference is not a conclusive argument against the reservoir right. The private right of wharfing out for purposes of navigation, differs materially from other water rights vested in the littoral proprietors. Unlike as these rights are, they are all alike in one respect, — they are all confined within the bounds of reasonableness. Within that limit, no reason is perceived for denying the reservoir right "founded on necessity & convenience, & maintained by uniform usage," through the long period in which it has been so exercised that it would have been questioned and contested, if it had not been universally recognized as a legal right growing out of the situation & circumstances of the people which are one of the chief sources of the common law.

"This is the whole point of the case," he told his colleagues. "The fact of universal understanding & usage should be asserted in the broadest & strongest terms, unless you find on inquiry that the outlets of ponds of more than 10 acres have not been used, from the first settlements, by unincorporated & incorporated persons, without any legislative grant of reservoir rights in the ponds." [35]

If the court adopted this solution, then the ruling made by Clark and himself at the trial term, "that the plfs have 'a perpetual right to a reasonable use of the lake as a reservoir & source of a reasonably uniform stream' was correct, & the supposed derivation of the right from statutory construction instead of the common law, was an error that did not affect the legal merits of the case or the judgment that should be rendered." [36]

Doe pleaded with Judge Chase to adopt as his opinion the thirty-eight page amicus brief, which needed only a few omissions and a slight shifting of emphasis to serve as a judicial decision. "If I should be silent, it is possible that the enclosed views would not be brought to light," he wrote. "The interests involved in this & many other similar cases are so great, that it would be a serious mishap if any material view were overlooked. In this state of things I concluded to send enclosed to you. If you don't approve the views there presented, no harm will be done. If you do approve them, you must, for obvious reasons, present them as your own. Everything said in consultation is told out of doors; i.e. you must assume it will be unless everyone is interested not to tell it. Much mischief has been & will be done in that way." [37]

What happened thereafter is unknown. For some reason — either because he did not share Doe's sense of urgency or because he remained true to his principle of not using "other folks' ideas" — Chase ignored the manuscript. Instead of adventuring on the broad road of judicial legislation, which Doe would have taken, he followed the narrow path of judicial restraint, which was not on Doe's map. Just as Doe was the type of judge who could not resist creating new law when the need arose, Chase was the type of judge who could not resist settling matters on a technicality or a point of fact. He knew that Doe's prime violation of the tenets of decision writing was his practice of extending issues beyond conventional limits in order to widen the range of discussion. This was how the chief justice, who had much to say, squeezed far-reaching opinions from unchallenging fact patterns. Chase's main strength as a judge was that he did the opposite and confined issues to their proper limits. He knew he had nothing to say.

Anyone reading Judge Chase's opinion would have no idea of the toil and worry Chief Justice Doe had given to the matter of defining the property interest possessed by mill owners in reservoirs formed from great ponds and lakes. Indeed, it would be difficult to guess that the point had even been considered an issue. Chase relegated it to a point of procedure and dismissed it in his first three sentences.

The finding that the plaintiff's charter conveyed to them rights in the lake, as stated in the case, is favorable to the defendants. Its tendency was to increase the market value of plaintiffs' real estate. The defendants have no occasion to object to it; and the plaintiffs have waived their objection by moving for decrees. [38]

Later, in the body of the opinion when discussing an issue of evaluation, Chase added: "This control of the lake as a reservoir is limited within the bounds of reasonableness, having reference to the rights of riparian owners upon the rivers forming its outlets." [39]

The only remnant of Judge Doe's labor was tucked away in the "Statement of Facts," so obscure and subtle as to go almost unnoticed. In the unpublished lower-court opinion Doe and Clark had stated that the legislature, by the acts of 1831 and 1846, had "granted to the plaintiffs a perpetual right to a reasonable use of the lake as a reservoir and source of a reasonably uniform stream, for the improvement of the Winnepiseogee and Merrimack Rivers." [40] In the "Statement of Facts" the court reporter, or Doe, or perhaps even Chase, changed this to read:

It was held that the state, by the acts of 1831 and 1846, granted to the plaintiffs a perpetual right to a reasonable use of the lake as a reservoir and source of a reasonably uniform stream for the improvement of the mill privileges upon Winnipiseogee and Merrimack rivers, *subject to the limitation that the right of navigation upon the lake should not be unreasonably impaired thereby, and also subject to the right of the owners of mill privileges upon said rivers to have the water of the lake come down its natural course, without unreasonable diminution or an unreasonable degree of irregularity caused artificially.*[41]

The words here italicized were taken from that part of Doe's memorandum written originally as an amicus brief for the attorney general. They state the principle of ownership which the chief justice wanted to establish, but they do not explain the theory of social usage upon which it is based. And of course they meant little, for even if the principle of reasonable use were noticed and its importance appreciated by the bar, the opinion makes clear that it was not adopted as law in New Hampshire. At the very most, it rested on a judgment at the trial term; a judgment founded on an erroneous construction of the acts of 1831 and 1846.

By most standards Judge Chase was right and Chief Justice Doe wrong. At least Chase showed himself a more faithful adherent to the common-law process. The usefulness of the judicial decision, after all, is limited to the facts of each case, and its function is to settle controversies which arise in bona fide actions between competent parties. As Chase knew, an opinion's utility is jeopardized when it becomes a peg for solving potential problems not yet in litigation. This was too confining for Charles Doe. The function of a common-law judge, he believed, is to make law with bold strokes and not to avoid issues by using technicalities. In that New Hampshire of 1893 large business enterprises, involving thousands of people and vast expenditures, were caught in a legal dilemma resulting from the discovery that private rights in reservoirs may conflict with the public ownership of great ponds. Was it not, he asked, the duty of the court to set minds at ease and avoid expensive litigation by declaring, at the first opportunity, the correct principle of property law which solved the dilemma? His critics — and there were many — would have answered no; that the chief justice should have learned a lesson from the consequences of his decision in *Robertson.* Had Doe restrained himself there, had he not deliberately formulated a new rule of substantive law uncalled for by the facts of that case, the dilemma would never have existed. Judge Doe believed that one of the evils of legislation was that it bred the need for more legislation. His critics could have said that he had proved the same of judicial legislation.

Perhaps this was what Chase told him; that he had gone too far and that the time had come to call a halt. Chase may have been awed by Doe's industry and sympathetic with his desire to rewrite New Hampshire law according to the dictates of reason, but he refused to be the instrument through which Doe formulated the doctrine of reasonable usage for private reservoirs in public waters. It is mainly because he created law in this manner that Charles Doe is remembered as one of the greatest judges in American legal history. Judge Chase is remembered because he was an associate of Chief Justice Doe.

PART FOUR

THE
CONSTITUTIONAL THEORIST

Chapter Sixteen

THE FIRST CHAPTER
OF THE CONSTITUTION
Civil Rights

FOR the biographer of a state judge no topic is more difficult than constitutional law. Constitutional issues do not crowd state dockets as they crowd federal dockets, and since most American judicial biographies deal with federal judges, tradition has made the subject a main area of discussion. Convention as well as interest require that attention be devoted to constitutional decisions. This is justified in the case of Chief Justice Doe only because the extraordinary length of his service on the New Hampshire bench made it possible for him to develop a unique body of constitutional doctrine.

There is also an historiological problem. When judicial biographers venture to treat constitutional matters, they usually concentrate on issues which divide their own generation. Today, for example, they are apt to emphasize civil rights. This is rendered fair, and placed within the canons of the historical method, when the writer reminds his readers not to judge the decisions of yesteryear by the standards of today. But the emergent picture is still distorted, since the biographee is presented to posterity in terms of passions he could not have felt and issues never called to his attention. This cannot be avoided, for if history — and especially legal history — is to be made meaningful and to serve a pragmatic function, it should join in the search for answers to the questions of its own time. Yet something is amiss when a topic, presently rife, is magnified in isolation from its original context and thrust upon stage center to be accorded an importance it never before enjoyed. Issues which during their own epoch were in the limelight are brushed into relative obscurity, and the fact that it was on them that earlier judges bent their best efforts is forgotten now that the heat of battle has been dissipated by the cool airs of solution. But answers can still be found in the struggle for civil rights long since waged, and inspiration is to be drawn from analogies and precedents both won and lost. The crosscurrents of American constitutional law provide a greater degree of changeless continuity than is usually revealed by the topical approach to historical comparison.

Charles Doe's work in the civil-rights field is a case in point. A recent comment has dismissed his views on personal liberties as wedded to nineteenth-century concepts of equality and to a discarded theory concerning the limitations of government.[1] The implication is that his decisions hold meaning only for a less troubled era and reflect the needs of a more simple economy. On the other hand, those contemporaries who became Doe's biographers did not even mention his decisions dealing with the bill of rights, which simply did not seem significant at that time. Thus at both ends of the historical ladder Chief Justice Doe's views concerning law and human freedom have been ignored, not so much because men thought them wrong or untenable, but because every historian must make a value judgment concerning the pertinency of material. What Doe had to say on the subject of civil rights then seemed overstressed and now seems misdirected. Both appraisals are wrong: civil rights can never be overstressed, and Doe's opinions are even more pertinent to today's issues than they were to those of his own times.

Judge Doe fought great battles on behalf of civil rights. But his rulings tell only part of the tale. More significant are the passionate sense of urgency with which he pleaded man's cause against the state and the techniques he used. He placed liberty on an impregnable foundation by his method of constitutional construction, and he did so by making John Locke's theory of the social compact the measure of New Hampshire's organic law. Surprising as it may be, he had solid legal as well as theoretical argument for doing this. The founding fathers had written the social compact into at least six sections of the constitution. These provisions, Doe claimed, justify calling the constitution a "social compact." [2] He passed no judgment on Locke's thesis. For legal purposes it is of no consequence that political scientists question the whole idea.[3] "Whether this is or is not the true theory of government in general, it is, in its legal sense, a statement of New Hampshire theory, sufficiently accurate for legal purposes. It is the theory which the people of this state, in 1783, voted to adopt, and which, since that time, has been the constitutional theory that the court is bound officially to support." [4]

Because he viewed the social compact as political theory which the court must accept but need not justify, Chief Justice Doe did not bother to define it. At most he restated it, either by paraphrasing the constitution or by summarizing Locke:

Locke's statement of it is, Men being, by nature, all free, equal, and independent, no one is subjected to the political power of another without his own consent: the only way whereby anyone divests himself of his natural liberty, and puts on the bonds of civil society, is by agreeing with other men to join and unite into a community for the preservation, security, and enjoyment of their lives, liberties, and estates. Thus the origin of government is in mutual consent or contract, and its object is the common benefit. Men, when they enter into society, give up rights which they had in the state of nature into the hands of the society, to be exercised for the preservation of themselves, their liberty, and their property.[5]

In place of political definition, Judge Doe turned to the law of contracts. As he put it, the government of New Hampshire had been formed "by the mutual contract of the people." [6] "It is the theory of the constitution that government originates from the people, is founded in consent, and created by a mutual contract." [7] Since Doe never had occasion to develop a common-law theory of contracts, he may have thought it unnecessary to formulate a constitutional theory. When deciding commercial matters, he usually was able to turn problems of definition into issues of construction by saying that a contract is "the ascertainment of the fact of the parties' intention from competent evidence." [8] Transposing this to constitutional interpretation, Doe construed the social compact as he would have construed an ordinary business contract. "The people having voluntarily agreed with each other to form themselves into a body politic, the legal meaning of the written agreement is their intention and understanding, shown by competent evidence." [9] They are the "grantors," [10] the constitution is the "grant," [11] and government officials are the "grantors' agents." [12]

Political scientists may think Doe's dependence on legal orismology unimaginative — proof that the law-trained man is trapped by the traditional thought patterns of his profession. There are two reasons why this belief does not hold true. One is that Locke, while not a lawyer, had himself phrased the social compact in concepts which, if not borrowed from the doctrines of English common law and equity, were at least easily adaptable to them. [13] The second is that Doe deliberately chose legal terminology; that he did so is his chief contribution to the cause of civil liberty. For he recognized that the social-compact argument can be used to guarantee the immutability of the bill of rights.

By the ordinary rules of constitutional construction, under which a constitution is organic law, not a social contract, the government is held to have inherent powers limited by certain enumerated provisions (as, for example, the federal Bill of Rights). In such a case, when the liberty of a citizen is pitted in litigation against the authority of the state, the citizen must depend on specific wording in the organic law to prove that he is protected and the government powerless. To make the constitution a "grant," on the other hand, leaves no room for inherent sovereign power. Whatever authority the state enjoys is "manufactured" — created by the people through the social compact. [14] By starting with the theory that the government, under the "contract," is an agent, while holding that the privileges of the citizen are absolute except when specifically surrendered by that "contract," Judge Doe relieved the citizen of the burden of proving that the government's power is limited. Instead, the burden falls upon the state to prove that it has been delegated the authority which it claims to exercise.

Today we seek to curb government by emphasizing a widening area of individual immunities grouped within a not very precise category called "civil rights." Judge Doe was more exact. "Civil privileges," he wrote, are those "which society has engaged to provide in lieu of the natural liberties so given up by individuals" under the "contract." [15] Personal freedom is thus placed in the strongest possible position, for in the state of nature liberty was absolute. The function of a constitution, therefore, is not to define the state's power. To see the constitution as a "contract," not merely as organic law, is to acknowledge that governmental authority is designed primarily to protect civil liberty;[16] even the principle of separation between the three branches of government has as its main function the preservation of "private rights." [17]

This last point may seem theoretical, but again Doe was on solid ground. In New Hampshire separation of powers is not a theory implied in the constitution by an arrangement dividing governmental authority; rather, it is a right guaranteed the people by the bill of rights. It is to Doe's credit that he recognized this and that he was bold enough to act upon it. Indeed, it epitomizes the spirit of Doe's constitutional interpretation. The bill of rights must not be treated as an adjuvant of the constitution — it is the heart of the constitution; the blueprint of liberty. "The bill of rights," Doe argued, "is a bill of their equal, private rights, reserved by the grantors of public power." [18] While it might more properly be called "the declaration of rights," [19] it is best understood as a "reservation," [20] made by the people of New Hampshire when they entered into the social compact. "By the reservation they limited their grant, and exempted themselves, to the stipulated extent, from the authority of the government they created." [21] This would be true even without the social-compact theory, because of the position of the bill of rights in the New Hampshire constitution. Unlike the federal constitution, for example, the New Hampshire bill of rights is not a series of amendments glossed on at the end as a belated afterthought. If anything, it is a qualifying preamble, a point Charles Doe strongly stressed. Before creation of the government, he observed, the people "lay the foundation, and therein reserve those personal liberties, which, upon the evidence of history and their own experience, they think cannot safely be surrendered to government." [22] Partly for this reason, though more especially for its preferred position in legal theory, Doe called the bill of rights "the first chapter of constitutional law." [23]

No enumerated right is trifling or conjectural. All civil liberties are absolute — an axiom which caused Judge Doe to insist on prophylactic safeguards many contemporaries thought excessive. Nowhere is this more evident than in his dissenting opinion in *Orr* v. *Quimby*. The defendant, a United States government surveyor, had entered upon and despoiled the plaintiff's property, cutting down and removing timber while making a survey of the Atlantic coastline pursuant to an act of Congress. In reply to the plaintiff's suit for damages, the defendant relied on a statute, passed by the New Hampshire legislature, authorizing entry upon private property for purposes of conducting the survey. The plaintiff contended that the statute was unconstitutional because it did not require an assessment of damages, and payment or tender of the sum assessed, *before* entry and injury to the land. The Supreme Court held the statute constitutional. "It is clear," Judge Hibbard wrote for the majority, "that, in cases in which it is impossible to ascertain the amount of damages in advance, a reasonable certainty of payment is all that should be required." [24] Doe was the lone dissenter.

Judge Doe admitted that his colleagues were probably correct in assuming that the state would eventually pay the plaintiff. But he thought their opinion irrelevant. "It relates to the future," he pointed out; "the confiscation is past. The wrong was committed some time ago." If a right is involved in a proceeding of this type, it is the right of a landowner not to have his property seized without compensation; not his right to payment at some future date.[25] The majority expressly recognized the right to compensation, but by leaving payment to the option of the government, they converted it from a legal into a moral right and denied the plaintiff legal justice. "The legal character of his right," Doe asserted, "is destroyed by the confidence of the court in the integrity and solvency of the public." [26] It is not secure and, not being secure, is not given the protection to which it is entitled as a constitutional right. The court's decision placed the plaintiff in the same predicament in which he would have been if there were no constitution or if the bill of rights provided that "Private property may be taken for public use without compensation." [27]

The difficulty lay in the fact that the New Hampshire constitution said nothing about compensation for eminent domain. Earlier judges had not troubled themselves with whether the point might be covered by some broad reservation even though not specifically mentioned. "Natural justice," they said, "speaks on this subject, where our constitution is silent."[28] The idea seems to have pleased everyone except Doe. "This is not a fit predicament for such a rule to be in," he asserted.[29] Either the right of each citizen to be secure in his property against the government exists as a reservation in the constitution or it does not exist at all. "Nothing so strict as a literal construction, or so loose as a general spirit, but the text, understood in the reasonable sense in which it would be likely to be understood by those who proposed and those who ratified it, is the constitution that was adopted and established by the popular vote. If it forbids the robbery of the citizen by the public authority, we may be sure the prohibition can be found in plain words. . . . Is there a single clause, or any number of clauses, by the plain meaning of which such robbery is prohibited?"[30]

Judge Doe found the answer in article two of the bill of rights, which provides: "All men have certain natural, essential, and inherent rights — among which are, the enjoying and defending life and liberty; acquiring, possessing, and protecting property; and, in a word of seeking and obtaining happiness." This article, Doe said, had been administered as a limitation on the legislative power to interfere with the natural right of "protecting" property, and "must be an equally operative reservation of the natural and common-law right of 'acquiring' and 'possessing' property."[31] "The power of eminent domain, or the public right of taking private property for public use by compulsory purchase, is not expressly granted. If it is a part of the general power of making constitutional laws, it is bounded by the reservation of the private right of ownership. . . . Neither the general power of constitutional legislation, nor the special power of taking property for public use, can, by robbing an individual under pretence of a compulsory purchase, override his reserved right of owning property."[32]

Orr v. *Quimby* sums up Judge Doe's position regarding the bill of rights and gives substance to his techniques for vindicating the liberties of individual citizens. It is, true enough, a dissenting opinion, yet it enjoyed wide influence during the remainder of the nineteenth century, for with time Doe's theories concerning the social compact came to dominate New Hampshire constitutional thinking. Under Chief Justice Doe's probing the right or reservation of equality became the cornerstone of constitutional jurisprudence, as will be discussed in the next chapter. His words concerning equality sound dated to post-New Deal lawyers, for he expounded a degree of equality which passed from the American legal scene with the advent of the progressive income tax. The same is true regarding his emphasis on the right to private property. By making protection of property against the public the chief function of the doctrine of equality, he gave attention to an individual privilege which has lost substance in recent years. It is little wonder, therefore, that the casual reader of his opinions might think his efforts on behalf of the bill of rights misdirected, or at least bearing no particular meaning for today's struggle over civil liberties. A conclusion such as this would be a misreading of Doe and an abuse of history. Chief Justice Doe made economic equality and private property the central theme of his defense of the absolutist theory of the bill of rights because they were the issues presented to his court by the economy of nineteenth-century New Hampshire. He took constitutional cases as they came and did the best he could with the fact situations which accident and circumstance called upon him to resolve. If he carried the doctrine of equality to an extreme, it was in order to vindicate all the fundamental liberties of the people. The unquestioned aim of law, he felt, is equality of rights, privileges, and capacities.[33] If he had been alive during the early 1960s Doe would have been inclined to regard the so-called freedom riders as misnamed. They should, in his terminology, more properly be called "equality riders." Equality is what they were really seeking.

Of course the equality sought by today's civil libertarians is not related to, but is in many ways a denial of, the right Doe was defending in *Orr. v. Quimby* — the right to private property. By tieing the doctrine of equality to the absolute security of private property, he removed himself in substance, not just in degree, from the philosophical tenets of today's more narrowly based concept of the bill of rights as a weapon for aiding special classes and groups. But again it would be an abuse of the historical method to evaluate Doe's attitudes toward current issues by his statements in the 1880s. He simply was not faced by a comparable situation. The fact that he believed absolute equality and absolute rights in private property inseparable furnishes no clue as to what attitude he would have adopted had he been asked to resolve twentieth-century issues which place equality and property in a framework which makes them incompatible. What Chief Justice Doe did, however, and what makes his theory concerning the bill of rights still of vital concern today, was to stress a truth which the United States Supreme Court and other apostles of civil liberty have forgotten: he recognized and sought to preserve the basic interdependence of the various reservations contained in the bill of rights.

It has become a dominant trend of thought lately that there are certain rights more fundamental than others — that there is, for example, a "firstness" to the first amendment.[34] Charles Doe would have rejected this notion. He believed in a "firstness" to the entire bill of rights; that it forms the "first chapter of constitutional law" in every sense. All rights are absolutely fundamental, since all had been reserved equally by the people when they made their grant of governmental power. That he gave more emphasis to the right of private property, and tied it more closely than other rights to the doctrine of equality, was due to two factors. The first was that most constitutional cases appealed to his court had to do with matters of taxation or confiscation by the state. The second was that he believed the right to private property was the one reservation then in danger in New Hampshire. Subscribing to a "falling dominoes" concept of defense, Doe concentrated on bolstering the right to property — the right currently under attack — as the best means of defending the entire bill of rights. This was why even the seemingly insignificant issue in *Orr* v. *Quimby* of encroachment on the plaintiff's land for the temporary purpose of making a survey had such importance. "If the right of property," he wrote in that case, "is not reserved the whole bill of reserved rights is a schedule of a general unconditional capitulation." [35] The right to property "could not have been more clearly retained; and if it is not inviolable, there is no constitutional right of any kind, and it is impossible to put in writing a reservation of rights that could not easily be changed into a surrender of them by judicial construction." [36] He summed up his position when he said, "If the plaintiff can be thus plundered, the legal rights of liberty and life are purely imaginary, for the reservation of these is no stronger than the reservation of the right of property." [37] In their haste to vindicate rights which are currently fashionable, the twentieth-century members of the federal judiciary have rejected, for better or worse, this interdependent concept of basic rights with which the nineteenth-century Chief Justice of New Hampshire attempted to safeguard all the liberties reserved by the people.

Judge Doe never claimed that private ownership of property was the highest right protected by the bill of rights. He merely insisted it be entitled to the same vigilance given those of a more political nature. He realized that it could, on occasion, collide with others and that one would have to be accorded priority. The occasion was rare in his court, but when it occurred, he did not hesitate to place such rights as freedom of religion above the right to property.

This result can hardly be surprising. Doe took a strong stand on the issue of separation of church and state. Opposition to public aid for sectarian schools, as has been shown, was part of his political creed.[38] He thought the church would be endangered more than the government, and he could not understand why some religious leaders were willing to risk their independence for the sake of monetary gains. "[A]n evangelical church, claiming an origin and character divine, in the supernatural sense, does not profane what it holds sacred by affixing itself forever to a society of human invention, binding itself to accept such teachers as that society may select through the vicissitudes of succeeding generations, and subjecting to a secular power the rights and the existence which it professes to hold by a divine and inalienable title. It does not voluntarily sink into an endless servitude so inconsistent with its pretensions, its faith, and its view of its own mission and the vital interests of mankind. . . . A church of any supernatural religion, choosing to be annexed by an inseverable tie to any human institution, like a fixture or a serf bound to the manor, would be a strange thing." [39] Perhaps so, but it was not strange to many upright citizens who saw the faith and the moral standards of the Puritans deteriorating all about them. Sin was common in the secularism of post-Civil War New Hampshire, especially the sin of drink. Men of piety could be forgiven if they recalled a society of saints back in the days when God's elect maintained His vigil, back before Isaac Hill and William Plumer disestablished the Congregational Church. As a judge, Doe could not argue with their dreams. Instead he questioned their history. Union of church and state was not only undesirable now, he argued, but had never been part of the New Hampshire way of life.

The history of religious liberty in New Hampshire was, in 1868, obscured by hearsay and legend. The official connection between the state and the Congregational Church had been dissolved, but confusion reigned as men, who had grown up in a community based on "Association," turned to the courts for clarification of the new order. Difficulties arose from the fact that disestablishment coincided with the emergence of Unitarianism. As Unitarian Congregationalists separated from Trinitarian Congregationalists, there were, inevitably, legal contests as to which was heir to the old society's property. In Massachusetts, where the union of church and state had been particularly strong, the judges had undertaken to settle common-law trust litigations by deciding which group was the successor to Puritan New England's orthodox theology. Naturally enough, their method began to seep into New Hampshire law.

The idea of an officially recognized religious body aroused Charles Doe. Determined to wipe all vestiges of the tradition from New Hampshire jurisprudence, and to free the court from the Massachusetts error of deciding property questions on doctrinal rather than on legal grounds, Doe devoted six months to the study of theology.[40] His explanation of the union between Congregationalism and colonial New Hampshire accommodates itself to nineteenth-century ideas of democracy and twentieth-century notions concerning the separation of church and state. Doe contended that the close cooperation and identity, during colonial times, between the civic body (town or parish) and the Congregational Church, could be explained by the fact that all were of the same faith, not "by a sacrilegious covenant unwittingly made," by early Puritan fathers, "in an inscrutable manner, never written or spoken by its makers, never heard of during the first two centuries of New England history, and never acquiesced in after it was heard of." No legal relationship had been contemplated or adopted. "The unity of spirit," he said, "had been the bond of peace." [41] Just as the town meeting had sprung up as a natural result of the native conditions of early New England, so too had the idea that the people of each town might select the form of worship they would follow. The essential factor was that, while the colony officially supported the religion selected by democratic process in each parish, it endorsed no creed or body of theology. It sanctioned a mode of ecclesiastical government, not a form of ecclesiastical worship. "The fundamental principle of parochial independence, established as the general law of the land, confirmed the natural right of each society to govern itself, and to choose and change its minister, and its religion, — the right of the majority to rule the parish in all ecclesiastical affairs. . . . It was religion established by law, but it was such religion as the majority of each town or other parish might choose and change every day in the year. It was, among other things, the right of apostasy. . . ." [42]

With this sweep of historical theory, Doe hoped to steer the court away from the quicksands of theological debate. By freeing the constitution of the suspicion that it had established Congregational sectarianism (not merely the Congregational covenant within a democratic context), he felt that there would be no need, and even less excuse, for settling legal issues by religious dogma or religious disputes by legal tribunals. The separation between state and church would become an actuality in fact as well as in principle.

In attempting to persuade his colleagues to accept this view of history, Doe was up against the fact that the bill of rights, while it reserved equal protection of the law to "every denomination of Christians, demeaning themselves quietly," laid special emphasis on the need to maintain Protestant teachers in public schools. Moreover, the constitution itself contained sections prohibiting major political office to anyone but a Protestant. While both provisions were, to a large extent, dead letters, at least for Roman Catholics and atheists, they were nonetheless still in the state's organic law, lending strength to the tradition of an official church-state relationship.

Doe challenged that tradition in the celebrated case of *Hale* v.

Everett. The issue was whether the Reverend Francis E. Abbott should be permitted to preach in the meeting house of the First Unitarian Society of Christians in Dover, the church of which Doe, while living in Dover before his marriage, had been a member. According to plaintiff's petition, Abbott, while pastor of the society, had announced he was not a Christian in the strict sense of the word and had declared "his disbelief in the doctrine of the Lordship and Messiahship of Jesus, and that the writings of some men now living are as highly inspired and as sacred as the Bible, and declared the doctrine 'that whenever a human soul has uttered its sincere and brave faith in the divine, and thus bequeathed to us the legacy of inspired words, there is the Holy Bible'. . . ." [43] If Abbott intended to shock the good people of Dover, he was wonderfully successful. The parish split over the issue of rehiring him, and after several bitter meetings, at which most of the congregation, if not the entire town, was present, his followers elected wardens whom they authorized to make a contract with the minister. The opposition then turned to the court and asked that the wardens be "jointly and severally strictly enjoined and forbidden to hire, employ, allow, suffer, or permit said Francis E. Abbott, or any other person, to preach and inculcate in the meeting house of said society doctrines subversive of the fundamental principles of Christianity, as generally received and holden by the denomination of Christians known as Unitarians; or to employ, suffer, or permit to preach in said meeting house any person who rejects Christianity altogether." [44]

This is surely one of the most amazing actions ever filed in a New Hampshire court — a prayer to enjoin "doctrines subversive of the fundamental principles of Christianity." How could a court enforce such an injunction, let alone define its terms? The majority of the supreme court knew it had to be done. Duty bound "to see that a trust or charity is administered according to the intention of the original founders," they granted the injunction. Judge Doe filed a dissent which ran to 143 pages.

Speaking for the court, Chief Justice Sargent stressed Abbott's renunciation of Christ as the Messiah and his rejection of Christianity. That this action involved a judicial determination of what it meant to be a "Christian" did not abash him. He paid no heed to the fact that men who called themselves "Christians" had elected Abbott their pastor. Nor did he comment on the constitutional right to freedom of religion. Rather he assumed authority to brand Abbott a non-Christian in law and enjoined him, and anyone else whom the defendants might hire, from preaching in the Unitarian church of Dover.

The majority thought themselves on solid ground. The meeting house and the other possessions of the parish were held in trust to support a true ministry, not to propagate heresy. Accepting basic legal premises, what was more logical than to protect the trust? This was exactly the type of reasoning which Doe believed endangered civil rights. Subordinating the matter of church property (fundamental though it might be in a different context) to the issues of religious liberty, he argued that they had decided a question, not of law, but of theology. By its very nature the subject was too sensitive for a court, sitting in a free society, to handle, and this case proved it. For what had the majority done to protect the trust property? They had done the only thing which they could do and the very thing which made it constitutionally advisable not to act at all. They had measured Abbott by their own concepts of the divinity of Christ and had, like an ecclesiastical court of old, found him a heretic.

Unless Abbott's religion is unconstitutional, the majority of the Dover parish, in allowing him to preach it "in the meeting-house of said society," did what they had a constitutional right to do. We cannot adjudge his faith to be a heretical departure from a state religion until we destroy the constitution, establish a state religion, and annex a supreme bishopric to the judicial office. If we condemn this man as a heretic, and his religion as an offense against the state . . . we can anathematize and outlaw any other person, and any other form of religion. Abbott's cause, strenuously opposed in the field of theology, becomes, in law, the common cause of religious liberty, and the indestructible interest of mankind. The decree cannot be aimed at him until it batters down constitutional bulwarks, erected by our ancestors for the defence of a possession, which, through ages of suffering and struggle, cost too much, and, after being long enjoyed in apparent safety, has been found worth too much, to be voluntarily surrendered.[45]

Judge Doe summed up his arguments in four sentences:[46] (1) The bill of rights reserves to the towns, parishes, or religious societies in the state the right "to make adequate provision, at their own expense, for the support and maintenance of public Protestant teachers of piety, religion, and morality." [47] (2) The power, if limited at all, is limited only by the Protestant test. (3) Abbott is a Protestant according to the constitutional meaning of that word. And (4) the pro-Abbott wardens of Dover's Unitarian Church were constitutionally within their rights when they elected him one of their public teachers.

These four logically arranged points contain the cold legal considerations upon which Doe based his dissent. But transcending them was the higher principle, the all-important issue of religious liberty, which the majority refused to acknowledge even though Judge Doe thrust it upon them in the most emotional judicial opinion which he ever wrote. "These questions," he pleaded, "concern interests of greater consequence than the doctrinal sermons to be preached, by leave of the court, in the meeting-house of this parish." His sarcasm was biting, but to no avail. His associates did not think Abbott's successor would take his place "by leave of the court." Nor did they see how their decision, which kept the trust property of a Christian parish safely out of the reach of a preacher who disowned Christianity, involved what Doe called "the comprehensive birthright of religious freedom and equality." [48]

Isolated in his position, and fervently believing himself to be upholding a fundamental liberty, Judge Doe ended his long dissent with one of the most memorable and ringing defenses of religious freedom ever penned by an American jurist.

When an infidel does not stand as well in law before the tribunals of justice as a Christian, in any sense of the word, our free institutions are a failure. To sneer at free-thinkers or free thought is to make a thoughtless use of free speech, and to scoff at a privilege which we are bound to protect. The constitution does not assume to create religious rights or to distribute them. It reverently recognizes and maintains them as original and universal, as rights which human government can neither grant nor withhold, which are not of human tenure, and which no man can give up. A single unresisted infringement, established as a precedent, subjugates the weak, and leaves them at the mercy of the strong. Every man and every parish is liable to hold unpopular theological opinions. And when the right to hold and inculcate such opinions is not sacred, and the violation of it is

not sacrilege; when the constitutional defences of that right are dis-
mantled, and it is left with no better security than the generosity and
tolerance of an ecclesiastical court, or the caprice of a ruling class;
when freemen are reduced to the consolation of remembering that
the writ for burning heretics is not obsolete, and of hoping that civilization will not suffer it to be revived, — the theory of our government
is exploded and its original authority at an end.[49]

It may be that some will think these words too warm to fit
the occasion, because Doe is defending not so much the separation of church and state in twentieth-century terms as the mere
cause of parochial freedom. But if Doe overstated his case, he
overstated the case for religious liberty, and this he would never
have acknowledged. Seeking to vindicate and preserve the constitutional right of religious apostasy, Charles Doe spoke the language of constitutional absolutism just as he had when he was defending the right of a landowner to prior compensation when
property is seized by the state. That he placed one right on a
higher level than the other is shown by the fervor of his words,
yet he was too shrewd a constitutionalist to have openly admitted
it. All civil liberties were equal because all were protected by the
same provisions of the constitution. If one is weakened or subordinated, all are weakened and subordinated.

Judge Doe's most valuable service to the cause of civil liberties
is the fact that his ideas concerning the fundamental guarantees
of the bill of rights are to be found mostly as *dicta* or in dissenting opinions. It was in this way that a great judge sitting on the
court of a small rural state was able to show his attachment to
the ideals of individual freedom. It is to be regretted that his
work has been forgotten, for his stress upon the absolutism of
each reservation has been echoed in recent years by such men as
Hugo Black and William O. Douglas, and what he had to say is
still pertinent in our era. They have recognized many rights
which he might have missed, and few would contest that they
may be more accomplished constitutionalists than he. But Doe
was a more subtle legal tactician and knew that liberty cannot
rest securely on the interpretation of mere words. His mastery of
the legal technique led him to seek firmer ground, and it is proof
of his genius that he rejuvenated the shopworn concepts of the
social compact. By adopting the revolutionary theory of the

ounding fathers, he converted the bill of rights from statutory exceptions to governmental powers into reservations withheld before the state was created, and he made it in every sense the first chapter of the constitution.

Chapter Seventeen

THE SUBSTANCE
OF THE CONSTITUTION
The Doctrine of Equality

WHEN interpreting civil liberty Charles Doe maintained a
marvelous consistency. The social compact had created absolute
privileges; therefore the privileges of the common man, even
when they conflict with governmental power, are absolute. But
not all constitutional issues are susceptible to such dogmatic
solution — on some questions the social compact theory demands
a finer line than Doe was able to draw, as he discovered with the
doctrine of equality.

The doctrine of equality is bone and marrow of Doe's social-
compact theory. Since all men had been equal in the state of nature and had "contracted" on equal terms to obtain equal privileges, it follows that equality is the principle "upon which our
institutions are founded." [1] Besides, it was clearly expressed in
the New Hampshire bill of rights; so clearly that Doe claimed that
the right of equality, if not secured by the state constitution,
"can never be secured by any written instrument." [2] Equality, he
wrote, is "practically the source and sum of all rights, and the
substance of the constitution." [3] These are strong words perhaps,
but Doe meant them. In his very first constitutional opinion he
had showed himself an absolutist on the question of equality.[4]
It would prove to be the only doctrine that circumstances forced
him to modify.

Chief Justice Doe's views on equality were shaped by his views of the times. There were, he believed, many nineteenth-century lawyers who did not consider equality an essential constitutional guarantee. Worse, Doe feared, a shortsighted few were willing to abandon the concept altogether. Writing to Congressman Austin Pike in 1881, he warned of the danger.

> I am glad you approve the doctrine of equal rights. It looks as if the 2nd century of our national existence is to see a renewal of the old fight over the fundamentals of the constitution. I suppose the majority, today, are on the wrong side; but I hope the popular intelligence will, in time, reassert the old doctrine of freedom & equality. I do not know any other ground of safety for life, liberty or property. If they of the true faith are faithful to their convictions, the right will prevail in the end, — perhaps not in our day; — but the older we grow, the more confidence we ought to have in the immutability & triumph of the eternal, natural law of justice.[5]

Surely Doe is overstating the danger. Many whom he accuses of straying from the faith objected to the uses, not to the theory, of equality. Like Doe, they thought it to be one of the constitution's immutable guarantees. But in recent times equality had become less a standard for testing personal liberty than a shield for protecting private interests. Perhaps Doe did not see the distinction; but it is more likely that he was too committed to the social-compact idea to pay it much heed. As he said, "equality that can be legally violated is not constitutionally protected."[6] Equality has to be absolute if the reservations in the social contract are not to be meaningless. When reformers demanded statutes to correct corporate abuses, Doe reacted: special legislation is by its very nature unequal. For a time he was more dogmatic about equality than about any other legal issue except civil liberties.

Most equality issues in nineteenth-century New Hampshire were concerned with taxation. Here, too, the social compact formed the cornerstone of Charles Doe's theory. As "the price paid for the protection which the payers are entitled to receive from a government constitutionally declared to be formed by the mutual contract of the people, taxes are, in a certain constitutional sense, debts created by contract."[7] By this contract, "The right of benefit and protection, and the duty of contribution, are reciprocal. The former is consideration for the latter. The latter is the price of the former." [8] Going to extremes of analogy, Doe suggested that taxes assessed to support the social compact "are much like premiums due from the members of a mutual insurance company" and that taxpayers are "purchasers of public benefits." [9] What they purchase is the protection of "life, liberty, and property," "the common benefits of the government established by the contract." [10] What they pay is their "share of the common expense incurred in the execution of the social compact," "a division made by themselves through their own agents, in pursuance of their original contract." [11]

Rooting it firmly in the social compact and the doctrine of equality, Judge Doe defined taxation as "an equal division of public expense." [12] It followed that "An unequal division of the public expense is not taxation." [13] Rather it is "an act of violence"; an act of "confiscation, destitute of that element of equal rights, which, under our constitution, is an essential part of the definition of law." [14] That each citizen pay his equal share is not merely his constitutional duty, "it is the constitutional right of his neighbors" [15] — for him to pay less than his share is to violate their constitutional rights.[16] "Any one's non-payment of his share is a compulsory payment of his debt by his neighbors, which is, in effect a compulsory gift of their money to him for his private use." [17] Equally free in the state of nature, the people did not contract to contribute disproportionally. "And so long as constitutional government continues to be the execution of a written agreement, creating a limited agency for the purchase of common benefit, protection, and security, by proportional contribution, the contract can no more be executed by an unequal division of the expense, than the right of property can be protected by such an unauthorized extinguishment of it." [18]

Here we find the vital principle of Charles Doe's constitutional absolutism. If, as he argued, some men are forced to pay their neighbor's share of the public expense, the community will divide "into inferiors and superiors." [19] Again he postulates constitutional guarantees upon extreme suppositions. If part of a man's property can be taken by unequal taxation, Doe would contend, then the government can "make the same disposition of the whole of it." [20] He even compared unequal taxation to Negro slavery, concluding that "Equality is not one of many grades of servitude, nor a partial freedom from legal inferiority"[21] but is, and by its very nature has to be, absolute.

To be equal, taxes had to be levied against the whole of society, and not merely upon some special branch. When the legislature required each railroad expressman to pay annually either 2 per cent of his gross receipts or $5 per mile, the court ruled the act unconstitutional. Doe wrote a seventeen-page concurring opinion in which he sought to lay down the principles governing equality in taxation. The special assessment on expressmen was unconstitutional because, irrespective of the form in which it was imposed (that is, a license), its practical effect was to levy a tax on the property of certain individuals or corporations from which all others would be exempt, throwing on that particular class a disproportionate share of the public expense, without any equivalent benefit.[22]

When he wrote this concurring opinion, Doe may have thought that he had settled once and for all the law of equality in New Hampshire. It was one of his best pieces of writing, clear, direct, and definitive. Anyone reading it could have had no doubt that in New Hampshire business need not fear special discriminatory taxes. It comes as a surprise, therefore, to find Doe, less than three years later, giving his blessing to a tax on bank deposits. "The savings-bank tax," he admitted, "is an anomaly, resting on peculiar grounds of public policy, and is universally understood to have acquired the position of an exception to the constitutional rule of equality."[23]

How could Doe possibly admit an exception to the rigid rule of equality? It is remarkable that he would even think that there could be an exception, let alone acknowledge its existence. He seems to have justified it as custom, for he said it was "universally understood" to be an exception. It could do no harm so long as everyone knew it was an "anomaly." In legal theory this exception should be classed with tax exemptions. Though exemptions from taxation are an obvious violation of absolute equality, they are nonetheless legal in New Hampshire, Doe said, because they had been legal at the time the bill of rights was adopted. The authors of the constitution had not thought tax exemptions violated equal rights.[24]

The savings-bank tax and the rule about exemptions clarify

one point: Judge Doe had no hope of applying absolute equality to the law of taxation. Nineteenth-century society was too diverse and complex to be taxed with mathematical precision; the time was bound to come when Doe had to admit there are degrees of equality. He had to allow deviations or else taxation would have been stunted. It was, he acknowledged, constitutionally permissible to tax one class of property, such as real estate, and not tax other classes, such as horses or furniture, if the taxed class was such that the distribution would fall equally on the entire community. This would not constitute "an exemption of any class of people," and, being equal, was different from taxing one occupation, such as that of expressman.[25]

As Doe discovered, equality can cut two ways. An obvious principle collateral to the doctrine of equality is that no property can be taxed twice unless all property is taxed twice.[26] But what if Massachusetts were to tax its citizens for the value of real estate which they own in New Hampshire? Are these landowners subject to a second tax in New Hampshire? Doe, of course, held that they were. Though it is true that the double tax which they pay and which others escape is unequal, it is not unequal in New Hampshire, and this is the test. For without the double tax New Hampshire citizens would be taxed unequally by paying the out-of-state owner's share of local expenses. For the sake of equality, some taxpayers had to pay more than others.[27]

Even the simple rule that local taxes should be equal locally and state taxes equal throughout the state became complicated as the government broadened its sources of revenue. In 1880 Doe was puzzled by a tax levied by the state upon railroad property. The state collected the tax and returned one-quarter of it to the towns in which the railroad property was located. The remaining three-fourths was divided by a rule of proportion based on the number of stockholders living in New Hampshire as against those domiciled outside the state; part went to the state and part to the towns in which the stockholders lived. Was it a town tax, a state tax, or a tax "of a triple character"? Doe could not make up his mind and sent the question back to the referee for factual determination. Taxes had to be equal, but it was not always easy to find an equation.[28]

Cases such as these taught Judge Doe that the rigid, uncompromising absolutism which he drew from the social compact in matters of civil liberties was not possible in tax law. Despite the absolute nature of equality in legal theory, it could not be absolutely applied in practical litigation. "It is," Doe had to admit, "to be intelligently applied as a broad, fundamental, and rational principle, not as an arbitrary formula or mere technical method, and with due regard for precedents, legislative and judicial." [29] The bill of rights might have a clear reservation of equality, and this might mean that no citizen could be forced to bear more than his "share" of the public expense, but the word "share" has a "legal" as well as an "arithmetical and common meaning." [30] The "prevailing constitutional policy of equality or inequality," not the form of a tax but its "legal character," is what determines the legality of an assessment.[31] "Mathematical equality of taxation being unattainable, an approximation, reasonably exact, as nearly proportional as possible in consideration of the difficulties of the subject, and sufficient for the practical purposes of substantial justice, is all that is required." [32] In his last opinion dealing with taxation and equality Judge Doe spoke of "the doctrine of an approximate equality," [33] thus admitting that the "equality" reservation in the social compact is, for purposes of taxation at least, relative and not absolute.

Partisan politics explain much of Doe's interest in taxation. The people's resentment against unequal taxation, he thought, was costing the Republican Party votes. In 1866 the state Supreme Court declared unconstitutional a tax of 25 per cent on income received from notes, bonds, and other securities. The tax would have been valid had it exempted securities of the United States government, but since they were taxed, the statute was declared void.[34] This opinion encouraged unequal taxation, for it allowed a New Hampshire citizen, to avoid his equal share of the local public expense, to convert his property into federal bonds. The court had no choice. It was bound to hold as it did because of *Weston* v. *Charleston*,[35] the decision in which Chief Justice Marshall had ruled that a state tax on stock issued for loans made to the United States is unconstitutional. When John Major Shirley published one of his exorbitant attacks on Marshall as a jurist,

Doe defended Marshall. But in a letter to Shirley he had to admit
that Marshall had made mistakes, the chief of which had been
Weston v. *Charleston:*

I have been reading up some subjects, that have called my attention to the history & work of the Sup. Ct. of the U.S. So far as I have
read, I cant agree to your estimate of Marshall. I think I can see
great errors that he fell into from his federal bias, & his natural tendency to establish a general rule upon extreme hypothetical cases on
one side, without regard to the opposite extreme cases at the other
end of the line, instead of taking a comprehensive view of the whole
situation, & construing the constitution, according to the well-known
historical intent of its authors. For instance, in the matter of taxation,
he introduced the exemption of government bonds, on the ground
that if a State could tax such a bond equally with all other property,
it could tax it unequally = 100 percent annually, — & thus veto the
federal power of borrowing money, — a most lame & impotent conclusion. Thompson dissented; but his dissent is one of those feeble
things that strengthens the opinion dissented from. He carried a good
legal reputation to the Bench; but the feebleness of his dissent in that
case, (*Weston* v. *Charleston*) was enough to ruin a better reputation
than his. I confess, I cant help envying him the opportunity he had,
to knock Marshall's exemption theory on the head — an exemption as
flagrantly unconstitutional in law, as it is injudicious & dangerous in
fact. It is a distortion of all legal ideas, a monstrous federal usurpation,
an insurrection against the fundamental principles of our institutions,
calculated to engender strife, social & political disorder, repudiation,
war between capital & labor, robbery & all the ruin of communism
& anarchy. If our government means anything, it means equality &
uniformity. Marshall was so possessed with the fear of state rights, &
the delusive arguments drawn from extreme hypothetical cases on
one side of a question, in disregard of such cases on the other side,
that he entailed on posterity the vicious heresy of exemption, & other
doctrines equally unsound.[36]

This looks like the pot calling the kettle black. By saying that
tax-free bonds will lead to repudiation of federal debts and to
war between capital and labor, Doe is acting as Marshall did —
he is arguing from extremes. But to Doe these were not hypothetical extremes. They were distinct possibilities. If he exaggerated the danger of "social disorder," he genuinely feared disaster for the Republican Party. "Our voters," he wrote William E.
Chandler in 1868, "are deserting us at a fatal rate because U.S.
bonds are not taxed. Resolutions are ineffectual. Nothing but ac-

tual & immediate taxation will save us." He was sending Chandler a bill to permit taxation of federal bonds. This bill had been pronounced constitutional by Judges Perley, Bellows, Sawyer, Foster, and by everyone "else to whom I have been able to show it," and now Doe wanted Chandler to find a "strong man" who would steer the bill through Congress, "& if Johnson should veto it, all the better." "If necessary we will send a petition of bondholders asking taxation," he promised. "You probably realize that nothing short of an effort to put bonds on a level with other similar property will satisfy the people." [37]

Judge Doe seems to be translating his constitutional predilections into partisan political strategy. For reason of legal theory he does not like unequal taxation and assumes the average New Hampshire voter agrees with him. He tries to do something about it on the national level, and the arguments he uses are unbecoming a judge. He was a Radical Republican and made no apologies for it, though he did tell Chandler to keep the matter secret. It is quite possible that Doe's constitutional theories were fed by his political fears. He thought that the Republican Party was hurt by the unequal-taxation issue and, while on the national level he could do little except propose an abortive bill, in his decisions he may have tried to smother the voters' cause for complaint. There is consistency between Doe's desire to tax federal bonds and his ruling that some forms of double taxation are not unconstitutional. He would not permit an out-of-state resident to escape local taxation just because the value of the property which he owned in New Hampshire had been taxed by the state where he lived. "To recognize such a right in another jurisdiction would introduce the most glaring inequality in the apportionment and collection of the public expense," Doe wrote. "To tax it elsewhere and not to tax it here would be to violate that fundamental principle of equality." [38] That this was the universal rule does not change the fact that Doe's acceptance of it may have been conditioned in part by political considerations.

Oliver Wendell Holmes once called equality the "last resort of constitutional arguments." [39] He was dealing with a problem of "equal protection" and was weary of the slogans used by a generation of American judges to strike down social legislation which they did not like. Judge Doe had helped to write these slogans.

He truly believed that equality was "the source and sum of all rights," not the "last resort" of desperate counsel. He tried to make equality what he thought it should be — "the substance of the constitution." He was doomed to fail on two grounds. The doctrine of equality was too sweeping a constitutional maxim for a democratic people to entrust to their judges; and it was too simple a legal rule to solve the problems of a complex society.

Chapter Eighteen

ALL THE SUMMERS
OF MY LIFE
The Limits of Government

CHARLES Doe's decisions on civil rights and equality are somewhat deceptive, since they give the impression that the social-compact theory furnished all his constitutional principles. In actual fact his method of interpreting the constitution was quite broad, and in many opinions he employed more conventional arguments. In decisions on government authority, for example, the social compact played a very small role. When grappling with issues of official power, Doe borrowed a wide variety of arguments, as is shown by the *Mink Case*.[1]

In the *Mink Case* the lower court had ruled that when a statute forbids the killing of minks, a person defending his property is privileged to kill minks which threaten that property only if the threat is real; but if the threat is merely apparent, he may be fined for violating the statute. Doe reversed the conviction on the grounds that, as applied by the lower court, the law was unconstitutional, having deprived the property owner of his "natural right," his "common-law right," and his "constitutional right of defence." [2]

By the "constitutional right" of property defense Judge Doe meant the specific reservation in the New Hampshire bill of rights which reserved to all men "the natural, essential, and inherent" right of "acquiring, possessing, and protecting property." [3] Enumerated in the constitution, it is a right which the legislature cannot abolish.[4] By the "common-law right" of defense Doe meant the common law as adopted by the constitution and found in human reason. "In the general terms of the common-law definition, the right of defence is the right to do whatever apparently is reasonably necessary to be done in defence."[5] Under the facts of the *Mink Case* it was reasonably necessary for the defendant, if he wished to preserve his property, to kill the minks; any statute denying him this right was void. By the "natural right" of defense Doe was referring to still a third right mentioned by the constitution. For, as noted above, the constitution specifically reserved to each man a "natural" right to protect his property. To some constitutional authorities, "natural" might be a superfluous word, but Doe decided that it had been put into the constitution for a purpose.

Higher and earlier in its origin, than the constitution or the common law, not superseded by those temporal and finite systems, but sustained and enforced by their declaration and sanction of the highest, primary, eternal, and infinite law of nature, the right of defence cannot be prescribed within the limits of a narrow technical rule. It is an original and comprehensive prerogative, necessarily ascertained and defined by natural reason. It is not established by any fallible authority, nor measured by any precedent, nor restricted by any arbitrary dogma. Long upheld by the common law, it has, under the administration of that law, theoretically been what it was before; and now, reinforced by a constitutional guaranty, it is what it has always been.[6]

Thus, in the *Mink Case,* Doe asserted three degrees of personal privilege which the government may not violate. He based them on arguments ranging from the specific words of the constitution to the broad principles of natural justice. In other cases, dealing with other issues, Doe curtailed government authority by using arguments just as broad and even broader. For instance, he neutralized discriminatory words in statutes by citing "the general drift of the constitution"[7] and by appealing to "the character of our institutions and the spirit of the organic law."[8] Perhaps his most sweeping arguments were drawn from what he called "American principles."[9] The best example is in *Robertson,* where in *dictum* Doe suggested that the executive department cannot constitutionally alienate the state's property interest in great ponds, because the king, when he governed New Hampshire, had held the great ponds in trust for the people. True, in England the king had had power to grant great ponds and tidelands to anyone he pleased; but in the colonies special conditions peculiar to American history had stripped him of that power.

> The private interest of the king in tide-land, and his power of conveying it to favorites to be held as a private interest, were parts of a social system which the settlers of New Hampshire considered oppressive and from which they endeavored to escape. . . . A private ownership of this wilderness, vested in the king, and a regal or executive power of conveying those reservoirs which the interests of the settlers required the government should hold for common use, would be in conflict with the general object of their migration. The mediaeval rule cannot be accepted without material modification.[10]

The power of the king, and therefore of the government, is limited by local American principles.

Why was it that Doe, who used the social-compact argument so effectively in civil-rights cases, did not rely on it when dealing with the closely related topic of governmental power? Surely the quintain of the social-compact theory is state authority. Using the social compact syllogistically, it is a logical deduction that the people of New Hampshire, when they entered into the "contract," had not agreed to create an omnipotent sovereign, that the contract itself circumscribes the state. This thought is basic to the very idea of a compact. Yet in the main Doe ignored the argument.[11] The reason seems to be that he was interested in more than New Hampshire problems of state authority. Most trends toward governmental power which disturbed him came from jurisdictions where the social compact had no standing in legal theory. These trends were based on broad arguments, and to combat them Doe sought counterarguments equally broad.

To discover what disturbed Doe it is necessary to recall his version of the social compact. The contractors, he believed, had placed a duty on the government "to countenance and inculcate the principles of industry, economy, and honesty." [12] By "honesty" Doe did not mean private or personal honesty alone. Usually he was referring to the Hamiltonian brand of constitutional honesty which had motivated Chief Justice Marshall, in *Fletcher*

v. *Peck,* to hold that a state legislature cannot repudiate a land grant even though the grant has been obtained by dishonest means. A legislative grant, said Marshall, is a contract between the state and the grantees and under the United States Constitution must be honored by the state.[13]

Fletcher v. *Peck* set a standard which did not last forever. By 1876 honesty was losing ground as a constitutional policy in some parts of the nation, but not, Doe hoped, in New Hampshire. Out on the prairies farmers were mounting attacks on railroads financed by eastern interests and were putting pressure on their state governments to amend the charters of common carriers, bringing them under government regulation. "The West & South," Doe wrote in a personal letter, "may favor an unlimited legislative power of confiscating property belonging to Eastern & Middle States or to foreigners, but in N.E. there is a strong element of honesty; & I cant believe our profession this side of Indiana & Virginia, is ready, or will soon be ready, to say that, in *F.* v. *Peck,* the Ga. statute ought to have been held valid."[14] Less than twenty years later Doe's optimism was gone. Property rights, he warned, were being "openly and directly attacked for the first time in this state since their safety was assured by the establishment of constitutional government at the close of the Revolutionary War."[15]

What had caused Doe's mood to change so radically? For one thing western ideas, spread by Populists and Grangers, had gained adherents among New Hampshire voters, and even the ranks of the legal profession had been breached. Many agreed with Senator Chandler that the greater menace to free society was corporate power, not government power. To smash the railroad oligarchy, the state should regulate what was only technically private property. Most important of all, there had been a shift in national law. Although some historians, conscious of later events, might not agree, Doe believed that the United States Supreme Court had abandoned the principles of Hamilton and Marshall. Perhaps no decision since *Dred Scott* alarmed him as did the verdict in the *Sinking-Fund Cases.* Speaking for his court, Chief Justice Waite had upheld a statute which amended the Union Pacific Railroad's charter, requiring it to establish a sinking fund for redemption of federal loans.[16] Waite's decision gave the United States wide powers of control over congressionally chartered corporations. In post-New Deal days this is familiar stuff; but in Doe's view it meant that anyone who invested in business enterprises could no longer feel secure in his personal property. Governmental good faith was no longer pledged by constitutional guarantee.

The judgment in the *Sinking-Fund Cases* was announced on May 5, 1879.[17] It was no accident that on July 10, just two months later, the New Hampshire Supreme Court published an opinion calculated to revitalize the Hamiltonian principle of governmental honesty. The House of Representatives had asked the justices to rule on the constitutionality of a law authorizing towns to exempt manufacturing property from taxation for ten years. The court might have answered in the negative and simply let the matter drop with an explanation that the statute conformed to the bill of rights, since its purpose was to encourage industry, not to favor a special class of taxpayers. But the court went further, surely at Doe's urging, and delivered a lecture on governmental honesty. A tax exemption, the judges said, is a "contract" between the state and the business enterprise which takes advantage of it. Therefore, they concluded (in what must be accepted as Doe's rebuke of Waite),

the credit of a trustworthy people, indispensable to the strength of the state in war or in peace, ought not to be weakened by any groundless distrust of the validity of public contracts. The constitution of New Hampshire makes it the duty of the legislators and magistrates to inculcate and consistently adhere to honesty and justice as necessary to preserve the blessings of liberty and good government. As magistrates, sharing that duty with the legislature, we are not prepared to hold that it would not be illegally violated by allowing the state or any of its municipal agencies to be guilty of the fraud and tyranny of breaking such contracts of ten-years exemption as have been made with manufacturers, railroads, and farmers.[18]

Doe really believed that "the blessings of liberty" depend upon governmental honesty. He risked too much on honesty's account not to have been sincere. He genuinely wanted to reestablish Hamiltonian principles throughout the United States. Ironically, he thought the root of the problem to be the *Dartmouth College Case* — the decision regarded as the finest expression of Hamiltonian legal theory.

Dartmouth College was the most important constitutional opinion handed down in nineteenth-century America. In 1816 Governor Plumer had persuaded the New Hampshire legislature to revoke Dartmouth's original charter. In its place the lawmakers substituted a new charter increasing the board of trustees just enough for control to pass to men appointed by Plumer. The old trustees appealed to New Hampshire's highest court, but Chief Justice Richardson held that, since Dartmouth was a "public" corporation, the legislature had power to reform its charter in accord with the needs of the day.[19] They then appealed to the Supreme Court of the United States, where Marshall ruled that the original charter was a "contract" and, since the so-called contract clause of the federal Constitution provides that no state shall make a law "impairing the Obligation of Contracts," the New Hampshire statute was unconstitutional.[20]

Both courts, Doe felt, had been wrong. A question so vital as this could not be resolved on such technical points as whether a college is a "public corporation" or whether a charter is a "contract." The real issue had to do with the "much more dangerous power to confiscate [Dartmouth's] property,"[21] a confiscation "morally equivalent to embezzlement."[22]

Of the two, Doe felt, Richardson's error had been the greater: he had been wrong in calling Dartmouth College a public corporation. It was private property, donated to trustees by private individuals for the education of young men. The property had not been given to the Province of New Hampshire, and at best it had been intended to benefit New Hampshire only indirectly. As private property, the trustees' title was owed "the same constitutional protection as any other property not held in trust."[23] Doe did agree with Richardson that the College charter could be repealed. This, however, was not the same as admitting that New Hampshire succeeded to the trustees' interests and rights. "What the govt has made, — corporate or corporate franchise, — the govt can destroy. But the property & the title of the donor's trustees, which the govt did not make, are protected by those [constitutional] provisions that protect your property & mine from confiscation. These provisions prevent the arbitrary legislative transfer of property from trustees to whom the donees conveyed their legal title, to other trustees appointed by the govt. If that is not so, what security have you & I against confiscation?" [24] Richardson's error was to award the College property to the new board of trustees created by Plumer's statute. He should have ruled that the repeal of Dartmouth's old charter was constitutional and that the attempted transfer of Dartmouth's assets was unconstitutional. The legal effect of repeal is to wind up a corporation's affairs and allow for a distribution of its property.[25] But even distribution is not necessary. "The property of the corporation would remain vested in the trustees, not as trustees of the dead corporation, but as trustees of the surviving funds." Chancery could enforce the use of the property in accordance with the design of the donors.

The short of it is, that the legislature may abolish the corporation of Dart. Coll. or change it as they please; but when they undertake to manage other people's property, i.e. the property the title of which is vested in trustees appointed by the former owners of the property, — when the legislature undertakes to change that title & transfer it to other trustees appointed by the gov't, — if they can do that, why cant they rip up all titles & appropriate all property to such uses as they please? [26]

Marshall's error had been one of tactics. His sense of honesty had revolted at Richardson's confiscatory decision; but he had selected the wrong grounds on which to reverse it. The contract clause of the United States Constitution had not been designed to prohibit the confiscation of property or to limit legislative authority but had been intended solely to protect executory contracts — contracts not yet performed — from state repudiation. The charter of Dartmouth College was not an executory contract in 1816. It had been performed. The property had vested in the trustees. Therefore, Doe concluded, the College charter was not a "contract" within the meaning of the federal constitution.[27] Marshall had been so worried by the implications of revocation that he converted the contract clause into a technicality with which to enforce government honesty. Marshall should have held, just as Richardson should have held, that even though the state could terminate the corporation, it could not assign the property to a new board of trustees.

The essence of Doe's argument turns on "the right of property." It does not need the contract clause to be protected from confiscation, because "the right of property includes the right that an equitable interest shall not fail for want of trustees." [28] When the old trust was terminated by revocation of the original College charter, the courts had power to protect Dartmouth's property by appointing new trustees.[29] When the legislature appointed its own trustees it usurped the province of the judiciary and overstepped its constitutional authority. This was the point Marshall should have made. He should have rested his decision on "separation of powers," not on the contract clause. He should have ruled that the New Hampshire legislature was attempting to perform a judicial act. By not doing so, Marshall had blundered, and "that blunder," Doe stated, "is the source of all our woe relating to the contract clause of the constitution." [30]

Although Marshall's moral position had been sound, his legal position, based on faulty interpretation of the contract clause, had caused a great deal of harm. The *Sinking-Fund Cases* demonstrated this. Waite had pointed out that the federal government was not bound by the contract clause — it applies only to the states — and therefore no constitutional reason prevented Congress from amending the Union Pacific's charter. Since Marshall had linked governmental morality so closely with the contract clause, the assumption had been that where the contract clause has no effect, there are no restraints on legislative power over private franchises. In the years since *Dartmouth College* every state in the Union had avoided the implication of Marshall's decision by inserting in business charters a "reservation clause," reserving the right to revoke or amend. These reservation clauses implied that the legislature reserved power to do as it pleased. Even Massachusetts' Chief Justice Lemuel Shaw, an outstanding defender of property, was baffled. "This power," he said, "must have some limit, though it is difficult to define it." [31] Charles Doe began his study of the *Dartmouth College Case* hoping to discover an acceptable definition. He knew the task was formidable. As late as 1864, he admitted, Marshall's contract-clause doctrine "was as well established in the general mind of the American

Bench & Bar as was the doctrine of the Trinity in the mind of Calvin." [32]

The seriousness of Doe's purpose was shown when he, the judge who carried public modesty to extremes, wrote two articles on the subject.[33] They are the only articles he published while on the bench — at least the only two that reveal him as author. But articles in law reviews were a mere scrimmage in his campaign. Case law provided the major battleground. In the decision in *Corbin's Case*, written with this issue in mind, Doe held that the reservation clause in the Concord Railroad's charter (that is, the reservation to amend or to modify the charter; not the reservation to purchase the railroad) did nothing more than release the New Hampshire legislature from the restraint placed on its lawmaking powers by the *Dartmouth College Case*. It permitted the legislature to amend the charter in the same manner that it could have amended it had Marshall not held incorporation to be a contract. But the reservation clause did not authorize confiscation of the railroad.[34] On the question of purchasing the Concord Railroad, we see Doe going out of his way to answer the *Sinking-Fund* doctrine. If anything, the New Hampshire legislature had a stronger claim to purchase the Concord than Congress had to impose a sinking fund on the Union Pacific. New Hampshire had specifically reserved the right to purchase; the Union Pacific's charter said nothing about sinking funds. Yet Doe ruled that the principles of constitutional honesty restricted the government; it could not "confiscate" property which belonged to stockholders of the Concord.

Even more significant was *Dow's Case*.[35] The legislature by special act had authorized the Northern Railroad to make a long-term lease of its track and equipment to the Boston & Lowell. Dow, a Northern stockholder who favored the interests of the Boston & Lowell's rival, the Concord Railroad, asked the court to enjoin the lease. Notwithstanding the regular reservation clause in the Northern's charter, reserving to the legislature the power to alter, amend, or repeal, Doe granted the injunction. The right of private property, he maintained, would be wrongfully taken from a Northern stockholder if without his consent a majority of the other owners were permitted to substitute a new business arrangement for the one to which he had agreed.

Judge Doe's opinion in *Dow's Case* has been called "the most vigorous and elaborate protest ever made against the decision of the Supreme Court of the United States in the 'Sinking Fund Cases.'"[36] Actually the case is not directly on point; to grant the injunction, Doe had to rely on private property law, not on constitutional property law. Much of what he has to say about legislature power is *dictum*. Even to raise that issue he had to gloss over the fact that the New Hampshire legislature had done nothing more than permit a change; it had not ordered that the Northern be leased. He also paid slight attention to the right of the majority stockholders to manage their property more profitably by converting from the role of common carrier to that of leasee. What he discussed was "valid" government power. The legislature, he said, could modify a corporate charter by altering or terminating the privileges granted by the state; it could not interfere with private property rights possessed either by the corporation or by its stockholders. More than a structural change, the authorization to lease the Northern was so fundamental that it required unanimous consent of the stockholders and could not be effected by majority vote even when sanctioned by legislative action.

In *Dow's Case* Chief Justice Doe was trying to undo the effects of a half-century of precedents which culminated in the *Sinking-Fund* doctrine. These precedents had concentrated on the reservation clauses in charters, and from this base it was easy to make an argument for unrestricted state control of business corporations. His solution was applauded by some, notably by Jeremiah Smith.[37] Others were critical;[38] they found his distinction between valid and invalid legislative action too vague to be practical. Corporation lawyers preferred the simplicity of the contract-clause approach, which, extended just slightly, could make corporate power impregnable. Considering this point we find the true root of Doe's constitutional argument limiting the powers of government. It lay, not in defining invalid legislative actions, but in enforcing valid judicial jurisdiction. For even if the contract-clause doctrine is accepted in its most extreme form, business corporations need not be immune from control.

"Suppose the charter is a contract & cant be altered," Doe wrote. "That isn't the end of the fight by a good deal. The question still remains, What is the contract?" In other words, there is always the problem of construction, and that is a judicial function. The popular will as expressed in the legislature is limited and the contract clause prevents political opportunists and sincere reformers alike from abusing private property. But the rule of law as enforced by common-law courts can still keep corporations within proper bounds. "In the *Dart. College Case*," Doe continued, "the charter-contract wouldn't be for the propagation of Federalism or Democracy, of Calvinism or Deism. It would be for the propagation of non-partizan, unsectarian knowledge, in harmony with the institutions & equal rights of a free country." A court construing this charter (not the legislature revoking it) was the proper forum for dealing with these matters. "I should fight out the battle on that line, if it took all the summers of my life, & the winters too." [39]

Applying this principle to current attempts by Grangers to regulate railroad rates, Judge Doe wrote, "So, in regard to the Western conspiracy to rob Eastern people of all their property invested in Western railroads by legislative action, I suppose that robber's right will be established as the law of the land. But suppose it were held that the R.R. charter is a contract, (that is not the ground on which robbery ought to be held unconstitutional,) it dont follow at all that the R.R. corporations have a right to fix their fares & tolls as high as they please. What is the contract on that point? Obviously the common-law, common-carrier contract [means] a reasonable compensation for a reasonable service, & a duty of performing such service without discrimination for such compensation." [40] Here Doe cited his own opinion in *McDuffee*, in which he had held that a railroad could not make an exclusive contract with one expressman, agreeing to serve no others. [41] He had based his decision on common-law principles and on the general spirit of the constitution as embodied in the reservation on equality. Though his holding was as broad as any statute demanded by a midwestern Granger, it did not depend on legislation altering the railroad's original charter, but on judicial construction of that charter and on the constitutional principle that the legislature lacked the authority to incorporate a railroad which could provide unequal service or establish discriminatory rates. As Doe said, speaking of another case in which he had made a similar ruling, this decision "shows what courts could do, even under the charter-contract theory, if they had the courage to stand up for the original faith of the fathers against the innovations of precedent." [42]

Doe's principle was not new. In place of the contract clause he wanted to establish the rule that when owners of private property, corporate or personal, abuse their privileges, correction is a judicial and not a legislative function. This was but an extension of what Jeremiah Mason and Jeremiah Smith had argued on behalf of the old board of trustees in the *Dartmouth College Case*. If the trustees did not properly perform their duty, Mason and Smith had contended, the courts might reform the trust but the legislature could not seize private property or appoint new owners. Behind this argument lurked the Federalist fear of unbridled democracy. As Smith asked when commenting on a section of Plumer's charter which appointed legislative visitors to oversee Dartmouth, "But who will visit the legislature?"

Smith's question posed a dilemma. Republicans were no more willing to trust the courts than Federalists were to trust the legislature. If ultimate power were given to the nonelective courts, how could a democracy "visit" the judges? Marshall had no answer — one reason why he turned to the contract clause, resolving the matter on the narrowest of grounds. Charles Doe was seeking an escape from Marshall's timidity. The court, he asserted, would be "visited" by the rules of constitutional construction. Judges not slaves to precedent and following the "drift of the constitution" can be trusted to adjust the interests of all elements of society. "Suppose," Doe explained, "all charters are contracts. Those contracts are to be construed by the court; & a court equal to its duty would seldom if ever be compelled, by sound rules of construction, to give them a construction inconsistent with the general laws that carry out the general theory of free institutions." Before this could be done, he admitted, the same rules of construction which he had reformed in will and contract cases would have to be introduced into constitutional interpretation. "The system of construing laws, constitutions, charters, & deeds by the literal meaning of particular words has been carried to inordinate excess. Everything in

America is to be construed, if possible, in harmony with American principles — the principles historically known to have been held by the authors of our constitution." [43] In this way private property will have greater security from the vacillations of popular government than it enjoys under Marshall's interpretation of the contract clause. At the same time property effected with the public interest, such as railroads, can be regulated by constitutional principles of equality and economic fairness.

The obvious defect in Charles Doe's solution of the dilemma posed by private property in conflict with government regulation was that the constitution entrusts public-policy decisions to the legislature. Doe was a firm believer in the doctrine of separation of powers, yet he claimed for the judiciary an area of competence effaced from American constitutional theory by the defeat of the Federalists. There is a simple, almost naive, assumption in Doe's argument. He envisioned constitutional principles so well defined that judges can satisfactorily settle issues of vast economic scope, keeping controversies over the regulation of private corporate property out of politics. He should have known better — surely *Corbin's Case* taught him a lesson. Senator Chandler, for one, did not think Doe's "constitutional principles" so clear that there was no room for debate.

In a way Senator Chandler, despite excessive language, summed up the arguments against Doe's attempt to limit legislative power. Decisions based on broad constitutional principles such as *Corbin's Case*, Chandler warned, meant that "no law can be devised by the ablest and most astute legislators that cannot be defied and nullified by the chief justice." These principles made Doe

the uncontrolled and mighty ruler and governor of New Hampshire; superior to the executive and legislative branches of the government; and high above any laws that can be conceived, drafted, or passed by the legislature of the people.

The passage of any law is useless. The briefs and arguments of lawyers are a waste of time and labor. The people and every one of their representatives in all the departments in the government; the corporations, manufacturers, merchants, farmers, and laborers of all kinds, exist only in subjection to the irresponsible, irrational, eccentric, and despotic will of one tyrant, the chief justice of New Hampshire.[44]

Though his language was reckless, Chandler scored a point. Doe would have made the court the originator, not merely the final arbitrator, of a great many policy decisions. Yet when his constitutional arguments are evaluated, it must not be forgotten that he did sincerely believe the judiciary to be confined by practical limitations. For the rules of constitutional construction which he formulated were designed to assure not only that the court would act boldly, but also that it would not act rashly. Rules of construction kept judges from excess just as they warned them against timidity. If the principles of the constitution were determined, the judges could be trusted. This is one explanation why some of Doe's constitutional decisions are burdened with discussions of correct rules of interpretation.[45]

To a certain extent all this is a lesson in "what might have been." Had Charles Doe been appointed to the Supreme Court of the United States in 1881, he would have brought these ideas to Washington. Who can say, given a national forum, what influence on constitutional law he might have exerted? Surely his ideas contained elements to please and dismay both conservatives and liberals. His distrust of legislative power would have added immeasurable support to the laissez-faire arguments of Stephen Field. His belief that the court could impose a common-law test of reasonableness upon business, on the other hand, would have furnished powerful intellectual stimulus to the positions taken by Waite, Miller, and Bradley. Perhaps his theory of government authority would have been out of place in Washington, where battle lines were revocably drawn around familiar landscape. It might have been too much of a shock to have had an original thinker on the national court. Of only one thing can we be sure: Doe would remain steadfast to his principles. This was the one fight to which he was prepared to devote all the summers of his life — and the winters too.

Chapter Nineteen

CHAOS AND CONTENTION
Railroad Regulation

WHEN Senator William E. Chandler warned New Hampshire that corporate power — not government power — was the greater menace to nineteenth-century liberty, Charles Doe paid no heed. It was not that Doe disagreed about the danger; he too was disturbed by the public-be-damned robber barons, who were turning sovereign states into personal fiefs. It was the senator's solution which Doe rejected. Chandler wanted the legislature to regulate the railroads. Doe did not object to regulation; it was legislative interference with private property that worried him. He never articulated a positive constitutional theory, but he did indicate that the then novel experiment in the economic regulation of business might more properly be developed through judicial remedies. In his analysis of the *Dartmouth College Case,* as has been shown, Doe suggested that in 1816, when the legislature first revoked Dartmouth's charter, the courts not only had had the power to preserve the property in the original board of directors as common-law trustees, but also had supervisory jurisdiction to keep them from violating their trust. In *McDuffee* he went further and held that correction of corporate abuses is a judicial function. If common carriers discriminate, there is no need for the legislature to pass a regulatory statute. The courts can protect the public's interests by suits at common law.

This was no mere speculation, thrown out by a reactionary judge as an excuse to declare legislative regulation unconstitutional. Doe believed that rights could be better adjusted and freedom made more secure if the courts extended their jurisdiction over business and enforced standards of fair play derived from common-law principles. He even thought the judiciary capable of the task and sought to demonstrate the practicality of this theory by regulating the railroads of New Hampshire. It became the one failure of his career.

A few months before Charles Doe was born, the Dover *Times* published pictures of a railroad carriage. The newspaper hoped to silence skeptics who called the railroad a visionary scheme.[1] Within a short time all doubt had vanished. Railroads reached into every section of the state, and the economy of New Hampshire soon depended on this one method of transportation. There was no significant effort at regulation until July 5, 1867, when the legislature passed "An act to prevent railroad monopolies" which forbade "the consolidation of competing roads through contracts or arrangements between them, by means of which competition is removed." It was expected that this so-called anti-monopoly law would solve New Hampshire's railroad problems.

Enforcement of the "anti-monopoly law" was left to the courts. There was a railroad commission, but it had few powers and even less inclination to use them.[2] Doe, on the other hand, had few reservations concerning the role and authority of the judiciary. Once, when counsel "admonished that courts ought to be slow to interfere" with management, Doe snapped back:

There is a case in another jurisdiction in which courts have been slow to suppress a corporate management illicitly directed to the benefit of the managers, and in which a peculiar system of railroad principles has been rapidly developed. A dominion of railroad directors arose on a foundation of fraud, intimidation, and corruption. It perverted corporate power and personal trust, trampled down the rights of stockholders and the public, defied the law, absorbed the local government, overwhelmed a powerful State, and spread the demoralizing influence of its success. In resisting the extension of such a system, it is not the duty of the court to be slow.[3]

On this excuse Doe prodded his court into action. "The procedure," he asserted, "will be such as is considered most appropriate for the work to be done."[4] His definition of the "public good" extended well beyond the antimonopoly policy of the act of 1867 and sounded like a judicial adoption of the program the Grangers would one day advocate. "It is the theory of New

Hampshire law," he wrote at a time when railroad charters limited annual dividends to 10 per cent of par value, "that a railroad is a public highway, designed, and put in operation, by legislative authority, for the public accommodation; that its managers are public servants; and that a rate of fare or freight, higher than is necessary for paying ten percent and keeping the road in a reasonable repair and a suitable condition for public use, is an oppressive public tax assessed and collected by a corporate monopoly created by the legislature." [5]

Since railroads could be built, in length, only in the great valleys — the Connecticut, the Merrimack, the Ashuelot, and the Piscataqua and Saco — the key to the vital commerce flowing between New Hampshire's industrial heartland and the markets of the world was the control of the Merrimack valley. It was dominated by two of America's exemplary roads, the renowned Boston & Lowell and the remarkably affluent Concord, which extended from Concord through Manchester to Nashua, where it linked with the small Nashua & Lowell, which in turn joined the Boston & Lowell, forming one route to Boston. The struggle to unite New Hampshire's railroads under one system became a struggle of the Concord to control other railroads and of other railroads to control the Concord.

Typical of the smaller railroads which operated in the Merrimack valley was the Manchester & Lawrence. A stepchild of legal theory in action, it had been incorporated because Manchester businessmen, taking the railroad laws into consideration, decided that competition was the best way to protect themselves from the Concord, which controlled traffic southward. They therefore established the Manchester & Lawrence, linking their city with the Boston & Maine at Lawrence, Massachusetts, and providing an alternate route to Boston. A railroad owing its existence to legal theory rather than economic realities rests on financial quicksand. Before long the Manchester & Lawrence was in trouble, and the Concord, after vainly seeking legislative permission to purchase the Manchester, received executive consent to lease it. In the five years that passed before the Supreme Court ruled the lease invalid, the relations of the two roads became so intermixed that they continued to be operated jointly during the next fifteen years.[6] This circumstance uncovered the first defect inherent in the judicial process when dealing with management matters in a supervisory capacity. The antimonopoly act of 1867 might be on the books and might be sympathetically interpreted by the Supreme Court, but as long as the court was governed by traditional common-law procedure the act could not be enforced with effective dispatch.

A second and more obvious defect to judicial supervision of business soon cropped up: the court could not act until an abuse was brought to its attention in a law suit. Once Doe became chief justice, he made this less of a drawback by extending his holdings beyond the specific fact patterns presented and by refusing to be tied down by the exact wording of statutes. Indeed, to prove that the judiciary could do the job and that there was no need for legislative interference, he often ignored statutory authority even when on point, relying instead on common-law principles. In 1870, for example, he invalidated a contract which transferred management of the Concord to the Northern railroad for five years. Rather than base his decision on the antimonopoly act of 1867, he developed a broad theory of corporate power which the Concord's board of directors had exceeded when negotiating the lease.[7]

Effective as the opinion may have been in realizing the immediate results Doe sought, its consequences exposed yet a third shortcoming in the judicial process. The court, while correcting existing violations, was not equipped for long-range policymaking. The Northern Railroad, which extended from Concord to White River Junction, Vermont, and the Boston, Concord & Montreal, which ran from Concord to Groveton Junction, where it met the Grand Trunk Railway of Canada, provided alternate routes over which the Concord sent its trains to the cities of Quebec. In turn, they depended on the Concord for shipping their freight to Boston markets. Consolidation seemed inevitable, and each line sought to dominate the other two. Doe had prevented the Northern from taking over one rival when he broke the Northern's lease of the Concord. Almost immediately the intent of his ruling was frustrated by a "ring" of speculators who took advantage of the instability in which termination of the lease had left the Concord and sold control of that railroad to both the Northern and the Boston, Concord & Montreal. As Harry Bingham, counsel for the Concord's minority shareholders, put it, "this road was in the hands of the Philistines." [8]

Bingham appealed to the courts. Again there was a delay of about five years — demonstrating still a fourth weakness to judicial administration of railroads. It was difficult to obtain a quorum, since three of the directors who were being sued were justices and a fourth judge was a heavy stockholder in the Concord.[9] When the court finally decided the case — with three members not sitting — it again ignored the antimonopoly act of 1867. Even though a referee had found the contracts made by the Northern and the Boston, Concord & Montreal with the Concord to be fair, they were invalid per se on the grounds that they had been negotiated by representatives of the northern companies who, acting as directors of the Concord, had been contracting with themselves. The court appointed a trustee to handle the Concord's business with its rivals until these directors could be replaced.[10]

The Concord was truly a prize worth fighting for. Its main line may have extended only from Concord to Nashua, but along those thirty-five miles was funneled the trade of half the state. If the northern roads regarded it with covetous eyes, so too did those to the south. The rich old Boston & Lowell, squeezed out of potential eastern routes by the Boston & Maine, had only one way in which to expand — into the territory of the Concord. Few questioned the advantages of a union between the Boston & Lowell and the Concord. Together with the small Nashua & Lowell, they formed a continuous line from Boston to Concord, where geography dictated a division of traffic between the Northern and the Boston, Concord & Montreal. But how could they be united legally? For many years there had been working agreements between the two roads. But when on August 19, 1881, they entered into a five-year arrangement which Doe described as a "general partnership contract," [11] several Concord stockholders filed a bill in equity seeking to enjoin its performance. Doe granted relief on the grounds that the Concord, under its charter, was not authorized to form a partnership with another corporation. Finding that the defendant had failed to show that what could be done by a partnership could not be done as well and as cheaply by each road's working independently, the chief justice held that under the facts the agreement was neither reasonable nor necessary. Again ignoring the antimonopoly act of 1867, he based his decision on the Concord's charter and on common law.[12] To the directors of both the Concord and the Boston & Lowell it surely seemed that Doe was defying the laws of nature, economic reality, and plain common sense. Everyone, including the chief justice, conceded the logic of a union, yet Doe persisted in creating legal obstacles unrelated to business actualities. His theories of corporate responsibility were impeding commercial progress, as became even more apparent when, following the injunction, the two railroads entered into a new arrangement. Again they were taken to court and again Doe invalidated the agreement as a violation of the Concord's charter.[13]

This decision proved a turning point in New Hampshire railroad history. Had the two wealthy dowagers of New England transportation been able to unite, they would have formed an unbeatable combination. The Boston & Maine, whose trains were strung together from dilapidated stock, was as yet in no position to challenge them, and the two northern roads would have fallen into line. But the moment had passed. The Supreme Court, led by Doe, rewrote the laws of economic inevitability when it destroyed their carefully built structure of consolidation. Moreover, these decisions forced the legislature into second thoughts about its railroad policy. It had been expected that if any two railroads could unite under the antimonopoly act of 1867, they would be the Concord and the Boston & Lowell. Yet, try as they might, they could not satisfy the requirements of the Supreme Court. Several small railroads, which had looked forward to being sheltered by the protective wings of their union, were now "physical wrecks," with nowhere to turn, and, it was later charged, there was "practically a Chinese wall around northern New Hampshire . . . preventing the location of manufacturing." It was apparent that the theory of New Hampshire's railroad laws was bankrupt. Even the court felt the policy it had been enforcing to be a failure.[14]

Chief Justice Doe agreed that the keynote of the future must be consolidation, not competition. He took pains, when invalidating the Concord's union with the Boston & Lowell, to point out that his objection was to the form chosen, not to the idea. Both roads could hire the same manager, but they must do so separately. "The distinction to be observed is between an authorized joint employment of an agent, by two companies as joint principals, in work which they are not authorized as joint principals to do, and an authorized several employment of the same person, by each, in those parts of the same work which each is authorized severally to do." [15] That Doe resorted to so uncharacteristic a legalism shows the desperation with which he sought to escape the dilemma of his own making. He even tried to work out a legal formula, based on common-law agency, which would have obtained the benefits of consolidation without formal merger.[16] Indeed, by way of *dictum*, he expressed his most extreme claims for judicial supervision when he said that a union of effort by roads forming a continuous line, such as the Concord and the Nashua & Lowell, was a public right which his court could order even if it had to invent new remedies.[17]

Such talk was ominous. It was difficult enough for railroad attorneys to advise clients on how Doe's court might act, without giving him free rein to follow unpredictable whim according to fact patterns over which they had no control. All the railroads in the state agreed that the legislature had to take a hand. At the 1883 session of the General Court they supported a "consolidation bill" known as the Colby act, granting them the right to enter into management contracts and to lease or be leased, with the approval of two-thirds of the voting stock in each of the contracting companies. Moreover, while the combination of competing roads was still prohibited, outright union between two or more railroads was authorized if the Supreme Court found it promoted the "public good." The Colby act had four purposes: (1) to furnish the state a general railroad incorporation law; (2) to provide a new policy of railroad consolidation; (3) to combine into one system the lines running north from Lawrence, Massachusetts; and (4) to unite the Boston & Maine, which extended from Lawrence to Dover, with the Eastern, which ran parallel with the Boston & Maine along the seacoast from Newburyport to Portsmouth. Two of these objectives were realized. The second and third were frustrated by Chief Justice Doe.

The initial coups under the Colby act were carried off by Massachusetts railroads. The Boston & Maine was the first to move into a position of strength by absorbing the overextended Eastern, practically doubling its size and ending the most costly rivalry in southern New Hampshire. The Boston & Lowell, which had earlier acquired the Nashua & Lowell, sought to realize its raison d'être by leasing both the Northern and the Boston, Concord & Montreal, thus bottling up the Concord and laying claim to the consolidated northern railroad which the Colby act had envisioned. It appeared that these two roads would divide New Hampshire between them — the Boston & Maine controlling the south and east, the Boston & Lowell the north and west. Then Doe struck two blows which sent the Boston & Lowell limping to the sidelines.

First, the decree freeing the Concord railroad from the "Philistines" became final. Doe's injunction forbade the Northern and the Boston, Concord & Montreal to vote the Concord stock which they had purchased from the "ring" of speculators, and as a result a board of directors hostile to the Boston & Lowell was elected. The new leadership of the Concord then set about escaping the vise in which it found itself between the Boston & Lowell to the south and the Northern and Boston, Concord & Montreal to the north. A pro-Concord owner of Northern railroad stock instigated a bill in equity challenging the ninety-year lease of the Northern by the Boston & Lowell. This action resulted in Doe's second blow to the Boston & Lowell's dream of New Hampshire railroad empire — the decision in *Dow's Case*.

As mentioned in the last chapter, Doe used *Dow's Case* as a vehicle for attacking the *Sinking-Fund* doctrine.[18] He was reacting against legislative interference with private property. The Colby act had provided that a railroad could be leased with the consent of two-thirds of its stockholders. Doe held this provision to be unconstitutional, since it deprived dissenting stockholders of their rights, he said, relying on common-law principles of partnership and contracts to establish a constitutional privilege which took precedence over the intent and spirit of the Colby act. The plaintiffs, when they had purchased their stock in the Northern, had entered into a "partnership" for the purpose of providing transportation, not for the purpose of being lessees.

"The lease violates the partnership contract," he concluded, "and takes from the plaintiffs an equitable estate of ninety-nine years without their consent, and without prepayment of the value of the estate taken." [19]

The decision in *Dow's Case* stunned railroad men and their lawyers. "The integrity and ability of our court cannot be challenged," one Boston & Lowell attorney wrote, "but it never in its history announced a conclusion of its judgment which caused so much disappointment to the people of New Hampshire as this." [20] In its report for 1888 the railroad commission summed up the effects:

> The decision emasculated the Colby act. It wrenched apart the Boston & Lowell system, which had been built up under that act. It compelled the unwilling owners of the Northern to take and, for the time being, operate the road independently. It invited a contest in the courts for the Boston, Concord & Montreal, and it precipitated upon the Legislature a railroad war more expensive, more demoralizing, and, in its results, more unsatisfactory to all the contending parties than any other that ever destroyed the substance and sacrificed the peace and dignity of the State.

"Beyond this," the commission added the following year, "all is chaos and contention." [21]

The most immediate effect of Doe's opinion in *Dow* was that the Boston & Lowell lost the will to fight. At the beginning of 1887 it had been the logical railroad to gain control of New Hampshire's heartland. By leasing the two northern lines, it held the Concord a virtual serf, and its position seemed impregnable. Now the tables were reversed. The Boston & Lowell, stripped of one of its newly acquired northern roads and with only the slenderest hold on the other, was bottled up between the expanding Boston & Maine and the revitalized Concord. And so, as one writer summed it up, "the Boston & Lowell shorn of a vital part of its mileage and shell-shocked by the court's decision, saw nothing else to do but give up the fight. In disgust and despair, the B. & L. directors sought peace of mind by leasing their system to the Boston & Maine for 99 years." [22] Thanks in part to Doe, the protagonists in New Hampshire's railroad drama were now the Boston & Maine and the Concord. They were to fight their short-lived struggle for supremacy in both the legislature and in the courts.

The battle was first joined in the legislature. No sooner had the *Dow* injunction been issued than the Boston & Lowell entered into another lease with the Northern, hoping to cure defects with special legislation. The Boston & Maine, now in control of the Boston & Lowell, then set about to lobby a bill through the General Court. It wanted legislation validating the Boston & Lowell's lease of the Northern and protecting its lease of the Boston, Concord & Montreal, whose board of directors had recently been taken over by interests friendly to the Concord. Moreover, it sought a law securing its hold on the Manchester & Lawrence, which it had just acquired, before the Concord could challenge it in Doe's court. The Concord, hemmed in on all sides and needing at least one of the northern roads to survive, turned to the General Court to recover the Manchester & Lawrence, to block the Boston & Lowell's new lease of the Northern, and to obtain permission to merge with the Boston, Concord & Montreal. Passage of the Boston & Maine's bill would have meant that eventually all New Hampshire railroads would be united under one system, dominated by the Boston & Maine. Passage of the Concord's bill would have meant division of the state between two transportation consolidations, one under the Boston & Maine, the other under the Concord. Pitted against the twin bugbears of monopoly and out-of-state financiers, the Concord presented the more emotional case by begging the legislature not to toss "the railroads of central New Hampshire into the capacious maw of the Boston & Maine." [23] The Boston & Maine's position seems sounder in the light of history. The Concord, it insisted, was too isolated. Even merged with the Boston, Concord & Montreal, it would have been a railroad which "begins nowhere and terminates at the other end of the same place." [24]

Precipitated by Doe's decision in *Dow's Case*, the "railroad session" of 1887 became the only New Hampshire legislative term with which scandal has been associated. After a long and bitter struggle, the House and Senate enacted the Boston & Maine's bill. Then, with the Boston & Maine on the very threshold of victory, Governor Charles H. Sawyer vetoed the bill, not because he objected to its provisions, but because "corrupt methods have

been extensively used for the purpose of promoting its passage."
Although he acknowledged that no evidence has been uncovered,
he asserted "there had been deliberate and systematic attempts at
wholesale bribery." [25] Chief Justice Doe could not suppress his
admiration. Governor Sawyer's investments and private business
interests would have prospered along with the Boston & Maine,
Doe believed, and his veto was therefore an act of true integrity.[26]

The Boston & Maine quickly pushed through a second bill
authorizing it to lease the Northern, which the governor also
vetoed because sections were "in substance and effect a reenact-
ment of an essential part" of the earlier bill. In the end the Boston
& Maine had to content itself with a law approving its lease of
the Manchester & Lowell and providing for the purchase of stock
from dissenting stockholders (hopefully satisfying the constitutional requirement laid down in *Dow*). This result was all that
came of the fierce legislative battle Doe had wrought. The Concord gained nothing besides stalling its opponent, while the
Boston & Maine emerged with only the leanest spoils. As the
railroad commission summed it up:

> Thus the one result of this memorable struggle, so far as it appears
> upon the statute books, is the confirmation of the lease of the Man-
> chester & Lawrence to the Boston & Maine. The Northern and
> Boston, Concord & Montreal, which were the grand prizes contended
> for, were left as they were found, the one to be operated independ-
> ently or under some makeshift arrangement, the other to be scrambled
> for in the courts.[27]

It was almost as if Doe's thesis of legislative incompetence had
been borne out. New Hampshire once more turned to her
Supreme Court to settle questions with which the legislature
could not cope.

In October, following the prorogation of the General Court, the
Concord attempted to lease the Northern. The directors of the
Northern, still under Boston & Lowell domination, rejected the
offer and leased their road, at less favorable terms, to the Boston
& Maine. At the same time the Boston & Maine assumed the
Boston & Lowell's lease of the Boston, Concord & Montreal.
These leases, together with the statute permitting it to absorb the

Manchester & Lawrence, placed the Boston & Maine in exactly the position it would have been in had the governor not vetoed its bill.[28] It seemed that all it had to do was wait for the Concord to topple into its lap. But first it had to reckon with Chief Justice Doe.

The Concord, still the wealthiest New Hampshire railroad, was not about to give up the fight. It had a strong card of its own to play — its control of the Boston, Concord & Montreal. Concord money had gained a majority on the Montreal's board of directors, and when the Boston & Lowell, acting for the Boston & Maine, insisted that its lease of the Montreal be honored, the pro-Concord directors appealed to the courts. After filing a bill in equity to invalidate the Boston & Lowell's lease, they brought a writ of entry against the Boston & Maine, which was in virtual control of the Montreal's property. By agreement the matter was to be settled in the state court, the Boston & Maine pledging not to remove any question to a federal tribunal. Although the actions were combined, Chief Justice Doe decided to treat them separately. He assigned to himself the opinion dealing with the bill in equity to invalidate the lease, while he gave to Judge Clark the opinion dealing with the writ of entry to recover possession.

Doe's decision in the equity suit is significant because, forced to meet the Colby act head on, he gave it his approval. No matter what the law had been under the antimonopoly act of 1867, he said, railroad consolidation was now official policy. The lease of the Boston, Concord & Montreal was valid since it conformed to the prerequisites of the Colby bill. "Neither the state, nor any Montreal stockholder who voted for the lease can maintain a suit to set it aside." The only persons who might were those minority stockholders whose rights under the corporate charter had been violated, as in *Dow's Case*. But the minority stockholders had not prosecuted with equitable expedition; they had waited nearly three years before bringing suit, probably to see how *Dow* would be decided. Because of this delay, Doe ruled, the objection of dissenting stockholders was waived by laches, and the bill in equity had to be dismissed.[29]

Laches could not bar the writ of entry. In the second opinion Judge Clark found that the Boston & Lowell, when it originally leased the Boston, Concord & Montreal, had covenanted that it would not "assign or underlet the premises hereby demised, or part with the possession thereof, except with the written consent of the [Boston, Concord & Montreal]." By its lease to the Boston & Maine, the Boston & Lowell had "voluntarily parted with its power to control the operation of the Montreal road, and has become the agent and servant of the Boston & Maine." Since this action was taken without the consent of the Boston, Concord & Montreal, Clark ruled (with three judges dissenting) that it constituted "a breach of the covenant of the Montreal lease and a forfeiture of the estate granted by it." [30] As a result, the lease was terminated, the Boston, Concord & Montreal was returned to a management which represented Concord interests, "and the circulars formerly issued by the Boston & Lowell telling the employees to use physical force to retain the road became of no avail." [31]

To many railroad men this decision seemed the last straw. Once again the Supreme Court had prevented consolidation. What good was it to have legislative approval for mergers if the larger railroads were not able to include dependent roads in their lease arrangements? The court was applying traditional notions of common law to situations for which they were no longer meaningful. Both the Northern and the Boston, Concord & Montreal, as the railroad commission reported, were "steadily deteriorating; their operation is of make-shift order, their dividends are unearned, patrons have no guaranty that contracts made with their managers will be executed, or that needed facilities will be furnished in the future." Even more deplorable, the moral fiber of the state had been undermined while the two northern roads became "prizes to be wrangled and struggled and schemed for by the Boston & Maine and Concord, as bones of contention in the Courts, causes of bitter and discreditable strife in the legislature, and corruption and demoralization in political parties." [32]

By June 1889 the Concord and the Boston & Maine had decided that matters had gone far enough. Seeking to avoid further litigation in Doe's court and to become the masters of their own fate, they signed a "truce." Under this agreement, as enacted by the General Court, the Concord was united with the Boston, Concord & Montreal to form a new corporation called the Concord & Montreal, which was permitted to purchase twelve small railroads. The Boston & Maine was allowed to lease six railroads, including the Northern, and to purchase several lines which it already held by lease. As a result all New Hampshire roads, outside the Connecticut Valley, were merged into two systems, the Boston & Maine and the Concord & Montreal, which together controlled nearly nine-tenths of the mileage in the state. In a series of opinions, Doe and his colleagues upheld the "truce." [33] With the Colby act's policy of consolidation finally established on a basis acceptable to the judges, the Supreme Court was ready to bow out of its role as a quasiadministrative watchdog. Economics, a reversal of political theory, and the limitations of the judicial process had passed it by.

The inevitable was not long delayed. On January 1, 1893, the Boston & Maine brought under its sway New Hampshire's other remaining independent railroad system by leasing the Connecticut River and its subsidiary lines. The Concord held out for only two more years. With Judge Doe no longer willing to bar its way, the Boston & Maine in 1895 leased the Concord & Montreal, thereby obtaining control of 937 miles of track out of a total broad-gauge mileage of 1,165, exclusive of lumber roads, in New Hampshire. The economic results were remarkable: shipping costs fell by as much as one-half in some parts of the state; a political calm such as had not been known for two decades settled over New Hampshire; and the Supreme Court relinquished its supervisory role as the final arbiter of railroad-management matters.

Doe had made a valiant try. If any judge in American history could have made the court an effective instrument for business regulation, it was he. That his solution did not solve but only compounded the problems posed by railroad monopoly proved the necessity for different methods and novel institutions. In Doe's failure lies the justification for administrative agencies with quasijudicial and quasilegislative powers. Doe's theory of constitutional limitations upon governmental regulation of private property had to be modified. Common-law courts are not equipped to settle most disputes between official policy and business enterprise.

It was a remarkable effort nonetheless. At a time when the governments of other states were knuckling under to the magnates and violence frequently erupted between the hirelings of rival speculators, the struggle to dominate the railroads of New Hampshire was refereed by what one economic historian has called the "metaphysical genius" of Charles Doe. It was he and his court who determined how the game would be played and gave the ultimate victory to the Boston & Maine by staying the hand of the Boston & Lowell. "Whether he cared if consolidation were voted up or down, his decisions did not state directly; but, by condemning the short cuts taken to secure it as a violation of the laws of the state and of more fundamental equities, he did his judicial best to postpone it for years." [34]

The years during which Doe postponed consolidation were the years between the periods in which Winston Churchill set his two great novels of American politics — *Coniston* and *Mr. Crewe's Career*. *Coniston* describes New Hampshire at a time when the railroads were weak and small towns dominated the government. *Mr. Crewe's Career* comes a decade after Doe's death, when New Hampshire, including her courts, belonged to the Boston & Maine. It was this transition of power, from the rustic political boss to the alien corporate manager, that would have been prevented by Doe's legal theories. While Doe was chief justice a New England conscience sat on the New Hampshire bench and in the name of nineteenth-century constitutionalism shielded the state from corporate domination, temporarily stemming the tide of monopoly, the demands of progress, and the inevitability of economic laws.

Chapter Twenty

THE TOMBSTONES
OF OUR ANCESTORS
Constitutional Principles

D ID the fact that Charles Doe tried to regulate public utilities
from an appellate bench mean that he abjured orthodox constitutional principles, such as separation of powers? The very
idea would have shocked Doe. He regarded himself the most
orthodox of men on the doctrine of checks and balances. He
usually spoke of it as an absolute principle upon the inviolability
of which liberty and "private rights" depend. Quoting Montes-
quieu, Doe wrote, "There is no liberty, if the judiciary power be
not separated from the legislative and executive." [1] In most decisions which involved the principle Doe was perfectly conventional. The legislature, he repeatedly stated, decides "what the
law shall be"; other public agents decide what the law is or
apply the law to the facts.[2] Legislative power cannot be delegated,
either to the courts, to the towns, or to the people.[3] Nor can the
court interfere with the legislature by settling membership disputes.[4] During his years as a judge Doe departed from the safe
side of theory only once, directing the General Court to stop
playing politics and elect a United States Senator — an order the
legislature refused to obey, on the grounds that the opinion of
Doe and his court was entitled to no more weight than that of
"any six good lawyers." [5]

But espousal of orthodox theory reveals only part of the story;
application of theory is what counts. And in this respect Charles

Doe's concept of checks and balances was more radical than conventional. As the railroad cases illustrate, he was inclined to assign to the judiciary a rather large role in the tripartite division of government. The prime constitutional function of courts, he believed, is to guard against abuses by the executive and legislative branches. Protection of private property especially is entrusted to the judiciary by the constitution, and judges have an absolute duty to see that the legislature does not trespass on their domain. This is one reason why Marshall should have decided *Fletcher* v. *Peck* and the *Dartmouth College Case* on the separation-of-powers principle. In *Fletcher* v. *Peck* the Georgia legislature, when it declared the land grant void for fraud, had invaded the judiciary's province. Under the doctrine of checks and balances, Doe asserted, "the legislature has no more power to exercise the judicial functions of declaring a grant or contract void for fraud, than the court has to exercise legislative power." [6] The same was true of *Dartmouth College*. The legislature had attempted to reform a trust by appointing new trustees. "The administration of the law of trusts is either legislative or judicial; it cannot be both." [7] Since it is judicial, it follows that the New Hampshire lawmakers had exceeded their constitutional prerogatives when they assigned college property to new trustees.

Doe found the division between the executive and judicial branches less easy to define. Judicial power, he had to admit, is not limited to the courts. Selectmen, when making tax assessments, act judicially and are not liable for errors. Similarly, since taxes are debts collectable by suit at common law, and since assessment and liability are of "a judicial nature," the courts cannot be denied a supervisory role. The constitutional guarantee of equality demands no less. "Without . . . a judicial remedy for illegal taxation, there would be a power of arbitrary and unequal assessment." [8]

As these cases make clear, in Judge Doe's hands the separation-of-powers principle became a means of enlarging the court's jurisdiction. In the same spirit, he was not above extending the principle if he thought this would lend constitutional respectability to one of his common-law reforms. When arguing that the court cannot invade the fact-finding province of the jury, he contended that the constitution, by adopting the common law, had divided the office of judge and jury. For the court to over-step these bounds would "destroy the check and balance which have been deemed essential to the judicial branch of the government." [9] Here is exemplified one of Charles Doe's most irritating tactics; the easy facility for converting his common-law prejudices into constitutional principles. He had developed his theory concerning the law-fact distinction entirely from English legal history, yet he thought nothing of making it a constitutional dogma. [10]

In most cases it is impossible to tell where common-law theory ends and constitutional principle begins. Undoubtedly there were times when the constitution did inspire his common-law reforms; but generally it was an afterthought, a means of strengthening his arguments by cloaking them with the immutability of organic law. This is certainly true of his procedural reforms. Correction of remedial injustice was his purpose and motivation. To help the cause along, Judge Doe would quote the article in the bill of rights which provides that "every subject of this state is entitled to a certain remedy." [11] With perfect confidence Doe asserted that this provision not only supported, but even required, the adoption of his procedural reforms. The common-law proposition that each party is entitled to such remedy, "including form, method, and order of procedure, as justice and convenience require," was eventually postulated as a constitutional principle. [12] "Adequate remedies," he maintained, "are incidents of substantial constitutional rights." [13]

One constitutional issue which Doe settled with the principle of adequate remedies was the right of women to be admitted to the bar. "The law regulating the admission of attorneys," Doe argued, "is a part of the law of procedure; and our common law allows such procedure as justice and convenience require. Justice requires that a party should be permitted to conduct his cause in person (subject to reasonable requirements of propriety), or by any agent of good character, and that the test of the agent's character should not be so rigorously applied as to imperil the constitutional right to a fair trial." [14] To rest this basic constitutional right on the principle that litigants are entitled to adequate procedure has caused some to think Doe admitted women by the back door. Much better, it is said, had he emphasized the changed social position of women in nineteenth-century America.[15] In other words, he should have established their right to be lawyers on grounds similar to those which motivated Chief Justice Earl Warren to hold segregated school unconstitutional. But Charles Doe was too shrewd a constitutional lawyer to depend on debatable assumptions. The question, he pointed out, should not be "whether women could lawfully be admitted, but whether they could lawfully be kept out." [16]

Judge Doe also knew better than to make the provision in the bill of rights which requires adequate remedies a cure for all procedural injustices. It had to be reconciled with other constitutional principles, one of which was the prohibition against retroactive laws. The rule had been that if a statute introduced procedural rather than substantive changes, it was not covered by the provision.[17] Doe considered this distinction too simple. A remedy, he pointed out, "may be changed as to affect a right injuriously, oppressively, and unjustly, within the meaning of the prohibition." The question is not whether the change effects the remedy, but whether it effects the remedy only. The test should be "not the distinction between right and remedy, but between right and wrong." In one case the court had held that a certain action of debt could not properly be maintained by three plaintiffs. Subsequently the legislature passed a law which provided that, "when two or more are joined as plaintiff, the writ or other process may be amended by striking out the name of any other plaintiff." Thereupon one plaintiff moved to strike the names of the other two. Despite the fact that the statute specifically said it was applicable "to existing suits," Judge Doe held that it could not constitutionally be applied to this action. To do so would "change no cause of action into a good cause of action, and operate as a substantial creation of a new suit that could be maintained, in place of an old one that could not." [18]

Had a constitutional principle not been at stake, Judge Doe might have permitted the amendment. In many a common-law case he had been faced by a more difficult problem, yet he usually found ways to brush aside technicalities and to try the matter on its merits. But constitutional technicalities were not easily dismissed. Consistency with the social-compact theory forbade compromise. Sound constitutional construction could not be sacrificed to the expediency of temporarily reaching a just result. As the organ which regulates the delicate balance between social conflicts, the constitution is too fragile an instrument to be tampered with by the shifting tides of judicial fiat. "It would be a serious misfortune," Doe wrote, "if, by construing the constitution strictly in its general direction, and liberally in other directions, or by adopting any arbitrary rule or eccentric habit of construction, it was rendered necessary to constantly amend the constitution by inserting such specific guarantees of the original instrument to changed circumstances and new conditions of society. Such a custom of amendment would propagate erroneous ideas of the original, break the uniformity and shake the permanency of its principles, and materially impair its efficacy." [19] Doe felt so strongly about this point that he likened amendments proposed by some constitutional conventions to the work of vandals seeking to despoil the tombstones of their ancestors.[20]

In some states [he warned] they tinker the constitution as readily as they tinker the statute law; the constitution becomes a mere statute annually altered; & ceases to be a constitution in any useful sense. I wouldn't propose a constl amendt except in a dire extremity, on any subject. I fear we are fast losing what the fathers meant by permanent constl liberty; that we are losing it by erroneous constructions on the one hand, & by amendments that ought to be unnecessary, on the other. For ought I can see, in some of the Western States, they might as well abolish their constitutions, & go along without any, as to be all the time altering them. When they find the constitution in their way, they alter it; it ceases to be a protection of life, liberty & property. There is sound doctrine enough in the N.H. Const for a state to run on, several hundred years.[21]

More than any other paragraph written by Charles Doe, this quotation summarizes his view of a proper constitution. A constitution should contain broad principles, nothing else. Implementation and resolution of those principles should be left to the legislature and to the courts, not to constitutional conventions. In short, Doe expected constitutions to be organic law, not statutory law. This is all he meant by the permanency of constitutional principles. Yet he may easily be misunderstood. Was he not in fact confusing constitutional-law principles with natural-law principles? Did he not advocate interpreting the constitution as though it embodied the law of nature? There is evidence to support the contention that Charles Doe was an exponent of natural law. His writings, even his private correspondence, are replete with references to the law of nature. Speaking of the constitutional principle of equality, for example, he associated it with "the immutability & triumph of the eternal, natural law of justice." [22] And in many of his opinions Doe gave greater weight to what he called "the system of legal reason" than to statutes, implying that he might even seek guidance from sources higher than specific constitutional provisions.[23] As previously mentioned, in the *Mink Case* he based the property owner's right to defend his property, even in violation of a statute, upon his "natural" as well as upon his "common-law" and "constitutional" right of defense. But these statements must not be read out of context. Charles Doe did not confuse constitutional principles with natural law. In the *Mink Case* he took pains to point out that the drafters of the New Hampshire constitution had specifically reserved to all men a "natural" right to enjoy and defend their lives and their property.[24] This meant nothing more than a right defined by natural reason, not limited by common-law precedents. "If any discrepancy should be found in the definitions of it given by common-law precedents and by natural reason, the latter must prevail, because the right is explicitly asserted in the bill of rights as a natural right, and not as one defined by common-law authorities." [25] But, as he made clear in another decision, the fact that a right is "natural" does not mean it cannot be superseded by the law of society. The meaning is, "not that society cannot legally prohibit self-defence, but that, in certain cases, society cannot in fact provide a substitute or equivalent for it. In those cases of emergency and necessity in which individuals cannot resort for protection to the law of society, because the law of society cannot furnish protection, that law recognizing its own inability to supersede the natural remedy, adopts and maintains it as a legal one." [26]

Illustrative of what Charles Doe meant by "natural reason" is his definition of the term "natural law." He used it in a rather narrow sense, as when he pointed out that a tax on whiskey is not paid by the manufacturer. His customers know he is passing it on to them. "By natural law, he is a collector of the tax, and the customers of his products are the payers of the tax." [27] This is a natural law of economics. Doe derived a law of physical nature from the fact that the Androscoggin River has the natural capability of floating logs. In 1825 Chief Justice Richardson, seeking a way around the ancient rule that waters above the ebb and flow of the sea are not "navigable" for legal purposes, held that a river may, by usage, become a public right of way. Doe held this to be contrary to authority and reason. Rivers are highways by nature, not by prescription. The first man to use a New Hampshire river as a right of way, whether "under Indian or English law," had a "legal right" to do so. "Though not 'navigable' in the English technical sense (that is, not tide water), it is a highway by the law of nature, adopted by the English common law, which in this respect, being suited to the condition of this state, is a part of our common law." For legal purposes, then, the river is a highway. [28]

Despite this narrow definition, it has been said that Doe based the social compact on the law of nature; that he believed the court to have a duty "to protect the natural law underlying the constitution." [29] By implication Doe is placed among that class of American judges who rely on divine or natural law to invalidate statutes of which they disapprove. In truth, there was no method of constitutional interpretation which Doe execrated more. Even in New Hampshire, he thought, "the constitutional view has been darkened by doctrines of natural justice, and theories of the highest law." [30] A judge, Doe maintained, has no authority to read into the constitution principles which are not there.

The constitution authorizes the legislature to make constitutional laws: and it requires the court to be sworn to officially support the constitution, and to perform the duties of their office agreeably to the constitution and the human laws of the state; not agreeably to that constitution and those laws supplemented or modified by the divine, natural, or moral law, or the principles of reason and justice. While it recognizes the divine government and the unalienable rights of conscience, it does not establish anarchy by legalizing every principle and practice that may be approved by anybody's interpretation of the higher law, nor authorize the court to destroy the constitution and laws which they are commissioned to administer. [31]

These words may have astonished some members of the New Hampshire bar. For Doe, who based so many sweeping pronouncements on natural justice and natural reason, is now condemning the practice. He tells lawyers to heed only the specific provisions in the constitution. Yet what about *Orr* v. *Quimby?* In that case, it will be recalled, he attempted to establish the broad principle that the state may not seize private property without first tendering compensation, even though the constitution says nothing about eminent domain. Closer inspection shows that Judge Doe was consistent. It is a matter of proper construction. In *Orr* v. *Quimby* he construed the constitution in terms of history: history explained why there was no eminent-domain provision in the bill of rights; the generation which had drafted the constitution had been unaware of the "danger" of government confiscation; therefore the bill of rights could not be expected to mention eminent domain. Instead this guarantee, if it existed, would be found in some general provision reserving to the people their right to property. In this way Doe arrived at the conclusion that the New Hampshire constitution protected private property from uncompensated government seizure.[32] He followed rules of construction, not arguments from natural law. Indeed, he specifically rejected the idea that such a right could be based on natural law. Other New Hampshire judges had also been troubled by the fact that the bill of rights was silent on eminent domain and, finding no other means for avoiding the inevitable, had turned to natural law. The first had been Chief Justice Richardson in 1826. Ignoring rules of construction, he made the sweeping assertion that "natural justice speaks on this point, where our constitution is silent."[33] Far from approving, Judge Doe regarded this the worst of all possible grounds for sustaining a constitutional principle, since it rested on the quicksand of social ethics by substituting moral suasion for legal force and moral probability for legal security.[34] Calling it "the higher law gospel," he pointed out that it could lead to "the destruction of all govt & the disintegration of society."[35]

Charles Doe admitted that he was "somewhat violent" on the subject of natural law. He had much to be violent about: it was commonly used as a method of constitutional interpretation. Richardson was by no means the only judge to employ it; New

York's Chancellor Kent had also "buried the constitutional law of eminent domain & compensation" under the natural-law gloss. So too had Mr. Justice Johnson when concurring with Marshall in *Fletcher* v. *Peck*. In all of Doe's correspondence there is no other passage now extant quite as bitter as his denunciation of Johnson's "higher law."

He holds that a state cant revoke its own grants, because to do so, would violate "the reason & nature of things"; by which he means the laws of the universe, the higher law of natural justice. No more higher law for me, if you please. The lower law of the constitution, is as high as the oath to support the const allows a judge to go in his judicial capacity. Johnson's higher law is the highest I ever heard of. It "will impose laws even on the Deity", says Johnson. There have always been crazy fellows at the South, & a few in Mass. who indulge in that kind of declamation when they put themselves outside the regulations of the organized society in which they live, set up an independent govt of their own, & become a law unto themselves. From all such, the Lord deliver us.

If Johnson were still around in 1876, Doe wrote, and "if he had lived through the distractions that have afflicted the country from his decision in 1810 to this day, I hope I could convince him that his higher law is the most detestable & ruinous heresy the world has yet heard of."

Johnson is satisfied with indulging in such platitudes, & "the reason & nature of things", as constitutional ground for holding a statute void. I have no patience with such stuff. We cant hold a statute void for unconstitutionality without [saying] which constitution it violates (the const. of Ga. or of the U.S.), & putting our finger on the particular clause of a particular const, & demonstrating, by fair, reasonable, & well-settled rules of construction, that the legal meaning of that particular clause prohibits the statute in question. When a man undertakes to convince me of the unconstitutionality of a statute, he wont make any headway until he gets through all such twaddle as "the reason & nature of things". . . . Those phrases I never saw in a constitution. I want to see the book, the page, the line, the very words of the written const with which the statute is said to be in conflict, before I hear any argument on the invalidity of the statute.[36]

Judge Doe may be uncompromising, but he is not backtracking; he is not rejecting in constitutional law the search for abstract justice which was the theme of his civil-law reforms; he is not saying that there is no place in constitutional interpretation for "morality" or "justice" or "right reason." On the contrary, he wants to place them on firmer ground than "higher law." The constitution had been written by men dedicated to "morality," "justice," and "right reason." Proper rules of construction seeking their intent is the one sound method of establishing principles. As constitutional principles, not natural-law principles, they will be guaranteed for tomorrow as well as for today. But was Doe being realistic concerning his rules of construction? He claims that they should be used, rather than natural-law arguments, to establish constitutional principles. But what was the chief rule of construction upon which he relied when interpreting the constitution if not John Locke's social-compact theory? This was natural law in its purest form — the view that governments derive authority from the consent of men voluntarily abandoning the state of nature in return for a society based on liberty and equality. Only the divine design could be higher law. By making it the key to constitutional absolutism and the test by which all fundamental principles are defined, was not Charles Doe making natural law the determinant of constitutional construction?

The answer is that he was not. A method of constitutional interpretation must not be confused with a belief as to the source of law. Chief Justice Doe did not adopt Locke's theories; they had been adopted by the drafters of the New Hampshire constitution. He had no alternative but to treat their instrument as a social contract.[37] This was not the same as making it the test of right, privilege, and power for all times and all places. Far from taking a stand on the validity of Locke's premise, Judge Doe acknowledged that Hobbes's view of an absolute state was probably good constitutional theory in contemporary England. "The omnipotence of parliament is the only English principle that is constitutional in the American sense of the word." Parliament might be restrained by custom, history, precedent, traditions, expediency, and "the moral sense of the influential class," but not by what Americans call constitutional principles.[38] This had been even more true for New Hampshire between the Declaration of Independence and the adoption of the first constitution. The provisional state government had possessed "undefined and boundless authority, hastily assumed and arbitrarily exercised." Fundamental principles were "superseded by what was regarded as necessity." [39] For both societies, contemporary England and Revolutionary New Hampshire, Doe agreed with John Austin that law is the command of the sovereign; no legal or theoretical restraints rested on these governments. Doe did not claim that the Lockeian theories which he expounded in nineteenth-century New Hampshire should have been binding upon them. Lockeian principles of liberty and equality had validity only because they had been adopted by the constitution of June 2, 1784. "We had no inviolable rights, no rights constitutional in the American sense, before the second day of June, 1784. The constitution that went into operation on that day terminated the era of unlimited power, and introduced an era of liberty and equality secured by a supreme written law, and an organic division of government into three branches, each vested with limited authority." [40]

It was the realization of divergent theories on the origin of law that furnished Charles Doe his most rigid principle of constitutional interpretation. "On the question of power," he warned, "English precedent and the pre-constitutional practice in this country establish either boundless despotism or nothing." [41] English constitutional decisions are useful only when "counteracted by a close attention to the difference between the supremacy of parliament and the limited power of an American legislature." [42] Nothing is more dangerous than justifying American state action from British example. "That is one of the arguments that excites my wrath," Charles Doe wrote a friend. "If that argument proves anything, it proves that there is no such thing as an American constitution — that a minority hold their lives, liberties & property at the mercy of the majority in this country as is the case in England. When I read such arguments, I cant help feeling either that the counsel making them are not lawyers, or that they believe the court is extremely deficient in law and authority." [43]

In *Thompson* v. *Androscoggin River Company* the defendants' attorney made this mistake. He cited an English decision as holding that a railroad, which is without fault, is not liable for damages resulting from a fire started by one of its locomotives. Other American judges might treat this case as common-law authority, but Doe dismissed it on constitutional grounds:

It was so held not because a careful use of fire on the defendants' railway was a reasonable use which the former owner of the land could have rightfully made of his own property at common law, but because the defendants' careful and skilful use of fire in their locomotives was authorized by parliament. The decision was put upon the ground that an act authorized by parliament was not a violation of the criminal law, nor in any sense unlawful. If, by authority of parliament, the defendants had carefully and skilfully consumed the plaintiff's house as fuel in their engines, without compensation, the decision would have been the same, and would have proceeded upon the same principle of arbitrary and unlimited legislative power, which is not a principle of American institutions. Such authorities, followed in this country, would put an end to our entire constitutional system of government.[44]

Similarly Judge Doe would not consider precedents drawn from New Hampshire's anteconstitutional past. To him they were precedents "of absolutism and inequality," which "serve for warning, though not for constitutional example." [45] The fact that during the Revolution the legislature had permitted towns to pay bounties for enlistments can have no bearing on whether the constitutional legislature in 1874 could authorize towns to reimburse those who had purchased substitutes during the Civil War. "The revolutionary evidence does not show that in voting bounties for enlistments in the continental service, a town was understood to legislate upon the subject of American independence as a local, municipal matter. Towns could vote those bounties, because, against the public enemy, anyone could do anything permitted by the general court or the committee of safety." [46]

It is apparent that Charles Doe's fundamental constitutional principle was nothing more or less than the supremacy of the constitution. This he made clear in his discussion of the *Dartmouth College Case*. Some claimed the King had granted Dartmouth an irrevocable charter. Doe denied this. But even if the King had done so, it would have had no bearing on the authority of New Hampshire's government to repeal that charter. "Our legislature inherits no power from the king or Parlt or anybody else. It derives its power from the const." [47] It was to the constitution and to the constitution alone that he had looked to resolve the *Dartmouth* issue to his own satisfaction. It did not matter that in other jurisdictions the rights of property were not as absolute as he made them in New Hampshire; it was the social compact which gave them "organic security." As long as he was chief justice, "They would not be overthrown here by proof that there are governments under which they are defenceless." [48] There is, therefore, no need for natural law. The constitutional principle of liberty and equality can better be preserved by construing the constitution with consistent and proper rules of construction. If this is done faithfully and uniformly, vandals will not despoil the tombstones of our ancestors.

PART FIVE

THE LEGAL PHILOSOPHER

THE LAST LAWMAKER
Judicial Power[1]

THERE is no field of legal scholarship more woefully neglected than the jurisprudence of our state judges. The leading
treatise on American legal theory, summarizing the thoughts of
dozens of the law's "prophets," discusses only three judges —
Story, Kent, and Holmes; and they are mentioned for their extrajudicial writings, not for their court opinions.[2] But American law
has been made by its judges, not by its prophets. It is questionable to portray "the legal mind in America" by quoting long passages from semipolitical speeches delivered by Robert Rantul,
Jr., and David Dudley Field without so much as mentioning
Lemuel Shaw and John Bannister Gibson. Yet this is what one
recent book attempts to do.[3]

The result is obvious: the development of American legal
theory is only partially known, and the assumption of history has
to be that the jurisprudential lodestars which have guided decisionmaking came from without rather than from within the
courts. The legal philosophies of individual judges are categorized
as belonging to this or that school or following this or that academic theorist. Practicing jurists are credited with slight originality and sometimes with none at all. John Henry Wigmore dismissed Charles Doe as a judicial thinker in this way. No man
praised Doe's great reforms more than did Dean Wigmore, yet
Wigmore apparently assumed them to have been promulgated ad
hoc, unrelated to any jurisprudential pattern. Considering a number of distinguished state judges, the Dean wrote, "Justice
Holmes seems to me the only one who has framed for himself a

system of legal ideas and general truths of life, and composed his opinions in harmony with the system already framed. His opinions present themselves as instances naturally serving to exhibit this general body of principles in application. The frame-work is his own, and not some orthodox commentator's." Wigmore then mentions twenty other judges — including Doe — stating that none "give the impression of having worked out, themselves, and for their own use, an harmonious construction of general principles." [4]

There is as much truth in Wigmore's summary appraisal as there is in Professor Leon Burr Richardson's offhand remark that Doe's "one interest was jurisprudence." [5] Chief Justice Doe had no "one interest," but if he had, it was surely the mechanics of case law rather than abstract legal theory. Yet there is more truth to Richardson's statement than in Wigmore's implication. Charles Doe was not only a student of applied jurisprudence, he also endorsed a composite set of general principles, which he adhered to with remarkable consistency. True, Doe's intellectual interests differed from Holmes's. Doe was concerned primarily with expounding law and administering justice. He was a practical, working judge, prepared to meet each problem as it arose. Holmes was a philosopher first and a lawyer second. He hesitated to enroll at Harvard Law School for fear of not finding the mental stimulation which he craved. The development of their divergent tort theories demonstrates the differences in their outlooks. It was Holmes the philosopher who led Holmes the jurist astray in the *Goodman* case. Yet Doe's contrasting holding in *Huntress* was as firmly based on principle and legal theory. [6] The reason Wigmore could not recognize a jurisprudential pattern in Doe's work was because Doe never wrote articles or books to explain his conception of the correct arrangement or classification of law. On this side of the Atlantic only Holmes was doing so. Wigmore's appraisal is therefore misleading. He purports to be speaking of Holmes the judge; yet when comparing him to other judges, he is really discussing Holmes the author of *The Common Law* and the editor of *The American Law Review*. It is these works that make it easy to discover a "system." To have worked out a rigid "framework" and then to have explained it to the world would have been out of character for Doe and might have stifled him.

But there was framework; a bare skeleton if you will, but a skeleton nonetheless.

Surely Wigmore was wrong in one respect: Doe did work out for himself a harmonious construction of general principles. He applied them consistently in a broad pattern — even in those matters in which he seems most radical, as is shown by his theories on judicial power. To read one or two of his opinions leaves the impression that he acted on expediency; that no matter what the problem, he believed the court had authority to act. There is no denying that Doe found excuses for exercising judicial power whenever he felt the need. Nevertheless, if his reach was wide, it was consistent. Before acting, he justified action. He did have a theory of judicial power; he did follow a philosophy which required restraint as well as initiative.

Judicial lawmaking did not enjoy favor during the last four decades of the nineteenth century. The doctrine of separation of powers placed it in an anomalous light, since almost everyone except Charles Doe thought judges had power to act only if directed by precedent or authorized by statute. Prior to the Civil War there had been a need for lawmakers on the courts. Kent, Marshall, Story, Gibson, Smith, and even Shaw had made their share of law for a new nation in a new industrial age. But periods of growth are followed by periods of retrenchment. It was Doe's lot to live in an era suitable to the theory that law is found and not made — when precedents were regarded as settled, rules as formulated, and principles as defined. Judicial lawmaking was so out of fashion that Roscoe Pound, surveying the scene in 1914, concluded that there had been only "one judge upon the bench of a state court who stands out as a builder of the law since the Civil War." His one exception was Charles Doe.[7]

We have already seen much of what Pound meant. Doe's new-modelling of the writs, his development of the modern approach to criminal insanity, and his reform of rules of construction in line with reason mark him as a law builder extraordinary in any age or place. It is characteristic of Doe's theory of judicial power that he was willing to "legislate" at the trial term as well as the law term.[8] The common-law process being what it is, however, we must turn to his appellate decisions to discover the underlying legal philosophy by which he was guided. Charles Doe's concept of judicial power was grounded upon the logic of necessity and the function of the court to furnish a remedy for every right. If under a specific fact situation an order, decision, or decree is required, the court has power to act. As he expressed it, "When the law commands a thing to be done, it puts in requisition the means of executing its command. From tribunals charged with the correction of judicial errors, indispensable process is not withheld." Thus any grant — contractual, testamentary, statutory, or common-law — conveys the rights and powers without which it would be of no effect. That is, it conveys "the means reasonably necessary for the enjoyment of the granted property or right, the exercise of the granted power, and the accomplishment of the object of the grant." [9] This is the doctrine of necessity which, carried to the conclusion to which Doe was prepared to carry it, meant that the court's jurisdictional authority is limited mainly by the factual problems which arise.

An example of Doe's application of the doctrine of necessity is *Attorney-General* v. *Taggart*, a case involving executive disability. The governor, David H. Goodell, being ill, his constitutional successor, Senate President David A. Taggart, refused to act until his duty was clarified by adjudication. Goodell directed the Attorney General to petition for *mandamus* ordering Taggart "to exercise the powers and authorities of the governor." Doe's method of approach was direct and, if one accepted his premises, logical. Starting with New Hampshire's organic law, he built an argument for judicial power. All that the state constitution provided was that the president of the Senate should fill the vacancy caused by the governor's "death, absence from the state, or otherwise." [10] Transforming the word "otherwise" into "disability," Doe said that the "mischief" which the constitution sought to prevent "was the suspension of executive government by the governor's death, absence from the state, or disability." [11] Next he found the necessity by saying, "The services of a substitute may be necessary when the governor's absence or disability is temporary, as well as when it is permanent." [12] Finally he established the right for which the court was bound to furnish a remedy. "The state's right to the executive service of the president of the senate," he wrote, "is no less enforceable than its right to the judicial service of a juror. There is no express or implied exemption of the executive substitute from the compulsion of legal process." [13] From these premises the Chief Justice concluded that the issue of whether a gubernatorial vacancy existed could be determined on a petition for *mandamus* brought by the Attorney General.

It is not suggested that Judge Doe's decision, while novel, was unexpected. It was what all parties desired — a determination that the president of the Senate, while temporarily governor, would be acting *de jure*. The significance of *Taggart* is that it illustrates Doe's method. Where he found necessity, he never hesitated to exert judicial power. Where he determined that a right existed, he was prepared to devise a sufficient remedy.

It was of little consequence to Chief Justice Doe that one pattern of legal thought, then perhaps prevalent, might have delayed decision until the matter arose in an orthodox law suit. To Doe such a technicality was unworthy of consideration. If necessity exists now, he argued, then now is the time to act, and not the time to quibble over such barren topics as judicial power. "The existence of an executive vacancy is a question of law and fact within judicial jurisdiction. If the defendant exercised executive power without a previous judgment on that question, the legality of his acts could be contested and determined in subsequent litigation; and the judicial character of the question does not depend upon the time when it is brought into court. With adequate legal process, the consideration and decision of such a question may be prospective as well as retrospective." [14]

In one sense this case marks the outer reaches of Judge Doe's theories on judicial power. If he set any limitations upon it, they were negative. That is, when there was no necessity to act, he would not act, but where he found necessity he also found power. In the *Taggart* case, as one professor of constitutional law has expressed it, he made the New Hampshire court "the leading exponent of the judicial method for dealing with executive disability," and set a precedent for using the court as the implement in the orderly transfer of governmental power. [15]

The doctrine of necessity was the pragmatic argument Chief Justice Doe employed to justify the exercise of judicial power. One of the theoretical underpinnings upon which he propped it came from legal history. He asserted that the Supreme Court had a "common-law jurisdiction of general superintendence," inherited not from Chancery, but from King's Bench.[16] In the United States, unless statutes provide otherwise, this general judicial superintendence is vested by common law in the highest court of common-law jurisdiction.[17] This means that "There is authority to do whatever is necessary to be done to accomplish the purpose of the superintendence of lower courts 'for the prevention and correction of errors and abuses where the laws have not expressly provided a remedy.' The duty of correction being imposed by law, everything requisite to attain the end is implied." [18] It is difficult to conceive of any claim to judicial power more broad in scope or far-reaching in implication.

Where a statute was involved, Judge Doe contended that a party was entitled to a process which would carry into effect the expressed will of the legislature.[19] It did not matter whether the legislature had failed to provide a remedial process or even to foresee the possibility that one might be needed; Doe was prepared to devise it from the doctrine of necessity and the jurisdiction of general superintendence. A striking instance of this occurred when the Concord & Montreal Railroad petitioned the court to select a site for a union station in Manchester. Its rival, the Boston & Maine, claimed that the court had no jurisdiction but admitted that the station was required for the public good and that the only obstacle to its erection was the inability of the two roads to agree on a site. Doe held that the court did have jurisdiction. The fact that the legislature had created a railroad commission, but had not expressly invested it or any other tribunal with power to locate depots, was not an indication that the legislature had intended that no tribunal should be able to decide the matter. The defendant's admission that a union station was in the public good acknowledged a legal duty to build and maintain it "as public necessity requires." [20] Therefore a right existed which had to be vindicated through an appropriate remedy furnished by the Supreme Court. When, he said,

there is judicial work to be done, and no court of limited and special jurisdiction is authorized to do it, the duty of affording relief is imposed upon the court of general jurisdiction. . . . In the absence of a court of special and limited jurisdiction authorized to administer a particular law requiring judicial action, legal rights are maintained by the court of general jurisdiction performing its ordinary duty of rendering judgment and issuing process in cases in which there is no other judicial mode of administering the law. The right of these parties and the public to have the union station at Manchester located in the proper place is a legal right, the enforcement of which is not prevented by the circumstance that the remedial power is not conferred upon a tribunal of special and limited jurisdiction. It is a right which can be judicially determined at the trial term upon a petition or bill in equity seeking such remedy as is considered most appropriate for the work to be done.[21]

If judges could determine the "proper place" to build a railroad depot there was not much Doe thought they could not do. As he put it, where no other forum is available, a question may be settled in the Supreme Court, since it has to be settled somewhere.[22]

While many of Judge Doe's decisions involving substantive manifestations of judicial power were phrased in terms of jurisdiction, a few made no pretense at being anything but assertions of the court's power to make law whenever necessary. The case most significant to the development of his jurisprudential theories, and one which we have had occasion to mention several times, is *Concord Manufacturing Company* v. *Robertson*. Doe used that case to decide who holds title to the hundreds of lakes and ponds in the state. He could have avoided the issue, and he probably should have; but his theory of judicial power removed the restraints which might have held back other judges, and his jurisprudential notions convinced him that a decision was needed. Until the matter of ownership was settled by local common law, littoral proprietors could never be sure just what rights they had to the timbered lakes and silver ponds which gave upper New Hampshire much of its rustic character and made it a mecca for summer visitors. Since a good share of the state's water system was used as reservoirs by cotton mills, large commercial interests were at stake, and Doe decided that it was necessary to let everyone — fee holders, tourists, and fishermen — know what rights he possessed.

The Chief Justice was correct in disregarding English and Irish precedents. The number and size of lakes in the British Isles bore no comparison with America or even with New England, and physical conditions (as well as the more significant social, economic, and historical conditions which he stressed in line with his philosophy of law[23]) were completely different. But Doe went to extremes and showed his professional penchant for lawmaking in his rejection of American precedents as well. His first move was to discard the old English tidal test, which made the crown owner of salt water and gave inland bodies to abutting land proprietors. Although the conservatism of his colleagues may have kept him from coming right out and saying so, Doe acknowledged that he was making law when he stated that it was necessary to choose another test and candidly admitted that it would probably "be impossible to find one that is not arbitrary." [24] To have based it on commercial or economic factors, would have defeated his purpose; it would not have furnished a uniform rule for every lake and pond. If the test was one of usage, the status of each body of water would have to wait until some future date when its ownership would be contested in a law suit and the court could determine the facts as they then existed. This outcome was just what Doe did not want. Years earlier the Supreme Court had decided that Sanbornton Bay was public and not private property.[25] Since that time the question had lain dormant. At such a rate it would be centuries before ownership of all the lakes and ponds in New Hampshire could be resolved.

As Doe viewed his duty, the court was obliged to exercise its full power by handing down a test now, at the earliest opportunity, rather than to let the matter hang in the air any longer. "Parties," he wrote, "are entitled to judgments in which their legal rights are ascertained and established. How far the marine territory of a nation extends from high-water mark, is a question which the courts may be compelled to decide on other evidence than written law." In other words, the judges could, out of the necessity of the case, make law. Since he was after a uniform test, one of size was handiest and surest. "A standard of size seems indispensable," he concluded, and for the court to set. "However slight the argument in favor of any particular dimension in determining whether a pond is public or private property, the law requiring a decision of the question authorizes the adoption of a necessary rule." [26] The size Judge Doe decided upon, after a rather dubious explanation of New Hampshire and Massachusetts history, was ten acres. It might as easily have been five or twenty.

As he admitted, it was "arbitrary," but accepting his arguments of necessity, power, and duty, it was inescapable that some figure be adopted. As a result, all ponds of ten acres or more in extent became public property, held by the state in trust for the people, leaving abutting landowners with only the right of reasonable use.

The *Robertson* decision has been criticized as brash lawmaking. "It was," one counsel argued, "the absolute creation of Chief-Justice Doe." [27] Even if Doe's theories concerning judicial power and the duty of the court to exercise that power are accepted, it can be argued that no necessity existed to lay down such a far-reaching legal doctrine at that time. But Doe seems to have made part of his theory of judicial power the proposition that any unresolved legal question should be settled, that doubt alone is enough to create necessity. In his haste to make law, however, he failed to anticipate the consequences of the rule he laid down. As has been shown, he tried to correct matters by using the *Winnipiseogee* case to make even more law, but his associates held back, preferring to wait for an actual fact situation to raise the problem rather than to act on another hypothetical "necessity." [28]

No matter what one might think of *Robertson* and *Winnipiseogee,* it cannot be denied that Charles Doe was following a jurisprudential pattern. This was his trouble: he was too theoretical and not practical enough, he was too intent on giving expression to his judicial philosophy. Justice did not demand the holding in *Robertson,* but theory did. Had it not been for theory, Doe might have avoided embarrassment. The same is true for his railroad cases. While motivated by constitutional rather than jurisprudential considerations, Doe's railroad decisions demonstrate the potential reach of his theory of judicial power.

The most remarkable claim of power made by Doe appears in a railroad opinion. It is by way of *dictum,* written at a time when the antimonopoly act, forbidding the consolidation of competing railroads,[29] of 1867 was still on the books. Yet Doe showed his willingness to shade the spirit of legislative intent by saying that if a union of effort by roads forming a continuous line (here the Concord and the Nashua & Lowell) became, under economic circumstances, a public right, the court could enforce that right if necessary, without assistance from the legislature either in laying down a general policy or in devising an appropriate procedure.

It may be found, should this point ever be presented for consideration, that these roads, running, the one from Nashua north to Concord, and the other from Nashua south to the Massachusetts line towards Boston, are highways authorized to be located and constructed for public use, there is, by necessary implication, a judicial power of compelling the corporations to work them as parts of a continuous line, in such a business connection as is required by the reasonable necessities of public convenience and public economy. In the public character of railroads, and the public purpose for which railway corporations are created, is included an extensive public right of convenient and economical use, for the enforcement of which the common law may afford more adequate methods than there has been occasion in this state to employ.

. . . And in case the Concord and Nashua & Lowell companies should neglect their duty of making a business connection as economical, convenient, and efficient as the public have a right to demand, it would be strange if the judicial introduction of numerous forms of action and process during the last one or two thousand years had so exhausted the resources of the common law that it could no longer produce the simple remedies needed for the maintenance of such an ordinary prerogative as the public right of reasonable use of connected highways.[30]

Here in stark, bold outline is Doe's theory of judicial power brought to bear on a vital area of commercial life. To tell railroads with whom to consolidate hardly seems a proper task for a court of law. But Doe thought differently, and he would have acted had "public convenience and public economy" presented the proper set of facts proving a public necessity.

The holding was to remain speculation, never going beyond *dictum*. Doe may have been preparing the bar for a decision he might one day have to write. But the legislature cut the ground out from under him by passing laws permitting railroad consolidation, and he never had to face the question. We can be certain of only one thing. The little matter of inventing a remedy would not have stood in his way. As he said, "it would be strange" if the court which he headed could not produce "the simple remedies" needed to vindicate a right. He had produced them many times before. It was in the area of adjective law that Judge

Doe's theories of judicial power had their greatest impact. In fact, he could not have effected his procedural reforms had he held a different philosophy.

Since Judge Doe regarded procedure as a mere formality, he had less need to establish a necessity for "new-modelling the forms" than when making substantive law. Even so, he remained consistent to his jurisprudential principles and did not act without first satisfying the doctrine of necessity. He proceeded with such ease that in two cases decided the same term he seems to be mocking the notion of judicial restraint. In the first case he makes it clear that necessity alone should be all the justification needed for the power to act.[31] In the second he lays claim to unrestricted creative authority by contending that need to make "the form and substance of relief at law more ample, specific, and equitable" is itself a "permanent necessity."[32] From such a springboard Doe could justify practically any procedural experiment.

Boody v. *Watson* was Judge Doe's great decision on procedural lawmaking.[33] Some taxpayers in the town of Northwood had brought suit contesting the decision of the selectmen to exempt from taxation certain industrial property. The court had ruled the exemption illegal,[34] thus establishing the plaintiff's constitutional right to have the town collect back taxes. Before final judgment was handed down, however, the terms of the selectmen had expired. The plaintiffs thereupon commenced a new action praying for a writ of *mandamus* ordering the selectmen to make the required adjustment and assess the tax. The defendants replied that the plaintiffs' right was worthless, even though it had been adjudicated, for there was no appropriate remedy with which to enforce it; that the writ of *mandamus* did not confer sufficient authority on the Supreme Court because *mandamus* could direct the selectmen to perform legal acts only, and since they were out of office, any assessment they might make would be extrajudicial. Doe was not to be bridled by so technical an argument. Since it was settled that the plaintiffs were entitled to relief, Doe contended that a decision that *mandamus* is not a sufficient remedy would only demonstrate the court's duty to issue some other writ or to issue a *mandamus* not limited by precedent.[35] He might well have stopped here and rested his decision on an expanded interpretation of the scope and function of *mandamus;* instead, he decided to go further. Doe believed that the board of selectmen, when it first assessed the taxes, had constituted a judicial tribunal and was therefore subject to the Supreme Court's superintendence.[36] He based the judicial nature of tax assessment partly on "the doctrine of necessity." [37] Considered from this point of view, the defendant was arguing that the lower court — the selectmen — no longer existed. Therefore there could be no remedy, because there was no tribunal in which the matter could be settled. But Doe's theory of judicial power could not acknowledge impotence. "The inability of that court," he said, "to voluntarily repair its own error would be reason for repairing it in the general jurisdiction from which the correction of such error is not excepted." [38] What he meant was that, since the Supreme Court had correctional authority to reverse a tax exemption, and since a reversal would be meaningful only if accompanied by a tax assessment, it followed from the very necessities of the case that the Supreme Court also had authority "to make the assessment or cause it to be made." [39] There was, therefore, no need to expand *mandamus.*

Judge Carpenter was appalled. What the Chief Justice was proposing, as he saw it, was either to convert the Supreme Court into a board of assessment, something the constitution had never contemplated, or to turn the task over to a lower tribunal which — since none now existed — the Supreme Court would have to create out of thin air. Proving that two could play the game of legal history, he argued that Doe was claiming a power even King's Bench had never possessed. "The unquestioned authority of that court," Carpenter pointed out, "to keep all inferior tribunals within their jurisdiction, and to correct their errors of law, does not include the power to create such tribunals, to confer upon them authority, or to do the work, which the law declares shall be done exclusively by them." [40]

The broad range of Doe's theory of judicial power easily swallowed Carpenter's objection. To restrain Doe, the legislature had to do more than give sole authority to selectmen to assess taxes. If it did not want the Supreme Court to correct otherwise remediless tax exemption by making necessary assessments, the legislature should say so in clear, unequivocal language which more or less covered the specific fact situation of the case. To prove his point, the Chief Justice drew a rather extreme analogy: "A repeal of every statute that authorizes the assessment of taxes by tribunals of special and limited jurisdiction [that is, by select-men] would evince, not a design to bring all local government to an end by cutting off its revenue, or to bankrupt or cripple the body politic, . . . but an intention that such statutes . . . , dividing the public expense and imposing contributory liability, if executable in no other way, should be carried into effect by the court of general jurisdiction performing its ordinary duty of rendering judgment and issuing process in cases in which there is no other judicial mode of administering the law. Nothing less than a positive declaration of intent to render all such statute in-operative could justify a belief that the law-making power have adopted a measure so subversive of civil society." [41]

Here, defending his ideas against the legalism of Carpenter, Judge Doe was careful to speak of the legislature as the lawmaker and to put his claims of judicial power in terms of inherent juris-diction. But the jurisdiction of general superintendence, as he described it, was just another way of saying that the court pos-sessed authority not only to create new remedies for lower statutory tribunals, but also to create boards of tax assessment when none existed — that is, to create a tribunal performing a largely executive function.

In *Boody* v. *Watson* Doe held that the Supreme Court's power of superintendence does not depend upon the jurisdiction of the lower court; nor is it limited by the authority of the lower court to correct its own errors. The Supreme Court not only can deliver a judgment which the lower court could have handed down, but it can go beyond and render such judgment "as ought to have been given." Even the existence of the lower court is no more necessary to the correction of its errors than its own reversing power. "The corrective power of superintendence," Doe stated, "depends on no irrelevant conditions of that kind." Thus in this case, where the assessment of property is necessary to vindicate the plaintiffs' adjudicated right to equal taxation, and the lower court has no power to perform the task, the Supreme Court will make the assessment. "Anything less than an enforceable assess-ment," he concluded, "will fail to answer the purpose for which the law has established the court for the correction of errors." [42] Carpenter called this assumption of authority judicial legislation;[43] Doe called it judicial power and justified it partly on the grounds of necessity, partly on the Court's inherent authority of general superintendence, and partly on plain common sense. "Without such an assessment," he pointed out, "there would be no practical difference between a reversal of the exemption and an affirmance of it." [44] If there was anything Chief Justice Doe disliked, it was a result which made the law ridiculous.

Boody v. *Watson* is sprinkled with a number of bold assertions on behalf of judicial power. One was Doe's suggestion that, under the statute conferring general superintendence, the court had power to invent whatever writs and processes it needed to accomplish its task.[45] This, he said, is part of the court's inherent authority and depends neither on its jurisdiction of general superintendence nor upon statutory grant.[46] His theory was supported by two considerations: first, the argument that procedural precedents do not have the force of law, but are, at most, evidence of what is convenient and just;[47] and second, a rather shaky historical thesis based on the belief that what the courts could do in Anglo-Norman times they can still do until some legislative body says otherwise. This doctrine must have struck the nineteenth-century legal mind as one of Doe's most radical, if not one of his most unsound pronouncements. Judge Carpenter spoke for the majority of American lawyers when he argued that to devise a new remedy is to create a new right and that both are beyond the power of a common-law court.[48]

An essential detail of Doe's doctrine concerning the formality of writs was that their validity depends on usefulness rather than on precedent. "The test of the legality of a former action," he asserted, "is utility as a method of vindicating rights." [49] Had Carpenter's argument concerning immutability prevailed in former times, "there would have been no common law procedure." [50]

The objection to the invention of a form of action is based on the idea that the remedial forms of the common law come from some other source than human design; or that courts, continuously charged by that law with the duty of allowing convenient forms of remedy to be used, are empowered by the same law to permit the use of forms capable of prohibiting the performance of the duty by themselves and their successors; or that the introduction of the whole existing remedial system of the common law, by progressive development through many ages, recent and remote, has been an unlawful usurpation of legislative power by judges who should have defeated justice by permitting no common-law procedure whatever, but whose illegal precedents are law. Until it is shown whose and what authorized edict, of ancient or modern date, annulled the common-law principle that requires the invention and use of common-law procedure, and commands common-law courts to allow convenient remedies, the duty imposed by that principle cannot lawfully be left unperformed. The test of the legality of a form of action, or other pleading, is not the time of its invention, but its utility as a method of vindicating rights entitled to the best forms and methods that can be produced.[51]

In the case of *Walker* v. *Walker* Chief Justice Doe turned this theory into practice and invented a new form of action. It is doubtful if any other common-law judge ever went so far in exercising judicial power for the primary purpose of demonstrating just what a court could do.

During the last century, before the advent of annuity plans and social security, it was not unusual for farmers who were childless to provide for their own retirement by conveying their farms to younger men in return for bed and board or a share of the income. In *Walker* v. *Walker* the plaintiff adopted a sophisticated variation of this practice; he conveyed his farm to himself for life, with the remainder vested in the defendant on condition the defendant support him in the style and manner to which New Hampshire farmers were accustomed. When the defendant failed to keep his end of the agreement, the plaintiff brought a bill in equity praying that the deed be declared void. The defendant moved to dismiss on the grounds that, since real estate was involved, he had a right to a jury trial and that a court of equity was not the proper tribunal for determining title to land. The plaintiff replied that he did not have an adequate remedy at law: he could not maintain a writ of entry, for he had possession; trespass would give him only nominal damages and leave the deed in full force; an action at law could give him nothing but compensation for damage committed up to the time of the suit; and only equity could grant the relief to which he was entitled.

Judge Doe spent little time considering the conflicting points. While he did not say that they were correct, he chose to treat them as though they were, because taken together, they meant that no satisfactory remedy existed at either law or equity, giving him the excuse to invent a new form of action.

First Doe established the parties' right to a writ which would adjudicate their interests. He based it on the argument that when a fee simple in a single tract of land is claimed by two persons, each has a right to a real action "in which an explicit determination of their conflicting claims will be made and recorded." His rationalization for holding that the right required a real action for vindication was somewhat jejune: "As a matter of common law, each is entitled to a convenient and adequate form of procedure; and, as a matter of fact, a real action is such a form." The Chief Justice widened the inventive faculties of the court as far as possible by adding, "This right is not affected by a possibility or a certainty that a like result would be reached in trespass, or some other personal action." [52] Apparently only the existence of an adequate, Doe-approved real action would have limited the court's power of invention in this case.

Next Doe established the necessity. "The question," he said, "is . . . whether in any case of extreme necessity a real action lies for a remainder of land in fee expectant upon a life estate." [53] His exact reason for using the word "extreme" is not clear. After all, it was his contention that as a general rule of common law a necessity is always present when there is need for "a plenary remedy for the infringement of a legal right" and that this necessity authorizes "the use of convenient procedure for ascertaining and establishing the right and obtaining the remedy." [54] Necessity and convenience together create forms of action to be employed in cases where they are appropriate remedies. [55] Necessity justifies creation, and convenience determines the shape creation will take. Applying the rule to the particular facts in *Walker* v. *Walker*, Doe stated, "The vested estate of the remainder-man, conveyable by his deed, and applicable on execution in payment of his debts, but incapable of being adjudged to be anybody's property in any suit brought to ascertain who the owner is, would exhibit a serious defect, imposed by a misconception of the necessity and convenience which are the common law of procedure." [56]

A real action is needed, and it is not enough to say that after the life tenant dies his heirs can vindicate his right by bringing a writ of entry. "In an action of some form, the plaintiff is entitled to judgment settling the disputed ownership of this remainder." The court, Doe argued, has no more authority to deprive the claimant of a remainder (which might be worth a hundred times as much as a short-lived freehold) of a full and appropriate remedy than it does "to turn the claimant of the freehold out of court without a trial, and compel him to resort to a personal action that may be indecisive and inadequate." [57] Since the court cannot deny relief, and since no adequate remedy exists for furnishing relief, it follows that the court has power to invent an adequate remedy. This Doe did, devising what may well be the only real action ever formulated by an American judge. He called it a writ for the enforcement of a forfeiture and the divesting of an estate in land for breach of condition subsequent.

Commenting upon *Walker* v. *Walker*, Professor Hening concluded that Doe had been "swept beyond the bounds of reasonable certainty and safety"; that, "conceding the existence of the judicial power of inventing actions, there was clearly no occasion for its exercise." [58] From one point of view Hening was right: a remedy was available in equity. But whether that remedy was adequate or not depended partly upon whether Doe's theories regarding judicial power are accepted. Doe held it to be inadequate because parties are entitled to "something more speedy, less harassing, and less expensive" than a personal action at law to settle the question of title and a subsequent suit in chancery for removal of the cloud. [59] Such roundabout procedure, even if a fiction, is "an unnecessary inconvenience," and this fact alone constitutes a necessity justifying the invention of a new real action. Hening would have replied that inconvenience is beside the point; that the equitable remedy is adequate by the very fact of its availability. Carpenter, who dissented without opinion, would have gone further and denied judicial power to invent forms of action, no matter how inadequate the old remedy.

Whether the available equitable remedy was adequate or not, Doe was correct on one count: it was hardly the best possible mode of procedure. Accepting his premise that the court must provide the most convenient method possible for vindicating rights, he may still be criticized for devising a wholly new writ. He might have done what he did in *Attorney General* v. *Taggart*, and what he said he could have done in *Boody* v. *Watson* — he might have expanded or reconstructed existing writs. He himself admitted that "By less exercise of the inventive faculty, a judgment for land, enforceable by a writ of possession, could be rendered in trespass, or other personal action in which the title is settled. . . ." [60] But as Hening said, Doe had been "carried too far by the momentum of his zeal for reform." [61] He presented the old forms in their strictest light because he wanted to invent a new cause of action. Doe had to have this case to round out his explanation of judicial power. His pattern of thought, his theory of necessity and convenience, his string of precedents breaking the stranglehold of the old notions concerning remedial law, all would have been incomplete had he not invented a new form of action. Perhaps in his eagerness to demonstrate his theory and show what could be done by an enterprising judge he went too far. "But," as Hening admits, "he believed that in the common law there are no lost arts. His imagination was captivated by the idea that if Glanvil could invent *replevin* and the assize of *novel disseizin,* if Rolle could invent ejectment, and the Elizabethan judges *indebitatus assumpsit*, the power to invent new writs by virtue of the famous statute of Edward I still existed to-day in any common law judge." [62]

Chief Justice Doe's theory of judicial power is difficult to place within the framework of American legal history. It was out of tune with the spirit and philosophy of his own times; a spirit and a philosophy summed up by Oliver Wendell Holmes when he wrote, "I recognize without hesitation that judges do and must legislate, but they can do so only interstitially; they are confined from molar to molecular motions. A common-law judge could not say I think the doctrine of consideration a bit of historical nonsense and shall not enforce it in my court." [63] Charles Doe would not have agreed. While he might not have quarreled, at least openly, with Holmes's thesis, he would never have acknowledged that common-law judges cannot cleanse the law of historical nonsense. He never got a chance to pass judgment on consideration, but he encountered an equally venerable doctrine in *Edgerly* v. *Barker* when he held that a contingency in excess of twenty-one years may be reduced by judicial construction to the maximum valid period.[64] Finding the historical harshness of the Rule against Perpetuities unreasonable nonsense, Doe felt no Holmesian restraints about not enforcing it in his court.

Judge Doe's isolation from the mainstream of American legal thought can be seen by comparing his ideas with the judicial method employed by Chief Justice Edward G. Ryan of Wisconsin in writing in 1874 one of the great decisions of their era — *Attorney General* v. *The Railroads.*[65] Ryan had been appointed for the very purpose of delivering the judgment he handed down; a judgment upholding the authority of the state to regulate the rates and to audit the expenses of common carriers.[66] The opinion contains two parts, one sustaining the constitutionality of Wisconsin's regulatory statutes and the other affirming the power of the Supreme Court to enjoin the railroads from violating the law. Both are masterful and show that Ryan was a keener student than most of his contemporaries (including Doe) of the relationship between economics and legal institutions. But he arrived at his conclusion that the court possessed injunctive power by struggling with the distinction between prerogative and judicial writs (a technicality Doe would have ignored), by dissecting precedents from other jurisdictions which he seemed to think represented the force of law (Doe would have treated them as mere evidence of best law), and by extending the implications of his holding no further than the facts required (Doe would have left openings to meet future needs). His method of approach, then, was in sharp contrast to Doe's. It seems safe to suggest that Doe, once he had established the constitutionality of the state's right to regulate rates and fares, would have needed only to find the necessity of employing some process for vindication of that right to have held that the court had judicial power either to expand the traditional scope of injunction or to invent other appropriate remedy. While he and Ryan would have arrived at the same result, the routes followed would have been totally different, primarily because Doe, unlike Ryan, would have based his decision on his theory of judicial power. Ryan's way was tortuous, but this alone made it more orthodox — and seemingly more sound. His opinion was hailed as a masterpiece in his own times, and it has recently been described as ranking among the foremost American judicial pronouncements in terms of judicial boldness and creativity.[67] While it was a brilliant example of the conventional legal method employed to accomplish a more than conventional result, compared to some of Doe's work its "boldness and creativity" seem pale. Its method of solution and the reception which it received, taken together, show the lonesomeness of Doe's jurisprudential position.

It would be a mistake to contrast Doe's theory of judicial power with the jurisdictional notions of Felix Frankfurter or Learned Hand or to relate it to recent lawmaking by the United States Supreme Court in such areas as segregation, reapportionment, and prayer in public schools. Doe's work was less controversial, since he was involved with mundane common-law problems rather than with vibrant constitutional issues and since he justified results on grounds of justice and convenience rather than political theory. On this substance of difference hangs the substance of criticism. Reaction toward the lawmaking of today's Supreme Court usually turns upon the observer's predilections in politics and sociology. But with Doe, few questioned the validity and worth of his purpose. Even Carpenter admitted that Doe's innovations brought a welcomed degree of justice and convenience into New Hampshire law and did much to smooth the harsh edges of doctrine.[68] Carpenter objected to judicial lawmaking per se, not to the results. Today's Supreme Court, while it might easily show greater respect for precedent, has to render decisions on constitutional affairs, and no matter which way it moves, some will inevitably claim that it has usurped the legislature's province. Doe, on the other hand, did not have to make the law he concocted — unless one accepts all his premises regarding judicial power, including those placing on the court a positive duty to act when there is necessity for action. And these premises were exactly what Carpenter, and most of his contemporaries, refused to accept. They objected to Doe's lawmaking because they opposed the idea of judge-made law. No matter how much they approved his results, even the finest and most valuable ends could never justify such means.

Chief Justice Doe himself appreciated that, even if the power of judicial initiative, as he theorized and applied it, was more or less unlimited, its use was and should be limited. While he sometimes let his enthusiasm run unchecked, as in *Walker,* Doe seldom threw all caution to the winds. He made law only when he was satisfied that a necessity existed for making it. Although his idea that necessity included the repair of academic gaps in substantive law (as in *Robertson*) may have struck some contemporaries as somewhat farfetched, he knew the value of judicial restraint, especially in constitutional matters.[69] He was unwilling to create a remedy or multiply the number of available remedies when adequate process already existed at statutory or common law.[70] And as could any judge worth his salt, Doe could at the right moment insist that he was powerless to act, that only the legislature could remedy a given fact situation. One such case has been cited to suggest that Doe may not have been the lawmaker he is usually held to be. It is said that in *Davis* v. *George* he refused to construe a lease of a furnished hotel as including an implied covenant that it was suitable for occupation, partly on the grounds that only the legislature could relieve future tenants of any hardship imposed by such a rule of law.[71] Actually Doe had found, more as a matter of fact than a matter of law, that the parties to the lease had not intended to warrant inhabitableness. His opinion indicates that he did not believe justice under the fact situation to be on the plaintiff's side,[72] and from this point of view the case falls squarely within his theory of judicial power. For without the pressure of justice, there was no necessity for lawmaking; and without necessity, creation of a new rule would be beyond the court's authority.

This manner of restraint — built as it was within Doe's theory of judicial power — may have reassured his contemporaries. Arguments from necessity and justice are calculated to win approval and to soften the strictures against action. It is significant that lawyers of that day complained less about Doe's flights into judicial legislation than they did about his manner of ignoring the law of precedent. Of course this emphasis arose in no small measure because the violation of precedent is more striking than are the manner and method used to violate it. Doe did some of his most effective legislating without even mentioning the theory of judicial power as a central theme in his opinions. His rejection of precedent was sure to catch the eye, and he probably saw no reason to furnish further ammunition to the enemy camp by antagonizing any more readers than he had to.

Articulating the theory of judicial power, however, was not important. Everyone was aware of what Doe was doing, even if some failed to catch the significance of the doctrine of necessity or the jurisdiction of general superintendence. It all came down to judicial legislation in the end. Hening somehow missed the point by saying that Chief Justice Doe was "Austin in action." [73] Doe did more than fill the gaps and build by analogy; he was a creator within the framework of the common-law tradition, not proof that the common law should be scrapped for a code. No one knew this better than Jeremiah Smith. While not so original as Doe, Smith had been inspired at times to strike out on new paths. Years later, while he was a Professor at Harvard Law School, he was asked whether judges make law. "Do judges make law?" he is said to have repeated. "Course they do. Made some myself." [74] He made it mainly by concurring with Doe.

It remained, however, for an obscure lawyer by the name of Waite to provide the most fitting epithet. He was from the town of Claremont near the Vermont line, and he had come up to Concord to attend the opening session of the Supreme Court's appellate term. During the invocation the minister asked for a blessing on the lawmakers. Immediately after he concluded, Waite turned to a colleague and whispered, "He prayed for the lawmakers — that's Doe." [75]

He might have added that they were watching the last of the breed.

A FRIVOLOUS FORMALITY
The Law of Precedent

THE most unconventional theory of judicial power would have little impact if it were held by a judge with a conventional theory of the law of precedent. It must be obvious, just from the manner in which he exercised judicial authority, that Doe's view of precedent was far from conventional. Any American state judge who rewrote the entire law of civil procedure, who rejected the M'Naghten Rules of criminal insanity, and who relaxed the rigidity of the Rule against Perpetuities would have been an iconoclast in the nineteenth century. Some of Chief Justice Doe's pronouncements regarding the doctrine of precedent seem startling, even today. He referred with disdain to the "proverbial reverence for precedent." [1] And in an often quoted sentence he said, "The maxim which, taken literally, requires courts to follow decided cases is shown by the thousands of overruled decisions, to be a figurative expression requiring only a reasonable respect for decided cases." [2] Indeed, he not only questioned precedent as law, but even doubted whether it had much utility. "As there was a time," he wrote, "when there were no common-law precedents, everything that can be done with them could be done without them." [3] Chief Justice Doe's theory of the law of precedent forms an important segment of his jurisprudence, not only because it clarifies his definition of "law," but also because his attitude toward precedent was motivated by his belief that legal principle has greater authority than pronounced doctrine.

Despite its frequent use, the term "precedent" escapes precise definition — especially in the case of Charles Doe. No other important American judge, it is believed, has been more severely criticized for abandoning precedents; yet his critics never defined the term. For that matter, neither did Chief Justice Doe. Disliking the notion of authority for authority's sake, he treated the concept loosely. He never spoke of *stare decisis,* nor did his critics. Both he and they lumped together "binding precedents" — decisions handed down by the highest local court — with "analogous precedents" — decisions from other jurisdictions. When dealing with New Hampshire cases, Doe was as likely to cite an unreported *nisi prius* opinion as to cite a reported Supreme Court opinion. From his point of view they carried about equal weight.

While this may seem careless, it should not be surprising. Even professional jurisprudents are vague as to the meaning of "precedent." [4] Doe's critics had no reason to define the word; they were not interested in how he treated out-of-state as compared to New Hampshire authorities. They were concerned rather with his making law uncertain by abandoning familiar guideposts. Judge Doe on the other hand had no reason to define precedent because he did not think of reported opinions in terms of binding authority. Even the great English cases which laid down the rules of common law were not precedents which had to be followed, but merely evidence of legal customs. Doe was interested in principles, and he did not care where he found them. He seldom bothered to distinguish between *obiter dictum* and *ratio decidendi* but cited both indiscriminately. If the principle was stated clearly in the *dictum* of one case and merely implied by the *ratio* of another, Doe would treat the first as more persuasive, and so it was to him. Principle, not holding or *stare decisis,* was the authority Doe followed.

If it were necessary to catalogue Doe, it might be said that he followed the "evidentiary theory of precedents." That is, he respected precedents as evidence of what is law. Other judges — such as Coke, Hale, and Blackstone — also treated judicial opinions as mere evidence of law; but they seem to have done so on the ground that judges cannot make law, they only find it. Charles Doe was more pragmatic. He made the value of a precedent a question of fact, removing from it most elements of law. While this may have been consistent with some of his other notions, such as the idea that judicial discretion is primarily a fact-finding process, it leaves little of what we traditionally call precedent.

This whole attitude, of course, fits perfectly with his theory of judicial power. As mentioned in the last chapter, proper use of this power — the inherent power of a court to protect privileges and promote justice — is not judicial legislation. Doe could never have agreed with Lord Campbell's statement, made in the House of Lords two years after Doe became a judge, that an appellate court should be bound by its own decisions, for otherwise it would "be arrogating to itself the right of altering the law, and legislating by its own separate authority." [5] Quite the contrary, Doe thought. Courts do not legislate when they correct error by overturning precedent. It is the court introducing error which is guilty of "judicial legislation." [6]

If this outlook was not unorthodox enough, Doe carried it to its logical conclusion by implying that the law of precedent itself is "arbitrary legislation" when it prevents correction of judge-made error.[7] Since the court has a duty to overturn error, not to perpetuate it, the one "precedent to be followed is the performance of this duty, not a violation of it." [8]

It was by twisting conventional legal theory about in this manner — by saying that adherence to erroneous precedents, not their correction, is judicial legislation — that Judge Doe found his jurisprudential justification for new-modelling the law of civil procedure. After all, the rules which at that time governed common-law pleading were largely judge-made precedent. Each of these rules, he wrote, "is presumed to have been introduced because it was deemed reasonably necessary for the convenient ascertainment or vindication of some legal right. And the introduction of each was a precedent for introducing as many more as, at any subsequent time, should be found reasonably necessary for the same purpose." [9] Thus the one "precedent" in the law of procedure which under the principle of reasonable necessity Doe acknowledged was the "precedent" that since rules of pleading had been invented by judges for the convenience of parties, they can, for the same reason, be altered by judges. To hold otherwise, he wrote, would be an admission that all common-law remedies are "judicial usurpations of law-making power" which, in turn, would be "a strained and quibbling interpretation, a strict observance of frivolous formality, and a disregard of substance and principle." [10]

It is apparent that Charles Doe did more than ignore precedents which he did not wish to follow. Every judge to some degree does this. Doe formulated an antiprecedent theory which denies the binding force of reported opinions. Syllogistically it was one of his soundest theories; but his associates looked beneath the veneer of logical argument and recognized its implications. The antiprecedent theory was one which they simply could not bring themselves to accept. This fact is seen by what happened to one of the evidentiary reforms Charles Doe tried to introduce in *Lisbon* v. *Lyman.* In that case, he demolished the rule which shifts the burden of proof when facts are peculiarly within the knowledge of the defendant. His colleagues agreed with what he said, but they were able to bypass the question without a ruling. Three years later, however, they came face to face with a case in which they either had to follow Doe or follow precedent. Asked to choose between principle and precedent, the six justices of the Supreme Court split three against three. Once more they all agreed with Doe that "as a matter of legal principle" the rule, shifting the burden of proof from a mover and placing it upon his opponent, "is erroneous." But the "error" was established by at least four precedents and distinctly recognized in five others. To overrule nine cases was asking too much of three of the judges. In two graphic sentences their *per curiam* opinion sums up the issue of *stare decisis* as seen by Charles Doe's court.

Three of our number, while agreeing with Richardson, C.J., . . . that "where a long usage, however erroneous, has become the foundation of the title to property, 'the law so favors the public good that it will permit a common error to pass for right,'" are yet of the opinion that it is never too late to correct an error like this, which is constantly liable to lead to other errors, and to mar the consistency and harmony of the law as a science. On the contrary, three of us, while not quite prepared to say in the language of Judge GOULD . . . "I might feel bound to submit and abide by the effect of the doctrine *stare decisis*, on the ground that what was so well settled might be right, although I might not be able to see it," yet, being of the opinion that this error has been found extremely convenient in practice, and is likely to be equally so hereafter, and that it has resulted in no practical injustice, and is not likely to result in any hereafter, feel bound to stand by the

decisions in this and other states, which have established a settled
rule of law that has been recognized in textbooks of standard authority.[11]

Thus the issue was joined. Doe, believing that it conflicted with
the general principle which places the burden on the mover, tried
to overrule the precedent which requires a defendant with
peculiar knowledge of the facts to carry the burden of proof.
Three associates, while for the principle, wanted evidence of injustice before disturbing precedent. The difference was not an
absolute gulf between slavish respect for authority and desire for
innovation. Rather, it was a difference in degree, turning on
certain value judgments, such as the law's need for certainty. No
American judge has placed less importance on certainty than has
Charles Doe, as is apparent from his effort to upgrade fact at
the expense of law and from his tort theory. Holmes, as we saw,
postulated a radically different theory of torts, chiefly because he
sought certainty in law. Doe may have had the best of that argument, since predictability cannot play a very significant role in
torts. As he said, things will "come to a strange pass" if a man
needs a course of legal study before he dares act in a reasonable
and necessary manner.[12] Too many legal rules would make tort
law inoperative. But Doe did not limit this argument to tort law;
he questioned the need for certainty in just about every legal
area, including that of the law merchant.[13]

Many others besides Holmes, especially practicing lawyers, preferred predictable decisions to "just" ones. At the initial meeting
of the Grafton and Coös Bar Association, William Heywood, the
association's first president, reflected the thoughts of most of those
present when he protested against Chief Justice Doe's willingness to allow the law to drift along without anchors. "It is," he
said, "frequently a matter of almost indifference to the course
of justice as to how a given point of law is decided, if it can be
decided so as to be certain, and the people in their dealings, and
lawyers in their advice, may certainly know what the law is. It
is a great wrong to overturn a well-considered case. It unsettles
the law and in effect has the practical injustice of an *ex post facto*
law." [14]

Far from being an appellate lawyer's expression of sour grapes, this call for clearcut precedents has been endorsed by judges from Francis Bacon, who felt law "cannot be just" without certainty, to Benjamin Cardozo, who said that without certainty the law as a guide to conduct would be "reduced to the level of mere futility." [15] But there were some sour grapes in the bitter denunciation of *Edgerly* v. *Barker* by John Chipman Gray, who had been consulted during the early stages of the litigation. Since he had no doubt that the trust violated the Rule against Perpetuities, Gray had confidently concluded that the court would invalidate the will and award the estate to the heirs at law. In a strict definition of "binding precedent" there was nothing to compel the court to do so. But as Gray pointed out, it would be hard to conceive of a case in which the claims of certainty and uniformity were stronger. "I submit it is a serious thing deliberately to break away from the *consensus* of the English speaking world on this subject. True, the matter is not one of commercial intercourse, and therefore it is not so important that the law should be uniform upon it; but persons often own land in States other than their own, and it is no slight evil that laws governing the settlement and devolution of property should differ." It especially bothered Professor Gray that "the view adopted by the Court was one which had never seemed possible to me, and to which I had not given any consideration." In other jurisdictions, he said, "any decently instructed lawyer" could answer promptly and with certitude questions about the Rule against Perpetuities. But in New Hampshire, "the more learned and acute the lawyer, the greater the perplexity in which such cases would plunge him." [16]

The local bar agreed with Gray. Harry Bingham, the state's leading practitioner, bemourned the fact that the Supreme Court tended to follow Doe's lead. "Formerly," Bingham wrote, "the experienced practitioner could advise his clients as to their cases and the law applicable to them with confidence, but now the greater the experience that the legal practitioner has had in our courts the less confidence will he feel in any opinion which he can give." Anyone seeking advice on New Hampshire law, Bingham thought, would do better "to consult a lawyer not familiar with the way and manner in which the law is authoritively expounded and applied to New Hampshire at the present time." [17]

Senator William E. Chandler put the matter more strongly.

"If," he wrote, "our court were asked whether 2 and 2 make 4; and whether 3 and 2 make 7 and were to answer Yes and No, the whole profession would be much amazed by the new and radical change of method adopted by the judges." [18] An editorial in one of Chandler's newspapers complained that under Doe "the practice of law in New Hampshire is more uncertain in its results than it is in Turkey and Russia."

No certainty is felt by any lawyer that his case will be decided according to legal principles, as able judges would work them out. It is notorious that the lawyers in the state are in a constant condition of apprehension concerning their strongest cases, believing they are as likely to be decided wrongly as rightly, owing to the eccentric and feverish, wild and wilful proclivity on the part of the court to decide questions contrary to what other courts would decide or have already decided, and contrary to the general and universal expectation of the bar. Lawyers draw a sigh of relief when an important case is decided correctly and according to precedent.[19]

Inevitably, the affair became the butt of professional humor. In a speech to the Grafton and Coös Bar Association satirizing Doe's opinions, Judge Carpenter's son told how Doe had held that four aces beat a straight flush. "His reason for this was, that the law had always been the other way." Judicial review, Carpenter said, was the only custom "over seven years old, that Doe did not upset." [20] A favorite story, which no one enjoyed more than did Judge Doe, had to do with an applicant for admission to the bar. The examining committee had tested him with conventional questions, and he had given them unorthodox answers. Puzzled, they asked Harry Bingham what he thought. "Gentlemen," he replied, "according to my conceptions of the law this young man's views on the points to which he has answered are startling, but on the whole I would recommend, if I were you, that he be admitted and let him have a hack at the Supreme Court, and God only knows but what he would convince them he is right." The story may well be true, for Doe is said to have remarked that it demonstrated Bingham's "utter contempt for the court." [21]

In one of the most important law books of the 1960s Karl Llewellyn has divided opinion writers into two groups — those of the Formal Style and those of the Grand Style. The Grand Style — which bases decisions on principle and policy rather than on precedents and maxims — is, according to Llewellyn, more predictable and certain; and Charles Doe is one of his chief examples of a master in the Grand Style.[22] Harry Bingham would have argued that Doe proves Llewellyn wrong. Bingham is proof that a legal scholar in active practice before a court employing the Grand Style is not necessarily going to feel that he can predict with any degree of confidence the outcome of a case. Let an attorney read an opinion of Doe's, he wrote, let him study all that Doe says about principle, and the most definite conclusion he would be able to arrive at would be that, "if he should bring a new suit just like the old one, resting on the same grounds, he might lose it and he might not." Doe could talk as long as he wished about "justice," and for the most part Bingham would agree with him. But "justice," Bingham said, is not found by ignoring precedent. "Sharp cuttings up, novel methods, sudden thrusts and incisive words dividing all precedents and dictated by the impulse of momentary inspiration, however entertaining they may be at all times to the unreasoning multitude, and however proper they may be on some occasions, are not the things to aid in the just disposition of legal causes and in that business are a poor substitute for the accumulated wisdom of the ages." [23]

Bingham's exaggeration must have been deliberate. His audience was largely anti-Doe, and he told them what they wanted to hear. Yet even Doe's critics knew that his genius could not be dismissed as "cuttings up" or "incisive words." As Harry Hibbard, while denouncing Doe to a roomful of lawyers, had resignedly admitted, "After all, there is a moral sublimity above that fellow's utter disregard of law which I must say commands my admiration." [24] Years later other lawyers made the same point when they eulogized Doe at a memorial session of the Supreme Court. They had gathered to praise the dead chief justice, but they were somewhat embarrassed by his theory of precedent. A few were almost apologetic. John S. H. Frink told them they were wrong:

Some of his critics have said that he has rendered the law fickle and uncertain. Uncertain in what? No lawyer who championed a just cause ever felt distrustful of the result, so far as Judge Doe could direct it.

It was too often, when we hoped to obtain results that our enlightened conscience did not approve, by arbitrary precedent and artificial rule that our legal education did approve, that we complained of his methods.[25]

Frink merely glosses the strictures; he does not answer them. Probably no lawyer with a "just cause" doubted that he would win in Doe's court. Yet this was exactly why Heywood, Bingham, and the others were unhappy. As Heywood put it, it did not matter how a case was decided, so long as it left the law certain. What, after all, was a "just cause"? Doe might think that he knew, but this did not mean everyone would agree with him. The thought apparently never disturbed him. It did disturb Judge Alonzo Carpenter to render an unjust verdict, yet when precedent dictated, he never hesitated to do so. When he died two years after Doe, no one had to apologize for him. He was eulogized as a judge who "believed in following established precedent absolutely no matter what the result might be." [26] Frink oversimplified the conflict by speaking of "arbitrary precedents" and by stating that they are "approved" only because lawyers have been brainwashed through legal education. This hardly answered Bingham's contention that a law without precedents is no law at all. Perhaps there is no satisfactory answer to Bingham, for the controversy between him and Doe has been raging for generations. If the common-law judge openly spurns precedents, it becomes absurd to pretend that he is finding rather than making law. Doe and other legal activists suggest too easy an answer when they ask how the common law can adapt itself to changing times if a judge cannot expand or bend it to meet new social challenges. Surely Bingham was not blind to this crux. He was no champion of codification; he knew growth had to come from judges. But Bingham wanted growth which retained guideposts and left lawyers feeling reasonably certain about the future. Doe did not care for guideposts or for certainty when they barred the way to justice and right reason. As an extremist he deserved the criticism that was leveled at him. But by being an extremist Doe mirrored the issue posed by precedent. His solution may have been too drastic, but his complaint was genuine.

Judge Doe might easily have dodged the controversy. In some ways the quarrel between him and his critics was as much a debate over techniques as over legal theory. For, in truth, there is an acceptable way to avoid precedents, and Doe did not choose to use it. Surely the practicing bar would have been less upset had he done things in the conventional manner, by distinguishing or limiting prior cases rather than by overruling them. It is a matter of tactics. By adding a fact here and ignoring a *dictum* there he could have obtained the results he wished while leaving everyone (except losing counsel) happy.

Judge Doe was not being reckless when he chose to overrule rather than distinguish prior decisions. He was, it must be remembered, more interested in principles than in results. Principles can be established on a sure footing only by eradicating false law. "Denials of truth are worse than useless," he explained to his colleagues: "they lead the world to regard the law as a dishonest system of government, & the habit of indulging in such denials has an unhealthy influence upon the mental & moral faculties. It tends to beget the state of self deception & confusion of thought incompatible with sound reasoning." [27] For this reason, in a letter to John Major Shirley, Doe referred to *stare decisis* as the doctrine "which has perpetuated so many deformities in all ages of the law." [28] Some of the most bizarre "deformities" have been fashioned by judges who, by distinguishing erroneous precedents they lacked the courage to overrule, distorted legal principles. Shirley was court reporter at the time, and in a note which he published in the New Hampshire *Reports* he tried to persuade the bar to see things Doe's way.

Some of the opinions in this volume deny, limit, qualify, question, or overrule previous opinions. . . . Since 1816, few cases in terms, and more virtually, have been overruled. The latter course seems to me the result of mistaken delicacy. In another state, such precedents have so honey-combed each other and shaken authority that suitors are said to feel reasonably safe, if they are unable to find any reported case in their favor.

No court however pure can always be right. The great matter of surprise is, that there have been so few mistakes. The court never lost anything by "revising without fear" prior decisions, when the case demanded it. This long tolerated practice of overruling cases in fact, but not in name, not only deeply embarrasses the court and the pro-

fession, but compels litigants to waste time and money fruitlessly, at
the expense of the reputation of both the bench and bar.[29]

If Charles Doe did not write this note — and he possibly did
— it was certainly inspired by him. It appears in the volume containing two of his earliest attacks upon precedent, and it is quite
likely that it was written while he was preparing a third.[30] The
note gives careful consideration to judicial function, and so did
Doe; he cannot be cast as a legal Hotspur. But to say as much
merely frees Doe from the indictment of blind recklessness; it
does not free him from the scorn of his indicters. He was guilty
of characteristics which they found unbecoming in a judge.
Temperament and inclination directed his thoughts toward judicial initiative rather than judicial restraint. "Intellectually," wrote
Jeremiah Smith, "he was above all things else, original." Professor Smith had been winning counsel in *Edgerly* v. *Barker,* but
aside from that he was bound to disagree with his fellow Harvard
faculty member, Professor Gray. Smith knew Doe too well to
dismiss him as a crank, yet even he admitted that Doe could not
balance the old with the new, that his jurisprudential prejudices
tipped the scales heavily on one side. "Novelty had, undoubtedly,
some charm for him, especially as to methods of reaching conclusions," Smith acknowledged. "He sometimes preferred to strike
out a new path of his own 'across lots', rather than go around by
the beaten path. His one controlling desire in every case was to
do exact justice, and if this end could not be accomplished save
by setting at naught the so-called 'wisdom of our ancestors', he
did not hesitate to go to that extremity." [31]
Smith put his finger on it. Right or wrong, Chief Justice Doe
was original. His mind could not be harassed by rules and precedents designed to solve another era's problems. "With him," an
admirer wrote while Doe was still alive, "law is a science, yet an
ever-moving science. No man is more glad of the to-morrow than
Judge Doe. He welcomes changed conditions of things, and is
ready to meet them with his strong, clear reason." [32] Doe did not,
however, seek change for change's sake but only to make improvements. "He once said that the new is good only when it is
needed." [33] Perhaps he believed this. If so, it may have given him
comfort, when he was attacked by Bingham, Carpenter, and the

rest, to think that their only disagreement was over what was needed. At least he must have found it ironic that, when urging him for the United States Supreme Court, the lawyers of New Hampshire had especially stressed his independence of mind and his refusal to be bound by precedent. "He is a man of marked individuality," Governor Bell had written President Arthur, "and not afraid to overrule a clearly erroneous opinion, of whatever standing." [34] Moreover, he served long enough to see many of his early "heresies" become "orthodoxies," [35] accepted by those who were howling over his latest strike.

It is these "orthodoxies" which now make Charles Doe tower above the other state court judges of his era. They mark him as one of the audacious builders of American law. Yet Bingham, Carpenter, and the other critics cannot be dismissed merely because history is catching up with Charles Doe. Forgetting his substantive achievements and thinking only of his method of building, even now his strong dislike of precedent leaves the image of a pertinacious judge — a faddish mutineer against traditional judicial restraints.

On balance the credits outweigh the debits. While Doe called precedent a "frivolous formality," he acknowledged that "long usage and common consent" might make it "unjust" to overrule a respected decision.[36] Again we find him turning to that vague test of "justice," and it is this which makes the debit side seem heavier on the scales. Chief Justice Doe placed so much emphasis on principle, justice, and reason that he completely disregarded precedent, certainty, and predictability. Despite Llewellyn, we must agree with Bingham that for those practicing in his court Doe made law unstable and chartless. Considering the sum of all his ideas and all he tried to accomplish, it seems almost as though Jeremy Bentham could foresee his work when he wrote: "Should there be a Judge who enlightened by genius, stimulated by honest zeal to the work of reformation, sick of the caprice, the delays, the prejudices, the ignorance, the malice, the fickleness, the suspicious ingratitude of popular assemblies, should seek with his sole hand to expunge the effusions of traditionary imbecility, and write down in their room the dictates of pure native Justice, let him but reflect that partial amendment is bought at the expense of universal certainty; that partial good thus purchased is universal evil; and that amendment from the Judgment seat is confusion." [37]

Still, there is more to law than certainty, and as time and progress remove us from the period of battle, certainty becomes less significant. It is through the perspective of history that Doe's credits begin to outweigh the debits. That Doe gave new meaning to case law is something Bingham could not see; but later generations can. Case law draws its strength from the conflicts of daily life; not from *stare decisis*. It is a law in close contact with practicabilities; a living law. Doe gave life to New Hampshire case law and willingly paid the price of uncertainty. It was a small price to a judge ready to gamble. Great law is written only by men who take great gambles, and Charles Doe wrote great law. In the chronicles of American legal history there are many judges who dominated the jurisprudence of their states; it is doubtful if there are any whose influence lasted as long as did Doe's. There are many who wrote their personalities, prejudices, and whims into the law of their states; it is doubtful if any wrote with the same indelible ink as Chief Justice Doe. There are many who changed the law of their states; it is doubtful if any changed law with the originality, audacity, and thoroughness of a Charles Cogswell Doe.

AN EVIL OF SOME MAGNITUDE

The Common Law

CHARLES DOE knew that most jurists would object to his theories of judicial power and of precedent on the ground that these theories give a judge license to stamp the law with his individual fancies and errors. Doe's answer was part of the theories themselves. Judges, he said, have a "judicial duty of rectifying 'the mistakes of former ages' — a duty we are not at liberty to neglect." The possibility that judges, under the guise of performing this duty, may introduce errors of their own is no argument against the exercise of judicial power or in favor of precedents. As Doe declared, he and his fellows have the satisfaction of knowing "that our mistakes can be corrected by our successors."[1]

Was this attitude realistic? If the theories of a law-building judge are unique — if other lawyers reject Doe's philosophy of judicial power and the nature of precedent — how can his mistakes be corrected? Judge Carpenter answered the question for New Hampshire. He might not approve of Doe's rulings, but once they were announced, they are precedents and as precedents have to be followed.[2] If Doe made errors, Alonzo Carpenter was not the man to correct them, and Carpenter was more typical than not. But even had American judges shared Doe's ideas on judicial power and on the authority of precedent, they could not have corrected his mistakes in the way he intended unless they also shared his theory of the common law. It was from this theory that Doe drew his arguments about "error," "right," and "reason."

Except for the few who favored codification, all nineteenth-century American judges endorsed the fundamental principle in Doe's theory of common law. "In every government of laws, a body of unwritten, common law is inevitable," he insisted. "No legislature can foresee the innumerable variety of complications in human affairs, or provide a statutory rule sufficiently precise and definite to meet each particular case." [3] An all-inclusive code is an impossibility. No matter how capable the drafters, they are sure to leave gaps. David Dudley Field heard this argument many times while trying to persuade lawyers to accept codification during the 1870s and 1880s. Doe's theory, however, did not stop at this point but implied much more. It was his contention that unwritten law is sounder than written law; it is better, safer, more comprehensive.

What Doe had in mind is shown by his dealings with a Massachusetts statute which extends the property rights of abutters on salt water. The English rule was that private ownership ends at the edge of high tide; the statute changed this to low tide. It seemed a more reasonable rule, since abutters have to use the area between low and high tide to build wharfs and to develop their land commercially. Why not, therefore, recognize the fact officially, and acknowledge that ownership extends down to low tide? The theory might be good, but Doe thought the statute contained errors typical of legislation which tries to improve on common law. It cannot do the job as well as can unwritten law. Common law, he said, gives owners of abutting property a reasonable use of the tide lands below the high-water mark. There is no need to transfer the fee. The Massachusetts statute makes matters worse rather than better by giving the owner a proprietary interest in the tideland but only for a limited time — twice each day, when the tide is high. For property to be developed for commercial purposes, the abutter still must claim a common-law right to improve and occupy space beyond the low-water mark. Since the statute merely clouds this right, it appears much better to recognize that a question of natural right is involved; a natural right which can only be determined by trying the issue of reasonable use in an appropriate action brought either by the owner or by the state. [4]

This was the argument Doe used in *Winnipiseogee*. Even though the state holds the great ponds in trust for the people, abutting mill owners have a common-law right to make reasonable use of them as reservoirs.[5] This natural right exists in a society dedicated to progress through free enterprise and is best defined as a question of fact by judicial determination. It is when courts interfere with the function of the jury by turning fact into law and the legislature interferes with the function of the court by clarifying judge-made errors that the common law encounters difficulty. This is why separation of law and fact is vital from a jurisprudential point of view — it is the one way to preserve "the ancient uniformity, consistency and symmetry of the law, as a system of general principles," based on reason.[6]

Statutory law has validity, of course. But it should not tread on the domain of unwritten common law. Even a statute which seeks to apply a constitutional guarantee "is to be construed by the reason of the common law."[7] To hold that a statute enacts common law means that it is "to be determined by the reasons of natural justice and practical necessity."[8] John Austin believed that case law has a tendency to make statutory law unsystematic. Doe was more concerned about statutes interfering with the logic and reason of the common-law system. He had a strong antidote: statutes can have little effect on matters traditionally covered by common-law rules, as is seen by his attempts to turn acts of incorporation into common-law trusts. Incorporation, he said, furnishes few benefits. He made this argument basic to his solution of the *Dartmouth College Case*. A business corporation and a nonprofit school can each have its charter revoked by the legislature or declared forfeited by the judiciary, yet both will continue to exist, one as an unincorporated partnership and the other as a common-law trust, just as lawfully as if no corporate franchise had ever been granted. "The educational substance" of Dartmouth College cannot be destroyed. "By our common law" a return from the corporate to the unincorporate form "would leave the substance of the truth unchanged."[9]

Judge Doe's great decision on the theory of common-law principle over statutory authority is *McDuffee* v. *The Portland & Rochester Railroad*. The defendant had made a contract with the Eastern Express Company to carry only its shipments, to the exclusion of all other expressmen. A rival firm brought suit alleging illegal discrimination, citing analogous precedents from other jurisdictions as well as a New Hampshire statute. Doe admitted that the precedents were on point, but he deliberately chose to ignore them, preferring to rest his judgment "on a general and fundamental principle, which does not need the support of, and could hardly be shaken by, decided cases." [10]

Since he wanted to establish for New Hampshire a principle of common law, Judge Doe also thought it better not to rely on the statute. In one of the best explanations of his antistatute theory he told why. In England Parliament had enacted many statutes regulating railroads. As time went by, English courts — and, even worse, American lawyers reading English precedents — had come to depend on these statutes and had forgotten that the general principle of equality is part of the common law; that at common law a common carrier is required to serve each member of the public on reasonable and equal terms.

With so much legislation on the subject as there has been in that country, and so much litigation upon the acts of parliament, it was not strange that the bar and bench should finally lose sight of the common law origin of the principle so many times enacted in different forms, and carried out in different methods prescribed by parliament. It seems to have been a result of anxiety of parliament, that, instead of merely providing such new remedies and modes of judicial procedure as they deemed necessary for the enforcement of the common law, they repeatedly reenacted the common law, until it came to be supposed that, in such an important matter as the public service of transportation by common carriers, the public were indebted, for the doctrine of equal right, to the modern vigilance of parliament, instead of the system of legal reason which had been the birthright of Englishmen for many ages. A mistake of this kind is an evil of some magnitude. It unjustly weakens the confidence of the community in the wisdom and justice of the ancient system, and impairs its vigor. When the understanding prevails that equality, in a branch of the public service so vast as that of transportation by common carriers, depends upon the action of a legislature declaring it by statute, and attempting the difficult task of accurately expressing the whole length and breadth of the doctrine in words not defined in the common law, public and common rights of immense value are removed from a natural, broad, and firm foundation, to one that is artificial and narrow, and consequently less secure; and many results of ill consequences flow from such a misconception of the free institution of the common law.[11]

Such is Charles Doe's antistatute theory. Legislative interference into areas traditionally guarded by common-law principles is not merely inconvenient or unnecessary. It may be downright harmful by undermining confidence in the common law and thus impairing its utility.

With this in mind it is little wonder Judge Doe did not rest his decision on the New Hampshire statute. A statute which requires all persons to be treated equally and reasonably is "merely declaratory of the common law." Of course he could have relied on the statute alone. "But the common law rule of equal right and reasonableness is the ground on which we stand. 'Common', in its legal sense, used as the description of the carrier and his duty and the correlative right of the public, contains the whole doctrine of the common law on the subject. The defendants are common carriers. That is all that need be said. All beyond that can be no more than an explanation or application of the legal meaning of 'common' in that connection." [12] The principle of common law is: "A common carrier is a public carrier. . . . His duty being public, the correlative right is public. The public right is a common right, and a common right signifies a reasonably equal right." [13] The Portland & Rochester had acted illegally when it made an exclusive contract with one express company. This conclusion is so clear from common-law principle that there should be no need for a statute.

Some lawyers might argue that there have to be some statutes, at least remedial ones; that a suit at common law to end discrimination will be ineffectual because of the difficulty of proving large damages or because a multiplicity of suits will not abate a continued grievance. But as has been shown, Doe thought that courts can regulate common carriers without help from either railroad commissions or the legislature. The common law always provides the remedy necessary for vindicating the rights which it guarantees. As Doe said, "in such cases there would be a plain and adequate remedy, where there ought to be one, by the reenforcing operation of an injunction, or by indictment, information, or other common, familiar, and appropriate course of law." [14] He seems to be saying that there can be a common law of crimes in business regulation, as well as court-invented civil remedies.

Accepting the ultimate consequence of his antistatute theory,

Doe tried to make it part of the law of pleading. He ended the *McDuffee* decision by suggesting that in discrimination cases "a good and sufficient count can easily be drawn for such a cause of action, without reference to the statute." [15]

This is a remarkable suggestion for a judge — that lawyers ignore an act of the legislature. Yet if a legal theory leads to the belief that statutes may be "an evil of some magnitude," it is perfectly logical. Charles Doe knew that his system of jurisprudence led to strange results, but he had the courage to be consistent.

THE PERFECTION OF REASON
The Nature of Law

THE term "common law" was applied vaguely by Charles Doe. He did not mean by it English common law or case law based on precedent. When Doe spoke of "common law" he was speaking of law itself. When seeking his definition of common law, therefore, we are seeking his answer to the question, "What is the nature of law?"

Judge Doe gave his answer when he said, "law is a science and the perfection of reason." [1] He meant "science" only in a broad sense — a science of general principles, not detailed rules, applied through a uniform pattern of fact finding, not through judicial experience. But when Doe said that law is the perfection of reason, he was giving his definition of the meaning of law. This, we suggested, helps explain why he and Holmes took such different positions on substantive points. Holmes wrote that the life of the law has been experience. "Reason," Doe said, "is the life of the law." [2]

Doe was paraphrasing Lord Coke, a jurist whom he often cited.[3] By "reason" Doe did not mean the syllogistic logic which Justice Holmes and the realist school of jurisprudence came to associate with his generation of judges in order to disparage them. Neither Doe nor most of his contemporaries used this approach to the solution of legal problems. Rather, by "reason" Doe meant the taught traditions of the legal profession, handed down through centuries of practice and study. His meaning was the same as Lord Coke's when Coke told King James that he might be the wisest of men, but without study of common law he could not know the reason of the law. This is an educated, not a native reason, yet it does not shut out experience. Doe agreed with Holmes up to a point. With Roscoe Pound he recognized that law "is experience developed by reason, and reason checked and directed by experience." [4] He did not say this himself, probably because he did not consider that reason can be separated from experience. Holmes tried to derive legal rules from daily experience. Doe preferred to judge the utility of a rule by reason. In his solution to the railway-crossing problem in *Huntress* he had considered experience when proposing answers to the factual question. In *Goodman* Holmes had laid down a rule based on experience without testing it by the standard of reasonableness.[5]

When Charles Doe spoke of "reason" he meant a process of decisionmaking which reconciles law with experience, not through the formulation of rules based on experience, but through application of felt and articulated "justice" discoverable in the norms and practices of changing society. Reason is the test of law. When the reason of a rule ceases, the rule ceases, he said in an opinion which held that under certain circumstances it is not necessary to use the word "feloniously" in an indictment. It had been necessary at English common law — and there had been good reason for the rule. But under the different conditions of American government the reason had disappeared. "What would 'feloniously' mean in this indictment?" Doe asked. "Would it inform the defendant that in England, felony was formerly punished by forfeiture, and generally by death? An indictment is an accusation, and not historical instruction. Would it inform him that New Hampshire punishes his crime either by death or state prison? That would be a statement of law, deficient in certainty; and an indictment is a statement not of law, but of fact." [6] There is no longer reason for the rule; therefore the rule no longer exists.

Conversely reason determines what rules are in existence, and these rules should be rules of reasonableness. At no time did Judge Doe better express the system of jurisprudence he hoped to bequeath to New Hampshire than when he wrote, "The doctrine of reasonable necessity, reasonable care, and reasonable use prevail in this state in a liberal form, on a broad basis of general principle." [7] This doctrine — the doctrine of reasonableness — permeates his decisions. Reasonableness was his solution to the *Winnipiseogee* case — owners of land on great ponds have a right to a reasonable use of waters which abut their property. It was his solution to the chaos in construction — documents should be construed reasonably and not by rules of law. It was his solution to many tort questions — the test of a person's liability is whether he acted on reasonable necessity and with reasonable care. Indeed, as mentioned earlier, Doe came very close to defining torts in terms of reasonableness alone.[8]

Reasonableness determines the presence of, and the weight to be accorded, each element at issue in a tort litigation. Doe's discussion of the occasions for the right of self-defense illustrates his method. "The chronological part of the doctrine of defence, like the rest of it," he wrote in the *Mink Case*, "is a matter of reasonableness; and reasonableness depends upon circumstances."[9] No question raised by the doctrine of defense should be settled as a matter of law. Even the probative value of each act committed by the person asserting the privilege of self-defense is a question of fact, to be determined by its reasonableness within the fact situation which existed at the time of the alleged tort. As Doe explained, reason is the best criterion.

In defence, it may be reasonable that a man should strike quicker for human life than for property; that he should strike quicker at a habitual fighter, professional robber, or notorious assassin, from whom there would be reason to expect sudden or extreme violence, than at a man previously inoffensive, from whom there would be little reason to apprehend a serious attack; that he would strike quicker at a strong man than a weak one; that he should shoot a dog quicker than he would shoot a man; and that he should shoot mischievous wild animals, which are the absolute property of nobody, quicker than he should shoot a valuable domestic animal, the property of his neighbor. The consequences of shooting, compared with the consequences of not shooting, are material to be considered on the question when he should shoot, as well as on the question whether shooting is a defence of a reasonably necessary kind.[10]

Here, in clear expression, is why Doe rejected preset formulas for such issues as self-defense. The concept of reasonableness will produce a truer, more just result. "Imminence of danger," he concluded, "in this broad and relative sense, creating a reasonable necessity, was the test of the defendant's right." [11]

By making reasonableness the norm for a ruling of law, Chief Justice Doe was not asking whether the ruling was more practical than its alternatives. As will be seen in the next chapter, Doe made pragmatism a vital part of his jurisprudence when explaining the origin of law, which he found in the customs of society. But as for the nature or essence of law, while Doe wanted law to be practical, practicality was not the only consideration. Above and beyond the workability of a ruling is the question of justice. In one case Doe called the "doctrine of reasonableness" the "doctrine of justice." [12] Common law, he said, is "determined by the reasons of natural justice and practical necessity." [13] Justice and reasonableness together are the two elements by which Charles Doe defined the nature of law.

Chief Justice Doe was not ashamed to appeal to the "dictates of justice and reason." [14] He settled administrative,[15] taxation,[16] and even constitutional questions[17] by inquiring into the requirements of justice. Most of his adjective reforms were based on "the convenience of justice." [18] This is another trait which separates Charles Doe from the mainstream of American law. From William Gaston[19] to Earl Warren[20] jurists have cited justice as a motivating force when speaking off the bench. But as one researcher has pointed out, "Few judges have felt sure enough of their own strength to risk presenting judicial choices naked except for arguments of their justice or expediency." Even Lemuel Shaw "preferred to dress them as consistent with precedents or their analogy." [21] The chief justice of New Hampshire had the courage to speak in the fashion of his actions.

Unfortunately Charles Doe never defined justice, thus leaving a gap in his jurisprudence. Those who feel law should be an exact science will find his legal theories deficient because of it. It would have been remarkable had Doe given much thought to definition, partly because judicial decisions do not lend themselves to explanations of this type and partly because there is a contradiction within his philosophical order. He was a man of practice, not an academician. He sought means, not ends. Yet he followed abstract principles, not concrete rules. This may be due to his emphasis on the means of the law — on rules of remedy and rules of construction. To reform these rules, he sought broad principles. The man of practice became a theorist in an area where theory is seldom applied. Yet he remained primarily a man of practice, not a philosopher who thought through concepts to their basic elements. He based much substantive law on the distinction between law and fact. Yet he never took time to define what he meant by "fact." Now we see him making "reason" and "justice" the criteria of his test of "law." Yet he does not define them. To compound the problem, he often held that whether justice requires the court to act is a question of fact which cannot be reviewed. For example, the justice of an amendment changing the form of action is a question of fact determinable at the trial term.[22]

One matter is clear: Charles Doe believed "reason" and "justice" to be definable terms. He used them so frequently that he could hardly have thought them catch-all phrases with which a lazy judge can disguise difficult problems or avoid unpleasant results. Perhaps he was naive; perhaps he thought "reason" and "justice" too obvious to need explanation. Surely Doe did not consider them subjective standards. He did not think that when he decided a case on grounds of reasonableness or justice he was applying only his idea of what is "reasonable" and "just." He was trained to make decisions in the felt and recognizable discipline of the common-law tradition. He expected other lawyers to understand the principle of reasonableness or justice even in cases where they disagreed with its application. During the last year of his life he was disturbed that Frank Nesmith Parsons, the newest member of the bench, doubted the utility of "justice" as a practical concept. Doe tried hard to reassure him. Parsons was the brightest of the young men on the court, and if Doe's work was to be carried on after he was gone, Parsons had to be won over. " 'What justice requires' is the test of many things in N.H. law," Doe assured him; "& if the court has a correct sense of justice, that test is something we need not be afraid of, however unsatisfactory it may be to mathematical & mechanical minds, & to judges who want to avoid the cultivation & laborious use of practical judgment on matters of fact by applying a two foot rule taken from the N.H. Reports." [23]

These words are a plea to Parsons not to abandon principles to which Doe had devoted his life. But they are also an affirmation of faith, faith in "justice" as a test of law. Of course the test is not precise; of course it will not satisfy those who wish to solve legal problems by the exact standards of mathematical measurement; it demands "laborious use of practical judgment." But law cannot be entrusted to men who will judge each action by what is said in the New Hampshire Reports.

Doe's critics might make the same argument against reasonableness that Judge Parsons apparently made against justice. They might claim it to be so vague that courts cannot apply it; the attempt would be too difficult. Doe admitted the difficulty — a difficulty of fact, not of law. "But," he answered, "such difficulty as there may be will arise from the breadth of the inquiry, the intricate nature of the matter to be investigated, the circumstantial character of the evidence to be weighed, and the application of the legal rule to the facts, and not from any want of clearness or certainty in the general principle of the common law applicable to the subject. The difficulty will not be in the common law, and cannot be justly overcome by altering that law. The inquiry may sometimes be a broad one, but it will never be broader than the justice of the case requires. A narrow view that would be partial, cannot be taken; a narrow test of right and wrong that would be grossly inequitable, cannot be adopted." [24]

Doe's manner of answering objections to reasonableness by saying that it is law, and that objections cannot be met by altering the law, is exasperating. Nevertheless, he does make his point. Reason and justice are not standards for the lazy. They are exacting. They take effort to apply — more effort than do rules of precedent, favored by most judges. They are determined by weighing the facts of each case. From the judicial decisions in which Doe did just that it is possible to seek the definition which he himself never framed. The task is not an easy one. Did he, for example, equate "justice" with morality? There is little doubt that Doe considered law ill equipped to settle controversies with norms of abstract morality; that is, morality in the sense of right and wrong as absolute guides for conduct. True, in one decision, which he did not write, his court questioned the "practical justice" of a rule which it nonetheless applied because "we feel quite confident that its application to the present case will do no wrong." [25] Yet in one of his own opinions Judge Doe implied that justice has little to do with morality; that it means "useful." An amendment, he held, may be allowed "if justice requires it." Since this was a question for the trial term, he did not decide it; but he did suggest that the amendment should be disallowed because it "does not appear that an amendment will be useful." [26] Nevertheless, it cannot be denied that there is a touch of morality in Judge Doe's use of the term "justice." He resolved one case by saying that justice did not require the court to correct an error because the error was not "injurious." [27] In this he expressed a lawyer's sense of morality. The idea of legal morals is close to what Charles Doe meant by justice. His concept of justice was related to the notion of "fairness"; a legal fairness to be sure, but fairness just the same. It weighed each case to determine which side had better claim on the court's legal conscience. It was not unlike the equity jurisdiction of the English chancellors in former times, when a petitioner had to have clean hands before he could obtain relief. Doe extended this principle. He balanced the interests of conflicting claims by considering personal, legal, and social factors. Such an approach does not imply that Charles Doe's principle of justice was a crude version of the jurisprudence of interests; he was too committed to the concept of law as a social phenomenon to feel that it could be reduced to a set of ethical values. But as a student of the role of social progress upon the development of legal rules, he recognized with Philipp Heck that law "operates in a world full of competing interests, and, therefore, always works at the expense of some interests." [28] The principle of "justice" permitted Doe to consider these interests as well as to take into account what is useful, what is desirable, and what is reasonable. In fact, Doe made the concept of reasonableness especially effective in this regard.

Judge Doe had in mind this balancing function of law through reason when, in *Brown* v. *Collins*, he rejected the rule of liability without fault.[29] That rule affords slight opportunity to weigh interests. The rule in *Rylands* v. *Fletcher* is almost as restrictive in that it makes a landowner automatically liable for certain consequences when he uses his property unnaturally but does not consider what interests he is developing or how the benefits to him compare with the inconvenience they cause to his neighbors. To Doe this is mechanical law. Reasonable use is a better rule, and in *Green* v. *Gilbert* he explained how it is to be applied. For a number of years owners of a mill had deposited surplus sawdust in a stream which flowed by the plaintiff's land. In 1873 the plaintiff improved his property by building a dam. The sawdust then began to accumulate on his premises, causing injury, and he brought action for damages. The issue, Doe said, was whether the defendants' use of the stream to carry away sawdust was a reasonable use of their rights as riparian owners. This was a question of fact, and among the facts to be considered was the reasonableness of the defendants' use of the stream before 1873, compared to the reasonableness of their use after the plaintiff's dam had been built. This question was resolved by balancing competing interests on the scales of reasonableness. "Whether the defendants' use, previously reasonable, became unreasonable in 1873 was a question of fact depending upon the circumstances of the case, including the defendants' benefit and the plaintiff's damage. The plaintiff's admission of the propriety of the defendants' use before 1873 would tend to reduce the broad issue of reasonableness to the narrower question whether it was reasonable that the defendants' old use should be discontinued on the introduction of the plaintiff's new one." [30] As Doe wrote in the headnote, the question of fact was to be resolved by the circumstances of the case, "including the purposes old and new for which the stream is used by each party, the amount of the defendant's benefit, the amount of the plaintiff's damage, and all the causes of the damage." [31]

Again the question of certainty in law arises. Do not the vague concepts of "reasonableness" and "justice" and the practice of measuring justice by weighing the degrees of reasonableness in competing interests make law unpredictable? Doe admitted that, like his theory of precedent, his theory of common law can cause uncertainty. "But," he explained, "the reason of the law has some regard for the fundamental principles of justice as well as the demands of convenience." [32] He did not intend to compromise those principles. In one case the issue was whether a certain statute violated the constitutional prohibition against retroactive laws. Doe could have resolved the matter by applying familiar maxims of interpretation; instead he relied on justice, though he was aware that lawyers might be dissatisfied. "It is natural," he acknowledged, "that courts, pressed by the difficulty and inconvenience of deciding causes in so broad a principle, and accustomed to the guidance of more limited rules and specific principles, should seek some path more restricted, sharply defined, and easily followed, than the unbounded expanse of justice. But it may be doubted whether some of the attempts made to lay out a path have not tended to disseminate contracted and obscure views of the principle on which the constitutional prohibition is based, and to embarrass its operation." [33] The constitutional prohibition against retroactive statutes is, like common law, based on the principle of justice. Those who would interpret it by any principle other than justice abuse law for the sake of certainty. Judge Doe believed that merely because the truth of a doctrine is undemonstrable to the satisfaction of everyone does not make its application unpredictable. While law is what is practicable, though not necessarily what is most convenient, certainty, though a norm, is not the test of its validity.

One consequence of Doe's common-law theory, especially his emphasis on "reasonableness," was that he did not judge every question in terms of rights; he gave occasional attention to duty. In the railroad discrimination case he looked at both sides of the tort. The public right against the common carrier, he said, is a "reasonably equal right," [34] while the public duty of the carrier is to furnish reasonable facilities on reasonable terms. [35] From either vantage point unreasonable discrimination is illegal. But this approach was not customary; generally Doe concentrated on right — the conventional pattern in those days. [36] In one opinion we find him discussing the use of property, not in terms of the owner's duty to employ the property reasonably, but of his neighbor's right that it not be used unreasonably. A landowner has the right to build a fire for domestic or commercial purposes if he manages it with care and skill. If, however, through his fault, the fire escapes to his neighbor's property and causes damage, he will be liable, not because he has violated a duty to use his land reasonably, but because his use, by his fault, is an invasion of his neighbor's right. [37] How seriously Doe took the distinction is not clear. But he did prefer to analyze the issue by holding it to be a property right, not to be injured by a neighbor making unreasonable use of his own land.[38] And in a discussion of convenient remedy he spoke of "the law of rights." [39]

Was this Charles Doe's view of the nature of law — that law is a bundle of rights founded on justice and determined by the perfection of reason? Most definitions of law are the work of jurisprudes. Few men who spend their lives on the firing line of law, as did Doe, have time to define it. A cynic, thinking of Doe's radicalism, his strength of character, and his mastery of argument, might consider that he agreed with Aaron Burr. "Law," Burr once remarked "is whatever is boldly asserted and plausibly maintained." [40] This statement describes Doe's actions, but not his philosophy. True, when Doe spoke of law, he referred, not to the process of administration, but to the process of adjudication. And in this limited context law in New Hampshire became to a large extent what he decided it should be. Yet he would have rejected Oliver Wendell Holmes's glib apothegm that law is "what the courts will do in fact." [41] The gulf separating Doe and Holmes on so many substantive issues continued to divide them here.

In one respect they were alike. Holmes also stressed the process of adjudication. Law, he said, is "a statement of the circumstances in which the public force will be brought to bear on men through the courts." [42] Doe would have been troubled by the word "force," which replaces reason and asperses justice. As applied by the disciples of John Austin, it permits no challenge to the commands of the sovereign state. It would make law the perfection of power, not reason. "Law," Doe said, "is a rule: not a transient sudden order from a superior to or concerning a particular person; but something permanent, uniform, and universal." [43] He was quoting Blackstone, and he made Blackstone's definition of the nature of law his own. He was saying that law is not the command of the sovereign. The state might demand confiscation of property, but the owner of that property has recourse to the law. Doe was not speaking only of "constitutional law" but of "law" in general. A confiscation decree of the Revolutionary government in 1778, seizing the estates of New Hampshire Tories, had been "law" in the constitutional sense. It had been "a law in the sense of being a lawful order issued by men holding all power, legislative and non-legislative." But it had not been "a law in the true legal sense explained by Blackstone." [44]

It is said that case law makes law amoral; that it overemphasizes "what is" at the expense of "what ought to be." [45] But in Doe's hands unwritten law was the conscience of the state and the scales which weighed the interests of private litigants. The common law, he said, "is, or can be, or ought to be, known to all who are subject to its government." It is "a rational system, and not a collection of rules, maxims, and definitions construed upon verbal distinctions, to be applied in an arbitrary or literal sense." [46] Law is not logical, it is systematic; it is not a science, but an art. By its very nature it is and has to be the perfection of reason and the experience of justice.

A MASS OF CUSTOMS
The Origin of Law

DID a theory that the best law is an unwritten law the essence of which are the principles of justice and reason mean that Charles Doe was an exponent of natural law? It has been shown that in constitutional matters he was not. Justice is not the test of constitutionality, he wrote in 1874.[1] And shortly before his death, in an intercourt memorandum, he reminded his colleagues that "The qualification of reasonableness does not affect the question of legislative power."[2] But what of nonconstitutional questions? Was he not an adherent of the natural-law school? Did he not use justice and reason as natural standards, as ideals with which to measure and maintain the purity and integrity of positive law?

Doe did not mean that law is found in justice and reason. He discovered many general principles by the process of reason, and to this extent he acted like a natural-law theorist; but his search for law itself was more confined. Justice and reason are the standards, the tests, the essence of law, not its source. True, in the "law of rights" Doe included natural rights. But he did not mean that nature is the fountainhead of a complete system of rules with which any and every problem may be solved. He took the idea of "natural rights" in a restricted sense, as he showed in *Haley* v. *Colcord*. The defendant had possessed a private way of prescription on the plaintiff's land, which the plaintiff obstructed. To avoid the obstruction, the defendant deviated from the private way by crossing the plaintiff's land at another reasonable and proper place. The plaintiff sued in trespass. Judge Doe not only held for the defendant, but said he lawfully could have taken more "natural" steps; he could have torn down the obstruction even if it had meant going into the plaintiff's field and doing more damage than by passing around the obstruction. This is "a natural right which no branch of government has given him." [3] It is a right which he possesses by necessity. "The necessity is generally a reasonable one, and determined by the application of reason to the circumstances of the case, and not prescribed as an arbitrary, verbal formula." The reason of law knows it cannot furnish an immediate remedy to meet every need. "The law adopts the natural right of self-defence, because it considers the future process of law an inadequate remedy for present injuries accompanied with force. It adopts the natural right of recapturing property, real and personal, by the mere act of the party injured, because legal process may be an inadequate remedy. It adopts the natural right of abating nuisances by the mere act of the party injured, because he cannot reasonably be required to wait for the slow progress of the ordinary forms of justice. These personal remedies are instances of the application of the rule of reasonable necessity. The division of common property in some cases, by the mere act of one of the owners taking his share, is another instance." [4] The right physically to abate a nuisance which interferes with the reasonable use of property is a natural right. Like other natural rights, it is determined not by a formula derived from the law of nature but as a question of reasonable necessity. The fact of reasonable necessity is resolved by the present conditions of society and the availability of sufficient alternatives.

If Charles Doe was not an exponent of the natural-law school, is there any group with which he may be classed? Certainly the utilitarian-analytical theory was not for him. It believes that the legislature, guided by the standard of utility, should determine law. The judge finds his principles in enacted law; he must not make law. [5] The opposite school — the historical school — was more suited to his ideas. Historical jurists place law above the command of the sovereign. Law results from historical and social circumstances. Doe lived during "the era of history"; the epoch when legal history was "the key to the science of law." [6] But as a rationalist, not a romanticist, he had little sentiment for the past as such. His emphasis upon the reason of law makes it difficult to classify him with a movement which reacts to reason. Moreover, Doe's decisions concentrating on legal history were usually directed at reform. He employed the history of law — the history of a doctrine or of a remedy — to attack current usage. His history-oriented opinions which created new law usually turned on social, economic, or political history, not on the more narrow history of law.

To say as much is not to discount Charles Doe's historical opinions. He was a judicial historian of the first rank,[7] although his method was somewhat careless. He traced doctrines to their source, and if he found that they had grown out of aristocratic privileges, he would call them "hostile to our system of society." [8] "Such things as these," he said of English rules which place the burden of proof on the less favored classes, "our emigrant ancestors intended to leave behind them when they came to New Hampshire. An English misunderstanding or perversion of the common law, is not necessarily our law." [9] This was good legal polemics, even though the historical premises were often questionable. It must be seen as polemic, not as legal theory. Doe was not saying that law originates either from politics or from conditions of government. True, an American constitutional issue such as freedom of religion "is to be decided upon American principles, indigenous or adopted." [10] But on nonconstitutional questions, when Chief Justice Doe compared aristocratic England to democratic America, he was not making political theory the genesis of law; rather, he was applying the familiar standard of the "American Reception" — the reception of English common law into America. He was saying that when our ancestors arrived on these shores they carried with them so much of the common law of England as useful and left behind so much as oppressive or unsuited to the new world. This is an argument of authority and of precedent familiar in American case law which has little to do with abstract legal theory. It was made by New Hampshire chief justices before and after Charles Doe.[11] There is no state in the union which has not heard its echo. It may not have been good legal history, but it was good legal argument and made a confident tool with which judges, less bold than Doe, were able to pick and choose between English precedents.

There are differences to be noted. First, Doe made it a broad, general argument against English precedents, not merely against selected precedents. Second, Doe gave it positive implications. He did not merely say that American conditions reject nonindigenous rules from English common law; he asserted that American conditions create their own common law, that there is a common law "that grows out of the institutions and circumstances of the country," a "common law that grows out of American conditions." [12] This is the origin, the source of law — the institutions, circumstances, and conditions of the nation and of the state. These institutions, these circumstances, and these conditions give rise to a law which is native, which is common, and which is workable. "I have been rereading your history of Exeter with great pleasure & profit," Doe once wrote to the historian of the town to which his great-great-grandfather, Sampson Doe, had moved late in the seventeenth century. "I get from it many ideas of what our common law must be." [13]

By "circumstances" and "conditions" Chief Justice Doe meant the sum total of the experience of the people for whom the court is making law. Undoubtedly this includes historical and political experience; but primarily it is economic and social, with emphasis on the present. The law "has not fixed a day when the precedents of its adaption to the mutability of human affairs shall no longer be in force." Thus doctrines such as the feudal tenure of land, "growing out of social conditions that have ceased, and incompatible with the increase of trade, productive industry, and personal estate, have become obsolete." [14] They have become obsolete because law keeps pace with the changes of society. These changes are not merely those resulting from settlement of a new world and rebellion from the mother country, but are social — changes in commerce, in manufacturing, and in the uses of private property. A common law which does not meet changes, which is a stagnated "code" enacted by the courts of olden times, "would be ill adapted to the situation and wants of the country, and repugnant to what are usually regarded as indispensable arrangements of modern life." [15]

On these terms Charles Doe defined common law. Common law, he said, is "in general a system of natural principles, necessarily adopted by custom and common consent, and necessarily conformable to the progress of society." [16] He had no reservations.

Law, he wrote, is "largely derived" from the "customs and conditions of society."[17] It is derived from the fact that men live in society. "The common law does not usually establish tests of responsibility on any other basis than the propriety of [men] living in the social state, and the relative and qualified character of the rights incident to that state."[18]

The salient manifestation is custom. "Custom is a great source of the common law," Doe wrote. "Indeed, the common law, properly so called, has been understood to be a mere mass of customs."[19] Admittedly elements of custom are "debatable subjects." "By what test," he asked, "are we to know when the individual understanding of a people, proved by hearsay, parol, and circumstantial evidence, becomes a matter of public history of which the courts take notice? The wonder is, not that there is so much conflict of authority on questions involving such considerations, but that there is so little. It is not easy to fix the bounds within which the judgment is to be exercised in determining whether a custom, usage, public policy, or historical fact, at variance with the general principles of the common law, is a legal custom, usage, policy, or fact, excepted from the operation of those general principles, and whether it is excepted from the literal and apparent meaning of the constitution."[20] Despite these difficulties, the bounds of custom can be fixed. Custom is not an historical determination but arises from today's society — today's needs, today's economy, today's norms. When Doe rejected historical jurisprudence, he rejected any idea of testing custom by immemorial usage.

History need not be neglected. The *Winnipiseogee* decision — the decision which his court refused to adopt[21] — is an example of Doe's employment of history to find a custom, to discover if New Hampshire's inhabitants recognized private rights to reasonable use of public waters. Doe turned to history to learn if the custom was in existence, if it had been universal, and if it worked. History was to prove validity, not antiquity. The time element was important because time establishes the indispensability of a usage, not its durability. As he told Judge Chase, history might show that land owners had always made reasonable use of the waters which abut their property. How else can the use be justified "if it had not been universally recognized as a legal right growing out of the situation & circumstances of the people, which are one of the chief sources of the common law?" [22]

Doe did not make custom serve novel questions only. "Differences of condition produce differences of law," he argued.[23] New law found in custom can change such old law as the rule that a devise of real estate to two or more persons creates a joint tenancy. The rule does not apply in New Hampshire, Doe held, because New Hampshire conditions do not favor a joint tenancy against a tenancy in common. "The English rule, that if there are no words of severance, devisees and legatees are joint tenants, is in this state reversed," he held. "By usage, and the general understanding of the people, promoted by seventy years' operation of the statute on conveyance and devises of real estate, it is a part of our common law that if an intention to create a joint tenancy is not expressed, legatees are not joint tenants." [24] When the type of tenancy is not in dispute, custom may still be useful. Thus Doe turned to custom to settle property rights in common in an action of *assumpsit* for the use of furniture brought by nine plaintiffs against the tenth tenant. Doe stated that "the unwritten rules" of ownership in common can be "prospectively implied from the exigencies of business by an enlightened public sense of expediency, obligation, and right." [25]

In these cases, as in others, Doe reminds us of Lord Mansfield. He too promulgated business customs with confidence.[26] But in nineteenth-century New Hampshire Doe's best opportunity to find commercial usages with which to build law came from the agricultural segment of the economy. Despite the Yankee exodus, there were still farmers grubbing their livings from the rocky hills.[27] It was on the strength of their experiences and practices that Doe held valid a parole agreement for the maintenance of a partition fence. "By the common law of New Hampshire, established by common custom and understanding, the unrescinded, oral contract, executed by one, bound the other." [28]

Doe's agricultural decisions are especially significant in rounding out his jurisprudence. Through them he showed that when the customs of one economic activity lag behind customs in other areas of the economy, law may also lag by recognizing an exception to general principles. In *Blaisdell* v. *Stone* the defendant verbally let his farm and stock to his son for a year. Some stock strayed from the pasture and damaged the plaintiff's land. Under ancient English common law the defendant, not his son, was liable regardless of facts; a liability without fault which "originated in barbaric ideas not now accepted as a ground of legal obligation." [29] As Doe had pointed out in *Brown* v. *Collins*, these ideas, based on ancient custom, had been valid in the era when they first operated.[30] "They were," he argued, "certainly introduced in England at an immature stage of English jurisprudence, and an undeveloped state of agriculture, manufactures, and commerce, when the nation had not settled down to those modern, progressive, industrial pursuits which the spirit of the common law, adapted to all conditions of society, encourages and defends. They were introduced when the development of many of the rational rules now universally recognized as principles of the common law had not been demanded by the growth of intelligence, trade, and productive enterprise, — when the common law had not been set forth in the precedents, as a coherent and logical system on many subjects other than the tenures of real estate." [31] Time and altered circumstances in commerce and industry have made these ideas obsolete. But the relationship of farmer to farmer had not changed to such an extent that new rules were needed. The question is not whether the old rule is "unsupported by its primitive reasons" but rather whether it "has no existing foundation in the succession of common customs, common necessities, or common sentiments, in which many common-law principles have an origin and a development that are continuous, authorized, and inevitable." Considering legal alternatives, practices of local husbandry, the issue of reasonableness, and the justice due competing interests, Doe concluded that "under the present conditions of New Hampshire agriculture, there may be less hardships in the defendant's liability than in a new rule putting the task of discovering the bailment, before suit, upon persons entitled to damages in such cases. It may be reasonably necessary that the risk of entrusting the custody of cattle to an irresponsible bailee, should so rest upon their owner as not to deprive injured third persons of the benefit of a common-law action, if the bailee is unable to pay the damages. The ancient rule, that the injured party may, at his election, maintain trespass against the owner or his bailee, is not so clearly devoid of modern reason as to acquire a decision that it has ceased to exist." [32]

Agricultural needs and practices had not progressed so far or changed so much that a doctrine of right handed down in ancient times had lost its validity. If custom still sustained it, then it was still good law. What makes this view remarkable is Doe's general tort theory. In *Brown* v. *Collins* he had attacked Lord Blackburn's *Rylands* rule, which puts landowners at their peril when undertaking certain activities which might escape and harm their neighbors. An unwarranted exception to the general rule governing inevitable accident, Doe had called it.[33] Yet in this instance he agrees with Blackburn. As an analogy to *Rylands,* Blackburn had cited the rule that an owner of cattle "must keep them at his peril, or he will be answerable for the natural consequences of their escape." [34] Oliver Wendell Holmes pointed out that in many prairie states the rule did not prevail.[35] Doe considered this aspect irrelevant for New Hampshire.[36] The economic and physical characteristics of the state were closer to both medieval and modern England than to the unfenced cattle country of midwestern America. The customs of that area of the nation had given rise to a different rule of law. In New Hampshire, customs and usages of industry and commerce had also made rules of absolute liability obsolete. They would have retarded the progress of society had they been applied against land owners using their property for manufacturing or for most other purposes. By the same reasoning the development of the open ranges did not favor doctrines making cattle owners absolutely liable for damage done by stray steers. But dairy farms in New Hampshire could still function safely under the old rule.

In this way Doe's legal theories clashed. It was a vital principle to him that the symmetry and harmony of the common law be preserved by discouraging exceptions to general rules. But general rules originate in the customs of society, and when customs of society create exceptions to these rules, Charles Doe placed the source of law above abstract principle. The theory of custom as the source of law took precedent in his jurisprudential scale of values. It also was the theory he carried to the greatest lengths of sophistication. The great case is *Concord Manufacturing Com-*

pany v. *Robertson,* in which he harmonized conflicting property rights by using the institutions and conditions of society to create one interest while preserving a competing one. This was the decision in which Doe laid down the rule that the citizens of New Hampshire own the great ponds and lakes of the state and that a great pond or lake is one of ten acres or more in extent. The controversy itself was not important. It is immaterial that he did not have to decide so sweeping an issue; that only rights to one pond were at stake. The fact that his philosophy of judicial power required him to settle the larger question has been discussed.[37] Here we need ask only how he used sociological arguments drawn from the historical and contemporary customs of New Hampshire's people.

Judge Doe began by considering the social and governmental background of England at the time the colony was first settled. In 1663, when Nicholas Doe landed at Portsmouth, the waters of the country he had left behind were controlled by a privileged few — either by the aristocracy who maintained them as private piscatory or hunting preserves, or, in the case of tidewater, by monopolies holding exclusive fishing rights. Little was left for the public. By the second half of the nineteenth century the likelihood existed that the same situation might soon hold true for the fresh waters of New Hampshire. There was no nobility, to be sure, but the best fishing and hunting spots could end up in the hands of sporting clubs. Doe made *Robertson* the vehicle for asking whether these private preserves were out of place among the democratic institutions of New England.

The question as he framed it was whether the lakes and ponds of the state belonged to the public. Doe sought the answer in the social and economic aspirations of New Hampshire's pioneers. "Beginning their settlement in the forest with many of the advantages of an original organization of society, exercising all the powers of self-government, and enjoying a large measure of practical independence, they had no time to adopt" the "unsound and useless" incidents of monarchy.[38] Their customs showed that they wanted the privileges denied them in England. They retained liberties of hunting and fishing, first in the wild and unoccupied districts of the colony, and later in large ponds and tidewaters after adjoining dry land had become private property.[39] As early as 1641 Massachusetts had codified these public rights. It is immaterial whether the statute extended to New Hampshire. "In this state, free fishing and free fowling in great ponds and tide-waters have not needed the aid of a statute for the abolition of written or the declaration of unwritten law. So far as the ordinance of 1641 introduced or confirmed these liberties, it was an enactment of New Hampshire law." In both jurisdictions, Massachusetts and New Hampshire, one acting by statute, the other depending on custom, the large ponds were "withheld from private ownership for reasons that are distinctly American." [40]

From this background and historical appraisal of custom Charles Doe ruled that title to the fresh-water ponds of New Hampshire divide into two classes — "the small, which pass by an ordinary grant of land, like brooks and rivers, from which, as conveyable property, they are distinguishable, — and the large, which are exempted from the operation of such a grant for reasons that stop private ownership at the water's edge of the sea and its estuaries. Tide-waters and large ponds are public waters." [41] In terms of legal doctrine, New Hampshire, "by uniform usage and a general concurrence of opinion," rejected the English rule that the distinction between public and private waters is based on tidal motion or on the presence of salt water. [42]

As Doe acknowledged, his decision was not without difficulties. How, for example, could he claim that New Hampshire people had recognized in their customs and common understanding public ownership of great ponds while they utilized them for private purposes? "The argument that the private use of tide-waters and large ponds by abutters disproves the public title, is not conclusive," he argued. "Like other general rules, the public title, and the king's want of capacity to convert such waters into private property, are applied with a due observation of private rights founded on necessity and convenience, and maintained by uniform usage." [43] In other words, in a society dedicated to progress through enterprise general customs which vest title in the state are modified by particular customs based on "the necessities of commerce." [44] Abutting proprietors cannot claim private title to public waters, but by custom, necessity, and common law they can claim a property right to reasonable use. "The dictates of justice and reason, which retain in the government, for common use, the fee of large ponds, and the shores and arms of the sea (and in some states, large fresh rivers), have vested a reasonable private right of using this public property in the owners of the adjoining land." [45] The extent of this private right cannot be defined but "is governed by the rule of reasonableness applied to the facts of his case." [46] Again Doe turned to custom. Custom determines what is a reasonable use and also shows that, while vague, it is not too vague to be practical. For by custom New Hampshire littoral owners have always been willing to accept such inconvenience as custom might cause. "This risk has been assumed, from the earliest settlement to the present time, without fear of loss; and if any public or private wrong or inconvenience has generally resulted, it is not generally known. The experience of more than 250 years has shown no practical difficulty in the question of the abutters' reasonable private use." [47]

To sum up his argument, Judge Doe wrote:

The doctrine that the soil under tide-water is a private emolument of the sovereign (subject to public rights of fishery and navigation), and that, without express or implied license, abutters cannot build wharves, or bathe in the sea, in front of their own land, is not introduced here by applying the dictates of justice and reason to the situation of the American people. The public title to the beds of large ponds, including a public right of fishery that cannot be impaired by prescription, and the private right of wharfing out, are not overthrown by [judicial] authorities. . . . If due weight is given to the axiom that the common law grows out of the institutions and circumstances of the country, the conclusion is unavoidable that the rights of abutters and the public in American public waters are the whole property, and not merely what was left for the subjects of the realm by the ancient monopolies of the English executive and the manorial lords. [48]

Many criticisms have been raised to Doe's reasoning in *Robertson*. Judge Putnam of the United States circuit court for the First Circuit objected that Doe had cited no authority when he ruled that the right of free fishing and free fowling on the great ponds does not need the aid of statutes. [49] While this objection is primarily to Doe's method of judicial lawmaking, it does call into question Doe's philosophy of law and custom. Doe was unable to cite a precedent partly because other judges had been less bold. In *Robertson* his assertion that law originates in the customs and usages of progressing society is a fundamental jurisprudential proposition. But Putnam apparently wants a precedent in the reports before he will accept it and this is the last type of authority Charles Doe could have furnished.

Another objection is that Doe offered no proof that as to ten-acre ponds a custom contrary to the laws of England obtained in colonial New Hampshire; nor could Doe cite evidence as to why New Hampshire should be different from other New England states which permit private ownership of great ponds.[50] Doe was aware of these points. He admitted that his ten-acre test was "arbitrary";[51] the general principle arose from customs and usages incapable of precision. The court settled on ten acres because it was convenient to have a standard, and ten acres seemed to conform to the spirit of the custom. Suitable standards might have been based on present use or on natural capacity for navigation, but since the custom was found in reaction to aristocratic privileges, commercial considerations would not answer the purpose. Of course he could cite no "authority," since the matter had not previously been raised. Other states had reached different results because they had followed English precedents on the issue of ownership and had ignored indigenous American conditions.

In Judge Putnam's opinion a statute existed which would have given Doe both authority and a test for measurement. This was the statute of 1887, which provided: "For purposes of this act, all natural ponds and lakes containing more than twenty acres shall be deemed public waters." [52] Doe did not mention this statute, and Putnam implies that had he relied on it, his judgment could have had the substance of legislative sanction. This statute certainly would have simplified the decision process, but it would have raised other problems. For if Doe had rested the rule of public ownership of great ponds on the statute rather than on custom, he would have been faced with a constitutional issue — what power did the legislature have to take over all waters of twenty acres or more? The court would still have had to decide who owned the great ponds at common law. If the state owned them, then the statute merely codified common law and served little purpose. If the state did not own them, then it was attempting to seize private property without compensation.

Putnam also saw merit in a Maine precedent which held that the right of fishing in the proprietor of the soil was of such a peculiar nature that the legislature might appropriate it at any time without compensation.[53] This ruling permitted the courts to recognize private ownership while protecting the paramount interests of the public in available recreational facilities. It was tidier than Doe's scheme of private reasonable use and public ownership, but would have violated his constitutional principles. He made this point clear in *Robertson* when he rejected a somewhat similar Massachusetts precedent which held that when the government grants lands on a stream flowing from great ponds, it retains a right to divert the pond. Doe said that in New Hampshire such a rule would be unconstitutional. If, for example, the government granted a mill privilege, it could not later grant to a second party use of the same water if that use interfered with the original grant. The grant of the mill privilege contained a private property interest in the public lake recognized by the custom of reasonable commercial use. The right of unlimited use which the government once possessed had ceased to exist, and the owners of the mill have a legal remedy when injured by an "unreasonable" use of the same pond.[54] This argument provides another example of the contradictory aspects so prevalent in Doe's lawmaking. The state has absolute title to the waters and soil of great ponds which it holds in trust for all the people. This title may not be alienated, as Doe suggests it may in Maine and Massachusetts. Yet once the state conveys or recognizes a private right of reasonable use in that same property, the private right is more firmly protected than is the higher right of fee simple in Maine and Massachusetts.

A more pertinent New Hampshire statute than the one referred to by Putnam made it an indictable offense for a trespasser to fish on "such ponds, streams, or springs as are wholly within the control of some person owning the land around the same, who has made some improvement or expended money or labor in stocking the same with fish for his own use." This law implied that for public-policy reasons the state recognized private rights in ponds which were developed and maintained for sporting or conservation purposes. But in two companion cases decided at the same term as *Robertson*, Doe nullified this statute. In the first, despite the fact that earlier convictions had been upheld, Doe dismissed an indictment because the pond in question was from 300 to 500 acres and, under *Robertson,* could not be private property.[55] In the second case he refused to enjoin an angler from fishing in a great pond stocked and maintained by a summer club which owned the abutting lands on all sides, again citing *Robertson.*[56] In these two cases Doe seems to tip his jurisprudential hand. He is a democrat bred to the struggles of his Yankee forefathers. In the political traditions and social customs of his native state — a state beneath whose soil six generations of Does already lay — he finds the resources and the motives for preserving the heritage which they and their fellows had left behind. The early settlers of New Hampshire had abandoned the England of their birth not only to seek their fortunes in an untamed wilderness, but also to escape the trappings of a state based on privilege and to form a compact of equality in a new world. They had rejected the social imbalance of aristocracy, and it was his task to see that new monopolies did not covet the bounties of a freeman's life. Perhaps he oversimplified the past and read too much into the present. But he was not prepared to turn in the other direction just because the claim of exclusive right was put forth by a conservation club, not by a courtier, which had obtained its franchise by purchase, not by favor. The law, he said, "grows out of the institutions and circumstances of the country."[57] In the history of those institutions he saw the threat, and from the spirit of those circumstances he drew his answer. The origin of legal doctrine is in progressing society, and Doe's version of nineteenth-century New Hampshire may have been idealized. Yet Henry James could have recognized it. Returning to New England after many years of European exile, James described the countryside as he saw it: "The teams, the carts, the conveyances in their kinds, the sallow, saturnine natives in charge of them, the enclosures, the fences, the gates, the wayside 'bits,' of whatever sort, so far as these were referable to human attention or human neglect, kept telling the tale of the difference made, in a land of long winters, by the suppression of the two great factors of the familiar English landscape, the squire and the parson."[58]

It was partly this, but much more besides. Charles Doe's

jurisprudence embraced greater tasks than the need to reset the common law of aristocratic England into the pastoral democracy of nineteenth-century New Hampshire. The customs which preserved fishing and fowling for every man could also preserve the vested interests of the few. In *Winnipiseogee,* the sequel to *Robertson,* Doe argued that the law which grew out of the economic customs and commercial usages of contemporary society guaranteed to mill owners a reasonable use of the reservoirs which they had built. The law, no matter what its origin, operates within a constitutional order and applies equally to all — even to manufacturers, who, along with the railroad barons, formed the closest equivalent New Hampshire had to an aristocracy. Just as the few may not buy up privileges to the exclusion of the many, so the many may not abuse the rights of the few. American conditions created the public ownership of great ponds. Custom, the needs of commerce, and the progress of society created the reasonable private use. And so Doe's version of New Hampshire society was not so simple, after all. While it may seem idealized, it was practical, rounded, and complete.

Robertson and *Winnipiseogee* go hand in hand. One is the work of Doe the democrat, the other the work of Doe the constitutionalist, yet both found the same rule of law in the same customs of the society. The democrat resurrected a forgotten right of the people; the constitutionalist refused to leave industrialists at the mercy of politicians. Law is not the outer vestments of the power of a dominant though changing elite, as Holmes would have it,[59] nor is it John Austin's command of the sovereign. Perhaps the very society from which Charles Doe drew his law explains his point of view. His Dover was too far removed from Holmes's Boston, with its alien immigrants, and from Austin's London, with its discontented masses, to permit him to see law in such blunt terms. New Hampshire had its minority groups — the French-Canadian coolies and the Irish servant girls — but the cousins of their employers were millhands and navvies. The social structure was too simple for an elite to ask the help of law; there were no great families and no appreciable classes. There were, of course, undercurrents of discontent; opportunity and reward were not equal for all. But solutions were sought from educators, not judges, and answers were furnished by the nineteenth-century method of gradual assimilation, not by the twentieth-century gloss of social legislation.

Charles Doe went onto the New Hampshire bench with a keen interest in politics and public affairs. But this waned as time passed. He became submerged in the law and the problems of remaking legal institutions. He was not asked to solve the burning issues of the Gilded Age. Even the questions of the fellow-servant rule and the property rights of women, common enough in those days, seldom came before his court. It was to new-modelling the old law as it affected the daily lives of an uncomplicated people that he directed his attention. He was a revolutionary, true enough; but it was law that Doe revolutionized, not the society which law reflects.

PART SIX

THE CHIEF JUSTICE

Chief Justice Charles Doe of the New Hampshire
Supreme Court. Sketched by T. E. Reid from a
photograph taken around 1890.

AN INCORRIGIBLE DESPOT

Relations with the Bar

FOR the first five years of his chief justiceship Charles Doe enjoyed a period of relative popularity. Not only did the more controversial of his unorthodoxies lie in the future, but the bar was still grateful that he and not former Chief Justice Sargent had been appointed. By 1881 he was riding the crest of the wave. On August 1 of that year he took his fellow judges to Old Orchard Beach, Maine, for what was called "a few weeks vacation." The idea was to keep them together in one place to prepare opinions. On August 24 they arrived in Concord for the law term.[1]

The term opened at nine o'clock on the morning of September 1. In a semibiographical novel about a young New Hampshire attorney, Herbert Goss described the scene as it appeared approximately four years later.

More than a hundred lawyers from various parts of the state assembled at the bar, and at length headed by C. Doe, then Chief Justice, the seven men who constituted the Supreme Court solemnly marched in and took their seats behind the bench, the Chief Justice being the central figure while the others were deployed on each side. Judge Doe was always noted for lack of formality, and on this occasion, after the learned man and associates had taken their seats, and each had deposited various bundles of papers on the desk before him, and had faced the assembled attorneys, Judge Doe pulled a paper from a package, spoke the name of a case near the head of the docket, and begun [sic] to read. The ceremony of opening court had been performed.[2]

The 1881 September session of the supreme court's law term did not commence in exactly that way. The first order of business was the swearing in of nineteen new lawyers. The judges then considered seventy-five matters and delivered several opinions, indicating that they had been busy during the three weeks at Old Orchard. The case which aroused the greatest interest concerned Frank J. Barbour's seeking admission to the bar. Some question had been raised concerning his ethics, and this could be serious in Doe's court. It is, Doe had said in 1876, "indispensable that an attorney be trustworthy," and the statutory definition of trustworthiness was not enough. If a lawyer did not measure up to Doe's standards, he was disbarred. Whatever Barbour had done, however, was forgiven. The court felt the "alleged offense was an error of the head, not of the heart, and the complaint was dismissed." [3]

The remainder of the law term was spent hearing oral arguments. In some ways this session of court marked the end of Doe's judicial serenity. After a lull following the Republican victory in 1876, controversial questions were again arousing men's passions. In particular there was the railroad issue, discussed earlier. While the judges were still at Old Orchard, the Concord Railroad entered into a joint contract with the Boston & Lowell. William E. Chandler, the Republican Party leader who made enforcement of the state's antimonopoly law his personal concern, protested to the governor and to the attorney general, both of whom refused to act. It was Chandler's right, under a special statute, to file a private action to enforce the law. He turned to a Democratic lawyer, John M. Mitchell of Concord, for help. "We must in some systematic way wage war on these souless creatures," Mitchell told him, "& to that end I am ready & willing in any honorable, legitimate way to lend my whole aid." Mitchell drew up a petition to enjoin the lease, and this he brought to Doe's house in Rollinsford. Doe agreed to hold a hearing in Concord the following week. Since the United States Circuit Judge was using the Mayor's office, where the court usually met, the hearing was conducted in Mitchell's law office — an illustration of the adverse physical conditions under which Doe worked: he not only lacked law clerks and secretarial help, but he did not always have chambers in the state capitol. [4]

At the law and equity terms Doe seldom interrupted counsel, one reason why he was thought a good presiding officer. At least lawyers found him less objectionable than during jury trials. But he still could not bear repetition or discussion of the obvious, and he would grow impatient when time was being wasted, as apparently happened in Mitchell's office. In a letter to Chandler, Mitchell described what he called an occurrence of a "most astonishing and extraordinary character." When Harry Bingham, one of Chandler's attorneys, tried to address the court, Doe told him to sit down. Next he denied another antirailroad lawyer "the privilege of *making* an explanation, which would not occupy over a minute or two." Since it is difficult to believe that Doe would have done anything but enforce the antimonopoly law and grant the petition, it now seems likely that he saw no reason to drag out the proceedings. Surely Mitchell's letter did not alarm Chandler. Doe was in touch with Chandler and had even offered to lend his notes. Such helpfulness is remarkable, for it indicates that before deciding the case, the Chief Justice was willing to show Chandler, a party to the action, which arguments had impressed him and which had not. Chandler's friends did not know of this cooperation and, like Mitchell, feared that the Chief Justice was hostile. The editor of Chandler's newspapers had earlier warned him not to trust Doe. "I suspect he will disappoint you in the R.R. case," he wrote. "Col. George [the Concord's counsel] wears a confident air, and he thinks he has Doe sure. I have very serious doubts of his friendliness towards you, in spite of your championship of his aspirations." [5]

Doe's "aspirations" were his candidacy for the United States Supreme Court — "aspirations" which were Chandler's doing, not Doe's. Nathan Clifford had died the previous June, leaving the "New England seat" vacant. Without consulting the Chief Justice, Chandler nominated Doe as Clifford's successor. "New Hampshire," he announced in an editorial printed two days after Clifford's death, "intends to have the appointment for Mr. Chief Justice Charles Doe. The Bar, the Congressional Delegation, and the people, will be united in their request, and ought not to be refused." [6]

Massachusetts also wanted the appointment. Even before Clifford passed away, Senator George Hoar of that state had stolen a march on Chandler by talking to President Garfield about the merits of the Massachusetts Chief Justice, Horace Gray. But Garfield was now dying in Elberon, New Jersey, and Hoar no longer had the advantage. At least one New Hampshire congressman, Ossian Ray, was confident that Doe's chances of appointment would be better with Vice President Chester A. Arthur than they had been with Garfield. This might be true, but the immediacy of Arthur's succession encouraged other men to enter the lists. Most notable was an old Massachusetts politico named George S. Boutwell. While not brilliant, Boutwell was considered "laborious" and "painstaking," qualities many Republicans preferred to brilliance in their judges. There was little doubt that Arthur would offer him a cabinet post, but Boutwell preferred to retire to the cataleptic sanctuary of the Supreme Court.[7]

A born optimist, Chandler set to work, and shortly after Garfield's death, President Arthur was bombarded with letters from private citizens, mostly Republicans, many instigated by Chandler. These letters were much alike, offering sincere appraisals of Doe's qualifications, for he enjoyed the respect of the community, though not necessarily its good will. Perhaps the most astute argument was made by Jeremiah Smith. "It must be apparent," he wrote Chandler, "that a sprinkling of radicals is necessary to counteract the natural tendency of such a tribunal to undue conservatism, and bring the court up to the golden mean of sound judgment." A few Democrats lent their support, but such leaders as Harry Bingham remained conspicuously silent. Even Chandler's editor, who was entrusted with the newspaper campaign, had doubts. "Why you should so much desire Doe's promotion is not plain to me," he wrote Chandler. "He has ability, but he is erratic. Some people question his truthfulness."[8]

Chandler's theme was that New Hampshire deserved the judgeship. Ever since the founding of the Republic, Massachusetts had received five Supreme Court justiceships and twenty cabinet appointments, while New Hampshire had been honored with only one justiceship and two cabinet posts, and these had gone to the same man. "Let Massachusetts now modestly stand back and give the old Granite State a chance, when she presents one like Chief Justice Doe," Chandler argued.[9] Before long the voters came to realize that their state had not received a fair share of the spoils. New Hampshire had been faithful to the Republican Party, but the Party had not been faithful to New Hampshire. Resentment was aroused, and with cool deliberation Chandler handed the Democrats, in a state where the two parties were precariously close, a campaign slogan which Republicans could offset only by appointing Doe to the Supreme Court or by giving a cabinet post to some deserving politician, such as Chandler himself.

Although Chandler appreciated the role politics would play in the selection, it was Jeremiah Smith who foresaw that the most telling point against Doe would not be the qualifications of Boutwell (since everyone but Boutwell admitted that he had no qualifications), or even those of Gray, but doubts aroused about Doe himself. Smith became alarmed when it was reported that Senator Hoar was using the *Mink Case* to poke fun at Doe. Hoar ridiculed Doe for ruling that a man might kill a mink contrary to the game law "if he *claimed* that he apprehended that the mink would kill his goslings." To undo the damage, Chandler followed Hoar around the Senate floor reading the headnotes to anyone who would listen, attempting to explain that by putting private property above state regulation, Doe had been defending sound Republican principles. But as Smith knew, this was not Hoar's point.[10] The merits of Doe's holding were immaterial to Hoar's argument. He criticized, not Doe's result, but Doe's method, especially his facetious discussion of the reciprocal rights, duties, and liabilities of the owner, the geese, and the minks. Typical of what Hoar had in mind is the following passage in which Doe answered the argument that the defendant, when protecting his geese from attacking minks, should have driven the minks off; that the fact they endangered his property was no justification for killing them out of season.

Requiring the defendant to drive away the minks if he could, is an admission that he had a right to drive them away, and that they had no right to remain on his premises without his consent. But requiring him, if he could not drive them away from the geese, to drive the geese away from them, is a practical denial of his right to keep geese in his own pond or on his own land, if he could only keep them there by killing minks. It amounts to this: it being impractical to permanently reject the assailants, he must banish the assailed; and the raising of geese being impossible, the raising of minks is compulsory.[11]

By calling the general frivolity of the opinion to the attention of the Senate, Hoar was questioning Doe's fitness to share in the august cerebrations of the United States Supreme Court. Although Smith would later deny that the *Mink Case* had kept Doe from receiving the appointment, he then thought Hoar's tactics serious enough to write Chandler a long letter explaining the special circumstances that lay behind the decision. It had, he said, been prepared when Doe was in a minority of one. It was an intracourt document, written in its mocking style not to ridicule an absurd theory advanced by counsel, but to ridicule the position of Doe's brethren. When they read it, they were won over, but Doe did not have time to rewrite his opinion, and it was printed in its original form. Smith's letter could not be made public, and before long the *Mink Case* was making the rounds of Massachusetts newspapers.[12]

By December the New York press had narrowed the choice to three men — Boutwell, a party stalwart, laborious and sincere; Gray, safe and solid; and Doe, brilliant but eccentric. The *Tribune* reported that the justices did not want Boutwell. What no one knew, however, was that some members of the court were supporting Gray. At least Justice Miller told Arthur that Gray was the choice of both Harlan and himself, and he may have said that the entire court wanted him. The *Herald* made what now appears the best evaluation when it reported, "Judge Doe and Judge Gray are equally esteemed for their fitness for the position. The probable selection of a member of the cabinet from Massachusetts would seem to indicate the appointment of Judge Doe." [13]

There was little doubt that Arthur favored Boutwell but was reluctant to force him upon a hostile court. He offered him the secretaryship of the navy, but Boutwell did not want the appointment. The next move was up to Chandler. Playing the trump he had all along been holding back, he suggested himself as a likely naval secretary. Since Arthur would surely refuse two important posts to New Hampshire, Doe's chances were dashed. At this point Hoar let it be known that Garfield had favored Gray.

No one believed Hoar, but with the posthumous blessings of the martyred president to prop him up, Arthur made his decision and sent Gray's name to the Senate. Four months later William E. Chandler was sworn in as secretary of the navy.[14]

Outside New Hampshire Gray's appointment was received with approval. It convinced many that Arthur's administration might prove better than they had feared. There were few complaints. Doe professed to be pleased. "The appointment of Judge Gray," he wrote Chandler, "is all the evidence anyone can want of the safety of some of the greatest interests in the country in the hands of Arthur. If his whole administration shall be as admirable as Gray's appointment, it will be as good as any administration possibly can be." Chandler disagreed. "You may think that Judge Gray's appointment was better than your own would have been," he replied. "I do not think so. I do not say I would like to see you the one *sole* judge of the U.S. Supreme Court nor even one of three judges but as one judge in nine you would have carried to the bench character and opinions which would have immensely stimulated and benefited that great tribunal." [15]

Chief Justice Doe had said nothing while his friends were at work. Indifference was the only posture he could assume. But after the waiting was over and Chandler openly referred to the matter, Doe decided that the need for discretion was past. Chandler sent him a collection of papers used in the campaign and wrote, "Allow me also to say (1) that the presentation of the subject to the President originated only in a sincere desire to secure for New Hampshire and one of her distinguished lawyers that recognition to which they were so fairly entitled; (2) that nothing was omitted to be done that could be wisely done in any way derogatory to the character & dignity of the State or of the gentleman whose name we had the honor to present to the President. No reply to this is expected." [16]

Doe thought that a reply was called for. Chandler's gratuitous nomination, he wrote, was "quite as inexplicable as anything you ever did." When Chandler protested that Doe had no grounds for anger, Doe replied that he was hurt, not angry. "If I were incensed by your volunteering the vigorous effort you made with reference to the bench commonly regarded as the highest,

I would be a more conspicuous figure than I am among the un-accountables. I am just as far from being pleased as from being vexed. What I know you did was simply incredible." [17]

This was all Doe said about the matter. He had done nothing to advance or encourage his cause, yet he was chagrined that his friends had exposed him this way. Mrs. Doe, on the other hand, was elated. She had the provincial's suspicion of the capital city and did not want her husband "down with that crowd." There is reason to suspect that the justices of the United States Supreme Court were equally relieved that they were getting Gray rather than Doe. But in one respect the choice may have made little difference: Gray shared Doe's fondness for fresh air in the courtroom, and his insistence on open windows did not endear him to his new colleagues.[18]

No sooner was Gray's appointment announced than Doe was put on notice that the era of good feelings was over. "Now that it is settled that our Court will not be depleted to give new blood to the Supreme Court of the United States," the *Monitor* editorialized the following day, Dec. 21, 1881, "won't their Honors give a little time to their opinions and bring the reports down to a period within the memory of men still living, to the great content of the bar?" The reporting of cases was so far in arrears that none had been published for five years. The problem was so acute that in December the lawyers of Grafton and Coös counties organized New Hampshire's first bar association, partly to put pressure on the court. "At that time," Frank N. Parsons later recalled, "one great advantage of a bar meeting seemed to be the opportunity it furnished to express something more than friendly criticism of the judges." [19] The principal speaker was Harry Bingham, who thought his strictures so severe that he would not permit his address to be printed until after his death. It was a general indictment of the court, with the bitterest remarks aimed at reporting delays, since Bingham implied that they were deliberate, perhaps even malicious.

I know of no reason for withholding these reports; I have heard none assigned. It seems to be a neglect without excuse or palliation. The court, with cool indifference, sees the bar struggling with their difficulties and groping in the dark while loaded with the responsibility of advising their clients rightly; complaints fall on deaf ears and are not heard, or if heard are not heeded. Nobody justifies the court in this matter; nobody will attempt to justify them. It is without parallel in any of the numerous state and federal courts of the Union; and yet the great body of our people are drifting along, apparently quiet and unconcerned, while these complaints, which everybody knows are real and not the mere vaporings of suitors and lawyers who have lost their causes, are ringing in their ears.[20]

Another speaker at that meeting was Philip Carpenter, the son of a recently appointed associate justice. Complaining that Bingham had stolen "my abuse of the court," Carpenter made Doe the target of his wit.[21] With an air of goodnatured fun, he described a recently discovered document left by some ancient inhabitants of New Hampshire.

Many centuries ago, a fellow by the name of Doe was chief Medicine Man in the tribe in which he lived. In this tribe, the educated, well-behaved and virtuous class, (the g.o.p. of moral ideas), were called, as now Republicans, while the low, uncultivated and vicious class were known, as now, as Democrats. Now these wicked and dissolute Democrats had, a few years before, bounced this Doe, who just then was a Republican, from his job as chief Medicine Man, and on his return to power he thirsted for revenge, (and he didn't keep dry very long.) He determined to kill off as many of this depraved class that I have mentioned as he could conveniently. He had always been more celebrated, as a doctor, for killing than for curing. He had fetched one poor fellow . . . with a prescription two or three hundred pages long, but he found now that such prescriptions would take too much time. He must write shorter prescriptions and kill more men, so a single word would now often suffice. His medicines were as powerful, however, as his prescriptions were brief, and the poor people over whom he was placed, apparently had to take them whether they wanted them or not. But he never took his own medicine, or at least, if he did, they did not relieve him from the terrible boils which he apparently suffered with, for it is frequently recorded . . . that "Doe did not sit." [22]

Today this jocular bit of published contempt seems more harsh than Bingham's unpublished address. At least Bingham's complaint about reporting delays was well founded. The supreme court proved this when it brought out volumes 58, 59, and part of 60 before the second meeting of the Grafton and Coös Bar Association. But since these omitted important cases which Doe was still researching, they did not quiet the criticism. Within two years the court was again in arrears, and at the 1885 meeting there was heated discussion by Grafton and Coös lawyers of the question, "What can the bar do to expedite the publication of the 61st and 62d volumes of the New Hampshire Reports?" Even the United States circuit judge complained of Doe's delays. Doe himself compounded the bar's frustration by inserting in old cases reference to newer ones. Thus in *Owen* v. *Weston* in *63 New Hampshire* he cited "*Dole v. Pike*, 64 N.H. — ." Both *Owen* and *Dole* were decided during 1885, but *64 New Hampshire* was not printed until two years after *63 New Hampshire*. A lawyer wishing to learn the significance of Doe's citation to *Dole* had to wait two years.[23]

It is hard to say what disturbed the lawyers more — these delays or Doe's radicalism. They probably complained most frequently about the delays, perhaps because they thought it more likely that remedial action could be taken. But when it came to the quality of vehemence, the unpredictability and the legislative nature of many of Doe's judgments aroused the strongest passions. By 1890 his critics were vocal, though for the most part respectful. It remained for Doe's old friend, William E. Chandler, the man who just a decade before had suggested him for the United States Supreme Court, to raise resentment to fever pitch.

By now Chandler had resigned as secretary of the navy and had been elected to the United States Senate. This event alone was remarkable, for he had a tendency to quarrel, especially with fellow Republicans and with the railroads of New Hampshire. Exactly what Chandler hoped to accomplish by fighting the railroads is not clear; his objectives were inconsistent, but not his opposition. It was he who had persuaded Doe to enjoin the lease between the Concord and the Boston & Lowell. He had sought to keep the Boston & Lowell independent, but, as has been shown, that railroad was no longer able to stand alone, and it merged with the Boston & Maine. This move had led the legislature to permit the union of the Concord with the Boston, Concord & Montreal. At this juncture Chandler became truly alarmed. New Hampshire's transportation system was dominated by two major corporations (the very thing he had sought to prevent when he broke the Concord's lease) which eventually might join, especially since the Boston & Maine was buying control of its rival. "If," Chandler wrote a friend, "the Reading–Boston & Maine combination gets the Concord railroad, and takes full possession of New Hampshire, the state will hardly be worth living in for freemen." [24]

Chandler thought he knew a way to prevent the inevitable. Under the Concord's charter granted in 1835 the state had reserved the right to acquire the road after twenty years by paying its original costs and making up arrears in dividends below 10 per cent. This provision was standard in most railroad charters and by the 1890s had become pretty much a dead letter, which few people expected the government to enforce, although it had been used from time to time as a threat "to bring the road to terms in other matters." [25] The Concord had cost $1,500,000 to build, and arrears in dividends below 10 per cent for the past fifty years came to $660,000. As a result the state, if it exercised its option, would need to pay only $2,160,000 for property with a market value of about $5,100,000. Even if the legislature chose to pay interest, New Hampshire still stood to gain a profit of between $2,000,000 and $3,000,000 on the deal. In 1891 Chandler persuaded Austin Corbin, a speculator with the resources to fight the Boston & Maine, to offer to buy the state's interest.

Corbin first proposed $500,000, later raised his bid to $1,000,-000, and finally suggested that the government's option be put up for auction. The Concord's stockholders objected and warned that any purchaser of the state's power to acquire their railroad would have to pay them interest. Corbin disagreed but proposed to try the question before the Supreme Court at his own expense. This offer placed the members of the legislature in a difficult position. The railroad lobby wanted Corbin's proposal rejected, yet the lawmakers were not so contemptuous of public opinion that they dared spurn $2 or $3 million. They therefore compromised: instead of allowing Corbin to take the sole issue of interest to court, the House of Representatives posed four questions for the justices to answer. The third question, pertaining to interest, was the one which every lawyer considered important, but as matters turned out, the first question proved to be the sleeper. It asked: "Has the state the right to purchase the Concord Railroad under section 17 of its charter?"

The hearing was conducted on March 30, 1891. With what has been termed "amazing alacrity" Doe and his colleagues rendered their judgment on the following day. Promising that the reasons would be given at a later date, the court held that the Concord Railroad was "no exception to the rule that private property may be taken for public use on payment of its value to its owners, and the property in question cannot be purchased or taken by the state for less than its value without the owner's consent." [26]

This was all that the judgment stated. On its face it seemed nothing more than an irrelevant truism summarizing the law of eminent domain. One of Corbin's attorneys called it "simply amazing" and urged Chandler to keep pressure on the judges to explain their reasoning. An out-of-state lawyer, he was not familiar with Doe's methods. "I confess I am entirely incapable of understanding your Supreme Court," he wrote. "I do not care further to express the impression the utterance has made upon me, except that it is exceedingly unfavorable; — indeed as it now stands, infathomable." [27] Senator Chandler hardly needed to be told to keep pressure on the judges. Vacillation was not one of his faults, and no person in New Hampshire knew this better than Chief Justice Doe. For years Doe had been warning his friend to curb what he called Chandler's "morbid pugnacity, quarrelsomeness, eagerness for personal brawl, & reckless efforts to involve the whole party in wrangles & private animosities." When Chandler told him that he enjoyed "useful controversy," Doe had replied that if Chandler would change "useful" to "useless," he would "express the unanimous opinion of New Hampshire of a failing that has done you much harm, and done no good to anyone outside of the Democratic party." Gilman Marston once told Doe that Chandler was one of the "unaccountables." "I entirely agree with him on that point," Doe had written. Chandler thought this judgment unfair and told Doe that he was accountable in some respects. As Doe should well know, for instance, "I love my friends dearly, especially my old friends, and never willingly give one up." Now in 1892 Chandler was ready to prove himself wrong and to sacrifice his friendship with the Chief Justice.[28]

The strategy employed by Senator Chandler to attack Judge Doe was as simple as the strategy he had employed a decade earlier to praise him: he sought to exploit Doe's reputation as a radical. The people of New Hampshire, went Chandler's theme, had come to expect novelty, obscureness, and tortuosity as natural and ordinary characteristics of an opinion of their Supreme Court, but on this occasion Doe had gone too far. "In searching for the meaning of the opinion of the judges," Chandler wrote in a newspaper editorial, "the fact that it was expressed in a round-about and peculiar mode did not surprise lawyers who had become familiar with the eccentricities of New Hampshire's judges, or some of them. That they did not answer directly or categorically any one of the questions asked them, but expressed such ideas as they entertained, in a way which no other judges would have thought of adopting, was not strange." [29]

It was maddening not to know what Doe was up to. After several months Chandler heard rumors that one of the judges promised a surprise; that the court would show that the state's right to purchase the Concord had been repealed by a statute passed more than twenty years before the merger; that when the judges went into consultation, one of them produced this statute, it was accepted as conclusive, and the opinion was based on it, although they agreed to keep its existence secret until the reasons for the opinion could be published in full. Chandler at first refused to credit this story, but when Chief Justice Doe was heard to remark that the decision rested on a point not alluded to in the arguments, he decided that it must be true. At his suggestion Corbin asked for a rehearing, but it was never granted. Chandler was outraged. "The judges are willing to give a rehearing if they can, after further argument, adhere to their former opinion," he wrote. "As they have discovered that they cannot so adhere, a rehearing is to be refused." [30]

It was not until two years after the hearing that the court published the reasons for its judgment. Even then they did not appear in the form of a regular judicial opinion printed in the official reports, but rather as a forty-two-page badly edited pamphlet which impressed many as a preliminary comment, a feeler or trial bal-

loon sent up to test public reaction. On close study Chandler saw
that it had, indeed, been based on arguments not presented at the
hearing. Yet it should have been predictable, for it turned
entirely on Judge Doe's pet constitutional theory — the doctrine
of equality.

Of all Doe's pronouncements on equality, *Corbin's Case* is
the most extreme, in many ways the culmination of his theories.
As was discussed, he agreed with Blackstone that a statute which
takes property unequally from different members of the community is a penalty, not a law. Therefore an enactment seizing
property without the owner's consent at less than market value
is not legislation but confiscation. In order to apply this argument
to *Corbin's Case* Doe let absolutism get the best of him. To force
an owner of property worth $400, he contended, to accept $399
for it would be the same as if he were forced to accept $1. "If
he can be deprived of half of his house by a special statute, taking so much without compensation, he can be deprived of his
liberty half of the time or be entirely despoiled and imprisoned
for life by the same arbitrary method, without trial and without
cause." [31] Should the legislature, "in unmistakable terms," pass a
"special" statute, Doe said, it would be the court's duty "to
inquire on what grounds it could be reconciled with the paramount law of equal right." [32]

It cannot be doubted that when the judges went into conference Doe was determined to invalidate the state's option. It
was unthinkable that at this late date the government should be
permitted to purchase the Concord at less than market value just
to benefit a speculator such as Corbin. Yet for all his indignation
at the inequality of the proposed "confiscation," the Chief Justice
was not so bold that he dared bar it solely as a constitutional
dogma. This was his impetus but not his excuse. Rather, he
rested his decision on the theory that the clause of the Concord's
charter reserving the state the right of purchase had been superseded by section 10, chapter 128, of the laws of 1844 which
enabled the state to take certain corporate franchises and certain
corporate property for public use if such property could not be
taken by eminent domain. Ignoring the argument that while the
law of 1844 was a general enactment, section 10 may not have
been and therefore perhaps did not apply to the Concord,

Doe ruled that it had been repealed (and with it all the state's interests in the Concord) when it had been realized that corporations were not exempt from eminent domain. It was his belief that the state had originally reserved the right to purchase the Concord because the power of eminent domain had not been fully appreciated, and he ignored the fact that the state had not reserved the right to purchase at market value — as it would if it were seeking merely to pursue a policy similar to eminent domain — but at original cost plus arrears in dividends. The Chief Justice reinforced this contention with the argument that the early legislatures had misconstrued the function of railroads and had granted them charters similar to turnpike franchises rather than as common carriers, even providing that any person be allowed to run his own locomotive and cars on the tracks for his own private use on the payment of a standard toll. He pointed out that the state had always intended to take over turnpikes when it could afford to do so, but that this intention had long since been abandoned as to railroads when it was realized that they were not highways but common carriers. Thus he felt that those who had bought Concord stock could not be held to constructive notice, since they had not realized the property could be taken at less than market value. "It was not believed," he said, "that the legislature would ever use, or ever desire, a power of despoiling those who could be entrapped by the operation of a law made for a different purpose." [33]

Chandler, who could scarcely believe his eyes when he read the pamphlet, quickly dubbed Doe "our judicial pamphleteer." "If the brains of the man or men who wrote this extraordinary paper are not in paresis," he wrote, "the legal science is utterly incomprehensible by the common mind." Quoting Jefferson on Marshall, Chandler put the blame on Doe. "An opinion is huddled up in conclave, perhaps by a majority of one, delivered as if unanimous, and with the silent acquiescence of lazy or timid associates, by a crafty chief justice, who sophisticates the law to his mind by the turn of his own reasoning." Chandler promised "no rest from surprises as long as our extraordinary and eccentric court existed." [34]

The doctrine of equality raised the Senator's wrath. He realized that it too could be carried to extremes. In Doe's hands "equality" meant that the people, the government, and all corporations "exist only in subjection to the irresponsible, irrational, eccentric, and despotic will of one tyrant, the chief justice of New Hampshire."

All of which is true, if it is meant that the chief justice nullifies every law, however plain, which he chooses to say is not uniform or is unequal in its operations. But such decisions have not been the fair and legitimate judicial restriction, by a reference to fundamental principles, of language of doubtful meaning; but they have been bold and indecent assumptions of arbitrary and tyrannical power, in defiance of law, from the continuance of which usurpations there is no escape except by the exercise of the people's right to reconstruct a faithless and worthless bench of judges.[35]

Senator Chandler meant what he said: he wanted Doe impeached. "That the chief justice will ever turn back after he has ventured upon a wrong course, can never be expected, when there is no direct appeal from his decision," he argued. "He is an incorrigible legal despot, who occasionally emerges from the lifetime seclusion of closet only to gratify his insatiable desire to say and do everything in form and substance differently from all other men, and to beat down all resistance to his will." In an open letter addressed to the presidents of New Hampshire's two bar associations, Chandler appealed to the profession, "confidently believing that they will, by apt measures, prevent the loss to the people and the stain upon the jurisprudence of the state which the judges are endeavoring to inflict." "How long the bar of the state will thus neglect to reorganize a court which juggles with legal principles, upturns legal landmarks, and constantly makes instead of declaring law, so that the practice of law in New Hampshire is more uncertain in its results than it is in Turkey or Russia, is for the lawyers to determine." If the bar did not act now, at a time when public opinion could be aroused, matters would only get worse. "The judges always, hereafter, in a like ruthless manner, when they prefer the wrong and hate the right, will erroneously decide any case which may come before them, and will cut the throat of any lawyer whom they dislike. The unhealed and bloody wounds of many victims are visible today. It is not the people alone whom the judges bleed." [36]

Chandler was clever. He associated the decision in *Corbin's Case* with all the complaints voiced against Doe over the years.

But political conditions were not ripe for judicial reform, nor was Chandler a leader around whom many lawyers cared to rally. The bar may have been amused by Doe's embarrassment, but it ignored Chandler's call to arms.

The decision could be scored. In order to sustain his position, Doe had ignored some potent arguments. For example, the law of 1844, which Doe had ruled as superseding the Concord's original charter, contained a section limiting its effect to corporations which adopted its provisions, and this the Concord had not done. Also, both the statute of 1887, which repealed the law of 1844, and the amendment to the Concord's charter in 1889, which authorized its merger with the Boston, Concord & Montreal, contained saving clauses reserving to the state all property rights it might otherwise have lost. In truth, Doe's statutory argument was weak, and the real explanation for his decision was to be found in the broad principles of constitutional equality. Chandler was not exaggerating when he accused the Chief Justice of sophisticating "the law to his own mind by the turn of his own reasoning." Even so, Chandler did not make these deficiencies the focal point of his attack. In his newspaper editorials he was speaking primarily to a lay audience and preferred *scandalum magnatum* to *reductio ad absurdum*. He was careful to be indignant over issues which the public could understand. When speaking of Doe's refusal to grant a rehearing, he came close to accusing the Chief Justice of corruption.[37]

This attack was too much for Doe's associates, who urged that Chandler be cited for contempt, an action that was generally expected. "Chief Justice Doe will prosecute you for scandalium magnalium won't he —," Senator O. H. Platt wrote his colleague. "Your article is vigorous and caustic — but my, what a rumpus there would be in Conn if I should attack the C. J. of *our* supreme court. But it gives me points as to how to talk about the Democratic party." Chandler's biographer feels that he would have welcomed a contempt citation: "Gladly would he have gone to jail for that offense and have used the penal institution as a sounding board to proclaim to the whole State and even to the country at large the story of a stout-hearted, fearless defender of public rights who was persecuted by the venom of a corporation-ridden court."[38] We may doubt if Chandler expected that Doe could be aroused. Eleven years earlier, when Chandler had tried to start a quarrel, Doe had waved him aside. "The official habit of twenty years has become second nature," the Chief Justice had told him. "It is impossible for me to quarrel with anybody; & anybody can quarrel with me with perfect safety, for he will have his quarrel to his own satisfaction without any participation on my part." He had, Doe added, "come to set too high a value upon this brief life, to waste any of it in the distractions of emotions unnecessarily disturbed." [39] Besides, Doe knew better than to place the crown of martyrdom on Chandler's brow, and he persuaded his associates not to press contempt charges. A motion to censure Chandler was introduced in the legislature, but without Doe's support it was defeated. [40] One day Doe encountered a friend who asked how he enjoyed his punishment in the newspaper. "What paper?" Doe asked.

"The *Monitor*," the friend replied.

"Oh!" said Doe in mock surprise. "Is that paper published now?" [41]

Judge Allen relates that Doe made an attempt at psychology to pacify Chandler. He wrote the Senator in Washington and asked him to purchase a book not available in New Hampshire. Poor Chandler must have felt much the same as had General Marston when Doe dropped in for pudding and milk. On his return home he brought the book. [42]

The affair was a depressing one. Yet the Chief Justice could count himself lucky: if he had been permitted to pick his enemy, he surely would have selected Chandler. Doe had been radical, he had deliberately overlooked precedents, and there was more than a touch of arbitrariness in the way he brushed the law aside in *Corbin's Case* to settle the question according to his own ideas of justice, reason, and equality. Yet Chandler was not the man to exploit the resentment. He had cried "wolf" too often during his career, and the call to impeach Doe did not sound convincing, coming from the man who had been singing his praises to President Arthur just a decade before. Doe had not changed during those years, but the cantankerous Chandler was never constant, and this was his undoing as a leader. The bar would not follow him. A prominent lawyer such as Harry Bingham could have caused much damage to Doe, but not Chandler.

Then, too, matters did not stand where they had stood during the 1860s. As Jeremiah Smith had told him when he was appointed chief justice, Doe now had friends at the bar. Chandler had begun his attacks at the time when, according to Judge Parsons, "the effects of Judge Doe's work as a reformer were bearing fruit." [43] A new generation of lawyers who had been brought up on Doe's philosophy were grateful enough for his procedural reforms to forgive his sins against precedent and his occasional lawmaking, as in *Corbin's Case*.

Charles Doe himself considered his relations with the bar good. Lawyers might use their meetings as forums for criticizing him and his court, but he took pride in the fact that they had adapted so well to his reforms. At the very moment that Chandler's fury was at its height, Chief Justice Doe wrote a confidential letter to the president of the Southern New Hampshire Bar Association praising the attorneys who practiced before his court. "Never before has the state had so learned, able, honorable, and trustworthy a bar as now," Doe wrote. "Instead of ignorance and weakness being introduced by sweeping away the technicalities of pleading, knowledge and strength more and more abound. The legal learning, capacity, and usefulness of our bar is far in advance of what it was forty years ago. The service it renders the community is of incomparably more value. Then very few thought of strenuous efforts to keep clients out of the law; now such efforts are made by substantially the whole body of successful practitioners. More lawyers try cases than formerly, because there are more men of learning and capacity who can try cases creditably." [44] Surely Doe felt no bitterness toward the bar in general.

Chandler's campaign had come too late. In his frustration he turned it into a personal vendetta against the Chief Justice, conjuring up the image of the judicial crank by running through a list of eccentricities from Doe's odd dress to the open windows. Earlier he might have struck a responsive cord, but not during the 1890s. As one of the most prominent members of the bar would say, there had been a time when he had doubts about the Chief Justice. "I had seen him for many years as a presiding judge, sharp, keen, and incisive in his rulings of the law, and at times there seemed to be peculiarities which led me to fear that my case might not have the quiet, calm consideration that I reasonably expected from such a man as Chief Justice Bellows or Chief Justice Sargent." Later he became acquainted with Doe and discovered he was not the "incorrigible despot" pictured by Chandler. "With personal association with him in 1892 and since, I revered him as a lawyer, but I loved him as a brother." [45]

Perhaps Herbert Goss spoke for most members of the New Hampshire bar when in his novel about a Coös County lawyer he had his protagonist say, "There is some fun in practicing the law when you are before a court that knows the law, isn't there?" [46]

THE WAGERS OF BATTLE
Colleagues

THERE were some who accused Senator Chandler of inconsistency. They said his criticisms of Chief Justice Doe were hardly compatible with his earlier efforts to put him on the national court. But irascible as they were, Chandler's views had a certain harmony. He always insisted that Doe would be safe only with strong colleagues to keep him in check. "I do not say I would like to see you the one *sole* judge of the U.S. Supreme Court," he had explained. Eight years earlier, when Doe had first been named chief justice, Chandler's newspaper had made the same point. "Chief Justice Charles Doe," it warned, "has erratic eccentricities of character resulting from too much secularism, tending to make him unsafe if a sole and autocratic judge. Originality of conception is not a judicial quality, nor is too much tenacity of opinion desirable in a judge; but better the latter than mental weakness or vacillation. As one of six able judges of diversified character and attainments, conferring, advising, controlling each other, Judge Doe deservedly stands as the Chief Justice." [1]

Chandler's complaint about *Corbin's Case* was that the balancing process had broken down — there had been no check upon Doe. He had come to dominate his associates to such an extent that he was now an incorrigible despot. If the other judges had dared stand up to him, everything would have been all right. But as matters stood, Doe had to be impeached. The Chief Justice would not have quarreled with Chandler. He too felt the need of strong-willed colleagues to keep a judge with an original mind in check. When a friend remarked that John Marshall had made too many mistakes for a great jurist, Doe replied that a judge such as Marshall, who sat without an intellectual peer at his side, could not be blamed for striking out on his own.

The trouble with Marshall's court, was, that although some of his associates were men of respectable talents, no one of them was strong enough to throw him, even when he was in error. If he had had but one associate capable of encountering him, those two would have made a court, in my judgment, superior to any the federal govt has ever had. If Marshall & Taney could have been together on the Bench, of equal age, from the start, that would have been a court after my own heart. They would have counteracted each other; or if they couldnt agree, they would have left opposing opinions (slavery excepted), from which their successors, & the leading intellects of the country could have selected the truth. I am inclined to think that they would both have taken extreme grounds; & that the impartial judge of the distant future, far removed from the political & other disturbing elements of Marshall's day, would have settled down upon an intermediate position, as the one consistent with the sovereignty of the Union, the sovereignty of State, & the sovereignty of the citizens, & the one intended by the fathers.[2]

Thus Chief Justice Doe agreed with Senator Chandler. A great judge needs at least one associate of his intellectual stride against whom he can sharpen his mettle and who in turn will provide a counterpoint for his theories. Doe did not have to rely on Marshall's example to prove this point; he could have used his own career. His colleagues had a decided influence upon his work. This is an obvious truism too often overlooked by judicial biographers. Most evaluations of judges are limited to consideration of the opinions to which they signed their names, ignoring the fact that their statements were often tempered by the objections of their associates or even incorporated memoranda written by others. A judicial decision may not be a team effort, but it is often a product of compromise. By the same token the biographer who does not consider the judicial writings of a biographee's fellow judges tells but half the story; his name may not appear on every decision, but he had a hand in the formulation of each. He assented to them just as much as he assented to his own opinions. A list of the cases to which he did not dissent may be as revealing as those which he wrote. Perhaps it is an imponderable which requires too much effort to measure, yet it must be measured before a judge and his work can be fully evaluated.

The means by which Doe employed astute management to sway the court to his point of view have been discussed. The other side of this coin is the effect his fellow judges had on his work. Their influence can be divided into three periods. In the beginning Doe wrote little law. Later, when he began to express himself, many of his important pronouncements appeared in dissenting opinions. Finally there came a time when his colleagues could no longer hold him in check.

The initial period of Judge Doe's judicial career gave no indication of his potential greatness. In the first eight volumes of the New Hampshire *Reports* published after his appointment he contributed less than eight pages per volume. Only two decisions written between June 1860 and July 1865 can be compared favorably to those he wrote in later years. He had one short opinion in *43 New Hampshire* and none in *44 New Hampshire*. From July 1861 to June 1864 he contributed nothing to the reports. "As late as 1866," Jeremiah Smith writes, "one of his ablest colleagues expressed the hope 'that Doe might *yet* make himself a name as judge.'" [3]

It was not that Doe was a new judge. William Bartlett, appointed in 1861, wrote more opinions than did Doe during this period. Nor was Doe unusually active at the trial term; his load of cases was no greater than that of the other judges. Surely malingering is so uncharacteristic of the man that it need not be considered. The best explanation seems to lie in the influence of his colleagues, especially of Chief Justice Samuel Dana Bell. They constituted a talented but conservative court, and Doe's originality had little chance of making headway among them. He might have dissented more often had not Chief Justice Bell had a strong distaste for dissenting opinions. Doe revered the older man, who had been a political ally of his father's during the 1820s. Bell was insistent that his judges refrain from dissent, and Doe honored his wishes. [4]

It is significant that the first two decisions written by Judge Doe, "which excited the general interest and commendation of the profession," were dissenting opinions filed after Bell retired. Ira Perley who had resigned as chief justice in 1859 was reappointed. Perley was cut from different cloth than Bell; indeed, it is difficult to think of two New Hampshire jurists more unalike. Samuel Dana Bell abhorred controversy; Ira Perley thrived on it. He had the most fearsome temper possessed by any nineteenth-century New Hampshire judge, and many a lawyer at the bar was whipped by his caustic tongue. Moreover, he was strongly opinionated and remarkably positive. If he was convinced of his position, Perley did not gloss over differences, as did Bell. It is little wonder that Charles Doe emerged from his judicial shell during Perley's tenure as chief justice.[5]

There are some who have insisted that Perley is the greatest legal mind which New Hampshire produced aside from Charles Doe. While this position is difficult to defend, it cannot be denied that Perley was able to exert more of a negative influence on Doe than any other judge during Doe's years as an associate justice. They had few quarrels over substantive law — Perley was as liberal as Doe on most questions. But he was opposed to any reforms of adjective law, and during his chief justiceship Doe's efforts at new-modelling the forms were accorded a premature death by the court.

One of the two dissenting opinions with which Doe began his climb to fame was, of course, *Boardman* v. *Woodman.*[6] It was, as has been shown, a double-edged dissent, involving both the test for insanity and the assertion that the opinions of nonexperts should be admitted into evidence. Doe scored his most impressive triumph as an associate justice two years later, when he persuaded Perley to adopt his insanity test in the *Pike* murder trial. But even then he could not persuade Perley to agree to his ideas on nonexpert opinion evidence. Perley was as reluctant to tinker with the rules of evidence as he was to reform procedure. This is seen by the second of Doe's important dissents, *Kendall* v. *Brownson,* in which the issue turned on legal presumptions and burden of proof. Perley spoke for the majority, and his decision, aimed directly at Doe's dissent, is perhaps the best example of his ability to keep his young colleague at bay.

The plaintiff was suing to collect a note which he produced, claiming that this established a *prima facie* case which, unless overthrown by evidence coming from the defendant, entitled him to a verdict. The defendant pleaded the general issue, admitting the note's validity, but averring that it had been paid. The point in controversy was whether the plaintiff could rest his case on the note alone or whether he had to prove that he had not been paid. The trial judge refused to put the burden of proving payment on the defendant. Rather, he instructed the jury that upon the whole case the plaintiff had the burden of proof. The plaintiff appealed. Doe felt that burden of proof was a smokescreen hiding the basic issue. He wanted the court to consider whether it was an invasion of the jury's province to create a presumption of non-payment simply because the plaintiff possessed the note. But Perley refused to be drawn into a discussion of presumptions, insisting instead that burden of proof was the issue. "An examination of the cases on this question," he wrote, "shows clearly, as I think, that in this State it has all along been regarded as a settled general rule of practice in civil actions, that, whenever a party in any stage of the cause, under any form of pleading, sets up an affirmative proposition in answer to his adversary's case, he has the burden of proof to maintain the affirmative fact on which he relies." [7]

Doe did not deny *stare decisis* that was against him, but he felt the rule fallacious and sought to demonstrate the weakness in Perley's argument by asking whether the affirmative fact upon which Perley relied (the defendant's contention that the note had been paid) was actually an affirmative. At best, Doe suggested, it was a literal affirmative which Perley had mistaken for a legal affirmative when it was in reality a legal negative. That the true legal affirmative (that the note had not been paid) was a literal negative should not change the burden of proof. "The obligation of proving any fact lies upon the party who substantially asserts the affirmative," Doe argued. "The averment of breach usually includes a formal negative because the promise is generally affirmative in form." [8]

The argument was too subtle for Perley. He understood Doe's intent, but he did not consider the time ripe for experimentation. The precedents were on Perley's side, and he knew how to keep the other judges in line. Doe was a minority of one, and the Chief Justice dismissed his arguments with an air more cavalier than judicial. "I do not think," Perley wrote, "we are warranted in disturbing what I understand to be the present rule of law in order to introduce a speculative novelty." [9]

Of the associate justices with whom Doe served from 1859 to 1874, at least two had a notable effect on his work. The first was the Democrat William Spencer Ladd, who more than any other colleague complemented Doe. They worked closely together, and Doe may have helped Ladd write some of his opinions. *State v. Jones,* the second criminal insanity case, is an example. Ladd is the author and is sometimes credited with formulating a compromise which made the doctrine more acceptable to the profession. Doe himself said that Ladd, along with Perley, deserved the praise. This statement is nonsense, although it is possible that Doe received more encouragement from Ladd than from any other judge. Ladd fully supported his procedural and question-of-fact reforms. On the other hand, Ladd may have been the instigator of the reforms which cleared New Hampshire law of outmoded rules of construction. It was he who wrote the important pioneering decisions, and which ideas originated with him and which with Doe is now impossible to determine. [10]

While Doe's closest judicial relationships were with Judge Ladd, his closest personal relationships were with Judge Jeremiah Smith, Jr. Smith was the only surviving son of Chief Justice Jeremiah Smith, born when the venerable jurist was seventy-eight years old. The elder Smith still had his sense of humor. "Nomine Jeremiae, anglice, Jeremiah," he recorded in his diary. "The boy is a source of pleasure to me far exceeding my expectations. I pray Heaven it may continue." He was also a source of pleasure to Charles Doe. He was appointed associate justice in 1867, at the age of thirty, thus furnishing Doe with his happiest professional comradeship. They worked harmoniously together, not only by collaborating with companion opinions in *State v. Pike,* the insanity case, but most notably by rewriting the law of partnerships in *Eastman v. Clark.* Smith demolished in America the doctrine that a profit-sharing agreement is enough, as a matter of law, to establish a partnership, concluding instead that it is only evidence of a partnership. Doe concurred, but apparently unsatisfied with Smith's research, he wrote a treatise-opinion on partnership, using prior English and American decisions to show that "the profit-sharing doctrine had only existed with such qualifications as to rob it of all force." [11]

Professor Samuel Williston stated that Smith's association with Doe on the bench was one of the educational influences of Smith's life. Unfortunately it was a short association. In 1874, worn down by tuberculosis, Smith resigned from the court. Asked by his doctor whether he felt better during cold or warm weather, Smith replied that his health improved during the winter. As a result he was sent to Minnesota, which the doctor thought even colder than New Hampshire. After a few years he returned to Dover and again practiced law. Doe had hopes that he would be reappointed associate justice, but in 1890 Smith accepted the Story professorship of law at Harvard. There he helped to shape a great deal of thinking as to torts, and thus he furnished a wider audience for Doe's ideas than could otherwise have been obtained. Previously classes in torts had considered mostly New York and Massachusetts law; Smith brought to the subject the New Hampshire point of view, largely shaped by Doe.[12]

During the second part of Charles Doe's judicial career — when he was chief justice — he did not sit on a court with the overall strength that had been known in the days when he was associated with Perley, Sargent, Ladd, and Smith. The men who served under Doe from 1876 to 1896 were competent, honest, and for the most part conscientious, yet only Alonzo Philetus Carpenter can be called outstanding. He belonged to the school of law opposed to Doe's, and he was emotionally and psychologically out of place on a court whose main impetus was reform. "I have the impression," one friend wrote, "that he looked with some distrust upon the freedom with which the old and recognized forms of procedure of common law had come in some respects to be dealt." [13] This was putting it mildly.

The fact that these two strong men, with contrary legal philosophies, were on the bench at the same time probably affected the style, the outcome, and the method of opinion writing more than anything else. Many of Doe's opinions owed their combative tone to the fight Carpenter put up before yielding, and in other opinions Doe disguised innovation and pretended to be following precedent chiefly to accommodate Carpenter.[14] Beyond doubt Carpenter was Doe's most talented sparring partner, and during

Doe's last decade he rallied whatever opposition could be mustered against the Chief Justice. Some thought that they struck the ideal balance.

The difference between Judge Carpenter's and Judge Doe's conception of the judicial function was fundamental. Judge Carpenter undertook to do no more than to interpret the law; Judge Doe, if he thought the occasion justified, did not scruple to alter it, abrogate it, or add to it. It is no doubt fortunate that neither extreme view has prevailed in our court of late years, but that the form which our jurisprudence has taken has been due in such large measure to the joint influence of these two powerful but strongly contrasted intellects.[15]

"Surely," Professor Hening added, "the frequent wagers of battle between these able and worthy champions must have satisfied even Judge Doe's fiercest denunciators at the bar."[16]

One argument led to another, one objection to the next. Wherever Doe turned in his search for better law, Carpenter was likely to pursue, warning, protesting, resisting. There was little of Doe's jurisprudence which Judge Carpenter did not question. Unawed by his chief's reputation, Carpenter was ready to fight for what he believed. Perhaps the best decisions to emerge from their judicial battles were Doe's majority opinion and Carpenter's dissent in the previously discussed case of *Boody* v. *Watson,* which involved four of the issues upon which they disagreed and which lay at the very core of Doe's lawmaking theories: (1) the creation of new forms of action; (2) judicial legislation; (3) the question whether a right's enforceability depends upon the prior recognition of a remedy; and (4) whether "justice" and "reason" are too abstract, too relative, and too vague to be pragmatic legal guides.

The town of Northwood had exempted from taxation industrial property belonging to a family named Pillsbury. The court had held the exemption unconstitutional, thus establishing the plaintiffs' right to have the property taxed.[17] Before final judgment was handed down, the terms of the defendants, the selectmen of Northwood, had expired. The plaintiffs prayed for a writ of *mandamus* ordering the selectmen to make the needed adjustment and to assess the tax. The defendants contended that since they were out of office, they no longer had authority; that the plaintiffs' right was worthless, even though adjudicated, because there was no appropriate remedy with which to enforce it.

Doe, of course, saw no difficulty. It was unthinkable that the plaintiffs could be denied an adjudicated right on so flimsy a technicality. "The merits of the case having been decided in their favor, the only remaining question is one of remedy." [18] Carpenter did not see how even an adjudicated right could exist without a remedy, and with the selectmen out of office there was no statutory procedure for making a tax reassessment; that is, there was no way in which the right could be vindicated. "If it cannot be so enforced," he argued, "the right does not exist." [19]

"The writs," Doe replied, "are not restricted to the uses that have been made of them. They may be modified and adopted to the wants of particular cases 'on grounds of convenience and expediency.' By a principle of our common law, for ascertaining, establishing, and vindicating legal rights, such procedure is to be invented and used as justice and convenience require." [20]

Carpenter said this would violate due process. If Doe was so concerned about rights, why not consider the defendants' right to be free of novel procedures concocted to meet a special situation? "It is not the plaintiffs' constitutional right to equal taxation; but their statutory right to the assessment of the particular tax on the Pillsbury factory, which is in question," Carpenter pointed out. "The Pillsburys have rights. Any view of the case which leaves them out of consideration is inadequate and deceptive. The plaintiffs' right and the Pillsburys' liability to the assessment, are coexistensive and correlative: the former cannot exist without the latter. If there is no provision of the statute requiring the assessment to be made, it is the Pillsburys' right that it shall not be made." [21]

Doe's answer was to balance these "rights." Surely the plaintiffs' constitutional right outweighed any procedural right which the Pillsburys might have. "The Pillsburys' non-payment of their statutory share [of taxation] would be a compulsory payment of that share by their neighbors, and, in effect, a payment to the Pillsburys, for their private use, of their neighbors' money," Doe wrote. "The plaintiffs' primary and substantive right is based, not on the defendants' duty of judicial assessment, or on their or our correctional duty, but on the legislative assignment to the factory of its share of a common expense incurred in the execution of the social contract." [22]

By admitting that the assignment of taxation was "legislative," Doe seemed to be conceding Carpenter's main point. "The whole matter of taxation rests in the control of the legislature, subject to the restraints of the constitution," Judge Carpenter asserted.[23]

"The constitution," Doe replied, "does not provide that judicial duties of the tax assessment shall not be imposed upon the highest judicial tribunal." [24]

But, Carpenter pointed out, the legislature had acted on this question by providing that reassessment could be made only in the year of error and not afterward.[25] "If justice requires that it should now be made, the remedy is with the legislature." [26]

This was the orthodox view of judicial power. It was not shared by Charles Doe. Power is created by need, not precedent. "When the law commands a thing to be done, it puts in requisition the means of executing its command," the Chief Justice contended. "From tribunals charged with the correction of judicial errors, indispensable process is not withheld. Correctional authority to reverse a tax exemption . . . is authority to make the assessment or cause it to be made." [27]

Carpenter's answer was perhaps the best protest ever written against Doe's jurisprudential principles. He lectured Doe on the dangers of judicial legislation and warned him about using "justice" as an excuse for making law. "The judiciary has never hesitated to exert its authority to keep the legislative department within its province," Carpenter pointed out.

It controls both that and the executive branch so far as to keep them from exceeding their constitutional powers. The court is the final arbiter of all controverted legal questions. Neither the legislature nor the executive can revise its actions or reverse its judgments. It is supreme. If it condemns without notice, adjudges without hearing, denies justice, or, what is equivalent, administers that which it pleased to call justice, in defiance of the legislative will, the people have no remedy except by impeachment and removal, or by revolution. It ought, therefore, while it is vigilant to restrain usurpations of the law-making and law-executing branches of the government, to be especially watchful that it does not itself trespass upon the domain of either. It is wiser to refer the correction of the occasional mischiefs incidental to all general laws to the legislature, which is always at hand, than to assume the exercise of a questionable jurisdiction.[28]

There was spirit as well as merit in Carpenter's argument, but Doe paid it slight heed. It assumed that functionaries who execute a court's order perform a personal role; that the fact the selectmen were no longer in office created an insurmountable barrier. To Doe it was immaterial whether an officer whose error is being corrected is in or out of office. "The court decides what the error is, and what amendment will be true. The order sets out in terms the precise alteration to be made. The officer, acting as scrivener without responsibility, decides nothing, and discharges no duty but obedience." [29]

This explanation seemed to Carpenter to imply that the court, not the selectmen, would be performing the reassessment. It gave him the excuse to argue that the writ of *mandamus* was the wrong form of action. If the plaintiffs had expected the court to correct the error, they should have brought a writ of error. "The plaintiffs," he contended, "can have no relief against the defendants except the writ of *mandamus* specifically asked for. If they are not entitled to that remedy their petition (in default of an amendment bringing in other parties) must be dismissed." [30]

Carpenter knew that Doe would not be stopped by so barren a point. But it was by pressing him in this way that he made the Chief Justice openly express the ultimate implications of his judicial theories — a step Doe might otherwise have avoided. To escape from Carpenter's trap, Doe had to lay claim to absolute remedial powers. "In this case," Doe wrote, "such technicalities are useless, and no time is to be wasted upon the inconvenient peculiarities of writs that cannot suppress or derange the best inventible procedure. A petition or motion to bring an action forward, and reverse or modify a judgment rendered at the trial term of this court, is an ample, simple, and convenient remedy; and for that reason a writ of error does not lie." [31]

Faced with so bold an assertion of judicial power, Carpenter could do little but return to *stare decisis*. "No case has been cited and none has been found in which it has been held that a writ of *mandamus* or other precept may be lawfully directed to a person not by law authorized and bound to execute it." [32]

Doe, of course, had an answer to this argument. "[A] demonstration or decision that a writ of *mandamus* limited, by precedent, is not the remedy, would merely show the duty of issuing some other writ, or a *mandamus* not limited by precedent, or adopting some other mode of defending a right that is as easily maintained as if such forms of action as *mandamus, certiorari,* and writ of error had not been devised." [33]

The gulf between these two men was absolute. They could find no common ground save Carpenter's respect for Doe's work. This is perhaps the most remarkable aspect of all. Carpenter could not follow Doe, but he nonetheless appreciated Doe's search for abstract justice. "Those who have dissented from his judgments would in most cases freely admit that the law ought to be as he held it was," Carpenter wrote of his chief justice. "And so it may be said that his judicial mistakes, if any there be, have been made in the interest of justice." Yet appreciation could never be enough for a judge with Carpenter's view of legal principles. As he wrote in *Boody* v. *Watson,* "It is the province of the courts to vindicate legal rights and redress legal wrongs; to administer not abstract justice, or justice as they may think it to be, but justice as declared by law." [34]

That Carpenter's appreciation of Doe was no eulogistic platitude is seen by a letter which he wrote to Jeremiah Smith a few months before his death describing a recent decision in which he had disallowed the claim of a seriously injured child. "The case has caused me great anxiety," he said, "and I feel by no means so sure as I wish I might, and as in ordinary cases, I do, that the decision is right. I have felt oppressed, not only by the decisions in a contrary direction, but by the humanitarian aspect. As a possible 'headnote', this has been constantly humming in my ears, viz., 'Man's inhumanity to man makes countless thousands mourn.'" [35] We cannot imagine Judge Doe writing such a letter. Technicalities and precedents would not have been permitted to make him mourn; he would have struck them down without hesitation or apology. One can almost feel Carpenter wishing that he had the courage of Doe's convictions, but perhaps his love for the law was too great. For Carpenter uniformity, certainty, and precedent were more important and more vital than vague, relative notions of abstract justice, no matter what the equities.

If one were to assert that Doe's concept of justice was highly personal, the same would have to be said for Carpenter's concept of precedent. Carpenter might have agreed that he was an adjudicator while Doe was a legislator; that his forte was exegetic while Doe's was nomographic. But he would not have conceded the prudence — though he admitted the justice — of his chief's nomology, any more than Doe would have conceded the foresight of his associate's jurisprudence. And it would be unfair to each to call Carpenter a legal sciolist and Doe a legal iconoclast; for Carpenter was a fine scholar of the law, while one of the purposes of Doe's procedural reforms was to strengthen traditional writs by preserving at least their names, thus maintaining historical continuity and forestalling their destruction by legislative codes. The best that can be said is that they complemented each other; that in Carpenter Doe found his Taney, although the extremes between them were greater than those which would have existed between Marshall and Taney.

Doe could not have been unaware of what Carpenter's presence meant to him. That the lavish praise which Carpenter heaped upon him was not reciprocated can be explained by the accident that Doe died first. It is known that they were personal friends; that Carpenter, while holding court in Dover, visited Doe in Rollinsford; that Doe showed special deference to Carpenter during intracourt conferences. In 1870 Doe had written, "There never was, & never can be a court more harmonious, sociable, cordial, free & easy, than the present one. We often differ in opinion on questions of law of course, but we are on perfectly good terms with ourselves, — which cannot be said for the court of 1855 & some other courts that have existed in N.H. and elsewhere." Doe might have written this about the court over which he presided.[36]

It has been mentioned that at the time of Chief Justice Doe's illness in 1878 his colleagues, rather than permit him to resign, had undertaken to divide his duties among themselves. "Either they are very skilful deceivers," Doe had commented, "or they

are anxious not to have somebody else in my place at present."
Later, after Carpenter had been appointed, they proved the
esteem in which they held him and the extent of their wish to
keep him from retirement by relieving him of all his trial work.
Then Doe could have written, as he had written in 1878, "It is
impossible for me to be more happily situated in respect to my
associates." [37]

A PECULIAR MODE
OF EXPRESSION
Common-Law Method

CHARLES DOE'S happy relations with his colleagues should be no surprise. Considering his personality and ability to manage men, he could be expected to maintain a spirit of fraternal cordiality. Yet from an ideological point of view it was a remarkable achievement. Always surrounded by strong men of conservative tendencies, opposed by some of the keenest legal minds in New England — Bell, Perley, Sargent, Carpenter, Parsons — Doe was never defeated on a major reform. Even his dissents were only temporary setbacks. Except for those dealing with constitutional issues, he lived to see them all become law.

What explains his success? Certainly not that his colleagues, even those of limited ability, lacked the will to oppose him. Associate Justice Chase was a conservative not inclined to follow Doe. Alone Doe might have overwhelmed him. But with Carpenter as a crutch upon which to lean, Chase could have stood his ground. Instead we find him following Doe as often as he followed Carpenter. To be sure, some judges may have been inclined to let Doe have his way, since he did most of the work; to argue with him took more effort than they cared to expend. But once Carpenter joined the court, they could let him do the arguing. How, then, did Doe win so many battles and still keep antagonism at a minimum? The best explanation seems to be that he made his views attractive for his colleagues. His method of argument was tailored to lull them into ag. eement.

Above all, Charles Doe was a master of the common-law technique. Few judges have had a firmer grasp on the workings of the case system or have known how to manipulate it to such advantages. He had an intuition for developing its strengths and seizing upon its weaknesses; to make those challenging his views debate issues along lines he set down. His legal instincts permitted him, even when he was advocating radical ideas, to force opponents onto the defensive. Reasonableness, approximation, and justice were the general principles guiding his course. He tried to make them the lodestars of legal progress, but he knew them to be impotent weapons in the arsenal of common-law polemics. To try to persuade nineteenth-century judges to abandon a well-established rule sanctioned by precedent merely on the ground that it was unreasonable was to battle against their educated instincts. Besides, it would have been a tactical mistake in most cases, resulting in a fruitless wrangle over the definition of "reasonableness." Doe therefore turned to more pedestrian aspects of law, such as the distinction between law and fact, which provided added leverage for wedging reforms through traditional barriers. It is his common-law method which accounts for much of his success.

One of the most difficult hurdles for Doe to surmount was the law of precedent. In the few instances when his position was so sound and his public policy so impregnable that he faced no opposition, Doe could rely on his antiprecedent theory. But such cases were rare. Judges, as Holmes pointed out, do not like to discuss questions of policy or to appear to be making new law, since to do so costs them "the illusion of certainty which makes legal reasoning seem like mathematics." To abate the qualms of his fidgety fellows, Doe played one of the common-law's oldest games of deception. He would, as Professor Hening put it, "burn incense to the time-honored judicial idol — a common law rule existing from time beyond memory, a law fixed and unalterable however incorrectly expounded, a law perhaps even unknown until at last judicially discovered." [1]

If Hening was implying that Doe pretended to "find" rather than to "make" law, he misinterpreted Doe's work. Doe was not so hypocritical. His practice was to state a general principle. To lend this principle common-law respectability, he cited analogous cases in which the principle was genuine authority, or he quoted *dicta* from which the principle could be culled. This technique may have been ancillary to his main argument that the principle, supported by reason, should be followed and the old rule, supported only by precedent, should be rejected; but it softened the impact of novelty by coating the reality of innovation with the color of authority.

Charles Doe was a modest man, but his efforts to hide his own originality by pouring new wine into old bottles had nothing to do with modesty. Rather, it was a manifestation of his tact — a kind of judicial tact designed to make reform as painless as possible. It had to be painless if he hoped to keep his colleagues in line. With what Judge Ladd called "his diabolical skill in dialectics," Doe was usually able to find some authority to support his argument; or, as Chief Justice Peaslee later phrased it, "to show that his conclusions have always been law." [2] It was "diabolical" because his authorities were often based on *dictum,* came from decisions ungermane to the question at bar, or were broad expressions of principle as yet unadopted by common-law courts. But so impressive was their number, and so respectable their source, that they overwhelmed his colleagues, sometimes even Carpenter.

That Doe mesmerized the other judges by flashing a string of authorities before their eyes may seem farfetched. Yet this apparently happened. Associate Justice Isaac W. Smith may have been one of those whom he fooled. Seeking to prove that Doe was not as radical as some critics claimed, Smith admitted that when necessary Doe made free use of the maxim *cessante ratione legis, cessat et ipsa lex.** But, Smith insisted, "a closer inspection of his opinions will disclose the fact, that he was accustomed to cite authorities with as much, if not greater freedom than other judges." [3]

Smith was not the only member of the court to count Doe's citations and find safety in numbers. All the judges did so in *Lisbon* v. *Lyman* — the case in which Doe overruled the common-law doctrine that a judgment is inseverable; that if a new trial is

---

* The reason of the law ceasing, the law itself also ceases.

granted, it extends to all issues, even if granted for error on one issue only. On the strength of this doctrine — well established elsewhere if not in New Hampshire — the defendant in *Lisbon* had claimed "a legal right to a new trial." Doe disagreed on the ground of general principle. Of the flood of opinions from other jurisdictions which he cited, none had thoroughly investigated the question, nor had any distinguished the English precedents which held otherwise. Moreover, the principle which Doe established — that the common law of new trials "preserves, as far as possible, what is good, and destroys only what is erroneous when the latter can be severed from the former" — was extracted from quotations found in English cases which either were not on point or which had held the other way.[4] Those most qualified to comment have written that in this decision Judge Doe brought about a departure from the common-law rule of the indivisibility of verdicts,[5] yet his colleagues, impressed by the authorities he cited, reacted as though they were accepting a doctrine of respectable stirps. At the same term of court, in a different opinion, Chief Justice Sargent called it "a rule somewhat new in this state, though long since established in some other jurisdictions."[6] Doe may not have fooled them; but he did make them more comfortable by seeming less original.

Perhaps it is only to be expected that Judge Doe's three favorite areas of reform gave him his three favorite techniques for justifying reform. The most effective methods he found for disarming the opposition were to turn substantive issues into adjective issues, to turn rules of construction into inferences of probability, and to turn matters of law into questions of fact.

It was not until he became chief justice that Doe began highlighting the remedial rather than the substantive aspects of an innovation. He did this not only because he himself felt few restraints about new-modelling the forms or believed his colleagues had come to accept the principle that procedure is a formality. There was also the fact that his new-modelling was so obviously successful — the one area where his reforms, after initial opposition, were immediately felt and to a degree appreciated by the practicing bar. Doe could expect less resistance when tampering with adjective than with substantive law. Thus a certain monotonous repetition appeared in his later opinions: the refrain that many rules of law are "inconvenient peculiarities" which must never be allowed to "suppress or derange the best inventible procedure."[7]

In *Smith* v. *Furbish,* for example, the issue was whether a reservation of real estate, not specifically identified by the deed in which it is reserved, should be enforced by a court of law. The old rule was that such a reservation is void for uncertainty. Doe jettisoned a long string of well-established precedents by postulating a rule of his own which, he suggested, was found in the reason of the law. That rule is that reservations "reducible to certainty by such means as the law appoints, are not void for uncertainty." The difficulty which makes the reservation "uncertain" is a difficulty of evidence not a difficulty of procedure. It is a question of how the intent of the person who made the reservation can be ascertained; that is, how to overcome the vagueness in the deed. Yet Doe focused attention on remedy rather than on proof by arguing that his more reasonable rule should not be "rendered inoperative by an obsolete system of deficient procedure." On the pretext of providing the best inventible process for vindicating the claimant's right to the reservation, he introduced a reform of substantive property law. While procedure was a legitimate issue, he used it primarily as a stalking-horse to make the reform more attractive to the bar.[8]

There is an ironic note in Doe's use of procedural arguments to effect substantive reforms in opinions such as *Smith* v. *Furbish,* written toward the end of his career. Earlier, while new-modelling the writs, he had often felt it necessary to disguise adjective changes by employing the most effective technique in his common-law methodology — the question-of-fact approach. When we recall that his new-modelling was done largely through the instrument of permitting a liberal system of amendments, we should also recall the technique he used for solving most of the issues posed by amendment. Whether a plaintiff should be permitted to amend mistakes or omissions by substituting a good writ for a faulty writ or by amending an action at law into a bill in equity is determined by the requirements of justice; and whether justice requires an amendment is a question of fact. It was this technique — the question-of-fact approach — which permitted Doe to free remedial law from its technical snare. As was pointed out above, by leaving each case to be determined on its merits as a question of fact he made certain that a new set of justice-defeating rules would not rise up to take the place of the old, as happened in many code states.[9]

Doe knew that he was turning the law of procedure largely into a question of fact, and he appreciated the risks of so haphazard a method of practice. But he was willing to take the chance in order to accomplish his objective — abolition of rules and exceptions which are laid down by appellate courts to solve one particular case but which perforce must be applied in all subsequent cases. For this reason Doe employed the distinction between law and fact as a means of extending the trial court's discretion.

It is proper common-law jargon to speak of a court's power to act in areas not yet settled by uniform rules as its "discretion." Doe called the term unfortunate, apparently because it smacks of arbitrary authority and confuses ministerial with judicial error.[10] One of its consequences has been to obscure the rules governing the relevancy of evidence.[11] Because discretionary power "is exercised by weighing evidence on a question of fact" and, "in its technical legal sense, is the name of the decision of certain questions of fact by the court," Doe insisted that matters within the court's discretion were best treated as questions of fact, especially since there is "no appeal and no power of revising the decision." [12]

The change was more than one of nomenclature. For if the expression "discretion of the trial court" conjures up the idea of arbitrariness which appellate judges are duty bound to confine within definite limits by formulating rules and presumptions, then the expression "question of fact" implies a decision which should be unfettered by judicial restraints — or so Doe hoped. As his court said, speaking of the admissibility of a confession (which is a question of fact for the trial judge in New Hampshire), the "finding upon this question is a finality as much as the verdict of a jury upon a question of fact." [13] The same held true concerning admissibility of unwritten foreign law and the construction of a foreign statute.[14] Both matters, along with how far cross-examination of a witness should be carried, and how far the trial of collateral issues can justly and reasonably go, Doe held, are questions of fact for the trial judge.[15] So are the questions whether all or part only of the issues in an action should be tried at one time, and which should be tried first; whether a verdict should be set aside because of excessive damages or because the finding wos against the evidence; whether a new trial should be granted by reason of newly discovered evidence; and whether justice requires a recommittal of a verdict to a jury and whether justice will result from doing so.[16] By labeling such decisions "questions of fact" rather than "discretion," Doe hoped to induce his colleagues to refrain from substituting their judgment for that of the trial judge. The more they refrained, the fewer rules and exceptions would be introduced into New Hampshire law by appellate intervention.

Doe even found the question-of-fact approach convenient for reforming doctrines of trial practice not previously within the trial court's discretion. He used it to overturn the rule that a recorded verdict cannot be amended by a jury once the jurors have separated. Separation, Doe admitted, increased the danger of wrong being done and thus raised the question whether justice required a recommittal of the case for reconsideration, which in turn raised the second question whether if reconsidered and amended, justice required a judgment on the amended verdict. "Both questions," Doe said, "were matters of fact to be determined at the trial term." [17] The question-of-fact approach was a side door through which reforms could be slipped into the common law. Some of Doe's associates resisted, but even they found it easier to accept an innovation framed as a question of fact rather than as a new, precedent-shattering rule of law.

Judge Doe's astute use of one polemic tool to support another is also seen in his manipulation of the question-of-fact argument to reinforce his rules-of-construction reforms. It has been noted how his dislike of rules of construction served as an excuse for altering several common-law doctrines, most notably "words of limitation." The law at that time provided that full title to real estate could be conveyed only if the property was granted to the grantee "and his heirs." If granted to the grantee alone, a life estate, not a fee simple, was conveyed. As previously discussed, Doe thought this a rule of construction which ascertained the grantor's intent by relying on a redundancy which only a lawyer could appreciate.[18] Here is one of the most impressive examples of Judge Doe's common-law method. He did not attack the doctrine of "words of limitation" directly. That is, he did not place it in its usual perspective — as a principle of real property which defines the interests or estates created by conveyances. Had he framed a proposed reform in this light, he would surely have been accused of judicial legislation. Possibly his colleagues would have felt that he was going too far and would have voted against his reform. Perhaps to avoid this risk Doe elected to follow the line of least resistance by attacking the doctrine indirectly, placing it within the broad perspective of his general theories concerning rules of construction, legal presumptions, and the distinction between law and fact. "Words of limitation," he argued, is not so much a principle of real property as a rule of construction, which not only presumes that no grantor or testator intends to convey a fee simple unless he uses the phrase "and his heirs," but also presumes that every grantor and testator has been trained in legal terminology. Placed within this perspective, the doctrine of "words of limitation" was easily dismissed as a presumption "contrary to the fact." [19]

In few other instances was Doe's mastery of the common-law method so vividly demonstrated. Mesmerized by common-law habits of thought, other judges had confused fiction with reality and had convinced themselves that they were giving expression to intention while actually defeating it. Using the question-of-fact approach as his lock and key, Doe opened compartments of the law long since closed. He did not challenge the significance of the words "and his heirs"; for all Doe knew, they might be the words which prove intent. But whether they do is a question of fact, to be determined as other questions of fact, "by the aid of all competent evidence, and not by the expulsion of evidence otherwise competent, nor by the mechanical application of antiquated forms of expression erroneously supposed to express legal principles." [20]

Chief Justice Doe's most perspicacious combination of the question-of-fact approach with the rule-of-construction argument occurred in *Edgerly* v. *Barker*. The testator, it will be recalled, had created a class gift to take effect forty years after lives in being, and the heirs-at-law claimed that since the remainder might not vest within the period prescribed by the rule against perpetuities, the gift was void and the estate passed as intestate property. By saying that it must not be permitted to defeat the testator's intent, Doe converted the rule against perpetuities from a rule of substantive property rights into a rule of construction.[21] To make it a workable rule of construction, he turned to the distinction between law and fact. "The construction of the will," Doe wrote in the first sentence of the decision, "including the question whether the testator intended the remainder, which he devised to his grandchildren, should vest in them before they became entitled to a distribution of it, is determined as a question of fact, by competent evidence, and not by rules of law."[22] Even the issue whether the court could make a division of a defective will was to be settled as a question of fact by examining the testator's intent.[23] As a judicial tool the question-of-fact and rule-of-construction combination was wonderfully effective. By turning the rule against perpetuities into a rule of construction it left in force an established common-law doctrine. And making the application of the rule a question of fact nullified the rule's harshness. Almost as important was its value as a tool of judicial polemics. Even Carpenter, who earlier had argued that the court was powerless to reform substantive doctrines of this type,[24] did not dissent in *Edgerly* v. *Barker*.

Judge Doe used the question-of-fact approach to supplement and reinforce other reforms besides those involving rules of construction. He found it particularly effective in furthering his efforts to make the norm of reasonableness the underlying principle of tort law. Though reasonableness is the legal test, there is no need to define it — indeed, it should not be defined — because it is a question of fact for the jury. By treating reasonableness as a question of fact, Doe removed rigidity from New Hampshire tort law, rendering it a matter of degree and giving it flexibility. Much of the disparity between his and Holmes's tort theories can be explained by their disagreement over how much freedom should be given to the deciders of fact.[25]

By 1890 Doe had made the question-of-fact approach his most effective judicial weapon, and lawyers at the New Hampshire bar were thoroughly familiar with its use. Some may have even thought it the main object, rather than the tool, of his reforms.

He probably welcomed this belief, since it kept their attention focused on means rather than on ends and permitted him to effect changes in substantive law which appeared less radical when viewed as part of the question-of-fact pattern. But in the wider arena of national law reform this feature of his common-law method was not so successful. Out-of-state lawyers who did not regularly read the New Hampshire *Reports* approached his opinions from a different vantage point. To them the substantive innovation loomed large, while the question-of-fact theory seemed an isolated argument thrown in to lend historical probity to a doubtful departure from precedent.

Surely no one suffered greater shock on reading a Doe opinion than did John Chipman Gray when he read *Edgerly* v. *Barker*. In a blistering, bitter article, calculated to draw blood, he criticized it from every angle and denounced it on every ground. Yet when he came across the question-of-fact argument as it related to giving expression to the testator's intent — the very heart and motivating force of Doe's decision — he dismissed it with the words, "This mode of expression is peculiar to the learned court." He had either become weary of encountering it in Judge Doe's decisions or decided it was a smokescreen laid down by Doe to cover his real purpose. In any event, Gray considered it of little importance, and readers, relying on his summary, never got an accurate idea of what the chief justice had said. Since the article has been reprinted in every edition of Gray's treatise, most American lawyers have depended on his presentation.[26]

Misinterpretations by out-of-state lawyers are minor considerations. What counts are the reforms Doe accomplished for New Hampshire by using the question-of-fact approach. It would be impossible to say what was more important to him, the immediate reforms or the general need to reestablish the distinction between law and fact. Perhaps in *Edgerly* v. *Barker* the common-law argument, as it related to finding the testator's intent, was more motivating than any desire to remodel the rule against perpetuities. With the New Hampshire insanity doctrine, however, it is possible that dissatisfaction with the right-wrong test weighed more heavily and that the question-of-fact theory was the means to an end.[27] It does not matter; what is unique is the formulation and the use. Only an astute scholar of the common-law process could have formulated the theory; only a master of the common-law method could have used it to purify so many unrelated rules and principles.

Many judges have shared Charles Doe's desire to reform law by eliminating harsh rules and abolishing technicalities. Yet few have brought about a fraction of the reforms which he accomplished. Lacking his genius and insight, they did not appreciate the need to master the more pedestrian tools in the common-law arsenal. Where he used the question-of-fact approach to outflank an entrenched legal dogma they conducted frontal assaults and were driven short of their goals. Instead of placing their colleagues on the defensive by contending that inferences, presumptions, and rules of construction should be treated as questions of fact, they offered alternative inferences, presumptions, and rules of construction. Alternatives based on notions of justice drawn from the factual circumstances of particular cases are not likely to sway judges devoted to *stare decisis*. Chief Justice Doe seldom debated facts, realizing that to do so would be to waste time. Many besides Doe knew what causes had to be fought, but he found a more effective means of fighting.

It was in this manner — by using the distinction between law and fact as his leverage — that Judge Doe was able to influence many different areas of adjective and substantive law. He found a simple, unifying principle, which permitted him to reform seemingly unrelated legal rules, to eliminate legal technicalities, and to bring flexibility to previously rigid law. Doe's belief that the distinction between law and fact was the neglected principle underlying the common-law system seems hardly novel. But it was in the practical application of theories that the chief justice excelled. The idea that through it he could unify the common law is proof of his originality. The discovery that he could reform so many technicalities by using this one method of analysis as a reagent is proof of his genius. Professor Gray was wrong about Judge Doe's use of the question-of-fact argument: it was more than a peculiar mode of expression.

THE OBSCURITY OF OVER-ELABORATION

Style and Influence[1]

THAT John Chipman Gray found Chief Justice Doe's mode of expression somewhat peculiar helps explain why Doe's influence on the course of American law has been less than might be expected. No other nineteenth-century judge was better able to translate his judicial psyche into the law of one jurisdiction than was Doe. Yet he failed to convert this ability into national significance. One reason may be his style of opinion writing — the style which Gray found peculiar. Doe could when he wished produce the well-turned phrase, demolish in a few words an established legal rule, or explain his own position in clear succinct language. He appreciated the value of the rounded sentence, the rhythmic flow of words, the richness of vocabulary, the lucidity of statement, and the precision of definition. But all too often these were lost in a maze of details and arguments, buried in an avalanche of repetitions and cross-references, or pushed into obscurity by lengthy quotes and exhaustive citations.

Doe's friends recognized the problem of his style — the "obscurity of over-elaboration," as John Major Shirley characterized it. Professor Smith worried that it might diminish his eminence. "The length of Judge Doe's opinions in some cases and the combative tone sometimes noticeable, may perhaps be made the subject of unfavorable comment," Smith warned in 1881. Sixteen years later he was so concerned that he devoted almost two pages of his thirty-page biography to answering the question, "Why should a man, who had shown himself capable of writing such admirable short opinions, so often write extremely long ones?" Smith suggested three explanations: 1) "he was in the minority in some of these cases, and was naturally anxious to fully justify his dissent"; 2) "he foresaw, and answered in advance, objections not yet raised"; and 3) he was unwilling "to adopt implicitly the statements and reasoning of other men." [2]

An explanation Smith did not mention was Doe's fondness for research and his habit of inserting into opinions material which had little business being there. Research was his "intellectual hobby." [3] When the Democrats "legislated" him from office in 1874, he had two years with no other occupation but writing opinions. Even in all that time he never caught up with arrears — as he explained to the court reporter in April, 1876.

Every point I go to work upon branches out into the whole universe of law; I get in a constant snarl over the question where to stop on incidental sidepaths; & to keep my studies in order I find no easy job. I believe I am beginning to make some headway; but to get my lines of study & thought into a close & convenient method, so as to make the most profitable use of time, is an art of difficult acqui——t [?]. I am just now completely worn down, & must stop & take time to breathe & collect my scattered ideas. [4]

There was "no end to the amount of drudgery he would go through," Professor Smith wrote of Doe — a fact New Hampshire lawyers, weary of the lengths of Doe's opinions, did not have to be told. When he died, it was discovered that he had been working on the opinion in *Dow's Case* for ten years, and it still was not finished. The draft had never been submitted to his colleagues, and obviously he had planned extensive reversions. The court appointed an editor to arrange it in digestible form, which he did by omitting arguments "fully stated" in other parts of the decision and by deleting "numerous lengthy" quotations better handled by mere reference to authorities. Even so, the decision came to over sixty-four printed pages, or, as one lay historian complained, it still "embraced long excursions" of "more than the customary erudition." No wonder Holmes called Doe "long-winded" and Chandler could accuse him of concealing "gross error" by making his decisions "long, verbose, and obscure." [5]

In sum, Doe was a poor editor of his own work. He could not bring himself to omit or sum up material he had spent weeks researching. The official reports were the only publications in which New Hampshire lawyers could read about local law, and perhaps Doe felt that if he did not make his disclosures known in a regular opinion, they would be lost. All too often what he had to say was irrelevant to the issue in controversy, diminishing the readability and therefore the influence of many of his more significant decisions. He devoted six months to the study of books and tracts on theology and church history while preparing his dissent in *Hale* v. *Everett,* the decision in which he passionately defended the absolutism of religious liberty. His liberal and far-sighted views, combined with this vast scholarship, should have produced a document of social and historical value. Instead, his inability to edit out many of his discoveries and observations resulted in a labyrinth of quoted authorities calculated to frighten off potential readers. The most widely circulated obituary of Doe dismissed *Hale* with the observation, "it was a religious squabble, Mr. Justice Doe's dissenting opinion is only 144 pages long." [6]

There is merit to such sarcasm. The written opinion is, after all, the heart of the common-law system. The judge who fails to master this basic working tool of his profession will not influence the course of law. Doe mastered it. He authored some of the classics of American law, and when he wished to he could write as compendious an opinion as anyone. Yet he frequently forgot the primary function of the common-law opinion, and using it for instruction or as a debating platform, he decreased its efficiency. With him this was a failure of creation, an artistic lapse. Later, looking at the finished product on the printed page, he sometimes recognized that his work suffered from the obscurity of overelaboration and regretted that he had not maintained tighter control over his flow of words. Thus he warned the editor of the *Medico-Legal Journal* not to follow his example of cluttering an argument for reform of criminal insanity with irrelevant discussions about burden of proof. "The average reader will be in danger of confusion if you allow anything to divert him from the real question which is whether the knowledge test or the N.H. rule is the true principle. Omit and protest against anything that is not an argument on that question, and you will strengthen your cause." [7] Doe's influence might have been larger had he possessed the discipline to act on his own advice.

Yet style is only one criterion. It is ironic that one of the faults which make Charles Doe's opinions difficult to read — his tendency to cram decisions with arguments and discussions ungermane to the controversy at bar — contributed to his fame and therefore to his influence. His unwillingness to be bridled by the patterns of common-law decision writing permitted him to avoid some of the handicaps connected with sitting on the bench of a small rural state. The fact that he is the only jurist from a small jurisdiction to be included by most scholars among America's great judges can be attributed in part to his unorthodox style as well as to his original reforms.

The size of a jurisdiction can be an immeasurable asset to fame, both for its impact on the general mind and, most significant to judicial prestige, for the attention it receives from writers. Judges in large states — in the market centers of manufacture and trade — are asked to decide more cases than are their brethren in small states. It is they who have the opportunity to build, year by year, a body of case law within specialized areas and, by demonstrating mastery of a subject, become its acknowledged authority. They are more likely to encounter the unusual fact situation, the conflict between precedents, and the "hard" cases upon which every judge must cut his teeth before he gains national recognition. On the very week that he was first proposed for the United States Supreme Court, and men were asking who he was, Doe handed down two decisions somewhat typical of the type with which he often dealt. In the first he held that agistment of cattle does not relieve their owner of liability for damage which they caused when they strayed from the agistee's field; in the second he held that a person pasturing another's milch cow may have a statutory lien upon it for the charge of pasturing. [8] These decisions were hardly calculated to impress the urban bar of other jurisdictions. Most city lawyers had forgotten what an agistment was and had never heard of a milch cow. A judge who hoped to influence the course of American law could waste his time on the bench of nineteenth-century New Hampshire. The odds of obtaining judicial immortality were very slim indeed.

There are, of course, counterconsiderations which could balance these factors. An obvious one is length of service. A judge with sufficient tenure will encounter a wide variety of cases regardless of the annual volume of business conducted in the jurisdiction, and a small-state jurist who stays on the bench long enough should match the output of his big-state colleagues with shorter tenure, although he would have to serve an unusually long time to encounter the hard cases that would make him a recognized authority or give his name to a legal doctrine. Doe's career seems to prove the point. His more than thirty-four years on the New Hampshire court are far above average. But even with so much time Doe did not write anywhere near the number of decisions within a given area that he might have had he been in a larger jurisdiction. For example, during those thirty-four years only three cases involving criminal insanity came before the court, and Judge Doe wrote a concurring opinion in just one of them. Yet these meager pickings constituted all the opportunities he had for formulating one of his strongest claims to fame. During the first decade after the District of Columbia judges handed down the *Durham* rule, they had about a hundred cases in which to redefine, explain, and defend it. It is little wonder that *Durham* overshadows the New Hampshire insanity doctrine in current literature. Except perhaps for his theory of constitutional equality, Doe seldom got the chance to reexamine his more important pronouncements and, by weaving them through a variety of different fact patterns, to justify them to the world.

How, then, did Chief Justice Doe gain national renown when his only working tools were those furnished by the litigation of a rural society in a small jurisdiction? One suggested answer is that he had the luxury of time; that the very fact he was on a small-state bench with comparatively little business gave him leisure to examine questions and research solutions which judges in Massachusetts and New York did not have.

While this argument is qualified by the fact that in Doe's day New Hampshire Supreme Court justices were burdened with *nisi prius* as well as appellate duties, it is the key to Doe's éclat. Few judges put leisure to better use than did Doe. Seldom absent from judicial labor, devoting every working hour to the study of law, he employed the additional time given nineteenth-century New Hampshire jurists to turning run-of-the-mill cases into definitive treatises and gathering up loose legal ends which only exhaustive research could uncover. Still, this circumstance alone would not have been enough. The explanation must go deeper, for no matter how much time a small-state judge has to track down authorities, develop answers, and rework materials, he cannot write opinions which will have an impact outside his jurisdiction and attract national attention unless he is asked to solve problems worthy of his mettle. Leon Richardson gave part of the answer when he wrote that Doe was accustomed "year by year, to mull over knotty points of the law and to arrive at conclusions concerning them which had nothing to do with the cases before the court. But, not infrequently in the course of time, a case would come up in which these issues were invoked and Doe would astonish everyone by his familiarity with the legal principles involved, as well as by his original and unprecedented solution of the problem presented." [9] This explanation tells only one third of the story. Doe did more than wait for the right case to "come up"; he often went out of his way to look for it, and occasionally he invented it.

Even waiting was sometimes hard. "Can you tell me," he wrote a colleague,

whether there is a case in the law term, raising the question whether setting aside a verdict as against evidence, is a question of fact or discretion for the Judge and Trial Term; or any other question of discretion?

I have some materials that I think I could work into an opinion on the distinction between matter of discretion and matter of law, and I should like to swap and get a question of that sort.

While Doe had to wait five more years before he found the case he wanted, the remarkable fact is that he had already researched the authorities on which he would base the distinction between appealable error in deciding a question of law and nonappealable error in deciding a question of fact.[10] He had formulated this prop to his law-fact theory long before he had a chance to announce it.

Another case for which Doe waited was *Concord Mfg. Co.* v. *Robertson,* in which he held that in New Hampshire the people own all ponds and lakes of ten acres or more in extent. The decision astonished those who read it. But as Doe explained to his associates four years later, he had been working on fresh-water questions for the past forty years. "I doubt if any man, living or dead, has spent so much time on them as I have," he added.[11] Thus, thirty-six years before *Robertson* Doe had started to research the issues, and when they finally "came up," he had so mastered his materials that he carried his colleagues in a direction no lawyer in the state could have predicted.

The most remarkable aspect of Judge Doe's manner of finding cases with which to develop the law along the lines which he wished was that at times he went beyond preparing material in the hope of finding the suitable fact pattern and even beyond forcing the material into decisions where it was not germane to the issue. He was not above inventing the right case if he could not get it through orthodox channels. Much of his new-modelling of the forms was accomplished in this manner. So too was a good deal of his work in the law of torts. As previously noted, *Brown* v. *Collins* was not a proper case for challenging the *Rylands* doctrine. Had Doe not stretched the facts there, he would not have been able to lay down the general rule that fault must be proven to sustain an action for accidental injury.[12] It became one of his most influential decisions; without *Brown* v. *Collins,* Doe's impact on the development of American tort law would have been appreciably diminished. Not stopping there, Doe occasionally went even further and actually created a fact situation when he felt the time had come to establish a new principle, as in the *Sawtelle* murder trial, or to overhaul what he thought an outdated legal doctrine, as in the *Almy* murder trial.

The *Sawtelle* situation was simple, and one can only guess at Doe's motives. It may be that he was concerned about the threat which the sensation-seeking newspapers of that day posed to the criminal jury system and wished to establish the principle that pretrial opinions would not disqualify an otherwise competent juror. If so, he chose an ideal case. Isaac Sawtelle was the most notorious fratricide in American history, and his trial contained all the ingredients of sensationalism: a worried father rushing to the bedside of his sick daughter; the long, well-publicized search for the missing man; the discovery of the headless body; and the identification of the corpse by the grief-stricken widow while a score of reporters looked on. Moreover, there was a possibility that despite convincing evidence of guilt the defendant might escape justice through a technicality. Sawtelle, a Massachusetts resident, had lured his brother from Boston to the New Hampshire-Maine state line where he killed him, partly in the hope that if he were caught the jurisdictional question might confuse the authorities. The press seemed to think that he would go free if neither state could prove where the crime was committed.

Citing a statute which excluded from jury duty anybody who was related to the principals, who had an interest in the outcome, and who entertained moral objections to capital punishment, Doe ruled that all others were qualified; the fact that a juror admitted that he had read and talked about the case and had listened to the views of others, did not bar him from service. In fact, he was competent even if he had already formed and publicly expressed an opinion concerning the defendant's guilt. All Doe asked the prospective juror was whether he thought himself able to render a fair verdict — that is, if he swore under oath that he could modify his views. The Chief Justice was so intent on establishing the principle that pretrial prejudice is not a bar to jury service that he forced the issue and did not attempt to find unbiased jurors. He selected a jury within three hours and called only fifty-two members of the ninety-three-member panel, accepting anyone who said that he could change his mind, without waiting to discover if thirteen impartial men could be found.[13] The defense took no exception and, as a result, waived all objections. But Doe, on his own motion and without urging from either side, reserved the issue for consideration at law term. He was intent on establishing new law and wanted the court's stamp of approval. Carpenter upheld him in an opinion written in the Doe style; it is probably the only decision signed by Carpenter which seems to have been authored by Doe. Its verbose length, swollen by battologization, the exhaustive research funneled into each page, the use of legal history to justify innovation, the argumentative tone which runs throughout, and the principle that a juror's qualification is a question of fact for the trial term, are all characteristics of Doe's work. The conclusion is inescapable that at some earlier day he became interested in the problem, investigated it thoroughly, decided that the law needed redefinition, and seized upon the *Sawtelle Case* as means to force the issue. Doe saw to it that the question was reserved for consideration by the full court, assigned the opinion to Carpenter who was willing to use his notes, then guided the matter through to its termination.[14]

The validity of this conclusion is reinforced by the fact that Doe at that time was in an experimenting mood. The *Almy* murder case occurred only eleven months later, and there is no need to guess about his actions on that occasion. Indeed, he went even further than he had gone in *Sawtelle,* and without a pretense of necessity he attempted to reform an ancient rule of common law.

Frank Almy had pleaded guilty to the murder of Christie Warden, and Doe presided at his trial which took place in Plymouth during November 1891. The sole issue was the degree of the crime. At the conclusion of the evidence the defense waived Almy's right to be present when sentence was imposed. One of Doe's biographers has claimed that Almy was afraid he might be lynched,[15] but this is doubtful. Admittedly feeling ran high, for Miss Warden was a local girl of good character, while Almy was from out of state. It is possible that violence had once been threatened, but there was clearly no danger at that time. Indeed, there was little excitement until word spread that Almy had been spirited out of town.[16] Professor Hening interviewed the county solicitor and the defense counsel, who told him "that no fear of being lynched was expressed by Almy, and that there was no apprehension of such an occurrence." [17] The majority of those attending the trial that last morning had been women, and they were so far from being a menace that the police not only led Almy out among them but two ladies were even able to whisper in his ear — the first time anyone except his lawyer had spoken to him in the courtroom. "On the way to the depot Almy appeared in the best of spirits and smiled several times in response to remarks from the spectators." Had the authorities suspected trouble, they surely would have kept him out of the public smoker and would have put him in a special car, as they had a month earlier when they took him to Woodsville for arraignment.[18] When he reached Concord, the site of the state prison, "there was no excitement, hardly a murmer escaping the crowd" of several hundred on hand at the station. He was not handcuffed. At no time was his life threatened.[19] The people of New Hampshire had been so restrained, in fact, that a local paper boasted that they had set an example of civilization by allowing the court to try the "miserable wretch Almy"; a statewide newspaper accused Doe of unjustly insulting them by implication when he failed to make Almy stand up to be sentenced in open court; a Maine newspaper congratulated them for teaching a lesson to those south of Mason-Dixon who surely would have lynched the murderer; and a New York newspaper complained that they had perhaps been too weak and might still have to "string him up."[20]

The Chief Justice was noncommittal when he was asked why he had discarded the practice of having the defendant in court when sentence was pronounced. "Judge Doe stated to the writer," one correspondent reported, "that as Almy was to go to Concord in any event, no matter what the decision was, he had been sent on this train; that's all there is to it." Almy's counsel, Alvin Burleigh, told the press that the idea had originated with his client. Almy "did not want to hear the sentence or face the demonstrations of the crowd, and above all else he did not want to take the long night's ride between Plymouth and the state prison." Burleigh probably informed Doe, who saw an opportunity to effect a reform he thought long overdue. "The futile practice," Hening writes, "of asking the convicted murderer why he should not be sentenced, when no reason which he might or could assign could possibly change the purpose of the judge, seemed to Judge Doe an intolerable relic of medieval barbarism." Doe called it "an idle, unnecessary and brutal performance that could serve no useful purpose whatever." He ordered Almy sent to the state prison and then, after deliberating on his fate, returned to the courtroom and ordered the clerk to read the verdict. A copy of the judgment, together with the date set for the execution, was to be read to Almy in his cell.[21]

Thus Doe, through a fact situation of his own creation, almost succeeded in breaking with years of tradition by abandoning a practice which he, but apparently no one else, found "idle, unnecessary and brutal." He almost succeeded but not quite, for the affair turned into a fiasco. Doe had apparently been unaware that seven months earlier the United States Supreme Court had ruled that "in all capital felonies it was essential that it should appear of record that the defendant was asked before sentence if he had anything to say why it should not be pronounced." Among the liturgical reasoning cited by Chief Justice Fuller was the argument that "the example of being brought up for animadversion of the court and the open denunciation of punishment might tend to deter others from the commission of similar offenses." [22] While Doe was hardly impressed by such thinking, he nevertheless felt constrained to recall Almy, to ask him if he had anything to say why sentence should not be pronounced, and then to condemn him once again to death by hanging. Perhaps he did not mind, for the experiment had not proved as humane as he had hoped. While Almy had been spared the ordeal of being condemned in open court before a hostile crowd of onlookers, he had been forced to wait over six days to learn his fate. Because of uncertainty and confusion the procedure set up to inform him had broken down. He was the last person in the state to hear the verdict, and public sympathy shifted toward him. "For six days after his trial," one newspaper complained, "he is made to endure a suspense as terrible as one can imagine, hoping for life one minute, despairing the next, but all the time kept in ignorance of his fate, — and this, too, in these days of express trains and fast mails." [23]

Doe was roundly censured. Making the most of the affair, Senator Chandler warned that by the bungling of the Chief Justice a "loop-hole of escape" had "carelessly been left open to the villain." He suggested that Almy would have been set free had not someone told Doe to resentence him. "New Hampshire thus narrowly escaped an everlasting stain upon her jurisprudence, although even now it is a matter of doubt whether Almy will be actually hung by a private citizen or by a sheriff, or by both, or by the chief justice himself." [24]

The *Almy* case certainly did not help Judge Doe's reputation,

·though it did spread his fame. Led by the New York *Sun,* the nation's newspapers began discussing the odd behavior of New Hampshire's judiciary.[25] The Brooklyn *Standard-Union* referred to Doe's "apparently strange carelessness." [26] A poll of the Boston bar showed most lawyers "astonished." [27] The cleverest witticism was attributed to a Massachusetts attorney who said that he disagreed with those who thought Doe did not know what he was about. "He believes the man who is such a crank on fresh air one of the ablest jurists in the country, and contends that Almy is not yet sentenced; and that Judge Doe is liable to call the court in Concord state prison and pronounce the doom of the murderer." To be sure, Senator Chandler made the strongest point, as reported in the same newspaper: "The plain people do not know about law," he wrote, "but they do not like to know that even Almys can be sentenced to death when not in open court, nor do they believe that even chief justices are justified in inflicting pneumonia upon innocent people by taking out the windows of court houses. This is, as has been often remarked, a bad year for dictators and the spirit of revolt which has knocked out a Balmaceda and a Da Fonseca may bounce a judge here and there." [28]

The *Almy* fiasco may not have advanced Charles Doe's prestige, but it does help to explain how he overcame the double handicap of a style made obscure by overelaboration and of the smallness of New Hampshire. For Doe's influence on the course of American law has been more in example than in doctrine, more in spirit than in deed. As Karl Llewellyn stated, Doe stood out "in powerful idiosyncratic contrast" to the other judges of his day.[29] Nowhere was this contrast more stark than in the contrary attitudes of Chief Justice Fuller and Chief Justice Doe in the *Almy* matter. Doe approached the problem with a certain flair and a will to experiment; Fuller approached it through the logic of the assumed premise and in the spirit of *stare decisis.* It is not important that Doe was wrong, for it was not the solution he proposed but his manner and his tactics which created the legend of judicial greatness. He was able to break free of the shackles of being in a small, insignificant jurisdiction, not in spite of *Almy,* but because of *Almy* — because he was willing to take such risks; to tinker with the law; to handle it as a living, growing force; to be more than merely prepared to expand, or bend, or reshape it whenever necessary, but to go beyond and seek out opportunities which lesser judges would not have found and to create issues which lesser judges would not have dared to touch.

If the *Almy* case helps to answer the question of why Charles Doe, despite his influence, has been called a "great" judge, it also helps explain why he was so frequently criticized and severely attacked during his own lifetime. Even friends were troubled by his sudden detours from familiar paths. But history cannot share their shock, for novelty wears thin with time. Far removed from the toxic aftereffects of his experiments, history admires Doe's sense of daring, his feeling for the untried, and his quest for justice. It finds in these qualities part of the reason for the greatness of a small-state judge. Yet the judgment of history does not quarrel with the observation of one contemporary who wrote that Doe "had a passion for reform, sometimes, as has been thought by others, carrying his ideas to such an extreme as to be almost a hobby." [30]

Chapter Thirty

BORN TO THE JUDGESHIP
The Heritage

C HARLES DOE'S critics were not the only ones who complained that he labored too hard. His friends, alarmed at what the work was doing to his health, also took note of his assiduity. It might be the death of him, they feared.[1] But Doe paid no heed. On the morning of March 9, 1896, he was in a hurry to travel to Concord for the adjourned term of the Supreme Court, and he may have forgotten that just three weeks earlier he had been taken home in a carriage from the local bank where he had "had a narrow escape from a shock."[2] He had been on the bench for almost thirty-five years. Only one English and four American judges had served the common law longer than he. Some people thought that much too long. "In New Hampshire today," Senator Chandler had complained just fifteen days before, "judicial tyranny has taken the place of a correct and just administration of the laws." While Doe's life lasted, Chandler thought, he could not hope by any future fidelity to compensate for his faithlessness and misconduct.[3] But few shared these sentiments. When it was rumored that Doe might resign, *The Dartmouth* reported that "the bar of New Hampshire, as well as the public, are united in the hope that our state will not be deprived of his eminent and acceptable services until the Constitutional limit of age shall be reached."[4] That would be April 11, 1900, when he was seventy years old. On March 9, 1896, Doe was barely a month short of his sixty-sixth birthday.

When the Chief Justice left home that morning, he was feeling "as well as usual."[5] The house itself was observing its centennial, having been built in 1796. A hundred years before that, the section of town in which it was located had been ravaged by a savage Indian raid. Now only the forces of nature brought devastation to the area. Eight days earlier Dover had been hit by the worst flood in its history; bridges had been destroyed and many merchants, caught without insurance, had been wiped out.[6] Now, as Doe passed out of his yard on the way to the Rollinsford depot, the river was calm again. Commerce no longer plied that part of the Piscataqua. The barges and gundalows which once floated downstream to Portsmouth were a memory of the past. But in that year of 1896 the United States was to build its first submarine, presaging the course of the future. For the economy of southern New Hampshire would come to depend on the submarine during most of the first seven decades of the twentieth century.

Immersed as he was in the daily problems of legal business, Charles Doe had little inclination to reflect on the changing world in which he lived. Yet 1896 would have been a good time to have taken stock. In the field of law there were momentous decisions for the future at the very hour when old traditions were passing into oblivion. During May the United States Supreme Court, with Horace Gray concurring and Jeremiah Smith's son serving as his law clerk, would announce the judgment in *Plessy* v. *Ferguson*, sanctioning racial segregation and writing the separate-but-equal doctrine into the federal constitution.[7] During November Isaac Charles Parker, the last of the great jurists to bring law to an untamed West, would die near his courthouse and gallows, stripped of his powers as the "hanging judge of Fort Smith" by eastern congressmen who thought him an anachronism no longer needed by a now-civilized nation. They lived in totally different legal environments, Parker and Doe, yet they shared the tragedy of being misunderstood by their contemporaries. If Doe knew of Parker, it was probably that Parker had been a promising judge who grew too fond of sentencing men to death. If Parker knew of Doe, it was probably through the popular notion that Doe was a brilliant jurist whose potential was stunted by personal and professional eccentricity.

It was also in this year that the political era in which Charles Doe had lived and worked came to an end in New Hampshire.

The even balance between the two major parties was shattered by forces from without the state. The Democrats, held together for so long by the past glories of Jacksonianism, floundered on the reef of Bryanism. Even Isaac Hill's son, a recent nominee for governor, was unable to support Bryan, and more Democrats deserted their party in 1896 than had deserted with Charles Doe during the Nebraska controversy. It would be decades before the Democracy was to regain its strength, and by then the tradition of addressing the judges out of office would be dead. A new age of judicial independence was made possible by this last great rush to the Republican ranks. Other events in 1896 marked the passing of the society and culture which Charles Doe had known. In a New York music hall an audience watched the first short movie, and motoring began with the Turin-to-Asti road race. The cinema and the automobiles were destined to end the isolation of the Piscataqua valley region, destroying forever the tight, small Yankee world which Charles Doe had known, and loved, and served. It exists for us today only in history books and novels, the finest of which is Sarah Orne Jewett's *The Country of the Pointed Firs,* first published in that very year of 1896.

Miss Jewett had not hoped to write a classic; she sought only to capture a fading way of life. The ethos of that breed of men for whom Charles Doe spoke in the area of law would be forgotten in a generation or two unless one who loved them composed their epilogue. And so she had written *The Country of the Pointed Firs,* a gentle, heavy-hearted apologia for the little corner of the American continent which she shared with Charles Doe. Their world — the world of the Piscataqua valley — had seemed destined to last as an American version of such tradition-steeped rural cultures as Wiltshire or the Cotswolds: self-contained worlds of folklore and tradition, such as the new West would never know; though nestled next to one another, as different as Cornwall is from Devon or Brittany is from Normandy; more different than Oregon could ever be from Wisconsin or Arizona from Texas. The population was so static that a man's home could be guessed by his name: a Wiggin came from Chatham, a Gilman from Exeter, a Saltmarsh from Concord.

The Country of the Pointed Firs told of the people by whose houses the Chief Justice passed that March morning on the way to the railroad depot, traveling in the family democracy wagon, driven by the hired man. It was for these people that he had devoted thirty-four years to making and remaking law. The tree stumps in their front yards used for chopping wood, the granite hitching posts, the barrels of apples and flour in the kitchens, the smell of baking bread through open doors were the symbols of his world. It was a world of intangibles as well as tangibles; a mood as well as a set of mores; an atmosphere as well as a way of life. The rollicking, freewheeling world of Joseph Doe had given way to a world of enervated men and cautious women, of a rigid propriety which could honor an eccentric judge but could not cherish him. It was an age of muddy streets and blazing autumns, of small farms and dingy shops, of historical societies and pride in ancestors as the Irish moved out of the mills into the professions and the French came down from Canada into the mills. It was not that the rollicking, freewheeling element had died out of the Yankee race; it had merely moved westward, leaving the less adventurous at home to share a world which ended at Seabrook on the Massachusetts line. If Charles Doe could not feel at ease in Boston, neither could his neighbors, and with them, he must have often thought of those who, like two of his brothers, had gone west many years ago. In Owen Wister's novel *The Virginian* a lady of Doe's generation meets the protagonist, that lean and fabled prototype of a thousand Western movies, who had been brought East by her grandniece, the girl he will marry. "There he is," the old lady said, pointing to a family portrait. "New Hampshire was full of fine young men in those days. But nowadays most of them have gone away to seek their fortunes in the West. Do they find them, I wonder." [8]

Miss Jewett also wrote of those men of her youth — the older men who had seen a greater, wider world during the days when local ports still served the China trade; a world about which the young of the 1890s could only read.[9] The Yankee nation seemed on the defensive now, and as new values fostered by a less-challenging existence began to efface the heritage of sturdy independence, she mourned the passing of a way of life. She imagined and loved the old too well to hope that the future could be as bright. The people of her little world were in decline, and by 1896 they were nearing the bottom step. In an age in which not only did men desert farms for factories, but boys of ten went into the mills to labor a nine-hour day for six cents an hour, the pride and self-reliance of their ancestors was remembered by very few.

Some of the more enterprising young people went away to work in shops and factories; but the custom was by no means universal and the people had a hungry, discouraged look. It is all very well to say that they knew nothing better, that it was the only life of which they knew anything; there was too often a look of disappointment in their faces, and sooner or later we heard or guessed many stories: that this young man had wished for an education, but there had been no money to spare for books or schooling; and that one had meant to learn a trade, but there must be some one to help his father with the farm-work, and there was no money to hire a man to work in his place if he went away. The older people had a hard look, as if they had always to be on the alert and must fight for their place in the world. One could only forgive and pity their petty sharpness, which showed itself in trifling bargains, when one understood how much a single dollar seemed when dollars came so rarely.[10]

Charles Doe could only have smiled at her despair. For him change and progress had charms all their own. What alarmed Miss Jewett gave him hope. Far from seeing "a hard look" in the faces of the old, he would have noticed, as did Henry McFarland, more "cheerfulness and good humor." McFarland had been born a year after Doe, and looking back on the decade of their birth from the decade of their death, he thought the elderly of the 1890s happier than the elderly of the 1830s. "This may be ascribed to the fact that life was a more serious business then," he wrote, "the fruits of toil were less, there were fewer amusements and fewer books, political differences were more bitter, and the tone of preaching was more severe, less helpful and less hopeful." [11] As Charles Doe drove to the railroad station, he had every reason to be optimistic. Thirteen months earlier he had written to Wigmore explaining his faith in a better tomorrow. Looking back over his life, Doe had assured his friend that while the reformer's lot was lonely and hard, it had been worthwhile.

It seems certain that the world not only has not ceased to move, but moves perceptibly faster than it did in ancient times, or even 40 years ago. In the law, while an increase of speed may not be visible every year, I have persuaded myself that the increase is visible every decade. Judging from ancient & mediaeval history, interruptions & even long stoppages are to be expected; but we may be sure that progress is the rule; & the more thoroughly changes are considered, the wider the views, the more far-seeing the wisdom, & the stronger the spirit of candor & moderation, with which changes are proposed, the less fluctuating is the advance likely to be. Of the old men who have been engaged on both sides of the eternal battle, those drop out of the fray with the greater satisfaction who have cogent evidence that they have been, for the most part, on what has been & will forever be the winning side, because they do not doubt that, in the long run, the right side will prevail.[12]

On March 9, 1896, Charles Doe, while confident that he was on the winning side, was not quite ready to drop out of the fray. There was still another battle to be fought. In his carpet satchel he was carrying a fifty-page manuscript opinion in a case which he had originally assigned to another judge. It illustrated what he meant about change and progress. The legislature had recently passed a statute providing for trial before police courts of crimes previously triable only after indictment by a grand jury. There were no traverse juries in the police courts, but the statute permitted anyone who had pleaded not guilty and had been convicted to appeal to the trial term of the Supreme Court, where the defendant would be tried again, this time by a jury. Carpenter thought the statute unconstitutional, on the ground that it interfered with a defendant's right to jury trial. Doe thought it practical and progressive. It should be sustained on its merits alone, as he explained in a memorandum prepared for his own use.

With a police court in session six days of every week, & a grand jury in session one, two or three days, twice a year, an opportunity for a trial or a judgment on the plea of guilty in a police court might often be for a defendant an advantage of a very substantial character. There are not so many sea-faring men in the state as formerly, but the number of persons going out of the state on errands of business, & migration, intending not to return, or to be absent a considerable time, is very great, & the delay caused by the paucity of grand-jury sessions were liable to be harassing & oppressive. The mental anxiety or distress occasioned by the suspension of justice for months at a time, & nearly all the time, was a grievance in many cases not regarded as trifling by human minds. Men, women & minors, presumed by the law to be innocent before conviction, were held constantly, many of them for months together, in the destructive moral atmosphere of jails, awaiting a session of the grand jury. Ten jails in which the old & young, hardened offenders & youth beginning a downward course are herded together are ten schools of crime, a disgrace to our civilization, & one of the evils which the legislature endeavored to diminish by the introduction of a reform school. Awaiting the action of the grand jury to open the course of reformation, the young were shut up, for a session, with such criminals as could be collected in the county. Instruction in all the branches of criminal education taught by experts in this high school of vice was a requirement for admission to the college of reform. The legislature have attempted to dispense with this requirement in the cases of misdemeanor mentioned in the act of 1895. And if a youth & his parents, or an orphan & his friends desire that he be spared the preparatory course of degradation & ruin, the constitution does not force it upon him, but leaves the legislature at liberty to extend the beneficence of the act of 1895 to other cases in which a reformatory education is needed, in observance of "the principles of humanity" which the 83rd article of the constitution commands them to countenance & inculcate.[13]

This would be the last question into which Charles Doe would pour his reforming zeal. How fitting, therefore, that Alonzo P. Carpenter should oppose him. Of the seven votes on the Supreme Court four were on Carpenter's side. Only Judge Clark and Judge Wallace agreed with Doe. The Chief Justice needed at least one more to prevail, and his best chance lay with the liberal but cautious Frank Parsons, who had only recently been appointed to the bench. Doe had been working on him, hoping to change his mind. Parsons thought the statute unconstitutional because in 1784, the year in which the constitution had been adopted, in cases in which the penalty was more than forty shillings a defendant's "right to a jury trial was not invaded by a trial in a court that had no jury with an appeal to another court that had a jury." [14] Doe had found a liquor-control statute passed in 1778 which provided a fine of ten pounds for every offense and for trial before "any two justices of the peace" sitting without a jury. Coupling this with an act of 1718 which gave an appeal to "any person sentenced for any criminal offense by one or more justices of the peace," Doe had asked Parsons if he still thought the law being challenged was an unconstitutional innovation without

preconstitutional precedent.[15] "I am going to convince those gentlemen that they are *wrong*," Doe had said three days earlier, undoubtedly thinking of Parsons.[16]

Half a mile from the railroad station Doe got out of the wagon
and sent the hired man back to the house. Those who saw him
may have smiled — he was indulging another of his eccentricities
well known in the neighborhood. Had his health been good, he
would have walked all the way. But even when he was driven he
never had himself taken right to the depot door. He wanted to
arrive on foot like anyone else. When it came to riding to the
railroad station, even the democracy wagon was ostentatious.
While most thought his action odd and did not try to rationalize
it, a few decided that there must be a reason for his habit. Undoubtedly, they concluded, he was trying to set an example of
simplicity for the poor, as he did by leading a life without lux-
uries. It is more likely that Doe had no cognitive motive, at least
none which he could have explained. He was simply following the
course which left him feeling the least ill at ease socially.

When Doe entered the waiting room of the Rollinsford depot,
he nodded to one or two acquaintances. None came over to
strike up a conversation because it was evident that he was deep
in thought. Perhaps he was speculating on the urgency of the
day's business. While he was disturbed that his colleagues were
intent on ruling the act of 1895 unconstitutional, he was even
more annoyed that they seemed in no hurry to announce their
judgment. Two appeals were pending, *State* v. *Williams* and
State v. *Gerry,* and he wanted them to use the *Williams* case for
making at least a preliminary decision this term. "I understand
that the trials in police courts under the act of 1895 are numerous," he had warned, "& it is unfortunate that the entire constitutional question cannot be satisfactorily settled, one way or
the other, in March. If it must go over to June, it would be some
relief for parties to know what kinds of cases are covered by the
decision in *State* v. *Williams.* In this view, what do you all say
of the act of 1778? & what do you think had better be done in
March?" [17]

Charles Doe never learned what they thought should be done.
The station master, noticing "heavy, peculiar breathing," went
over to the bench where Doe was sitting to see if he was ill and

found him unconscious. Three doctors were called — one from Somersworth, one from the village of Salmon Falls, and the Doe family physician from South Berwick. There was nothing they could do; he had suffered a stroke of apoplexy. By 8:30 A.M. on the morning of March 9, 1896, the Chief Justice of New Hampshire was dead.[18]

When Joseph Doe had been a representative in the New Hampshire General Court, it had taken him eight hours to journey by stagecoach from Dover to Concord,[19] and news traveled just as slowly. Matters moved faster now. United States District Judge Edgar Aldrich was on a trip through the southwestern part of the country on March 9, 1896. Less than two hours after the event he read of Doe's death in a local newspaper.[20] By coincidence both John Henry Wigmore at Northwestern and Jeremiah Smith at Harvard were discussing Doe's opinions with their tort classes. Wigmore was dealing with the *Mink Case* and "descanting to my class on the greatness of the writer of that opinion." "His death," Smith wrote, "has taken hold of me as few other events could." [21]

Judge Carpenter was informed by telegram. He spoke of an "overpowering loss" but decided not to adjourn court. Candidates were waiting to take their examinations for admission to the bar, and other work had to be conducted.[22] Later there would be a memorial service, but a bench and bar which had learned from Doe that judicial business takes precedence over judicial ceremony did not stop to pay tribute to their greatest figure on the day of his death. Nor did Mrs. Doe think it fitting to have ceremony at his funeral. Following a private service, he was buried in a small rise of land overlooking a secluded bend in the Piscataqua. His son Ralph had thought it the most beautiful spot along the river, and after the boy was killed by a prairie fire in Nebraska, the judge had purchased it. Now, in a manner as simple as the life he had led, he was laid to rest beside his son.

Death may seem "astonishing and unnatural" in a city, Sarah Orne Jewett had written; in the country it is different. "The neighbors themselves are those who dig the grave and carry the dead, whom they or their friends have made ready, to the last resting-place." [23] There is no fuss. Surely there was none for Charles Doe. Few men had served New Hampshire as long or as well as he, yet few have been less honored. No streets or schools were ever named for him, not even in Dover or in Rollinsford. His portrait has never been hung in the chambers of the Supreme Court, although there are pictures of judges who served with far less distinction. A state which commemorates its minor political figures and its insipid poets has not seen fit to mark either Charles Doe's birthplace or the site of his home. There are few in the old neighborhood today who can tell you where he lived.

The newspapers spoke mostly of his eccentricity. The Boston *Journal* published a page of letters praising his accomplishments, but most editorials preferred to dwell on his love for fresh air rather than on his love for justice. "In his harness," the Boston *Globe's* headlines announced. "Apoplexy swiftly carries off Judge Doe — Famous New Hampshire jurist reaches his journey's end — Eminent in counsel and swift in decision — Presided at Notorious Almy and Sawtelle trials — Eccentric and quaint, but with a warm heart." [24] For his old enemy William Eaton Chandler "all asperities are softened" by death. Doe might have been amused had he read Chandler's words. "While many differed with him, none can gainsay his consummate ability and his masterful personality which even his marked eccentricities were unable to cloak and which have their abiding witness in the history of law in the last four decades." [25] Chandler knew what Doe's death meant, for he had known the influence of Doe's personality. Few outside the bar could sense the loss. *The Granite Monthly*, "A New Hampshire Magazine, devoted to History, Biography, Literature and State Progress," which professed to record the changing New Hampshire scene, gave little more than half a page to Doe's obituary. Shoe manufacturers and grocers, more in tune with current fashions, were given much more space. Perhaps the most revealing estimate of Doe's worth was given by the state historian in a book, *Some Things About New Hampshire.* He listed forty-five distinguished New Hampshire jurists and lawyers, including the general counsel of the Illinois Central Railroad. The name of Charles Cogswell Doe was not included.[26] And when Wigmore dedicated his treatise to Doe and Thayer, the *Harvard Law Review* was able to remark, "Most of Professor Thayer's pupils would probably place him before

Judge Doe in such a dedication." [27] While some may have noticed the slight, it is doubtful if many cared to protest.

Jeremiah Smith was the man who should have preserved
Doe's fame. But Mrs. Doe felt that her husband would have objected to a formal biography, and Smith therefore limited himself to a thirty-page memoir, which he read to the Southern
New Hampshire Bar Association. A decade later a sketch of
Doe's life was included in the eight-volume series, *Great American Lawyers*. It was a tribute of sorts, but since Professor Hening's evaluation of Doe's decisions was distinctly second-rate,
readers may have wondered why Doe was included at all.
Roscoe Pound was the man who salvaged Doe's fame and created the legend of the eccentric genius. Pound started the
process of enshrining him in American legal history in 1916,
when he wrote that Doe was the "one judge upon the bench of
a state court who stands out as a builder of the law since the
Civil War." [28] And later, in 1938, when Pound announced that
Doe was one of the ten greatest judges in American history, the
memory of the unassuming chief justice of New Hampshire became encased in a mythical hall of fame.[29] Men who were not
sure what Doe had done nevertheless accorded him the stature
of a giant. He became one of those familiar names, used by law
writers and legal historians as a point of comparison or as a means
of reference. Many who mentioned his greatness could not have
explained why his fame had outlasted that of all his contemporaries. Roscoe Pound's imprimatur was enough to warrant judicial immortality.[30]

Charles Doe would have cared little about posterity's evaluation. He had been motivated by a sense of duty, not by a desire
for personal distinction. He was the unselfish scholar, the dedicated public servant in the best and richest traditions of civilized
society. Of all the tributes paid in the hours following Doe's
death, that of his former law student, Alvin Burleigh, came the
closest to expressing the Chief Justice's own wish. Let his life's
work be his monument, Burleigh said.[31] It was all that Doe had
ever asked. But then, he might also have been pleased by something Jeremiah Smith wrote for the *Harvard Law Review*. "Until
his memory is forgotten," Smith said, "cases in New Hampshire

will be tried expeditiously and upon their merits; justice will not be 'strangled in a net of form'; and witnesses will not be subjected to insulting and abusive treatment at the hands of cross examiners." [32]

History, however, has provided no better epitaph than that written by Judge John Elliott Allen — "The law was his life" — or spoken by David Cross — "It may be said of him that he was born into the judgeship of New Hampshire, that he there lived and wrought and died." [33]

ACKNOWLEDGMENTS
NOTES   INDEX

ACKNOWLEDGMENTS

The task of writing a judicial biography is not unlike that faced by an advocate who argues a case before a jury. Evidence must be gathered and arguments presented, legal issues clarified and technicalities brushed aside. In preparing this, "The Case of Charles Doe," we had the help of many individuals and institutions. For providing us with the evidence which we used to build our "case," thanks are due to Stanley M. Burns and E. Paul Kelly of the New Hampshire Bar, to the staffs of the New Hampshire Historical Society, the Dartmouth College Library, the Harvard University Library, and to Mark DeWolfe Howe, the biographer of Oliver Wendell Holmes, and William Robert Roalfe, the biographer of John Henry Wigmore. And for a grant which permitted us the means and the time to discover this evidence and to write this book, we are indebted to the trustees of the William Nelson Cromwell Foundation. Among those who personally knew Charles Doe, Miss Molly Flynn, Mrs. Gardiner Grant, and Miss Elizabeth Frost, served as our "character witnesses." Edward J. Bloustein, President of Bennington College, and Norman Dorsen, Director of the Hays Civil Liberties Center, generously provided advice as "experts" for those chapters within their special competence. Among the periodicals which published our arguments in the form of articles or "briefs," and thus permitted us to strengthen the case immeasurably, were the *American Journal of Legal History*, the *Boston University Law Review*, the *Columbia Law Review*, the *Dartmouth Alumni Magazine*, the *Journal of Legal Education*, the *New Hampshire Bar Journal*, the *New York University Law Review*, the *Northwestern University Law Review*, the *University of Pittsburgh Law Review*, the *Vanderbilt Law Review*, the *Villanova Law Review*, the *Virginia Law Review*, the *Washington University Law Quarterly*, and the *Wayne Law Review*. To each we acknowledge permission to reprint copyrighted material. Miss Gloria Yannantuono, who worked on the manuscript, and Teresa Reid, my mother, who prepared a sketch of Judge Doe, may be said to have furnished the "exhibits" for this litigation. Roy Liebman, Esq., of the New York Bar, checked our authorities. Professor William G. Hennessey, Professor Philip M. Marston, and Dr. John T. Holden served as "referees" at a preliminary hearing when they constituted the board which accepted the arguments presented in chapter five of this book in partial fulfilment of the requirements for the degree of Master of Arts at the University of New Hampshire. Finally, special thanks are due to Chancellor Russell D. Niles, of New York University, who may be said to have presided over the "equity" side of our case, and to Chief Justice Frank R. Kenison, of the New Hampshire Supreme Court, who presided over the "legal" side. Without the encouragement and active support of Judge Kenison, this biography of Charles Doe could not have been written.

John Phillip Reid

Vanderbilt Hall
Washington Square
August 30, 1966

NOTES

Chapter One. A Race of Yankees: *Ancestors*

1. Sybil Noyes, C. T. Libby, and W. G. Davis, *Genealogical Dictionary of Maine and New Hampshire* 197 (1928–1939).

2. 3 Rockingham County Records, Registry of Deeds 95a.

3. 1 Court Records in New Hampshire [40 New Hampshire State Papers] 348, 358 and 385 (Hammond ed. 1943); Charles B. Kinney, *Church & State: The Struggle For Separation in New Hampshire, 1630–1900* 17–18, 59–60 (1955).

4. Edwin D. Sanborn, *History of New Hampshire from Its First Discovery to the Year 1830* 93 (1875).

5. *Hale v. Everett*, 53 N.H. 9, 53 (1868); ibid. 193 (dissenting opinion).

6. Ibid. 200 (dissenting opinion).

7. Ibid. 193, 171 (dissenting opinion).

8. James Hill Fitts, *The History of Newfields, New Hampshire* 49 (1912); 7 Rockingham County Records, Registry Deeds 378; Worcester, "Early Colonial Laws of New Hampshire — No. II," 3 *Granite Monthly* 468, 470 (1880); *Piper v. Piper*, 60 N.H. 98 (1880).

9. Mary P. Thompson, *Landmarks in Ancient Dover, New Hampshire* 120 (1892); 8 Rockingham County Records, Registry of Deeds 241 (July 6, 1711); 5 Rockingham County Records, Registry of Probate 357 (June 8, 1714); ibid. 356 (June 14, 1714).

10. Elmer Doe, *The Descendants of Nicholas Doe* 139 (1917); Titus, "The Wedding in ye Days Lang Syne," 8 *Granite Monthly* 90, 91 (1885); 25 Rockingham Records, Registry of Deeds 249; 17 ibid. 156.

11. Elmer Doe, supra note 10, 144.

12. 34 Rockingham County Records, Registry of Deeds 65. See e.g. 39 ibid. 246 and 105 ibid. 274 and compare 28 ibid. 511 to 41 ibid. 163; Elmer Doe, supra note 10, 144; James Hill Fitts, supra note 8, 90, 105.

13. 107 Rockingham County Records, Registry of Deeds 468. See also 108 ibid. 121, 123; 29 ibid. 447; 30 ibid. 370.

14. Charles P. Whittemore, *A General of the Revolution: John Sullivan of New Hampshire* 3–5 (1961).

15. Compare Esther Forbes, *Paul Revere and the World He Lived In* 231–33 (1942) to Page, "The King's Powder, 1774," 18 *New England Q.* 83 (1945); Clough, "Colonel Alexander Scammell," 14 *Granite Monthly* 262, 264 (1892).

16. Nellie Palmer George, *Old New Market, New Hampshire: Historical Sketches* 38 (1932); James Hill Fitts, supra note 8, 242.

17. See below 231.

18. James Hill Fitts, supra note 8, 134, 105, 236, 243–44, and 252.

Chapter Two. Rout of the Doe-Faces: *Father*

1. Nellie Palmer George, *Old New Market, New Hampshire: Historical Sketches* 30, 41 (1932); Edwin D. Sanborn, *History of New Hampshire From Its First Discovery To The Year 1830* 234–36 (1875); William Plumer, Jr., *Life of William Plumer* 67, 75 (1857).

2. Batchelder, "Ancient Church Lore of New England", 12 *Granite Monthly* 296, 297 (1889); James Hill Fitts, *The History of Newfields, New Hampshire* 134, 313 (1912); Nellie Palmer George, supra note 1, 23; Folder 9629, Rockingham County Probate Records: 44 Rockingham County Records, Registry of Probate 285–86; Old Series Folder 6506, Rockingham County Probate Records.

3. Edwin D. Sanborn, supra note 1, 251, 264.

4. Quint, "Memorial Address", *The First Parish in Dover, New Hampshire* 11, 43 (Alonzo H. Quint ed. 1884).

5. Anon., *Biography of Isaac Hill of New Hampshire* 44 (1835).

6. Charles B. Kinney, *Church & State: The Struggle For Separation in New Hampshire, 1630–1900* 103 (1955).

7. George Barstow, *The History of New Hampshire, From Its Discovery, in 1614, to the Passage of the Toleration Act in 1819* 441 (2d ed. 1853).

8. *New Hampshire Patriot & State Gazette* (Concord), March 11, 1822 (hereinafter cited as *Patriot*).

9. *Journal of the House of Representatives of the State of New Hampshire, June Session, 1824* 34 (1824); *Patriot*, Nov. 29, 1824.

10. G. J. Chark, *Memoirs of Jeremiah Mason* 150–51 (1917).

11. *Stafford Register*, July 30, 1822; ibid., Aug. 12, 1822.

12. *Patriot*, Feb. 14, 1825; ibid., March 7, 1825.

13. Letter From Joseph Doe to Nathaniel Haven, Jan. 19, 1825, in *Patriot*, Jan. 31, 1825.

14. *Patriot*, March 7, 1825 ["extra"].

15. Ibid., Feb. 28, 1825.

16. Ibid., Jan. 10, 1825.

17. Ibid., March 14, 1825; ibid., June 6, 1825.

18. Elmer Doe, *The Descendants of Nicholas Doe* 182 (1917); 103 Strafford County Registry of Deeds 124.

19. *Journal . . . ,* supra note 9, 209.

20. *Patriot*, June 16, 1823; ibid., Dec. 13, 1824; ibid., Dec. 20, 1824; ibid., Dec. 27, 1824.

21. Ibid., July 10, 1826.

22. Ibid., July 26, 1826.

23. *Dover Gazette & Stafford Advertiser*, July 4, 1826 (hereinafter referred to as *Gazette*); *Patriot*, July 3, 1826.

24. *Patriot*, July 10, 1826.

25. Jeremiah Smith, *Memoir of Hon. Charles Doe* 4–5 (1897); Smith, "Memoir of Charles Doe," 2 *N.H. Bar Ass'n Proc.* 125, 126–27 (1897).

26. F. E. Robinson, *Isaac Hill* 83 (unpublished master's thesis, University of New Hampshire, 1933).

27. *Patriot*, July 10, 1826.

28. Portsmouth *Journal*, July 8, 1826; *Strafford Inquirer* (Dover), June

24, 1828; *The Times & Dover Enquirer*, Dec. 30, 1828; *Patriot*, Dec. 8, 1828; ibid., Jan. 5, 1829; *The Times & Dover Enquirer*, Jan. 6, 1829.

29. *Patriot*, Jan. 29, 1827; ibid., Oct. 29, 1827.

30. *The Times & Dover Enquirer*, Jan. 20, 1829.

31. *Gazette*, March 3, 1860.

Chapter Three. The Barbaric Course: *Education*

1. 2 F. B. Sanborn, *Recollections of Seventy Years* 579–80 (1909); Sanborn, "Ellery Channing in New Hampshire", 32 *Granite Monthly* 157 (1902).

2. Sanborn, "Book Review", Exeter (N.H.) *News-Letter*, Feb. 18, 1910.

3. Compare 248 Rockingham County Records, Registry of Deeds 157–60; 250 ibid. 238 and 330; 261 ibid. 465; 262 ibid. 49 and 178–79; 265 ibid. 191; 278 ibid. 269; 32 ibid. 96.

4. *Reminiscences of Henry Clay Barnabee* 38 (George Leon Varney ed. 1913).

5. John Hayward, *A Gazetteer of New Hampshire* 128 (1849).

6. *History of York County* 318–19 (Everts & Peck, 1880); Jewett, "The Old Town of Berwick", 10 *New England Mag.* 597, 604–05 (1894).

7. Pike, "President's Address — Memories of Judge Doe", 3 *N.H. Bar Ass'n Proc.* 463, 483 (1916).

8. Jewett, supra note 6, 603.

9. Ibid.

10. *The Centennial History of the Harvard Law School 1817–1917* 225 (1918).

11. *Record of Phillips Exeter Academy, 1822* (mss. Davis Library); *Catalogue of the Officers and Students of Phillips Exeter Academy for the Academy Year, 1843–4* (1844).

12. 1 Claude Moore Fuess, *Daniel Webster* 33–34 (1930).

13. Frank B. Woodford, *Lewis Cass: The Last Jeffersonian* 14 (1950).

14. Charles H. Bell, *Phillips Exeter Academy in New Hampshire: A Historical Sketch* 56 (1883).

15. Laurence M. Crosbie, *The Phillips Exeter Academy: A History* 95 (1924).

16. Percey C. Rogers, *History of the Phillips Exeter Academy* 29 (type-written mss. N.H. State Library, Concord); Laurence M. Crosbie, supra note 15, 98; Claude M. Fuess, *An Old New England School: A History of Phillips Academy Andover* 308 (1917).

17. 5 Cush. 295, 5 Am. Dec. 711 (Mass. 1850).

18. 1 George F. Hoar, *Autobiography of Seventy Years* 89 (1903).

19. Theron G. Strong, *Joseph H. Choate* 21 (1917).

20. Charles A. Warner, *Harvard: Four Centuries and Freedoms* 114 (1950); Samuel Eliot Morison, *Three Centuries of Harvard* 275–87 (1936).

21. Quoted in Mark DeWolfe Howe, *Oliver Wendell Holmes: The Shaping Years* 68–69 (1957).

22. Letter From Joseph Doe to Edward Everett, Aug. 22, 1846, Harvard Coll. Archives.

23. Leon Burr Richardson, *History of Dartmouth College* 458 (1932).

24. Ibid. at 472–75.

25. Letter From Charles Doe to Frederick Chase, Dec. 14, 1889, Dartmouth Coll. Archives, Mss. 889664.

26. Letter From Charles Doe to Fletcher Ladd, June 20, 1886, Dartmouth Coll. Archives, Mss. 884370.

27. Hall, "Charles Doe," 2 *Proc. So. N.H. Bar Ass'n* 84 (1896).

28. Jeremiah Smith, *Memoir of Hon. Charles Doe* 4 (1897); Smith, "Memoir of Charles Doe," 2 *Proc. So. N.H. Bar Ass'n* 125, 126 (1897).

29. Hall, supra note 27, 84.

30. Allen, "Charles Doe, 1849," 13 *Dartmouth Alumni Mag.* 283 (1921).

31. Jeremiah Smith, supra note 28, 4; Smith, supra note 28, 126.

32. "Charles Doe," 20 *Granite Monthly* 275 (1896); Concord (N.H.) *Evening Monitor,* March 9, 1896.

33. 17 *The Dartmouth* 122–23 (Nov. 1, 1895).

34. Letter From Charles Doe to John Major Shirley, n.d., Doe Papers, N.H. Sup. Ct.

35. Reid, "The Touch of History: The Historical Method of a Common Law Judge," 8 *Am. J. Legal Hist.* 157 (1964).

36. Henry McFarland, *Sixty Years in Concord and Elsewhere: Personal Recollections* 20 (1899).

37. 1 Alexander V. G. Allen, *Life and Letters of Phillips Brooks* 86–88 (1900).

Chapter Four. Joe Doe—Educated: *At the Bar*

1. William Plumer, Jr., *Life of William Plumer* 60 (1859).

2. Smith, "Charles H. Bell," in Charles H. Bell, *The Bench and Bar of New Hampshire* xii (1894).

3. Sargent, "Joel Parker," in *Memorials of Judges Recently Deceased, Graduates of Dartmouth College* 88 (1881).

4. Elmer E. Doe, *The Descendants of Nicholas Doe* 182 (1917); *Strafford Register* (Dover), June 4, 1822; 44 Rockingham County Records, Registry of Probate 273; 113 Strafford County Records, Registry of Probate 339; Baer, "The Ricker Inn: Home of the Late Chief Justice Doe and Family," 61 *Granite Monthly* 160, 162 (1929).

5. Jeremiah Smith, *Memoir of Hon. Charles Doe* 5 (1897); Smith "Memoir of Charles Doe," 2 *Proc. So. N.H. Bar Ass'n* 125, 127 (1897); Beale, "Jeremiah Smith," 35 *Harv. L. Rev.* 1, 2 (1921).

6. Daniel Hall, *Addresses Commemorative of Abraham Lincoln and John P. Hale* 149 (1892).

7. Hall, "Daniel Christie," 1 *Granite Monthly* 35, 39–40 (1877).

8. Pike, "President's Address: Memories of Judge Doe," 3 *N.H. Bar Ass'n Proc.* 463, 465 (1916); Smith, Obituary Note, 9 *Harv. L. Rev.* 534 (1896); Reid, "Doe Did Not Sit: The Creation of Opinions by an Artist," 63 *Colum. L. Rev.* 59, 64 (1963); Luce, "President's Address: Early Makers of New Hampshire Common Law," 5 *N.H. Bar Ass'n Proc.* 5, 23 (1925).

9. Smith, "Annual Address," 1 *Proc. So. N.H. Bar Ass'n* 57, 59–60 (1892); D. Hamilton Hurd, *History of Rockingham and Strafford Counties, New Hampshire* 590 (1882); *Dover Gazette & Strafford Advertiser,* Dec.

27, 1851 (hereinafter cited as *Gazette*); Pike, supra note 8, 465; Charles H. Bell, supra note 2, 259–62.

10. Jeremiah Smith, supra note 5, 5; Smith, supra note 5, 127.

11. Ibid.

12. Hall, "Charles Doe," 2 *Proc. So. N.H. Bar Ass'n* 84 (1896)

13. Exeter (N.H.) *News-Letter,* Feb. 18, 1910.

14. Joel Parker, *The Law School of Harvard College* 3–4 (1871); Letter from William Eaton Chandler to His Parents, March 13, 1853, Chandler Coll., N.H. Hist. Soc'y; Batchelder, "Old Times at the Law School," 90 *Atlantic Monthly* 642, 653 (Nov. 1902); *A Catalogue of the Officers and Students of Harvard University for the Academic Year 1853–54: First Term* 58 (1853).

15. *The Centennial History of the Harvard Law School, 1817–1917* 20 (1918); William E. Chandler, *Address Before the Grafton and Coös Bar Association* 10 (1888); 2 Charles Warren, *History of the Harvard Law School* 123–25 (1908).

16. G. S. H., *Joel Parker* 28 (1876).

17. Batchelder, supra note 14, 649.

18. Theron G. Strong, *Joseph H. Choate* 22 (1917).

19. 2 Charles Warren, supra note 15, 182.

20. *Britton v. Turner,* 6 N.H. 481 (1834).

21. *Delano's Case,* 58 N.H. 5, 6 (1876).

22. A. J. Collidge and J. B. Mansfield, *History and Description of New England: New Hampshire* 474 (1860).

23. *Gazette,* Oct. 7, 1854.

24. Jeremiah Smith, supra note 5, 8; Smith, supra note 5, 130.

25. *Gazette,* March 2, 1855.

26. Jeremiah Smith, supra note 5, 7; Smith, supra note 5, 129.

27. *Journal of the Honorable House of Representatives of the State of New Hampshire,* June Session 1855, 452–59.

28. See *Gazette,* Nov. 14, 1857; Obituary Note, 2 *Granite Monthly* 275 (1896).

29. *Gazette,* Dec. 3, 1839.

30. John Scales, *History of Strafford County New Hampshire and Representative Citizens* 32, 39–40 (1914).

31. *The New Hampshire Annual Register* 28 (1855).

32. *Gazette,* July 8, 1954; ibid. July 7, 1855; *Dover Enquirer,* July 10, 1856.

33. Charles H. Bell, supra note 2, 763.

34. 1 Claude Moore Fuess, *Daniel Webster* 86 (1930).

35. Sargent, supra note 3, 87–88.

36. *Gazette,* May 28, 1853.

37. William Plumer, Jr., supra note 1, 237–38.

38. John Lord Hayes, *A Filial Tribute to the Memory of William Allen Hayes of South Berwick, Maine* 12 (1886).

39. Will M. Cressy and James Clarence Harvey, *The Hills O' Hampshire* 243 (1913).

40. Hening, "Charles Doe," 8 *Great American Lawyers* 241, 245 n. 3 (W. D. Lewis ed. 1909); *State v. Gove and Wife,* 34 N.H. 510 (1857).

41. Jeremiah Smith, supra note 5, 6; Smith, supra note 5, 128.

42. *Kingman v. Judge of Probate*, 31 N.H. 171 (1855).

43. Jeremiah Smith, supra note 5, 6; Smith, supra note 5, 128.

44. Hening, supra note 40, 246 n. 4.

45. Hall, supra note 12, 84.

Chapter Five. Swallowing Himself: *Politics*

1. For a more detailed discussion of the material in this chapter see John Reid, *The Political Affiliations of Charles Doe During the Ordeal of the Union* (Ms. Master's Thesis, Univ. of New Hampshire, 1957).

2. Roy Franklin Nicholas, *Franklin Pierce: Young Hickory of the Granite Hills* 119 (1931); James O. Lyford, *Life of Edward H. Rollins: A Political Biography* 11–18, 79–80, 504–07 (1906).

3. *Dover Gazette and Strafford Advertiser*, June 18, 1853 (hereinafter cited as *Gazette*); ibid., Feb. 3, 1855; Pike, "President's Address: Memories of Judge Doe," 3 *N.H. Bar Ass'n Proc.* 463, 466 (1916).

4. *The Daily Patriot* (Concord), Dec. 19, 1850.

5. John Lord Hayes, *Remarks Made at a Democratic Meeting in Portsmouth on the 7th of January 1845 in Defense of the Course of John P. Hale Member of Congress From New Hampshire in Relation to The Annexation of Texas* 4 (no imprint); *Exeter News-Letter and Rockingham Advertiser*, Jan. 20, 1845 (hereinafter cited as *News-Letter*); *News-Letter*, Jan. 27, 1845, p. 2, col. 3; Ela, "Hon. John P. Hale," 3 *Granite Monthly* 404 (1880); *News-Letter*, Feb. 17, 1845, p. 2, col. 3.

6. Jeremiah Smith, *Memoir of Hon. Charles Doe* 8 (1887); Smith, "Memoir of Charles Doe," 2 *So. N.H. Bar Ass'n Proc.* 125, 130 (1897); *Gazette*, June 18, 1853, p. 2, col. 2.

7. *Gazette*, May 27, 1854, p. 3, vol. 4; ibid., June 10, 1854, p. 3, col. 3.

8. Dudley P. Fraiser, *The Antecedents and Formation of the Republican Party in New Hampshire* 44 (Ms. Thesis, Harvard University, 1945).

9. Letter From Charles Doe to J. Stevens, Sept. 27, 1856, Doe Collection, N.H. Hist. Soc'y.

10. Ibid.

11. Pike, supra note 3, 466.

12. Letter From Charles Doe to John H. George, Feb. 28, 1858, George Coll., N.H. Hist. Soc'y.

13. Jeremiah Smith, supra note 6, 10; Smith, supra note 6, 132.

14. Letter From Charles Doe to Charles Marseilles, April 2, 1872, Marseilles Coll., N.H. Hist. Soc'y.

15. Letter From Charles Doe to John Major Shirley, n.d., Doe Papers, N.H. Sup. Ct.

16. Jeremiah Smith, supra note 6, 10; Smith, supra note 6, 132.

17. Quoted in *The Daily Chronicle*, Feb. 1, 1859.

18. *Portsmouth Journal of Literature and Politics*, Feb. 5, 1859 (hereinafter cited as *Journal*).

19. *Gazette*, Feb. 19, 1859.

20. *The Independent Democrat* (Concord), Feb. 3, 1859.

21. *Journal*, Feb. 5, 1859.

22. The Dover *Enquirer*, Feb. 24, 1859 (hereinafter cited as *Enquirer*).

23. Ibid., Feb. 10, 1859.

24. *Gazette,* Feb. 12, 1859.
25. *News-Letter,* Feb. 14, 1859.
26. Pike, supra note 3, 466.
27. *Gazette,* March 5, 1859 (Letter to the Editor).
28. *Enquirer,* Feb. 17, 1859 (Letter to the Editor).
29. Ibid.
30. *Gazette,* Feb. 19, 1859.
31. *Enquirer,* Feb. 17, 1859.
32. The *New Hampshire Statesman,* Feb. 26, 1859.
33. Ibid.
34. *Gazette,* Feb. 19, 1859.
35. *The Independent Democrat,* Feb. 17, 1859.
36. *Gazette,* Feb. 19, 1859.
37. *Enquirer,* Feb. 17, 1859; *Gazette,* Feb. 26, 1859.
38. See ibid., Feb. 26, 1859; *The Independent Democrat,* Feb. 24, 1859.
39. *Dollar Daily Mirror* (Manchester), March 9, 1859.
40. *New Hampshire Patriot & State Gazette* (Concord), March 9, 1859.
41. *Enquirer,* March 17, 1859.
42. *Journal,* March 19, 1859.
43. *The Independent Democrat,* March 10, 1859.
44. *The Union Democrat* (Manchester), March 15, 1859.
45. Hall, "Charles Doe," 2 *Proc. N.H. Bar Ass'n* 85 (1896).
46. Jeremiah Smith, supra note 6, 10; Smith, supra note 6, 132.

Chapter Six. Entirely According to Doe: *Trial Judge*

1. *Enquirer,* May 26, 1859.
2. Portsmouth *Journal,* Sept. 3, 1859.
3. *Enquirer,* Aug. 4, 1859.
4. Ibid., Aug. 25, 1859; Portsmouth *Journal,* Aug. 27, 1859.
5. Manchester *Daily Mirror,* Aug. 10, 1859.
6. Pike, "President's Address — Memories of Judge Doe," 3 *N.H. Bar Ass'n Proc.* 463, 467 (1916); Great Falls *Advertiser,* Oct. 1, 1859.
7. See, *Enquirer,* Sept. 29, 1859; Great Falls *Advertiser,* Oct. 1, 1859.
8. *The Union Democrat* (Manchester), Sept. 27, 1859.
9. *Gazette,* Sept. 24, 1859.
10. *New Hampshire Patriot & State Gazette* (Concord), Sept. 28, 1859.
11. *Dollar Daily Mirror* (Manchester), Oct. 1, 1859.
12. Letter From Charles Doe to John Major Shirley, n.d., Doe Papers, N.H. Sup. Ct.
13. Great Falls *Advertiser,* Oct. 1, 1859.
14. Hening, "Charles Doe," 8 *Great American Lawyers* 241, 307 (W. D. Lewis ed. 1909).
15. Quoted in Portsmouth *Journal,* Dec. 10, 1859.
16. *Enquirer,* Nov. 24, 1859; see also ibid., Dec. 1, 1859.
17. Allen, "Charles Doe, 1849," 13 *Dartmouth Alumni Mag.* 283, 284 (1921).
18. Eastman, "Chief-Justice Charles Doe," 9 *Green Bag* 245, 248 (1897); Boston *Evening Globe,* Dec. 16, 1890.
19. 2 Hobart Pillsbury, *New Hampshire Resources, Attractions and Its*

People: A History 581 (1927); James O. Lyford, *Life of Edward H. Rollins* 344 (1906).

20. Eastman, supra note 18, 248.
21. Nashua (N.H.) *Telegraph*, Dec. 18, 1890 and Dec. 19, 1890.
22. Boston *Journal*, Dec. 22, 1890.
23. Boston *Daily Globe*, Dec. 19, 1890.
24. Pike, supra note 6, 470.
25. Ibid.; Eastman, supra note 18, 250.
26. Pike, supra note 6, 471.
27. See e.g. the Great Falls *Free Press*, Dec. 19, 1890.
28. Pike, supra note 6, 471–72.
29. Clark, "Charles Doe," 2 *Proc. So. N.H. Bar Ass'n* 105 (1896).
30. Parsons, "Address," 3 *N.H. Bar Ass'n Proc.* 209 (1912).
31. Pike, supra note 6, 467.
32. Ibid. 467–68; Eastman, supra note 18, 247.
33. Pike, ibid.; Eastman, ibid.; Jeremiah Smith, *Memoir of Hon. Charles Doe*, 12–13 (1897); Smith, "Memoir of Charles Doe," 2 *Proc. So. N.H. Bar Ass'n* 125, 134–35 (1897).
34. Jeremiah Smith, supra note 33, 12–14; Smith, supra note 33, 134–36; Eastman, supra note 18, 247.
35. Jeremiah Smith, supra note 33, 17; Smith, supra note 33, 139.
36. Eastman, supra note 18, 248.
37. Ibid. 248–49.
38. Jeremiah Smith, supra note 33, 15–16; Smith, supra note 33, 137–38.
39. Jeremiah Smith, supra note 33, 16; Smith, supra note 33, 138.
40. Eastman, supra note 18, 250.
41. Reid, "Almost a Hobby," 49 *Vir. L. Rev.* 58, 65–66 (1963).
42. Boston *Daily Globe*, Dec. 21, 1890.
43. Pike, supra note 6, 446.
44. Plymouth (N.H.) *Record*, Nov. 21, 1891.
45. Ibid. See also Dover *Enquirer*, *Nov.* 20, 1891; Boston *Evening Record* quoted in Concord *Evening Monitor*, Nov. 23, 1891.
46. Jeremiah Smith, supra note 33, 14; Smith, supra note 33, 136.
47. Jeremiah Smith, ibid., 15; Smith, ibid., 137.
48. Exeter (N.H.) *News-Letter*, Feb. 18, 1910.
49. Jeremiah Smith, supra note 33, 15; Smith, supra note 33, 137.
50. Frink, "Reminiscences of the Rockingham Bar," 2 *N.H. Bar Ass'n Proc.* 45, 61 (1904).
51. Letter From Charles Doe to Harry Hibbard, Sept. 29, 1870, Doe Coll., N.H. Hist. Soc'y.
52. Cross, "Charles Doe," 2 *Proc. So. N.H. Bar Ass'n* 94 (1896).
53. Letters From Charles Doe to Harry Hibbard, Sept. 29, 1870 and Sept. 26, 1870, Doe Coll., N.H. Hist. Soc'y.
54. Letter From Charles Doe to Charles Marseilles, Dec. 26, 1876, Marseilles Coll., N.H. Hist. Soc'y.
55. Luce, "President's Address — Early Makers of New Hampshire Common Law," 5 (No. 3) *N.H. Bar Ass'n Proc.* 5, 22 (1925).

Chapter Seven. New-Modelling the Forms: *Civil Procedure*

1. William Plumer, Jr., *Life of William Plumer* 154 (1857).

2. Batchellor, "The Development of the Courts of New Hampshire," 4 William Thomas Davis, *The New England States* 2295, 2306 (1897); Cross, "The President's Address," 1 *Pub. So. N.H. Bar Ass'n* 31, 36 (1895).

3. John Morison, *Life of Hon. Jeremiah Smith, LL.D.* 174–76 (1845).

4. Eastman, "Chief-Justice Charles Doe," 9 *Green Bag* 245, 246 (1897); Shirley, "Practice," 5 *Granite Monthly* 150, 154 (1882).

5. *Dalton v. Favour*, 3 N.H. 465 (1826).

6. *McDuffee v. Portland & Rochester R.R.*, 52 N.H. 430, 459 (1873); *Lisbon v. Lyman*, 49 N.H. 553, 595 (1870); *Walker v. Walker*, 63 N.H. 321, 328 (1885).

7. *Boody v. Watson*, 64 N.H. 162, 182, 9 Atl. 794, 809 (1886); *Edes v. Boardman*, 58 N.H. 580, 590 (1879).

8. *Brooks v. Howison*, 63 N.H. 382, 388 (1885); *Metcalf v. Gilmore*, 59 N.H. 417, 434 (1879); *Owen v. Weston*, 63 N.H. 599, 602, 4 Atl. 801 (1885); *Lisbon v. Lyman*, 49 N.H. 553, 589 (1870).

9. Eastman, supra note 4, 246.

10. Hening, "Charles Doe," 8 *Great American Lawyers* 241, 250–51 (W. D. Lewis ed. 1909).

11. *Brown v. Leavitt*, 52 N.H. 619 (1873).

12. *Stebbins v. Lancashire Ins. Co.*, 59 N.H. 143 (1879).

13. *Gamsby v. Ryan*, 52 N.H. 513, 517 (1872).

14. *Boody v. Watson*, 64 N.H. 162, 171–72, 9 Atl. 794, 802 (1886); *Owen v. Weston*, 63 N.H. 599, 603, 4 Atl. 801 (1885); *Metcalf v. Gilmore*, 59 N.H. 417, 434 (1879); *McKean v. Cutler*, 48 N.H. 370, 376 (1869).

15. *Morgan v. Joyce*, 66 N.H. 476 (1891).

16. *Crawford v. Parsons*, 63 N.H. 438 (1885).

17. *Owen v. Weston*, 63 N.H. 599, 603, 4 Atl. 801 (1885).

18. *Cole v. Gilford*, 63 N.H. 60 (1884); *Foster v. Foster*, 62 N.H. 532 (1883); *Hazen v. Quimby*, 61 N.H. 76 (1881).

19. *Lane v. Barron*, 64 N.H. 277 (1886).

20. *Elsher v. Hughes*, 60 N.H. 469 (1881). See also *Lyons v. Child*, 61 N.H. 73 (1881).

21. *Gagnon v. Connor*, 64 N.H. 276 (1886).

22. *Boody v. Watson*, 64 N.H. 162, 9 Atl. 794 (1886).

23. *Merrill v. Perkins*, 59 N.H. 343 (1879); 1 Richard H. Field and Benjamin Kaplan, *Materials for an Elementary Course in Civil Procedure* 254 (Temp. ed. 1952).

24. *Metcalf v. Gilmore*, 59 N.H. 417 (1879); Hening, supra note 10, 255–56.

25. Eastman, supra note 4, 246; Hening, supra note 10, 257; *Haverhill Iron Works v. Hale*, 64 N.H. 406 (1887); *Brooks v. Howison*, 63 N.H. 382, 389 (1885); *Sleeper v. Kelley*, 65 N.H. 206 (1889).

26. *Crawford v. Parsons*, 63 N.H. 438 (1885); Parsons, "The President's Address," 3 *N.H. Bar Ass'n Proc.* 209, 213 (1912).

27. *Brooks v. Howison*, 63 N.H. 382 (1885); *Cole v. Gilford*, 63 N.H. 60 (1884); *Chauncy v. German American Ins. Co.*, 60 N.H. 428 (1881).

28. *Hickey v. Dole*, 66 N.H. 336 (1890); *Sargent v. Sanborn*, 66 N.H. 30 (1889); *Owen v. Weston*, 63 N.H. 599, 604, 4 Atl. 801 (1885); *Sanborn v. Randall*, 62 N.H. 620 (1883).

29. *Cole v. Colburn,* 61 N.H. 499, 500 (1881). See also *Dearborn v. Nelson,* 61 N.H. 249 (1881).

30. *Rutherford v. Whitcher,* 60 N.H. 110 (1880); *Strafford v. Welch,* 59 N.H. 46 (1879).

31. *Webster v. Hall,* 60 N.H. 7 (1880).

32. *Dearborn v. Newhall,* 63 N.H. 301 (1885).

33. Scott, "The Progress of the Law — Civil Procedure," 33 *Harv. L. Rev.* 236, 248 (1918); *Lisbon v. Lyman,* 49 N.H. 553, 600 (1870).

34. Quoted in Cross, supra note 2, 34–5.

35. *Attorney-General v. Taggart,* 66 N.H. 362, 369, 29 Atl. 1027, 1031 (1890).

36. *Boody v. Watson,* 64 N.H. 162, 172, 9 Atl. 794, 802 (1886).

37. Jeremiah Smith, *Memoir of Hon. Charles Doe* 22 (1897); Smith, "Memoir of Charles Doe," 2 *So. N.H. Bar Ass'n Proc.* 125, 144 (1897). See also, Smith, Obituary Notice, 9 *Harv. L. Rev.* 534, 535 (1896); Eastman, supra note 4, 246.

38. Roscoe Pound, *Interpretations of Legal History* 139 (1930); Note, "Doe of New Hampshire: Reflections on a Nineteenth Century Judge," 63 *Harv. L. Rev.* 513, 515 (1950). See also Medina, "Judges as Leaders in Improving the Administration of Justice," 36 *J. Am. Jud. Soc.* 6, 8 (1952).

39. Quoted in Parsons, supra note 26, 211.

40. Willingham, "Georgia's Constitution of 1877 as Relates to the Judiciary: Some Comparisons with Other States and Some Proposed Changes," 30 *Report Ga. Bar Ass'n* 145, 149 (1913).

41. Arthur T. Vanderbilt, *Men and Measures in the Law* 99–100 (1949).

42. Arthur T. Vanderbilt, *The Challenge of Law Reform* 53 (1955).

43. *Metcalf v. Gilmore,* 59 N.H. 417, 434 (1879).

44. Parsons, supra note 26, 212.

45. Hening, supra note 10, 256.

46. Ibid. 261.

47. Parsons, supra note 26, 214.

48. *Concord Manufacturing Co. v. Robertson,* 66 N.H. 1, 23, 25, Atl. 718, 729 (1889).

49. *Lebanon Savings Bank v. Waterman,* 65 N.H. 88 (1888); *North Haverhill Water Co. v. Metcalf,* 63 N.H. 427 (1885); *School District v. Selectmen,* 63 N.H. 277 (1884); *Bergeron v. Dartmouth Savings Bank,* 63 N.H. 195 (1884).

50. *Winnipiseogee Paper Co. v. Eaton,* 64 N.H. 234 (1886).

51. Cross, supra note 2, 38.

52. Fuller, "General Sullivan as a Lawyer and a Judge," 1 *N.H. Bar Ass'n Proc.* 601, 607 (1902).

53. William Plumer, Jr., supra note 1, 156–57.

54. Quoted in *King v. Hopkins,* 57 N.H. 334, 336 (1876).

55. *Lisbon v. Lyman,* 49 N.H. 553, 604 (1870); Luce, "President's Address: Early Makers of New Hampshire Common Law," 5 (No. 3) *N.H. Bar Ass'n Proc.* 5, 19 (1925).

56. Jeremiah Smith, supra note 37, 22; Smith, supra note 37, 144.

57. John Morison, supra note 3, 177.

58. Clark, "Charles Doe," 2 *Proc. So. N.H. Bar Ass'n* 105 (1896).

59. Eastman, supra note 4, 247.

60. Letter From Charles Doe to Frank Nesmith Parsons, Oct. 28, 1895, Doe Coll., N.H. Hist. Soc'y.

61. Parsons, supra note 26, 212.

Chapter Eight. The Labyrinth of Authority:
The Law of Evidence and Criminal Insanity

1. Hall, "James Bradley Thayer, 8 *Great American Lawyers* 345, 354 (W. D. Lewis ed. 1909); Hening, "Charles Doe," ibid. 271–72.

2. *Gray v. Jackson,* 51 N.H. 9, 37 (1871).

3. *Huntress v. Boston & Me. R.R.,* 66 N.H. 182, 192, 34 Atl. 154, 157 (1890); for an extended discussion see Reid, "A Peculiar Mode of Expression: Judge Doe's Use of the Distinction Between Law and Fact," 1963 *Wash. U.L.Q.* 427.

4. *Lisbon v. Lyman,* 49 N.H. 553, 563 (1870).

5. *State v. Hodge,* 50 N.H. 510, 517 & 526 (1869). See also Note, "Province of Court and of Jury," 6 *Albany L.J.* 269 (1872).

6. *Lisbon v. Lyman,* 49 N.H. 553, 575 (1870).

7. Ibid. 569.

8. 2 *Wigmore on Evidence,* sec. 458, 474 (3d ed. 1940); 1 Edmund M. Morgan, *Basic Problems of Evidence* 172 n. 5 (1954).

9. *Boardman v. Woodman,* 47 N.H. 120, 146 (1865) (dissenting opinion).

10. *Darling v. Westmoreland,* 52 N.H. 401, 402 (1872).

11. *Greenleaf on Evidence,* sec. 52 at 819 (16th ed. 1899); 1 *Wigmore on Evidence,* sec. 39, 432 n. 2 (3d ed. 1940).

12. *Darling v. Westmoreland,* 52 N.H. 401, 403 (1872).

13. 2 *Wigmore on Evidence,* Sec. 458, 474–75 (3d ed. 1940).

14. Letter From Charles Doe to John Henry Wigmore, Feb. 4, 1895, Wigmore Coll., Northwestern Univ. Law Library.

15. *Amoskeag Mfg. Co. v. Head,* 59 N.H. 332, 337 (1879); *State v. Boston & Maine R.R.,* 58 N.H. 410 (1878); *Hovey v. Grant,* 52 N.H. 569, 580 (1873).

16. *State v. Pike,* 49 N.H. 399, 427 (1870) (dissenting opinion).

17. *Boardman v. Woodman,* 47 N.H. 120, 145 (1865) (dissenting opinion).

18. *Lisbon v. Lyman,* 49 N.H. 553, 571 (1870).

19. *M'Naghten's Case,* 10 Cl. & F. 200, 210, 8 Eng. Rep. 718, 722 (1843).

20. *Commonwealth v. McCann,* 325 Mass. 510, 515, 91 N.E. 2d 214, 217 (1950).

21. For an extended discussion see Reid, "A Speculative Novelty: Judge Doe's Search for Reason in the Law of Evidence," 39 *B.U. L. Rev.* 321 (1959).

22. *State v. Pike,* 49 N.H. 399, 438 (1870).

23. Letter From Charles Doe to Clark Bell, Jan. 10, 1889, in Bell, "Editorial: The Right-Wrong Test in Cases of Homicide By the Insane," 16 *Medico-Legal J.* 260, 264 (n.d.).

24. *Boardman v. Woodman,* 47 N.H. 120, 150 (1865) (dissenting opinion).

25. *State v. Jones,* 50 N.H. 369–70 (1871) (syllabus).

26. Wechsler, "The Criteria of Criminal Responsibility, 22 *U. Chi. L. Rev.* 367, 370 (1955).

27. Reik, "The Doe-Ray Correspondence: A Pioneer Collaboration in the Jurisprudence of Mental Disease, 63 *Yale L.J.* 183, 189–90 (1953); *Durham v. United States*, 214 F. 2d 862, 874–75 (D.C. Cir. 1954).

28. *Blocker v. United States*, 274 F. 2d 572, 573 (D.C. Cir. 1959); *Douglas v. United States*, 239 F. 2d 52, 59 (D.C. Cir. 1956).

29. For an extended discussion see Reid, "Understanding the New Hampshire Doctrine of Criminal Insanity," 69 *Yale L.J.* 367 (1960). See also, Reid, "The Companion of the New Hampshire Doctrine of Criminal Insanity," 15 *Vanderbilt L. Rev.* 721 (1962); Reid, "Criminal Insanity and Psychiatric Evidence: The Challenge of Blocker," 8 *Howard L.J.* 1 (1962); Reid, "The Working of the New Hampshire Doctrine of Criminal Insanity," 15 *Miami L. Rev.* 14 (1960).

30. Letter From Charles Doe to Clark Bell, Jan. 10, 1889, in Bell, supra note 23, 264.

Chapter Nine. A Private Conjecture: *Rules of Construction*

1. For an extended discussion of the substance of this chapter see Reid, "A Private Conjecture: Charles Doe and Rules of Construction," 39 *N.Y.U. L. Rev.* 20 (1964).

2. *Smith v. Furbish*, 68 N.H. 123, 132, 44 Atl. 398, 402 (1894).

3. *Sanborn v. Sanborn*, 62 N.H. 631, 640 (1882), quoting from *Goodale v. Mooney*, 60 N.H. 528, 535 (1881).

4. *Burke v. Concord R.R.*, 61 N.H. 160, 233 (1881).

5. *Sargent v. Union School District*, 63 N.H. 528, 530 (1885).

6. Opinion of the Justices, 66 N.H. 629, 651, 33 Atl. 1076, 1088 (1891).

7. *Hale v. Everett*, 53 N.H. 9, 193 (1868) (dissenting opinion); the second quotation is from Doe Papers, N.H. Sup. Ct., file 580 at 4–5.

8. Doe Papers, N.H. Sup. Ct., file 580 at 4–5.

9. *Brown v. Bartlett*, 58 N.H. 511 (1879).

10. *Sanborn v. Sanborn*, 62 N.H. 631, 643 (1882).

11. *Stilphen v. Stilphen*, 65 N.H. 126, 139, 23 Atl. 79 (1889).

12. *Bodwell v. Nutter*, 63 N.H. 446, 448, 3 Atl. 421, 422 (1885).

13. *Smith v. Furbish*, 68 N.H. 123, 129, 44 Atl. 398, 401 (1894).

14. Ibid. 133–34, 44 Atl. 403.

15. *Tilton v. American Bible Society*, 60 N.H. 377, 382–84 (1880).

16. *Brown v. Bartlett*, 58 N.H. 511 (1879); *Silsby v. Sawyer*, 64 N.H. 580, 585, 15 Atl. 601 (1888).

17. *Smith v. Furbish*, 68 N.H. 123, 157, 44 Atl. 393, 415 (1894).

18. Opinion of the Justices, 66 N.H. 629, 651, 33 Atl. 1076, 1088 (1891).

19. *Smith v. Furbish*, 68 N.H. 123, 44 Atl. 398 (1894).

20. *Sanborn v. Sanborn*, 62 N.H. 631, 645 (1882).

21. *Smith v. Furbish*, 68 N.H. 123, 158, 44 Atl. 398, 415 (1894).

22. *Sanborn v. Sanborn*, 62 N.H. 631, 641 (1882).

23. Ibid.

24. *Curtis v. Gardner*, 54 Mass. (13 Met.) 457, 461 (1847).

25. *Stevens v. Underhill,* 67 N.H. 68, 72, 36 Atl. 370, 372 (1883) (dissenting opinion).

26. *Smith v. Furbish,* 68 N.H. 123, 156–58, 44 Atl. 398, 414–15 (1894).

27. *Edgerly v. Barker,* 66 N.H. 434, 475, 31 Atl. 900, 916 (1891).

28. Ibid. 473, 31 Atl. at 915.

29. Ibid. 452, 31 Atl. at 904.

30. Gray, *Rule Against Perpetuities* sec. 871 (4th ed. 1942).

31. *Kendall v. Green,* 67 N.H. 557, 559, 42 Atl. 178 (1893).

32. *Sanborn v. Sanborn,* 62 N.H. 631, 643 (1882).

33. *Kendall v. Green,* 67 N.H. 557, 560, 42 Atl. 178, 179 (1893).

34. *Opinion of the Justices,* 66 N.H. 629, 651, 31 Atl. 1076, 1088 (1891).

35. Leach, "Perpetuities Legislation, Massachusetts Style," 67 *Harv. L. Rev.* 1349, 1352–54 (1954); Leach, "Perpetuities in Perspective — Ending the Rule's Reign of Terror," 65 *Harv. L. Rev.* 721, 735 (1952). See also, Leach, "Perpetuities: New Hampshire Defertilizes the Octogenarians," 77 *Harv. L. Rev.* 279 (1963).

36. *Boston, Concord & Montreal R.R. v. Boston & L. R.R.,* 65 N.H. 393, 399, 23 Atl. 529, 532 (1888).

37. *Smith v. Furbish,* 68 N.H. 123, 157, 44 Atl. 398, 415 (1894).

Chapter Ten. Experience or Reason: *A Theory of Torts*

1. For an extended discussion of the substance of this chapter, see Reid, "Experience or Reason: The Tort Theories of Holmes and Doe," 18 *Vand. L. Rev.* 405 (1965).

2. Holmes, "Book Notice," 5 *Am. L. Rev.* 340, 341 (1871).

3. I Jaggard, *Handbook of the Law of Torts* vi (1895).

4. Holmes, *The Common Law* 77 (1881).

5. Holmes, "Law in Science and Science in Law," 12 *Harv. L. Rev.* 443, 451 (1899).

6. See Mark DeWolfe Howe, *Justice Oliver Wendell Holmes: The Proving Years* 65–66 (1963).

7. Holmes, "The Theory of Torts," 7 *Am. L. Rev.* 652 (1873).

8. *Fletcher v. Rylands,* L. R. 1 Ex. 265, 279 (1866).

9. *Brown v. Collins,* 53 N.H. 442, 448, 16 Am. Rep. 372, 379 (1873).

10. Ibid. 443, 16 Am. Rep. 372.

11. Ibid. 450–51, 16 Am. Rep. 382-83.

12. Ibid. 451, 16 Am. Rep. 383.

13. *Rylands v. Fletcher,* L.R. 3 H.L. 330 (1868).

14. *Brown v. Collins,* 53 N.H. 442, 448, 16 Am. Rep. 372, 379 (1873).

15. *Lyons v. Childs,* 61 N.H. 72, 74 (1881).

16. *Thompson v. Androscoggin River Improvement Co.,* 54 N.H. 545, 547 (1874) [reporter's note].

17. *Huntress v. Boston & Maine R.R.,* 66 N.H. 185, 190–91 (1890).

18. *Thompson v. Androscoggin River Improvement Co.,* 54 N.H. 545, 551 (1874).

19. Ibid. 556.

20. Holmes, "Law in Science and Science in Law," 12 *Harv. L. Rev.* 443, 455 (1899); Holmes, *Collected Legal Papers* 210, 230 (1920).

21. *Fifield v. Northern Railroad,* 42 N.H. 225, 240 (1860).
22. *Demers v. Glen Manufacturing Co.,* 67 N.H. 404, 406 (1892).
23. See text to note 11 supra.
24. Note, "Doe of New Hampshire: Reflections on a Nineteenth Century Judge," 63 *Harv. L. Rev.* 513, 520 (1950).
25. *Underhill v. Manchester,* 45 N.H. 214, 218 (1864).
26. Ibid. 216.
27. *Brown v. Collins,* 53 N.H. 442, 450, 16 Am. Rep. 372 (1873).
28. Holmes, supra note 4 at 161–62.
29. Mark DeWolfe Howe, supra note 6 at 189.
30. *Baltimore & Ohio R.R. v. Goodman,* 275 U.S. 66, 69–70 (1927).
31. Pollock, "Mr. Justice Holmes," 44 *Harv. L. Rev.* 693, 695 (1931).
32. *Huntress v. Boston & Maine Railroad,* 66 N.H. 185, 190 (1890).
33. Holmes, supra note 4, 124.
34. Pound, Book Review, 44 *Harv. L. Rev.* 1303, 1304 (1931).
35. *Huntress v. Boston & Maine Railroad,* 66 N.H. 185, 191–92 (1890).
36. Ibid.
37. *Haley v. Colcord,* 59 N.H. 7, 8 (1879).
38. *McDuffee v. Portland & Rochester Railroad,* 52 N.H. 430, 452 (1873).
39. Howe, supra note 6 at 199; Holmes, supra note 7 at 654–55; *McDuffee v. Portland & Rochester Railroad,* 52 N.H. 430, 464 (1873).

Chapter Eleven. A Dose of Ozone: *The Public Man*

1. Felix Frankfurter, *Of Law and Men* (Philip Elman ed. 1956).
2. Pound, "Puritanism and the Common Law," 45 *Am. L. Rev.* 811, 815 (1911).
3. Roscoe Pound, *Social Control Through Law* 43 (1942).
4. Bohlen, "The Rule in Rylands v. Fletcher, Part I," 59 *U. Pa. L. Rev.* 298, 390 (1911).
5. Pound, "The Economic Interpretations and the Law of Torts," 53 *Harv. L. Rev.* 365, 383 (1940); Roscoe Pound, *An Interpretation of Legal History* 109 (1930).
6. Book Review, 18 *Harv. L. Rev.* 478 (1905).
7. Letter From Oliver Wendell Holmes to John Henry Wigmore, Jan. 14, 1910, Harvard Law Lib.
8. Holmes, "The Theory of Torts," 7 *Am. L. Rev.* 652, 654 (1873).
9. *Stewart v. Emerson,* 52 N.H. 301, 314 (1872).
10. For an extended discussion of this controversy see Reid, "Brandy in His Water: Correspondence Between Doe, Holmes and Wigmore," 57 *Nw. U.L. Rev.* 522 (1962).
11. *Brown v. Collins,* 53 N.H. 442, 445 (1873). See also 66 N.H. at 458, 60 N.H. at 509, 59 N.H. at 435.
12. Letter From Charles Doe to Isaac Ray, May 17, 1869, in Reik, "The Doe-Ray Correspondence: A Pioneer Collaboration in the Jurisprudence of Mental Disease," 63 *Yale L.J.* 183, 195 (1953).
13. Letter From Charles Doe to Clark Bell, Jan. 10, 1889, in Bell, "Editorial: The Right and Wrong Test in Cases of Homicides by the Insane," 16 *Medico-Legal J.* 260, 262–63 (n.d.).
14. Ibid. 261.

15. Mark DeWolfe Howe, *Justice Oliver Holmes: The Proving Years* 3–25, 268 (1963).

16. Hamilton, "On Dating Mr. Justice Holmes," 9 *U. Chi. L. Rev.* 1, 22 n. 30 (1941).

17. Cross, "Charles Doe," 2 *Proc. So. Bar Ass'n* 91 (1896).

18. Holmes, "In Memoriam: Frederic William Maitland," 22 *L.Q. Rev.* 137–38 (1907).

19. Letter From Charles Doe to Isaac Ray, March 23, 1869, in Reik, supra note 12, 194.

20. Smith, "Charles Doe," 9 *Harv. L. Rev.* 534 (1896).

21. Jeremiah Smith, *Memoir of Hon. Charles Doe* 14 (1897); Smith, "Memoir of Charles Doe," 2 *Proc. So. N.H. Bar Ass'n* 125, 136 (1897).

22. Smith, "Charles Doe," 2 *Proc. So. N.H. Bar Ass'n* 83 (1896); Burns, "Charles Doe," ibid. 89; Cross, "Charles Doe," ibid. 94; Mitchell, "Charles Doe," ibid. 99–100; Concord (N.H.) *Evening Monitor,* March 9, 1896. See also the letters to the editor in Boston *Morning Journal,* March 10, 1896.

23. Letter From Isaac Smith to Chester A. Arthur, Oct. 14, 1881, Doe Coll., N.H. Hist. Soc'y; Parsons, "Response," 5 *Proc. N.H. Bar Ass'n* 174, 179 (1924).

24. Bell, "Ira Perley," *Memorials of Judges Recently Deceased, Graduates of Dartmouth College* 76–77 (1881).

25. 1 George F. Hoar, *Autobiography of Seventy Years* 388 (1903).

26. Luce, "President's Address: Early Makers of New Hampshire Common Law," 5 *Proc. N.H. Bar Ass'n* 5, 22 (1925).

27. Cross, supra note 17, 94.

28. Eastman, "Chief-Justice Charles Doe," 9 *Green Bag* 245, 249 (1897).

29. Burns, supra note 22, 89.

30. Jeremiah Smith, supra note 21, 14–15; Smith, supra note 14, 136–37.

31. Luce, supra note 26, 22.

32. Boston *Evening Globe,* Dec. 19, 1890.

33. 1 George F. Hoar, supra note 25, 388.

34. Smith, supra note 22, 83; Chamberlin, "Charles Doe," 2 *Proc. So. N.H. Bar Ass'n* 98 (1896); Eastman, supra note 28, 251.

35. Letter From Charles Doe to Gilman Marston, Dec. 19, 1881, Doe Coll., N.H. Hist. Soc'y.

36. Allen, "Charles Doe, 1849," 13 *Dartmouth Alumni Mag.* 283, 285 (1921).

37. Exeter (N.H.) *News-Letter,* Feb. 18, 1910.

38. Letter From Charles Doe to William E. Chandler, Jan. 19, 1882, Chandler Coll., N.H. Hist. Soc'y.

39. Letters From Charles Doe to William E. Chandler, May 23, 1882, and April 20, 1882, Chandler Coll., N.H. Hist. Soc'y.

40. Luce, supra note 26, 21.

41. Allen, supra note 36, 284.

42. Luce, supra note 26, 23.

43. Frink, "Reminiscences of the Rockingham Bar," 2 *Proc. N.H. Bar Ass'n* 45, 61 (1904).

44. Doe Papers, Manuscript File 580, N.H. Sup. Ct.

45. Allen, supra note 36, 287.

46. *DeLancey v. Insurance Co.*, 52 N.H. 581 (1873).

47. Smith, supra note 20, 535.

48. *Aldrich v. Wright*, 53 N.H. 398, 401–2 (1873).

49. Cross, supra note 17, 95–96.

50. *Aldrich v. Wright*, 53 N.H. 398, 421 (1873).

51. Boston *Daily Globe*, Dec. 22, 1890.

52. Boston *Morning Journal*, March 10, 1896.

53. Boston *Evening Globe*, Dec. 20, 1890.

54. Hening, "Charles Doe," 8 *Great American Lawyers* 241, 310 (W. D. Lewis ed. 1909); Boston *Morning Journal*, March 10, 1896.

55. *Dover Gazette & Strafford Advertiser*, Aug. 20, 1859.

56. Allen, supra note 36, 284; Eastman, supra note 28, 250.

57. Quoted in Concord (N.H.) *Evening Monitor*, Nov. 23, 1891.

58. Hening, supra note 54, 312.

59. Boston *Daily Globe*, Dec. 22, 1890.

60. Concord (N.H.) *Monitor*, June 2, 1892.

61. Dover *Enquirer*, Dec. 26, 1890.

62. Boston *Daily Globe*, Dec. 22, 1890.

63. New York *Herald*, March 10, 1896.

64. Boston *Morning Journal*, March 10, 1896; Boston *Daily Globe*, Dec. 22, 1890; Boston *Morning Journal*, Dec. 20, 1890.

65. Allen, supra note 36, 285; Eastman, supra note 28, 251.

66. Boston *Morning Journal*, March 10, 1896.

67. *Independent Democrat* (Concord), Nov. 26, 1891.

68. 12 *The Dartmouth*, May 1, 1891. See also Nashua *Daily Telegraph*, Dec. 31, 1890.

69. Dover *Enquirer*, Dec. 19, 1890; Nashua *Daily Telegraph*, Dec. 16, 1890.

70. Jeremiah Smith, supra note 21, 30; Smith, supra note 21, 152.

71. Dover *Enquirer*, Dec. 13, 1889.

72. Letters From Charles Doe to Harry Hibbard, Sept. 20, 1870, Doe Coll., N.H. Hist. Soc'y; to John Henry Wigmore, June 2, 1890, Wigmore Coll., Northwestern Univ. Law Lib.; to William E. Chandler, June 1, 1878, Chandler Coll., N.H. Hist. Soc'y.

73. Letter From Charles Doe to Gilman Marston, Dec. 19, 1881, N.H. Hist. Soc'y.

74. Letter From Charles Doe to John Henry Wigmore, July 9, 1889, in Pike, "President's Address — Memories of Judge Doe," 3 *N.H. Bar Ass'n Proc.* 463, 478 (1916).

75. Letter From Charles Doe to William E. Chandler, June 1, 1878, Chandler Coll., N.H. Hist. Soc'y.

76. Luce, supra note 26, 21–22.

77. Knott, "Charles Doe," 5 *Dic. Am. Bio.* 354 (1930).

78. Foster, "Charles Doe," 2 *Proc. So. N.H. Bar Ass'n* 86 (1896).

79. Allen, supra note 36, 284.

80. Luce, supra note 26, 21.

Chapter Twelve. Wonder of the Neighborhood: *The Family Man*

1. *Dover Gazette & Strafford Advertiser*, March 3, 1860, p. 3., col. 4; *New Hampshire Patriot & State Gazette*, March 7, 1860, p. 3, col. 5.

2. A. J. Coolidge and J. B. Mansfield, *History and Description of New England: New Hampshire* 628–29 (1860); *Reminiscences of Henry Clay Barnabee* 73–74 (George Leon Varney ed. 1913); Thomas Bailey Aldrich, *The Story of a Bad Boy and Other Sketches* 28 (1897).

3. Charles W. Brewster, *Rambles About Portsmouth* 351 (1859); the Portsmouth *Herald*, Feb. 12, 1958 (see also, John C. Park, *Address at a Meeting of the Descendants of Richard Haven of Lynn at Framingham, Mass., August 29, 1844* [1844]); Portsmouth *Daily Chronicle*, March 1, 1859, p. 2, col. 4; March 2, 1859, p. 3, col. 1; March 3, 1859, p. 3, col. 1.

4. John Eldridge Frost, *Sarah Orne Jewett* 31 (1960).

5. Letter From Sarah Orne Jewett to Lucretia Fisk Perry, Jan. 28, 1872, in Cary, "Sarah Orne Jewett and the Rich Tradition," 4 *Colby Library Quarterly* 205, 207 (1957).

6. Winston Churchill, *Coniston* 97 (1906).

7. Jewett, "Jake's Holiday," 26 *The Independent* 13–14 (Feb. 19, 1874).

8. Letter From Charles Doe to John Henry Wigmore, July 9, 1889, in Wigmore Coll., Northwestern Univ. Law Lib.

9. 2 Mark De Wolfe Howe, *Justice Oliver Wendell Holmes: The Proving Years* 8 n. 17 (1963).

10. Boston *Globe*, March 10, 1896.

11. Jewett, supra note 7, 14.

12. *Sargent v. Union School-District*, 63 N.H. 528, 533 (1885).

13. Pike, "President's Address — Memories of Judge Doe," 3 *N.H. Bar Ass'n Proc.* 463, 480 (1916).

14. Boston *Daily Globe*, March 10, 1896.

15. Boston *Morning Journal*, March 10, 1896.

16. Boston *Daily Globe*, March 10, 1896.

17. Boston *Morning Journal*, March 10, 1896.

18. Boston *Record*, quoted in Concord *Evening Monitor*, Nov. 23, 1891.

19. Hall, "Charles Doe," 2 *Proc. So. N.H. Bar Ass'n* 79, 85 (1896). See e.g. Letter From Charles Doe to Austin Pike, July 26, 1884, N.H. Hist. Soc'y.

20. Aldrich, "Alonzo P. Carpenter," 2 *Proc. So. N.H. Bar Ass'n* 297, 303 (1899); Hening, "Charles Doe," 8 *Great American Lawyers* 241, 310 (W. D. Lewis ed. 1909); Eastman, "Chief-Justice Charles Doe," 9 *Green Bag* 245, 251 (1897).

21. Concord *Evening Monitor*, Nov. 23, 1891; Letter From Charles Doe to Gilman Marston, Dec. 19, 1881, Doe Coll., N.H. Hist. Soc'y; Letter From Charles Doe to Charles Marseilles, April 12, 1876, Marseilles Coll., N.H. Hist. Soc'y.

22. Boston *Daily Globe*, March 10, 1896.

23. See e.g. ibid.

24. *Dover Gazette & Strafford Advertiser*, March 3, 1860.

25. Census of 1870 (June), Town of Rollinsford, County of Strafford, State of New Hampshire, p. 37 (Strafford County Courthouse, Dover, N.H.).

26. Letter From C. W. Woodman to Chester A. Arthur, Oct. 12, 1881, Doe Coll., N.H. Hist. Soc'y.

27. Hall, supra note 19, 85; Hening, supra note 20, 242; *The Dart-*

mouth, June 14, 1895, p. 332; Concord *Evening Monitor,* March 9, 1896.

28. Medina, "Judges as Leaders in Improving the Administration of Justice," 36 *J. Am. Jud. Soc'y* 6 (1952).

29. See full page of letters in the Boston *Morning Journal,* March 10, 1896.

30. Hening, supra note 20, 312.

31. Ibid.

32. Letter From G. S. Frost to the Editor, Boston *Morning Journal,* March 10, 1896.

33. Hall, supra note 19, 85.

34. Frink, "Charles Doe," 2 *Proc. So. N.H. Bar Ass'n* 79, 88 (1896).

35. Burns, "Charles Doe," ibid., 89.

36. Jeremiah Smith, *Memoir of Hon. Charles Doe* 23 (1897); Smith, "Memoir of Charles Doe," 2 *Proc. So. N.H. Bar Ass'n* 125, 145 (1897); Smith, "Obituary of Charles Doe," 9 *Harv. L. Rev.* 534, 535 (1896).

Chapter Thirteen. Pudding and Milk: *The Private Man*

1. Allen, "Charles Doe," 13 *Dartmouth Alumni Mag.* 283, 284 (1921).

2. Pike, "President's Address — Memoirs of Judge Doe," 3 *N.H. Bar Ass'n Proc.* 463, 474 (1916).

3. Ibid. 475.

4. Jeremiah Smith, *Memoir of Hon. Charles Doe* 28 (1897); Smith, "Memoir of Charles Doe," 2 *Proc. So. N.H. Bar Ass'n* 125, 150 (1897).

5. G. J. Clark, *Memoirs of Jeremiah Mason* 39 note (1917).

6. John Morison, *Life of Hon. Jeremiah Smith, LL.D.* 223 (1845).

7. Reid, "The Touch of History: The Historical Method of A Common Law Judge," 8 *Am. J. Legal Hist.* 157 (1964).

8. Letter From Charles Doe to Frederick Chase, Dec. 14, 1889, Dart. Coll. Archives, Mss. 889664.

9. Letter From Charles Doe to Frederick Chase, Dec. 11, 1889, Dart. Coll. Archives, Mss. 889661.

10. See e.g. 66 N.H. at 226; 54 N.H. at 608; 53 N.H. at 135 (where Doe cited Stanley's *Life of Arnold*).

11. Letter From Charles Doe to Frederick Chase, Dec. 14, 1889, Dart. Coll. Archives, Mss. 889664.

12. See 4 Albert J. Beveridge, *The Life of John Marshall* 258–59 (1919).

13. Letter From Charles Doe to Nathaniel Bouton, Aug. 11, 1875, N.H. Hist. Soc'y.

14. Letter From Charles Doe to Nathaniel Bouton, Dec. 6, 1875, N.H. Hist. Soc'y.

15. Parker, "An Heroic Age in the History of the New Hampshire Bar," 6 (No. 3) *Proc. N.H. Bar Ass'n* 17, 47 (1932).

16. See Hall, "Charles Doe," 2 *Proc. So. N.H. Bar Ass'n* 79, 85 (1896).

17. Burns, "Charles Doe," ibid. 89; Allen, supra note 1, 285; Jeremiah Smith, supra note 4, 28; Smith, supra note 4, 150.

18. Smith, "Obituary Notice — Charles Doe," 9 *Harv. L. Rev.* 534, 535 (1896).

19. Letter From Charles Doe to John Major Shirley, March 9, 1876, Doe Papers, N.H. Sup. Ct.

20. Hall, supra note 16, 84.

21. Cary, "Sarah Orne Jewett and the Rich Tradition," 4 *Colby Library Quarterly* 205, 216 (1957).

22. Quoted in 1 *The [Berwick] Academy Quill* 5 (Jan. 25, 1935).

23. *Letters of Sarah Orne Jewett* 26 (Fields ed. 1911).

24. Ibid. 18.

25. Ibid. 45.

26. Sarah Orne Jewett, *A Country Doctor* 146 (1884).

27. Cross, "Charles Doe," 2 *Proc. So. N.H. Bar Ass'n* 79, 94 (1896); Letter From Henry Robinson to the Editor, Boston *Morning Journal,* March 10, 1896; Pike, supra note 2, 482; Jeremiah Smith, supra note 4, 29; Smith, supra note 4, 151.

28. Frink, "Charles Doe," 2 *Proc. So. N.H. Bar Ass'n* 79, 88 (1896).

29. Pike, supra note 2, 482–83.

30. Letters From Charles Doe to William E. Chandler, Jan. 13 and Jan. 19, 1882, Chandler Coll., N.H. Hist. Soc'y.

31. Frink, supra note 28, 88; Jeremiah Smith, supra note 4, 29; Smith, supra note 4, 151.

32. Merwin, "The Irish in American Life," 77 *Atlantic Monthly* 292 (March, 1896).

33. Harrison, "The Sale of Votes in New Hampshire," 25 *Century* 149 (1893); Leon Burr Richardson, *William E. Chandler, Republican* 166 (1940).

34. Clark, "Charles Doe," 2 *Proc. So. N.H. Bar Ass'n* 79, 105 (1896); Frink, "Reminiscences of the Rockingham Bar," 2 *N.H. Bar Ass'n Proc.* 45, 60 (1904); *The Dartmouth,* June 14, 1895, p. 333; Martin, "Annual Address," 4 *N.H. Bar Ass'n Proc.* 191 (1919); Hening, "Charles Doe," 8 *Great American Lawyers* 241, 306 (W. D. Lewis ed. 1909); Luce, "Early Makers of New Hampshire Common Law," 5 (No. 3) *N.H. Bar Ass'n Proc.* 5, 22 (1925).

35. Pike, supra note 2, 480.

36. Letter From John Henry Wigmore to Robert G. Pike, March 27, 1916, quoted in ibid., 476.

37. Letter From Charles Doe to John Henry Wigmore, Sept. 12, 1888, Wigmore Coll., Northwestern Univ. Law Lib.

38. Letter From Charles Doe to John Henry Wigmore, April 13, 1888, Wigmore Coll., Northwestern Univ. Law Lib.

39. Letter From Charles Doe to John Henry Wigmore, March 11, 1889, Wigmore Coll., Northwestern Univ. Law Lib.

40. Pike, supra note 2, 481.

41. Boston *Daily Globe,* March 10, 1896.

42. Letter From Charles Doe to John Major Shirley, n.d., Doe Papers, N.H. Sup. Ct.

43. *Hale v. Everett,* 53 N.H. 9, 274 (1868) (dissenting opinion).

44. Pike, supra note 2, 469.

Chapter Fourteen. A Political Football: *Nonjudicial Activities*

1. See e.g. Letter From W. B. Morrill to James M. Lovering, Jan. 30, 1861, Lovering Coll., N.H. Hist. Soc'y.

2. See e.g. Dover *Enquirer,* June 16, 1859.

3. *Congressional Globe,* 37 Cong., 1st Sess., p. 260.

4. *Democratic Standard* (Concord), Oct. 1, 1859.

5. Letter From Charles Doe to John Parker Hale, March 12, 1861, Hale Coll., N.H. Hist. Soc'y.

6. Letter From Charles Doe to William E. Chandler, Jan. 14, 1868, Chandler Coll., N.H. Hist. Soc'y.

7. Letter From Charles Doe to Charles Marseilles, April 12, 1876, Marseilles Coll., N.H. Hist. Soc'y.

8. 2 Hobart Pillsbury, *New Hampshire, Resources, Attractions and Its People: A History* 581 (1927).

9. Letter From Henry Robinson to the Editor, Boston *Morning Journal,* March 10, 1896.

10. Hening, "Charles Doe," 8 *Great American Lawyers* 241, 308–9 (W. D. Lewis ed. 1909).

11. Eastman, "Chief-Justice Charles Doe," 9 *Green Bag* 245 (1897).

12. James O. Lyford, *Life of Edward H. Rollins: A Political Biography* 212 (1906).

13. Shirley, "Practice," 5 *Granite Monthly* 150, 157 (1882).

14. See Letters From Charles Doe to William E. Chandler, Dec. 22 and 27, 1884, and Jan. 5, 1885, Chandler Coll., N.H. Hist. Soc'y.

15. Letter From Charles Doe to Harry Hibbard, Sept. 20, 1870, Doe Coll., N.H. Hist. Soc'y. See also Letter From Charles Doe to Charles H. Bell, Aug. 24, 1870, Dartmouth Coll. Archives, Mss. 870474.

16. *The Independent Statesman* (Concord), Aug. 12, 1870.

17. Reid, "Chandler! Name Your Man! — The Revolution in Judicial Appointments During the 1870's," 5 *N.H.B.J.* 11, 13–18 (1962).

18. Batchellor, "The Supreme Court of New Hampshire: An Historical Sketch," 17 *Medico-Legal Journal* 8, 16 (n.d.).

19. Letter From Charles Doe to Harry Hibbard, Sept. 29, 1870, Doe Coll., N.H. Hist. Soc'y.

20. Letter From Charles Doe to Harry Hibbard, Sept. 20, 1870, Doe Coll., N.H. Hist. Soc'y.

21. Upton, "The Independence of the Judiciary in New Hampshire," 1 (No. 4) *N.H.B.J.* 28 (July, 1959).

22. James O. Lyford, supra note 12, 328.

23. Letter From Charles Doe to William E. Chandler, June 9, 1876, Chandler Coll., N.H. Hist. Soc'y.

24. Letter From Charles Doe to William E. Chandler, April 4, 1876, Chandler Coll., N. H. Hist. Soc'y.

25. Letter From Charles Doe to William E. Chandler, Feb. 1, 1876, Chandler Coll., N.H. Hist. Soc'y.

26. Letter From Charles Doe to William E. Chandler, June 9, 1876, Chandler Coll., N.H. Hist. Soc'y.

27. Letter From Charles Doe to William E. Chandler, March 30, 1876, Chandler Coll., N.H. Hist. Soc'y.

28. Letter From Charles Doe to William E. Chandler, June 9, 1876, Chandler Coll., N.H. Hist. Soc'y.

29. Letter From Charles Doe to William E. Chandler, June 28, 1876, Chandler Coll., N.H. Hist. Soc'y.

30. Letter From Charles Doe to William E. Chandler, Feb. 14, 1876, Chandler Coll., N.H. Hist. Soc'y.

31. Letter From Charles Doe to William E. Chandler, June 28, 1876, Chandler Coll., N.H. Hist. Soc'y.

32. See Letter quoted in James O. Lyford, supra note 12, 344. For Doe's legal theory see *Opinion of the Justices,* 58 N.H. 621 (1877).

33. *Memorial of Hon. Harry Bingham* 166 (Henry Harrison Metcalf ed. 1910).

34. See letter quoted in James O. Lyford, supra note 12, 343.

35. Letter From Edward H. Rollins to Daniel Hall, May 11, 1875, quoted in ibid. 345.

36. *Bell v. Pike,* 53 N.H. 473 (1873); *Opinion of the Justices,* 53 N.H. 640 (1873).

37. *Opinion of the Justices,* 56 N.H. 574 (1875).

38. Letter From Charles Doe to Charles Marseilles, April 12, 1876, Marseilles Coll., N.H. Hist. Soc'y.

39. James O. Lyford, supra note 12, 343.

40. Letter From Charles Doe to Luther Dearborn, April 22, 1876, N.H. Hist. Soc'y.

41. Letter From Charles Doe to William E. Chandler, June 9, 1876, Chandler Coll., N.H. Hist. Soc'y.

42. 2 Conrad Reno, *Memoirs of the Judiciary and the Bar of New England for the Nineteenth Century* 55 (1901).

43. Letter From Charles Doe to William E. Chandler, June 9, 1876, Chandler Coll., N.H. Hist. Soc'y.

44. Jeremiah Smith, *Memoir of Hon. Charles Doe* 25 (1897); Smith, "Memoir of Charles Doe," 2 *Proc. So. N.H. Bar Ass'n* 125, 147 (1897).

45. Letter From Charles Doe to Charles H. Bell, Jan. 14, 1889, Dartmouth Coll. Archives, Mss. 889114.

46. Letter From Charles Doe to John Major Shirley, n.d., Doe Papers, N.H. Sup. Ct.

Chapter Fifteen. The New Hampshire Method: *The Court Leader*

1. For extended discussions by the author of material appearing in this chapter see "Doe Did Not Sit — The Creation of Opinions By an Artist," 63 *Colum. L. Rev.* 59 (1963) and "A New Light Dawns — The Judicial Operosity of Chief Justice Doe," 9 *Vill. L. Rev.* 233 (1964).

2. Hening, "Charles Doe," 8 *Great American Lawyers* 241, 304 (W. D. Lewis ed. 1909).

3. 68 N.H. 495, 38 Atl. 272 (1896).

4. Doe Papers, Folder 580, N.H. Sup. Ct.

5. Leon Burr Richardson, *William E. Chandler, Republican* 446 (1940).

6. Smith, "Charles Doe," 2 *Proc. So. N.H. Bar Ass'n* 81, 82 (1896).

7. Doe Papers, Folder 580 (Draft Letter to Judge Parsons, Feb. 26, 1896), N.H. Sup. Ct.

8. Doe Papers, Unnumbered File, N.H. Sup. Ct.

9. Doe Papers, Folder 580, 4, N.H. Sup. Ct.

10. Ibid. 5.

11. Doe Papers, Folder 582, 7, N.H. Sup. Ct.

12. 1 *Holmes-Pollock* Letters 258 (Mark DeWolfe Howe ed. 1941).

13. Max Lerner, *The Mind and Faith of Justice Holmes* 130–31 (1943).

14. Hening, supra note 2, 303–04.

15. *Hoitt v. Hoitt,* 63 N.H. 475, 3 Atl. 604 (1885).

16. Letter From Charles Doe to Isaac N. Blodgett, March 27, 1886, Dartmouth Coll. Archives, Mss. 886227.

17. Chase, "Isaac N. Blodgett," 2 *Proc. N.H. Bar Ass'n* 523, 532 (1909).

18. Eastman, "Chief-Justice Charles Doe," 9 *Green Bag* 245, 249 (1897).

19. Hening, supra note 2, 306.

20. Probably *State ex rel Rhodes v. Saunders,* 66 N.H. 39, 25 Atl. 588 (1889).

21. Eastman, supra note 18, 249.

22. Jeremiah Smith, *Memoir of Hon. Charles Doe* 21 (1897); Smith, "Memoir of Charles Doe," 2 *Proc. So. N.H. Bar Ass'n* 125, 143 (1897).

23. Letter From Doe to Chase, Doe Papers, Folder 579, N.H. Sup. Ct.

24. Hening, supra note 2, 305.

25. *Winnipiseogee Lake Cotton & Woolen Mfg. Co. v. Gilford,* 64 N.H. 337, 348, 10 Atl. 849, 850 (1887).

26. *Winnipiseogee Lake Cotton & Woolen Mfg. Co. v. Gilford,* 66 N.H. 621, 30 Atl. 1121 (1889), and *Winnipiseogee Lake Cotton & Woolen Mfg. Co. v. Gilford,* 66 N.H. 626, 30 Atl. 1121 (1891).

27. "Reserved Case," *Winnipisseogee Lake Cotton & Woolen Manufacturing Co. v. Gilford,* Belknap, ss., September Term, 1892, 180 *Briefs & Cases* 157, 159–161 (N.H. State Law Library).

28. "Brief for Plaintiff," ibid. 169.

29. *Concord Manufacturing Co. v. Robertson,* 66 N.H. 1, 25 Atl. 718 (1889).

30. Doe Papers, File 579, 3, 6–7, N.H. Sup. Ct.

31. Ibid. 20.

32. Bellows's decision was *Cocheco Manufacturing Co. v. Strafford,* 51 N.H. 455 (1871), Doe's "later" decision was *State v. Welch,* 66 N.H. 178, 29 Atl. 21 (1889).

33. Doe Papers, File 579, 39, N.H. Sup. Ct.

34. Ibid. 48.

35. Ibid. 43–44.

36. Ibid. 47.

37. Letter From Charles Doe to William Martin Chase, Nov. 24, 1893, ibid.

38. *Winnipiseogee Lake Cotton & Woolen Manufacturing Co. v. Gilford,* 67 N.H. 514, 517, 35 Atl. 945, 946 (1893).

39. Ibid. 520, 35 Atl. at 948.

40. "Reserved Case," supra note 27, 161.

41. *Winnipiseogee Lake Cotton & Woolen Manufacturing Co. v. Gilford,* 67 N.H. 514, 515, 35 Atl. 945 (1893) (emphasis added). (The quotation appears only in 67 N.H.)

Chapter Sixteen. The First Chapter of the Constitution: *Civil Rights*

1. Note, "Doe of New Hampshire: Reflections on a Nineteenth Century Judge," 63 *Harv. L. Rev.* 513 (1950).

2. *Boody v. Watson*, 64 N.H. 162, 165, 9 Atl. 794, 797 (1886).

3. *State v. U.S. & Canada Express Co.*, 60 N.H. 219, 253 (1880) (concurring opinion). See also *State v. Hayes*, 61 N.H. 264, 321 (1881).

4. *Orr v. Quimby*, 54 N.H. 590, 618 (1874) (dissenting opinion).

5. *State v. U.S. & Canada Express Co.*, 60 N.H. 219, 253 (1880) (concurring opinion).

6. *Edes v. Broadman*, 58 N.H. 580, 585 (1879).

7. Ibid. 587.

8. *Crawford v. Parsons*, 63 N.H. 438, 443 (1885). See also *Morrison v. Insurance Co.*, 64 N.H. 137, 138, 7 Atl. 378, 379 (1886).

9. *State v. U.S. & Canada Express Co.*, 60 N.H. 219, 255 (1880) (concurring opinion).

10. *Wooster v. Plymouth*, 62 N.H. 193 (1882).

11. *State v. U.S. & Canada Express Co.*, 60 N.H. 219, 255 (1880) (concurring opinion).

12. *Wooster v. Plymouth*, 62 N.H. 193, 197 (1882).

13. Frederick Pollock, *Essays in the Law* 85 (1922).

14. *Orr v. Quimby*, 54 N.H. 590, 618 (1874) (dissenting opinion).

15. *Wooster v. Plymouth*, 62 N.H. 193, 194 (1882).

16. *Orr v. Quimby*, 54 N.H. 590, 618 (1874) (dissenting opinion).

17. *Ashuelot R.R. Co. v. Elliott*, 58 N.H. 451, 452 (1878).

18. *State v. U.S. & Canada Express Co.*, 60 N.H. 219, 250 (1880) (concurring opinion).

19. *Aldrich v. Wright*, 53 N.H. 398, 399 (1873).

20. *Wooster v. Plymouth*, 62 N.H. 193, 194 (1882).

21. Opinion of the Justices, 66 N.H. 629, 631, 33 Atl. 1076 (1891).

22. *State v. U.S. & Canada Express Co.*, 60 N.H. 219, 250 (1880) (concurring opinion).

23. *Wooster v. Plymouth*, 62 N.H. 193, 201 (1882).

24. *Orr v. Quimby*, 54 N.H. 590, 601 (1874).

25. Ibid. 639 (dissenting opinion).

26. Ibid. 645 (dissenting opinion).

27. Ibid. 640 (dissenting opinion).

28. *Fay v. Parker*, 53 N.H. 342, 389 (1872) quoting from *Bristol v. New Chester*, 3 N.H. 524, 535 (1826).

29. *Orr v. Quimby*, 54 N.H. 590, 606 (1874) (dissenting opinion).

30. Ibid. 612 (dissenting opinion).

31. Ibid. 619 (dissenting opinion).

32. Ibid. 617 (dissenting opinion).

33. Opinion of the Justices, 66 N.H. 629, 663, 33 Atl. 1076 (1891).

34. Cahn, "The Firstness of the First Amendment," 65 *Yale L.J.* 464 (1956); McKay "The Preference for Freedom," 34 *N.Y.U.L. Rev.* 1182 (1959).

35. *Orr. v. Quimby*, 54 N.H. 590, 640 (1874) (dissenting opinion).

36. *State v. U.S. & Canada Express Co.*, 60 N.H. 219, 253 (1880) (concurring opinion).

37. *Orr. v. Quimby*, 54 N.H. 590, 640 (1874) (dissenting opinion). See also ibid. 618–19 and 655.

38. Letter From Charles Doe to Charles Marseilles, April 12, 1874, in Marseilles Collection, N.H. Hist. Soc'y.

39. *Holt v. Downs,* 58 N.H. 170, 173 (1872).
40. Eastman, "Chief-Justice Charles Doe," 9 *Green Bag* 245, 251 (1897).
41. *Holt v. Downs,* 58 N.H. 170, 174 (1872).
42. *Hale v. Everett,* 53 N.H. 9, 139 (1868) (dissenting opinion).
43. Ibid. 14.
44. Ibid. 134 (footnote).
45. Ibid. 276 (dissenting opinion).
46. Ibid. 227 (dissenting opinion).
47. *N.H. Bill of Rights,* Article 6.
48. *Hale v. Everett,* 53 N.H. 9, 275 (1868) (dissenting opinion).
49. Ibid. 275–76 (dissenting opinion).

Chapter Seventeen. The Substance of the Constitution:
The Doctrine of Equality

1. *DeLancey v. Insurance Company,* 52 N.H. 581, 592–93 (1873).
2. *Gould v. Raymond,* 59 N.H. 260, 275 (1879).
3. *State v. Express Co.,* 60 N.H. 219, 256 (1880) (concurring opinion).
4. *Gove v. Epping,* 41 N.H. 539 (1860).
5. Letter From Charles Doe to Austin Pike, March 22, 1881, Doe Collection, N.H. Hist. Soc'y.
6. *Gould v. Raymond,* 59 N.H. 260, 275 (1879).
7. *Edes v. Broadman,* 58 N.H. 580, 585 (1879).
8. *State v. Express Co.,* 60 N.H. 219, 251 (1880) (concurring opinion).
9. *Edes v. Broadman,* 58 N.H. 580, 585 (1879); *State v. Express Co.,* 60 N.H. 219, 251 (1880) (concurring opinion).
10. *Orr v. Quimby,* 54 N.H. 590, 617 (1874) (dissenting opinion); *Edes v. Broadman,* 58 N.H. 580, 584 (1879).
11. *Boody v. Watson,* 64 N.H. 162, 167, 9 Atl. 794, 799 (1886); *Edes v. Broadman,* 58 N.H. 580, 589 (1879).
12. *Willoughby v. Holderness,* 62 N.H. 227, 228 (1882).
13. *Morrison v. Manchester,* 58 N.H. 538, 559 (1879).
14. *State v. Express Co.,* 60 N.H. 219, 255 (1880) (concurring opinion); *Boston, Concord & Montreal Railroad v. State,* 60 N.H. 87, 94 (1880).
15. *State v. Express Co.,* 60 N.H. 219, 251 (1880) (concurring opinion).
16. *Morrison v. Manchester,* 58 N.H. 538, 549 (1879).
17. *State v. Express Co.,* 60 N.H. 219, 251 (1880) (concurring opinion).
18. Ibid. 254.
19. Ibid.
20. Ibid. 252.
21. Ibid. 255.
22. *State v. Express Co.,* 60 N.H. 219, 246–63 (1880) (concurring opinion); Note, 15 *Am. L. Rev.* 442 (1881).
23. *Boston, Concord & Montreal Railroad v. State,* 62 N.H. 648, 649 (1883) (*dictum*). But for *ratio* see *Somersworth Savings Bank v. Somersworth,* 68 N.H. 402 (1895).
24. *State v. Express Co.,* 60 N.H. 219, 260 (1880) (concurring opinion).
25. *Morrison v. Manchester,* 58 N.H. 538, 553–56 (1879).
26. *Telephone Company v. State,* 63 N.H. 167 (1884) (per J. Carpenter).
27. *Winkley v. Newton,* 67 N.H. 80, 83, 36 Atl. 610, 612 (1891).

28. *Boston, Concord & Montreal Railroad v. State*, 60 N.H. 87 (1880).

29. *State v. Express Co.*, 60 N.H. 219, 246 (1880) (concurring opinion).

30. Ibid. 251.

31. *Winkley v. Newton*, 67 N.H. 80, 81, 36 Atl. 610 (1891); *State v. Express Co.*, 60 N.H. 219, 246 (1880) (concurring opinion).

32. *Boston, Concord & Montreal Railroad v. State*, 60 N.H. 87, 94 (1880).

33. *Winkley v. Newton*, 67 N.H. 80, 81, 36 Atl. 610 (1891).

34. *Opinion of the Justices*, 53 N.H. 634 (1866).

35. 27 U.S. (2 Peters) 448 (1829).

36. Letter From Charles Doe to John M. Shirley, n.d., Doe Collection, N.H. Sup. Ct.

37. Letter From Charles Doe to William E. Chandler, Jan. 14, 1868, Chandler Collection, N.H. Hist. Soc'y.

38. *Winkley v. Newton*, 67 N.H. 80, 83, 36 Atl. 610, 612 (1891).

39. *Buck v. Bell*, 274 U.S. 200, 208 (1927).

Chapter Eighteen. All the Summers of My Life:
The Limits of Government

1. *Aldrich v. Wright*, 53 N.H. 398 (1873).

2. Ibid. 399.

3. N.H. Const., Part First, Article 2.

4. *Aldrich v. Wright*, 53 N.H. 398, 399 (1873).

5. Ibid. 400.

6. Ibid.

7. *De Lancey v. Insurance Co.*, 52 N.H. 581, 592 (1873).

8. *McDuffee v. The Portland & Rochester Railroad*, 52 N.H. 430, 455 (1873).

9. See e.g. *Orr v. Quimby*, 54 N.H. 590, 618 (1874) (dissenting opinion).

10. *Concord Manufacturing Co. v. Robertson*, 66 N.H. 1, 12, 25 Atl. 718, 723 (1889).

11. But see *Orr v. Quimby*, 54 N.H. 590, 618 (1874) (dissenting opinion).

12. *Corbin's Case*, Opinion of the Justices, 66 N.H. 629, 635, 33 Atl. 1076, 1079 (1891).

13. *Fletcher v. Peck*, 10 U.S. 87 (1810).

14. Letter From Charles Doe to John Major Shirley, March 9, 1876, in Doe Papers, N.H. Sup. Ct.

15. *Corbin's Case*, Opinion of the Justices, 66 N.H. 629, 635, 33 Atl. 1076, 1079 (1891).

16. *The Sinking-Fund Cases*, 99 U.S. 700, 719 (1879).

17. 3 Charles Warren, *The Supreme Court in United States History* 364 (1924).

18. Opinion of the Court, 58 N.H. 623, 524 (1879) (citation omitted).

19. *Dartmouth College v. Woodward*, 1 N.H. 111 (1817).

20. *Dartmouth College v. Woodward*, 17 U.S. 518 (1819).

21. Doe, "A New View of the Dartmouth College Case," 6 *Harv. L. Rev.* 161 (1892).

22. Ibid. 173.

23. Ibid. 171.

24. Letter From Charles Doe to John Major Shirley, March 9, 1876, Doe Papers, N.H. Sup. Ct.

25. Note, "A New View of the Dartmouth College Case," 27 *Am. L. Rev.* 71, 72 (1893).

26. Letter From Charles Doe to John Major Shirley, March 9, 1876, Doe Papers, N.H. Sup. Ct.

27. Letter From Charles Doe to John Major Shirley, April 29, 1876, Doe Papers, N.H. Sup. Ct.

28. Doe, supra note 21, 171.

29. Note, supra note 25, 72.

30. Letter From Charles Doe to John Major Shirley, March 9, 1876, Doe Papers, N.H. Sup. Ct.

31. Quoted in Hening, "Charles Doe," 8 *Great American Lawyers* 241, 294 (W. D. Lewis ed. 1909).

32. Letter From Charles Doe to John Major Shirley, n.d., Doe Papers, N.H. Sup. Ct.

33. Doe, "Lease of Railroad by Majority of Stockholders with Assent of Legislature," 8 *Harv. L. Rev.* 295 (1895); Doe, supra note 21, 16.

34. *Corbin's Case,* Opinion of the Justices, 66 N.H. 629, 642, 33 Atl. 1076, 1084 (1891).

35. *Dow v. Northern R.R.,* 67 N.H. 1, 36 Atl. 510 (1886).

36. Hening, supra note 31, 292.

37. Smith, "John Marshall," 1 (Old Series 6) *Proc. N.H. Bar Ass'n* 302 (1901).

38. See Russell, "Status and Tendencies of the Dartmouth College Case," 30 *Am. L. Rev.* 321, 342-43 (1896).

39. Letter From Charles Doe to John Major Shirley, n.d., Doe Papers, N.H. Sup. Ct.

40. Ibid.

41. *McDuffee v. The Portland & Rochester R.R.,* 52 N.H. 430 (1873).

42. Letter From Charles Doe to John Major Shirley, n.d., Doe Papers, N.H. Sup. Ct.

43. Ibid.

44. Concord *Evening Monitor,* May 6, 1893. See also *The Independent Statesman,* April 20, 1893.

45. *Stilphen v. Stilphen,* 65 N.H. 126 (1889); *State v. Varrell,* 58 N.H. 148 (1877); *Orr v. Quimby,* 54 N.H. 590, 608-612, 617, 634-35 (1874) (dissenting opinion); *Aldrich v. Wright,* 53 N.H. 398, 399 (1873); *De Lancey v. Insurance Co.,* 52 N.H. 581 (1873).

Chapter Nineteen. Chaos and Contention: *Railroad Regulation*

1. *The Times & Dover Enquirer,* Aug. 11, 1829.

2. 49 *Report N.H. Railroad Commission* 11 (1893).

3. *Fisher v. Concord R.R.,* 50 N.H. 200, 212 (1870).

4. *Concord & Montreal v. Boston & Maine,* 67 N.H. 464, 466 (1893).

5. *Fisher v. Concord R.R.,* 50 N.H. 200, 210 (1870).

6. George Pierce Baker, *The Formation of the New England Railroad System: A Study of Railroad Combination in the Nineteenth Century* 132 (1949).

7. *Northern R.R. v. Concord R.R.*, 50 N.H. 166, 179 (1870).

8. Harry Bingham, *Closing Argument . . . Before the Railroad Committee* 7 (Aug. 10, 1887)

9. Alvin F. Harlow, *Steelways of New England* 301 (1946).

10. *Pearson v. Concord R.R.*, 62 N.H. 537 (1883).

11. *State v. Concord R.R.*, 62 N.H. 375, 376 (1882).

12. *Burke v. Concord R.R.*, 61 N.H. 160 (1881).

13. *State v. Concord R.R.*, 62 N.H. 375, 378 (1882).

14. 49 *Report N.H. Railroad Commission* 10 (1893); Charles H. Burns, *Final Argument . . . Before the Railroad Committee* (Aug. 16, 1887); *Manchester & Lawrence v. Concord R.R.*, 66 N.H. 100, 127–28 (1889).

15. *State v. Concord R.R.*, 62 N.H. 375, 377 (1882).

16. *Burke v. Concord R.R.*, 61 N.H. 160, 242–43 (1881).

17. See below 305–06.

18. See above 261–62.

19. *Dow v. Northern R.R.*, 67 N.H. 1, 63–64 (1886).

20. Charles H. Burns, supra note 14, 10.

21. 44 *Report N.H. Railroad Commission* 6 (1888); 45 *Report N.H. Railroad Commission* 11 (1889).

22. Alvin F. Harlow, supra note 9, 304.

23. George S. Philbrick, *Argument . . . in the House of Representatives* 20 (Sept. 15, 1887).

24. George F. Page, *Argument . . . on Behalf of the Business Interests of New Hampshire Before the Railroad Committee [etc.] . . .* 14 (1887).

25. *Journal of the N.H. House of Representatives,* June 1887 Session 782 (1887).

26. Letter From Charles Doe to Charles H. Bell, Jan. 14, 1889, Dartmouth College Archives, Mss. 889114.

27. 44 *Report N.H. Railroad Commission* 9 (1888).

28. *Gregg v. Northern Railroad,* 67 N.H. 452 (1893); 44 *Report N.H. Railroad Commission* 9 (1888); 51 *Report N.H. Railroad Commission* 6 (1895).

29. *Boston, Concord & Montreal v. Boston & Lowell,* 65 N.H. 393, 400–401 (1888).

30. Ibid. 447–49.

31. George Pierce Baker, supra note 6, 170.

32. 45 *Report N.H. Railroad Commission* 12 (1889).

33. *Gregg v. Northern Railroad,* 67 N.H. 452 (1893); *Jones v. Concord & Montreal,* 67 N.H. 234 (1892); *Jones v. Concord & Montreal,* 67 N.H. 119 (1891); *Manchester & Lawrence v. Concord Railroad,* 66 N.H. 100 (1889).

34. 1 Edward Chase Kirkland, *Men, Cities and Transportation: A Study in New England History 1820–1900* 449 (1948); 2 ibid. 431 and 262.

Chapter Twenty. The Tombstones of Our Ancestors:
Constitutional Principles

1. *Ashuelot v. Elliott,* 58 N.H. 451, 452 (1878).

2. *Boody v. Watson,* 64 N.H. 162, 165, 9 Atl. 794, 797 (1886).

3. In re *School-Law Manual,* 63 N.H. 574 (1885); *Willoughby v.*

Holderness, 62 N.H. 227, 228 (1882); *State v. Hayes,* 61 N.H. 264 (1881).

4. *Bingham v. Jewett,* 66 N.H. 382 (1890).

5. *Opinion of the Court,* 60 N.H. 585 (1881); Richard Upton, *A History of the Doctrine of Separation of Powers in New Hampshire* (Unpublished Thesis, 1938, Harvard Law School).

6. Letter From Charles Doe to John Major Shirley, March 9, 1876, Doe Papers, N.H. Sup. Ct.

7. Doe, "A New View of the Dartmouth College Case," 6 *Harv. L. Rev.* 161, 169–70 (1892).

8. *Edes v. Broadman,* 58 N.H. 580, 585 (1879) and *Boody v. Watson,* 64 N.H. 162, 165, 9 Atl. 794, 797 (1886).

9. *Gray v. Jackson,* 51 N.H. 9, 37 (1871).

10. *State v. Hodge,* 50 N.H. 510, 522 (1869).

11. *N.H. Bill of Rights,* Art. 14.

12. *Owen v. Weston,* 63 N.H. 599, 600, 4 Atl. 801, 802 (1885).

13. Doe, supra note 7, 171.

14. *Ricker's Petition,* 66 N.H. 207, 225–26, 29 Atl. 559, 568 (1890).

15. Note, "Doe of New Hampshire: Reflections on a Nineteenth Century Judge," 63 *Harv. L. Rev.* 513, 519 (1950).

16. *Ricker's Petition,* 66 N.H. 207, 254, 29 Atl. 559, 583 (1890).

17. *Rich v. Flanders,* 39 N.H. 304 (1859).

18. *Kent v. Gray,* 53 N.H. 576, 578–80 (1873).

19. *De Lancey v. Insurance Co.,* 52 N.H. 581, 593 (1873).

20. Eastman, "Charles Doe," 2 *Pub. So. N.H. Bar Ass'n* 79, 81 (1896).

21. Letter From Charles Doe to John Major Shirley, n.d., Doe Papers, N.H. Sup. Ct.

22. Letter From Charles Doe to Austin Pike, March 22, 1881, Doe Collection, N.H. Hist. Soc'y.

23. See e.g. McDuffee v. Portland & Rochester Railroad, 52 N.H. 430, 456 (1873).

24. *N.H. Bill of Rights,* Art. 2.

25. *Aldrich v. Wright,* 53 N.H. 398, 400 (1873).

26. *Orr v. Quimby,* 54 N.H. 590, 610 (1874) (dissenting opinion).

27. *Morrison v. Manchester,* 58 N.H. 538, 554 (1879).

28. *Thompson v. Androscoggin River Improvement Co.,* 54 N.H. 545, 548 & 549 (1874). Also *Scott v. Wilson,* 3 N.H. 321 (1825).

29. Note, supra note 15, 521.

30. *Orr v. Quimby,* 54 N.H. 590, 647 (1874) (dissenting opinion).

31. Ibid. 611 (dissenting opinion).

32. Reid, "The Touch of History — The Historical Method of a Common Law Judge," 8 *Am. J. Legal Hist.* 157, 161–62 (1964).

33. *Bristol v. New Chester,* 3 N.H. 524, 535 (1826).

34. *Orr v. Quimby,* 54 N.H. 590, 649 (1874) (dissenting opinion).

35. Letter From Charles Doe to John Major Shirley, March 9, 1876, Doe Papers, N.H. Sup. Ct.

36. Ibid.

37. *State v. Hayes,* 61 N.H. 264, 321 (1881); *State v. Express Co.,* 60 N.H. 219, 253 (1880); *Orr v. Quimby,* 54 N.H. 590, 618 (1874) (dissenting opinion).

38. *Thompson v. Androscoggin River Improvement Co.,* 54 N.H. 545, 556 (1874).

39. *Gould v. Raymond,* 59 N.H. 260, 272 (1879).

40. Ibid. 274. See also *Ashuelot R.R. Co. v. Elliott,* 58 N.H. 451, 452 (1878).

41. Doe, "Lease of Railroad by Majority of Stockholders With Assent of Legislature, II," 8 *Harv. L. Rev.* 396, 407 (1895).

42. *Thompson v. Androscoggin River Improvement Co.,* 54 N.H. 545, 556 (1874).

43. Letter From Charles Doe to John Major Shirley, n.d., Doe Papers, N.H. Sup. Ct.

44. *Thompson v. Androscoggin River Improvement Co.,* 54 N.H. 545, 556–57 (1874).

45. *Gould v. Raymond,* 59 N.H. 260, 275 & 276 (1879).

46. Ibid. 274.

47. Letter From Charles Doe to John Major Shirley, April 29, 1876, Doe Papers, N.H. Sup. Ct.

48. *Corbin's Case, Opinion of the Justices,* 66 N.H. 629, 635, 33 Atl. 1076, 1079 (1891).

Chapter Twenty-One. The Last Lawmaker: *Judicial Power*

1. For the substance of this chapter with extensive notes see Reid, "The Last Law Maker: Charles Doe and Judicial Power," 10 *Wayne L. Rev.* 553 (1964).

2. Harold Gill Reuschlein, *Jurisprudence: Its American Prophets* (1951).

3. *The Legal Mind in America: From Independence to the Civil War* (Perry Miller ed. 1962).

4. Wigmore, "Mr. Justice Holmes," *Mr. Justice Holmes* 212–13 (Felix Frankfurter ed. 1931).

5. Leon Burr Richardson, *William E. Chandler, Republican* 446 (1940).

6. See above 141–46.

7. Pound, "The Place of Judge Story in the Making of American Law," 48 *Am. L. Rev.* 676, 690 (1914).

8. See Chapter VI.

9. *Boody v. Watson,* 64 N.H. 162, 177, 9 Atl. 794, 805–06 (1886).

10. N.H. Constitution, Part Second, Art. 49.

11. *Attorney-General v. Taggart,* 66 N.H. 362, 29 Atl. 1027 (1890).

12. Ibid. 365–66, 29 Atl. at 1029.

13. Ibid. 371, 29 Atl. at 1032.

14. Ibid. 366, 29 Atl. at 1029–30.

15. Dowling, "Executive Disability," 1 *N.H.B.J.* 14, 17 (Jan. 1959).

16. *Boody v. Watson,* 64 N.H. 162, 169, 9 Atl. 794, 800 (1886).

17. Ibid. 170, 9 Atl. at 800.

18. Ibid. 177, 9 Atl. at 806.

19. Ibid. 169, 9 Atl. at 799.

20. *Concord & Montreal Railroad v. Boston and Maine Railroad,* 67 N.H. 464, 465, 41 Atl. 263, 264 (1893).

21. Ibid. 466, 41 Atl. 264.
22. Ibid.
23. See below 356–64.
24. *Concord Manufacturing Co. v. Robertson,* 66 N.H. 1, 28, 25 Atl. 718, 731 (1889).
25. *State v. Gilmanton,* 14 N.H. 467 (1843); *State v. Gilmanton,* 9 N.H. 461 (1838).
26. *Concord Manufacturing Co. v. Robertson,* 66 N.H. 1, 27, 25 Atl. 718, 731 (1889).
27. Hening, "Charles Doe," 8 *Great American Lawyers* 241, 298 (W. D. Lewis ed. 1909).
28. See Chapter XV.
29. See above 268.
30. *Burke v. Concord Railroad,* 61 N.H. 160, 241–42 (1881).
31. *Brooks v. Howison,* 63 N.H. 382, 388 (1885); *Buzzell v. State,* 59 N.H. 61 (1879).
32. *Owen v. Weston,* 63 N.H. 599, 602, 4 Atl. 801, 802 (1885).
33. See above 102–03.
34. *Boody v. Watson,* 63 N.H. 320 (1885).
35. *Boody v. Watson,* 64 N.H. 162, 172, 9 Atl. 794, 802 (1886).
36. See above 283.
37. *Edes v. Boardman,* 58 N.H. 580, 584–85 (1879).
38. *Boody v. Watson,* 64 N.H. 162, 182, 9 Atl. 794, 809 (1886).
39. Ibid. 177, 9 Atl. at 806.
40. Ibid. 198, 9 Atl. at 821 (dissenting opinion).
41. Ibid. 188, 9 Atl. at 813–14.
42. Ibid. 180, 9 Atl. at 808.
43. Ibid. 207–08, 9 Atl. at 828 (dissenting opinion). See below 396–97.
44. Ibid. 180, 9 Atl. at 808.
45. Ibid. 171, 9 Atl. at 801.
46. *Concord Mfg. Co. v. Robertson,* 66 N.H. 1, 20, 25 Atl. 718, 729 (1889).
47. See below 321–22.
48. *Gage v. Gage,* 66 N.H. 282, 297, 29 Atl. 543, 551 (1890) (dissenting opinion).
49. *Walker v. Walker,* 63 N.H. 321, 327 (1885).
50. *Boody v. Watson,* 64 N.H. 162, 179, 9 Atl. 794, 807 (1886).
51. *Walker v. Walker,* 63 N.H. 321, 326 (1885).
52. Ibid. 323.
53. Ibid. 324.
54. Ibid. 322.
55. Ibid. 324.
56. Ibid. 323.
57. Ibid.
58. Hening, supra note 27, 260.
59. *Walker v. Walker,* 63 N.H. 321, 325 (1885).
60. Ibid. 325.
61. Hening, supra note 27, 260.
62. Ibid.

63. *Southern Pacific Co. v. Jensen*, 244 U.S. 205, 221 (1917) (dissenting opinion).

64. See above 128–30.

65. 35 Wis. 425 (1874).

66. Robert S. Hunt, *Law and Locomotives: The Impact of the Railroad on Wisconsin Law in the Nineteenth Century* 109–30 (1958).

67. Alfons J. Beitzinger, *Edward G. Ryan: Lion of the Law* 113–22 (1960).

68. Carpenter, "Charles Doe," 2 *Pub. So. N.H. Bar Ass'n* 103–104 (1896).

69. E.g. *Hale v. Everett*, 53 N.H. 9, 273 (1868) (dissenting opinion). See also *Bingham v. Jewett*, 66 N.H. 382, 29 Atl. 694, 695 (1890).

70. *Edes v. Boardman*, 58 N.H. 580, 590–91 (1879).

71. Note, "Doe of New Hampshire: Reflections on a Nineteenth Century Judge," 63 *Harv. L. Rev.* 513, 519 (1950).

72. *Davis v. George*, 67 N.H. 393, 398, 39 Atl. 979, 982 (1892).

73. Hening, supra note 27, 299.

74. Paul A. Freund, *On Understanding the Supreme Court* 3 (1951).

75. Luce, "Early Makers of New Hampshire Common Law," 5 *Proceedings N.H. Bar Ass'n.* (#3) 5, 21 (1925).

Chapter Twenty-Two. A Frivolous Formality: *The Law of Precedent*

1. *State v. Pike*, 49 N.H. 399, 438 (1869) (concurring opinion).

2. *Lisbon v. Lyman*, 49 N.H. 553, 602 (1870).

3. *Metcalf v. Gilmore*, 59 N.H. 417, 433 (1879).

4. For example, a Nebraska case which stated that it was bound by analogous precedents has been cited as a classic defense of the law of precedent. Roscoe Pound and Theodore F. T. Plucknett, *Reading on the History and System of the Common Law* 272 (3rd ed. 1927). See also, William F. Clarke, *The Soul of the Law* 192–93 (1942).

5. *Beamish v. Beamish*, [1861] 9 H. L. C. 274, 338.

6. *Haley v. Colcord*, 59 N.H. 7, 9 (1879).

7. See *Edgerly v. Barker*, 66 N.H. 434, 472, 31 Atl. 900, 915 (1891).

8. *Boody v. Watson*, 64 N.H. 162, 179, 9 Atl. 794, 807 (1886).

9. *Metcalf v. Gilmore*, 59 N.H. 417, 434 (1879).

10. *Boody v. Watson*, 64 N.H. 162, 179, 9 Atl. 794, 807 (1886).

11. *State v. Perkins*, 53 N.H. 435, 436 (1873).

12. *Aldrich v. Wright*, 53 N.H. 398, 420 (1873).

13. *State v. Hodge*, 50 N.H. 510, 524 (1869).

14. Heywood, "Address," 1 *Grafton & Coös Bar Ass'n Proc.* 85 (1882).

15. Catherine D. Bowen, *Francis Bacon: The Temper of a Man* 146 (1963); Benjamin Cardozo, *The Growth of the Law* 3 (1924).

16. Gray, "General and Particular Intent in Connection with the Rule Against Perpetuities," 9 *Harv. L. Rev.* 242, 246 & 254 (1895).

17. Bingham, "Certain Political Conditions and Tendencies Which Imperil the Integrity and Independence of the Judiciary," *Memorial of Hon. Harry Bingham, LL.D.* 240, 245–46 & 276 (Henry Harrison Metcalf ed. 1910).

18. William E. Chandler, *New Hampshire a Slave State: Commonly Known as the Book of Bargains* 76 (1891).

19. Concord *Evening Monitor*, May 15, 1893, p. 4, col. 4.

20. Carpenter, "Response to the Toast, 'The 58th N.H. Report,'" 1 *Proc. Grafton & Coös Bar Ass'n* 44, 47 & 46 (1883).

21. Hening, "Charles Doe," 8 *Great American Lawyers* 241, 308 (W. D. Lewis ed. 1909).

22. Karl Llewellyn, *The Common Law Tradition: Deciding Appeals* 423 n. 47 (1960).

23. Bingham, supra note 17, 246.

24. Eastman, "Chief-Justice Charles Doe," 9 *Green Bag* 245, 248 (1897).

25. Frink, "Charles Doe," 2 *Proc. So. N.H. Bar Ass'n* 87–88 (1896).

26. Sargent, "Alonzo Philetus Carpenter," 2 *Proc. So. N.H. Bar Ass'n* 262, 263 (1898).

27. Mss. p. 7, Folder 582, Doe Papers, N.H. Sup. Ct.

28. Letter From Charles Doe to John M. Shirley, n.d., Doe Papers, N.H. Sup. Ct.

29. *Reporter's Note*, 49 N.H. vi. viii (1872).

30. *Lisbon v. Lyman*, 49 N.H. 553 (1870); *State v. Pike*, 49 N.H. 553 (1869) (concurring opinion); *State v. Hodge*, 50 N.H. 510 (1869).

31. Jeremiah Smith, *Memoir of Hon. Charles Doe* 27–28 (1897); Smith, "Memoir of Charles Doe," 2 *Proc. So. N.H. Bar Ass'n* 125, 149–50 (1879).

32. Corning, "The Highest Courts of Law in New Hampshire, — Colonial, Provincial, and State," 2 *Green Bag* 469, 487–88 (1890).

33. Allen, "Charles Doe, 1849," 13 *Dartmouth Alumni Mag.* 283, 284 (1921).

34. Letter From Charles H. Bell to Chester A. Arthur, Oct. 14, 1881, in Doe Collection N.H. Hist. Soc'y.

35. Smith, Obituary Note, 9 *Harv. L. Rev.* 534, 535 (1896).

36. Doe, "A New View of the Dartmouth College Case, II," 6 *Harv. L. Rev.* 213, 214 (1892).

37. Jeremy Bentham, *Comments on the Commentaries* 214 (Everett, ed. 1928).

Chapter Twenty-Three. An Evil of Some Magnitude: *The Common Law*

1. *Lisbon v. Lyman*, 49 N.H. 553, 604–5 (1870).

2. Reid, "The Reformer and The Precisian: A Study in Judicial Attitudes," 12 *J. Legal Ed.* 157, 164–65 (1959).

3. *Concord Manufacturing Co. v. Robertson*, 66 N.H. 1, 6, 25 Atl. 718, 720 (1889).

4. Ibid. 26–27, 25 Atl. at 730.

5. See above 221.

6. *Kendall v. Brownson*, 47 N.H. 186, 205 (1866) (dissenting opinion).

7. *McDuffee v. Portland & Rochester Railroad*, 52 N.H. 430, 457 (1873).

8. *Boody v. Watson*, 64 N.H. 162, 171, 9 Atl. 794, 801 (1886).

9. Doe, "A New View of the Dartmouth College Case," 6 *Harv. L. Rev.* 161, 167–68 (1892).

10. *McDuffee v. Portland & Rochester R.R.*, 52 N.H. 430, 455 (1873).

11. Ibid. 456.

12. Ibid. 457.

13. Ibid. 447–48.

14. Ibid. 451.
15. Ibid. 459.

Chapter Twenty-Four. The Perfection of Reason: *The Nature of Law*

1. *Lisbon v. Lyman,* 49 N.H. 553, 571 (1870).
2. See above 145–46.
3. *Kendall v. Brownson,* 47 N.H. 186, 205 (1886) (dissenting opinion). See Hening, "Charles Doe," 8 *Great American Lawyers* 241, 300 (W. D. Lewis ed. 1909).
4. Pound, "Economic Interpretation and the Law of Torts," 53 *Harv. L. Rev.* 365, 367 (1940).
5. See above 144.
6. *State v. Felch,* 58 N.H. 1, 2 (1876).
7. *Haley v. Colcord,* 59 N.H. 7, 8 (1879).
8. See above 145–46.
9. *Aldrich v. Wright,* 53 N.H. 398, 403 (1873).
10. Ibid.
11. Ibid.
12. *McDuffee v. Portland & Rochester Railroad,* 52 N.H. 430, 454 (1873).
13. *Boody v. Watson,* 64 N.H. 162, 171, 9 Atl. 794, 801 (1886).
14. *Concord Manufacturing Co. v. Robertson,* 66 N.H. 1, 18, 25 Atl. 718, 726 (1889).
15. *Sargent v. Sanford,* 66 N.H. 30 (1889).
16. *Edes v. Broadman,* 58 N.H. 580 (1879).
17. *Kent v. Gray,* 53 N.H. 576 (1873).
18. *Owen v. Weston,* 63 N.H. 599, 603, 4 Atl. 801, 803 (1885).
19. Connor, "William Gaston," 3 *Great American Lawyers* 39, 84 (W. D. Lewis ed. 1908).
20. Warren, "Law and The Future," 52 *Fortune* 106 (Nov. 1955).
21. Nelles, "Towards Legal Understanding, I," 34 *Colum. L. Rev.* 862, 885 (1934).
22. *Morgan v. Joyce,* 66 N.H. 476 (1891); *Gagnon v. Connor,* 64 N.H. 276 (1886).
23. Letter From Charles Doe to Frank Nesmith Parsons, Oct. 28, 1895, in Doe Collection, N.H. Hist. Soc'y.
24. *McDuffee v. Portland & Rochester Railroad,* 52 N.H. 430, 453–54 (1873).
25. *Burleigh v. Clough,* 52 N.H. 267, 281–82 (1872) (per Foster, J.). looked up).
26. *Cocheco Aqueduct Association v. Boston & Maine R.R.,* 62 N.H. 345, 346 (1882).
27. *Edes v. Boardman,* 58 N.H. 580, 588 (1879).
28. Heck, "The Jurisprudence of Interests," in *The Jurisprudence of Interests* 31, 35 (Schock ed. 1948).
29. See above 135–36.
30. *Green v. Gilbert,* 60 N.H. 144, 145 (1880).
31. Ibid. 144.
32. *Rixford v. Smith,* 52 N.H. 355, 362 (1872).
33. *Kent v. Gray,* 53 N.H. 576, 580 (1873).

34. *McDuffee v. Portland & Rochester Railroad,* 52 N.H. 430, 448 (1873).

35. Ibid. 454.

36. Mark DeWolfe Howe, *Justice Oliver Wendell Holmes: The Proving Years* 67 (1963).

37. *Thompson v. Androscoggin River Improvement Co.,* 54 N.H. 545, 556 (1874).

38. Ibid. 552.

39. *Metcalf v. Gilmore,* 59 N.H. 417, 435 (1879).

40. Quoted in *Memoirs of Jeremiah Mason* 176 n. "a" (G. J. Clark ed. 1917).

41. Quoted in Max Lerner, *The Mind and Faith of Justice Holmes* 368 (1943).

42. *American Banana Company v. United Fruit Company,* 213 U.S. 347, 356 (1909).

43. *Corbin's Case, Opinion of the Justices,* 66 N.H. 629, 632, 33 Atl. 1076, 1078 (1891).

44. Ibid.

45. Palmer, "Defense Against Leviathan," 32 *A.B.A.J.* 328, 332 (1946).

46. *Stewart v. Emerson,* 52 N.H. 301, 314 (1872).

Chapter Twenty-Five. A Mass of Customs: *The Origin of Law*

1. See above 285–86.

2. File #579, p. 12, Doe Papers, N.H. Sup. Ct.

3. *Haley v. Colcord,* 59 N.H. 7, 9 (1879).

4. Ibid. 8 (citations omitted).

5. Roscoe Pound, *An Introduction to the Philosophy of Law* 53 (1922).

6. Pound, "My Philosophy of Law," *My Philosophy of Law: Credos of Sixteen American Scholars* 249, 258 (Julius Rosenthal Foundation, 1941).

7. Reid, "A Touch of History: The Historical Method of a Common Law Judge," 8 *Am. J. Legal Hist.* 157 (1964).

8. *Lisbon v. Lyman,* 49 N.H. 553, 569 (1870).

9. Ibid. 581–82.

10. *Holt v. Downs,* 58 N.H. 170, 173 (1872).

11. *State v. Rollins,* 8 N.H. 550, 561 (1837); Peaslee, "Common Law in the Making," 5 *Proc. N.H. Bar Ass'n* 111, 119 (1924).

12. *Smith v. Furbish,* 68 N.H. 123, 149, 44 Atl. 398, 411 (1894) and *Ricker's Petition,* 66 N.H. 207, 226, 29 Atl. 559, 568 (1890).

13. Letter From Charles Doe to Charles H. Bell, Sept. 7, 1892, Mss. No. 892507, Dartmouth College Archives.

14. *Brooks v. Howison,* 63 N.H. 382, 386–87 (1885).

15. Ibid. 386.

16. Ibid.

17. *Stratton v. Stratton and Ladd,* 58 N.H. 473, 474 (1878).

18. *Brown v. Collins,* 53 N.H. 442, 448, 16 Am. Rep. 372 (1873).

19. *Orr v. Quimby,* 54 N.H. 590, 636 (1874) (dissenting opinion).

20. Ibid. 637.

21. See above 220–23.

22. File #579, p. 43, Doe Papers, N.H. Sup. Ct.

23. *Concord Manufacturing Co. v. Robertson,* 66 N.H. 1, 6, 25 Atl. 718, 720 (1889).

24. *Pierce v. Baker,* 58 N.H. 531, 532 (1879).

25. *Brooks v. Howison,* 63 N.H. 382, 387 (1885).

26. *DeLancey v. Insurance Co.,* 52 N.H. 581, 590 (1873); *Gray v. Jackson,* 51 N.H. 9, 38 (1871).

27. Harold Fisher Wilson, *The Hill Country of Northern New England* 107 (1936).

28. *Page v. Hodgdon,* 63 N.H. 53, 54 (1884).

29. *Blaisdell v. Stone,* 60 N.H. 507, 509 (1881).

30. See above 135–36.

31. *Brown v. Collins,* 53 N.H. 442, 450, 16 Am. Rep. 372 (1873).

32. *Blaisdell v. Stone,* 60 N.H. 507, 509 (1881).

33. See above 135.

34. Quoted in *Brown v. Collins,* 53 N.H. 442, 447, 16 Am. Rep. 372 (1873).

35. Holmes, "The Theory of Torts," 7 *Am. L. Rev.* 652, 653 (1873).

36. *Morse v. Boston & Lowell Railroad,* 66 N.H. 148, 149 (1889), quoting *Avery v. Maxwell,* 4 N.H. 36 (1827).

37. See above 303–05.

38. *Concord Manufacturing Co. v. Robertson,* 66 N.H. 1, 15, 25 Atl. 718, 725 (1889).

39. Ibid. 6, 25 Atl. at 720.

40. Ibid. 24, 25 Atl. at 729.

41. Ibid. 4, 25 Atl. at 719.

42. Ibid. 4–5, 25 Atl. at 720.

43. Ibid. 17–18, 25 Atl. at 726.

44. Ibid. 22, 25 Atl. at 728.

45. Ibid. 18, 25 Atl. at 726.

46. Ibid. 19, 25 Atl. at 727.

47. Ibid. 20, 25 Atl. at 727.

48. Ibid. 19, 25 Atl. at 726–27.

49. *Percy Summer Club v. Astle,* 145 Fed. 53, 59 (C.C.D. N.H. 1906).

50. Hening, "Charles Doe," 8 *Great American Lawyers* 241, 298 (W. D. Lewis ed. 1909).

51. See above 304–05.

52. *Percy Summer Club v. Astle,* 145 Fed. 53, 60 (C.C.D. N.H. 1906).

53. Ibid.

54. *Concord Manufacturing Co. v. Robertson,* 66 N.H. 1, 29–30, 25 Atl. 718, 732 (1889).

55. *State v. Welch,* 66 N.H. 178, 28 Atl. 21 (1889).

56. *Percy Summer Club v. Welch,* 66 N.H. 180, 28 Atl. 22 (1889).

57. Supra note 12.

58. Henry James, *The American Scene* 23 (1946).

59. Max Lerner, *The Mind and Faith of Justice Holmes* 45 (1943).

Chapter Twenty-Six. An Incorrigible Despot: *Relations with the Bar*

1. Concord *Daily Monitor,* Aug. 2, 1881; Concord *Daily Monitor,* Aug. 25, 1881.

2. Herbert I. Goss, *T. Thorndyke Attorney-at-Law: The Romance of a Young Lawyer* 455 (1907).

3. *Delano's Case,* 58 N.H. 5, 6 (1876); Concord *Daily Monitor,* Sept. 1, 1881.

4. Concord *Daily Monitor,* Oct. 11, Oct. 12, and Oct. 14, 1881; Leon Burr Richardson, *William E. Chandler, Republican* 276–79 (1940); Letter From John Mitchell to William E. Chandler, Dec. 10, 1881, Chandler Collection, N.H. Hist. Soc'y.

5. Eastman, "Chief-Justice Charles Doe," 9 *Green Bag* 245, 251 (1897); Letter From John Mitchell to William E. Chandler, Dec. 10, 1881, Chandler Collection, N.H. Hist. Soc'y; Letter From Charles Doe to William E. Chandler, Dec. 3, 1881, Chandler Collection, N.H. Hist. Soc'y; Letter From W. E. Stevens to William E. Chandler, Oct. 6, 1881, Chandler Collection, N.H. Hist. Soc'y.

6. Concord *Daily Monitor,* July 27, 1881.

7. Letter From Ossian Ray to William E. Chandler, Oct. 3, 1881, Chandler Collection, N.H. Hist. Soc'y; New York *World,* Dec. 17, 1881; New York *Times,* Nov. 13, 1881; for an extended discussion see Reid, "Of Men, and Minks, and a Mischievous Machinator: Did the Mink Case Keep Judge Doe Off the United States Supreme Court?" 1 (No. 2) *N.H.B.J.* 23 (1959).

8. Letter From Jeremiah Smith to William E. Chandler, Oct. 22, 1881, Chandler Coll., N.H. Hist. Soc'y; Letter From W. E. Stevens to William E. Chandler, Dec. 12, 1881, Chandler Collection, N.H. Hist. Soc'y.

9. Concord *Daily Monitor,* Oct. 18, 1881.

10. Concord *Daily Monitor,* Oct. 18, 1881.

11. *Aldrich v. Wright,* 53 N.H. 398, 421 (1873).

12. Letter From Jeremiah Smith to William E. Chandler, Oct. 20, 1881, Chandler Collection, N.H. Hist. Soc'y; Concord *Daily Monitor,* Oct. 24, 1881.

13. New York *Tribune,* Dec. 19, 1881; Charles Fairman, *Mr. Justice Miller and the Supreme Court* 384 (1939); New York *Herald,* Dec. 18, 1881.

14. New York *Tribune,* Dec. 29, 1881; New York *Times,* Dec. 19, 1881; New York *Tribune,* Dec. 20, 1881.

15. *Harper's Weekly,* Dec. 31, 1881; *The Nation,* Dec. 22, 1881; New York *Herald,* Dec. 21, 1881; New York *Daily Graphic,* Dec. 20, 1881; New York *Tribune,* Dec. 20, 1881; Letter From Charles Doe to William E. Chandler, Jan. 5, 1882, Chandler Collection, N.H. Hist. Soc'y; Letter From William E. Chandler to Charles Doe, Jan. 11, 1882, Chandler Collection, N.H. Hist. Soc'y.

16. Letter From William E. Chandler to Charles Doe, Dec. 26, 1881, Chandler Collection, N.H. Hist. Soc'y.

17. Letter From Charles Doe to William E. Chandler, Jan. 5, 1882, Chandler Collection, N.H. Hist. Soc'y; Letter From Charles Doe to William E. Chandler, Jan. 13, 1882, Chandler Collection, N.H. Hist. Soc'y.

18. 1 Merlo J. Pusey, *Charles Evans Hughes* 275 (1951).

19. Concord *Daily Monitor,* Dec. 21, 1881; Parsons, "The President's Address," 3 *Proc. N.H. Bar Ass'n* 209, 210 (1912).

20. 1 *Proc. Grafton & Coös Bar Ass'n* 22 (1882); Bingham, "Certain Political Conditions and Tendencies which Imperil the Integrity and Independence of the Judiciary," in *Memorial of Hon. Harry Bingham, LL.D.,* 240, 251–252 (Henry Harrison Metcalf ed. 1910).

21. 1 *Proc. Grafton & Coös Bar Ass'n* 43–44 (1882).

22. Carpenter, "Address," ibid. at 45–6.

23. 1 *Proc. Grafton & Coös Bar Ass'n* 301 (1889); *Percy Summer Club v. Astle*, 145 Fed. 53, 57, 58 and 64 (C.C.D. N.H. 1906); *Owen v. Weston*, 63 N.H. 599, 605, 4 Atl. 801, 805 (1885).

24. Letter From William E. Chandler to C. J. Amidon, March 13, 1893, Chandler Collection, N.H. Hist. Soc'y.

25. 47 *Report N.H. RR. Comm.* 23 (1891).

26. *Opinion of the Justices* (popularly known as *Corbin's Case*), 66 N.H. 629, 33 Atl. 1076 (1891).

27. Letter From Wayne MacVeagh to William E. Chandler, April 7, 1891, Chandler Coll., N.H. Hist. Soc'y; Letter From Wayne MacVeagh to William E. Chandler, April 3, 1891, Chandler Coll., N.H. Hist. Soc'y.

28. Letter From Charles Doe to William E. Chandler, March 31, 1885, Chandler Coll., N.H. Hist. Soc'y; Letter From Charles Doe to William E. Chandler, March 27, 1885, Chandler Coll., N.H. Hist. Soc'y; Letter From Charles Doe to William E. Chandler, Jan. 5, 1882, Chandler Coll., N.H. Hist. Soc'y; Letter From William E. Chandler to Charles Doe, Jan. 11, 1882, Chandler Coll., N.H. Hist. Soc'y.

29. William E. Chandler, *New Hampshire a Slave State: Commonly Known as the Book of Bargains* 75–6 (1891).

30. William E. Chandler, *New Hampshire's Enslavement By the Free Passes, the Ale and Rum and the Corruption Money of the Railroads* 4–5 (1891).

31. *The 42-Page Pamphlet of the Judges* 3 (reprinted in William E. Chandler, *The People's Interest in the Concord Railroad* 5 [1895]).

32. Ibid. 35.

33. Ibid. 15.

34. Concord *Evening Monitor*, May 6, 1893; *Independent Statesman*, March 30, 1893; Concord *Evening Monitor*, May 6, 1893.

35. Concord *Evening Monitor*, May 6, 1893; *Independent Statesman*, April 20, 1893.

36. Concord *Evening Monitor*, May 15, 1893; *Independent Statesman*, Aug. 3, 1893; Concord *Evening Monitor*, May 15, 1893.

37. Concord *Evening Monitor*, May 6, 1893.

38. Letter From Orville Hitchcock Platt to William E. Chandler, May 9, 1893, Chandler Coll., N.H. Hist. Soc'y; Leon Burr Richardson, supra note 4, 458.

39. Letter From Charles Doe to William E. Chandler, Jan. 19, 1882, Chandler Coll., N.H. Hist. Soc'y.

40. Richard Upton, *A History of the Doctrine of Separation of Powers in New Hampshire* 156–59 (Unpublished thesis, 1938, Harvard Law School Library).

41. Hening, "Charles Doe," 8 *Great American Lawyers* 241, 309 (W. D. Lewis ed. 1897);

42. Allen, "Charles Doe, 1849," 13 *Dartmouth Alumni Mag* 283, 285 (March, 1921).

43. Parsons, "William Martin Chase," 4 (No. 2) *Proc. N.H. Bar Ass'n* 152, 154 (1918).

44. Cross, "Charles Doe," 2 *Pub. So. N.H. Bar Ass'n* 91–92 (1896).

45. Ibid.

46. Herbert I. Goss, supra note 2, 217.

Chapter Twenty-Seven. The Wagers of Battle: *Colleagues*

1. Letter From William E. Chandler to Charles Doe, Jan. 11, 1882, Chandler Coll., N.H. Hist. Soc'y; *Independent Statesman* (Concord), July 27, 1876.

2. Letter From Charles Doe to John Major Shirley, n.d., Doe Papers, N.H. Sup. Ct.

3. Jeremiah Smith, *Memoir of Hon. Charles Doe* 18 (1897); Smith, "Memoir of Charles Doe," 2 *Proc. So. N.H. Bar Ass'n* 125, 140 (1897). The two decisions were *Underhill v. Manchester,* 45 N.H. 214 (1864) and *Fifield v. Northern Railroad,* 42 N.H. 225 (1860).

4. But see *Stevens v. Merrill,* 41 N.H. 309 (1860) (Bell for court; Fowler and Doe dissenting); *Davis v. School District* in Haverhill, 44 N.H. 398 (1862) (Bartlett for court; Bell and Doe "doubted").

5. Jeremiah Smith, supra note 3, 18; Smith, supra note 3, 140.

6. 47 N.H. 120 (1865) (Doe dissenting at 140).

7. *Kendall v. Brownson,* 47 N.H. 186, 191 (1866) (dissenting opinion).

8. Ibid. 196 (dissenting opinion).

9. Ibid. 192. Doe's views were adopted by the court in *Tenney v. Knowlton,* 60 N.H. 572 (1881).

10. *Rice v. Society,* 56 N.H. 191 (1875); *Cole v. Lake Co.,* 54 N.H. 242 (1874).

11. Laurence M. Crosbie, *The Phillips Exeter Academy: A History* 74 (1924); Luce, "Early Makers of New Hampshire Common Law," 5 (No. 3) *Proc. N.H. Bar Ass'n* 5, 19 (1925); *Eastman v. Clark,* 53 N.H. 276 (1872) (Smith at 279; Doe concurring at 290); Note, "Doe of New Hampshire: Reflections On a Nineteenth Century Judge," 63 *Harv. L. Rev.* 513, 520, n. 56 (1950).

12. Williston, "Jeremiah Smith," 30 *Harv. Graduates' Mag.* 153, 156 and 158 (1921); Beale, "Jeremiah Smith," 35 *Harv. L. Rev.* 1, 5 (1921).

13. Wait, "Alonzo Philetus Carpenter," 2 *Pub. So. N.H. Bar Ass'n* 268, 270 (1898); For an extended discussion of the Doe-Carpenter relationship see Reid, "The Reformer and the Precisian: A Study in Judicial Attitudes," 12 *J. Legal Ed.* 157 (1959).

14. Peaslee, "Common Law in the Making," 5 *Proc. N.H. Bar Ass'n* 111, 112 (1924).

15. Ladd, "Alonzo Philetus Carpenter," 1 *Proc. N.H. Bar Ass'n* 185, 187 (1899).

16. Hening, "Charles Doe," 8 *Great American Lawyers* 241, 303 (W. D. Lewis ed. 1909).

17. *Boody v. Watson,* 63 N.H. 320 (1885).

18. *Boody v. Watson,* 64 N.H. 162, 164, 9 Atl. 794, 796 (1886).

19. Ibid. 207, 9 Atl. at 828 (dissenting opinion).

20. Ibid. 171, 9 Atl. at 802.

21. Ibid. 200, 9 Atl. at 823 (dissenting opinion).

22. Ibid. 167, 9 Atl. at 799.

23. Ibid. 205, 9 Atl. at 827 (dissenting opinion).

24. Ibid. 175, 9 Atl. at 804.

25. Ibid. 196, 9 Atl. at 820 (dissenting opinion).

26. Ibid. 206, 9 Atl. at 827 (dissenting opinion).

27. Ibid. 177–78, 9 Atl. at 806.

28. Ibid. 207–08, 9 Atl. at 827–28 (dissenting opinion).

29. Ibid. 181, 9 Atl. at 809.

30. Ibid. 194, 9 Atl. at 819 (dissenting opinion).

31. Ibid. 173, 9 Atl. at 802–03.

32. Ibid. 197, 9 Atl. at 821 (dissenting opinion).

33. Ibid. 172, 9 Atl. at 802.

34. Carpenter, "Charles Doe," 2 *Proc. So. N.H. Bar Ass'n* 102, 104 (1896); *Boody v. Watson,* 64 N.H. 162, 198, 9 Atl. 794 (1886) (dissenting opinion).

35. Aldrich, "Alonzo P. Carpenter," 2 *Proc. So. N.H. Bar Ass'n* 297, 304–05 (1899).

36. Hall, "Alonzo Philetus Carpenter, 2 *Proc. So. N.H. Bar Ass'n* 265, 267 (1898); Letter From Charles Doe to Harry Hibard, Sept. 26, 1870, Doe Coll., N.H. Hist. Soc'y.

37. Letter From Charles Doe to William E. Chandler, June 1, 1878, Chandler Coll., N.H. Hist. Soc'y; Letter From Charles Doe to Mason Tappan, May 15, 1878, Doe Coll. N.H. Hist. Soc'y.

Chapter Twenty-Eight. A Peculiar Mode of Expression: *Common-Law Method*

1. Holmes, "Privilege, Malice, and Intent," 8 *Harv. L. Rev.* 1, 7 (1894); Hening, "Charles Doe," in 8 *Great American Lawyers* 241, 302 (W. D. Lewis ed. 1909).

2. Hening, ibid. 302; Peaslee, "Common Law in the Making," 5 *Proc. N.H. Bar Ass'n* 111, 112 (1924).

3. Smith, "Chief Justice Doe," 2 *Proc. So. N.H. Bar Ass'n* 81, 82 (1896).

4. *Lisbon v. Lyman,* 49 N.H. 553, 583 (1870).

5. Millar, "Notabilia of American Civil Procedure, 1887–1937," 50 *Harv. L. Rev.* 1017, 1051 (1937); Scott, "Progress of the Law — Civil Procedure," 33 *Harv. L. Rev.* 236, 249–50 (1919); See also Hening, *supra* note 1, 258.

6. *Janvrin v. Fogg,* 49 N.H. 340, 354 (1870).

7. *Boody v. Watson,* 64 N.H. 162, 173, 9 Atl. 794, 803 (1897).

8. *Smith v. Furnish,* 68 N.H. 123, 133, 44 Atl. 398, 403 (1894).

9. See above 105–06.

10. *Darling v. Westmoreland,* 52 N.H. 401, 408 (1872); *Colburn v. Groton,* 64 N.H. 151, 153, 28 Atl. 95, 96 (1889); *Boody v. Watson,* 64 N.H. 162, 186, 9 Atl. 794, 812 (1886).

11. *Darling v. Westmoreland,* 52 N.H. 401, 408 (1872).

12. *Edgerly v. Barker,* 66 N.H. 434, 471, 31 Atl. 900, 914 (1891); *Colburn v. Groton,* 66 N.H. 151, 153, 28 Atl. 95, 96 (1889); *Darling v. Westmoreland,* 52 N.H. 401, 408 (1872); *Attorney-General v. Taggart,* 66 N.H. 362, 369, 29 Atl. 1027, 1031 (1890).

13. *State v. Pike,* 49 N.H. 399, 407 (1869); *Colburn v. Groton,* 66 N.H.

151, 153–54, 28 Atl. 95, 96 (1889). See also *Holman v. Manning,* 65 N.H. 92, 18 Atl. 746 (1889).

14. *Jenne v. Harrisville,* 63 N.H. 405 (1885).

15. *Merrill v. Perkins,* 59 N.H. 343, 345 (1874); *Amoskeag Mfg. Co v. Head,* 59 N.H. 332, 338 (1879).

16. *Owen v. Weston,* 63 N.H. 599, 605, 4 Atl. 801, 805 (1885); *Bemis v. Morey,* 62 N.H. 511 (1883); *Merrill v. Perkins,* 61 N.H. 262 (1881); *Colburn v. Groton,* 66 N.H. 151, 154, 28 Atl. 95, 96 (1889); *Fuller v. Bailey,* 58 N.H. 71 (1877); *Brooks v. Howard,* 58 N.H. 91 (1877); *Dearborn v. Newhall,* 63 N.H. 301 (1885).

17. *Dearborn v. Newhall,* ibid. 302–03.

18. See above 126–27.

19. *Kimball v. Bible Society,* 65 N.H. 139, 149, 23 Atl. 83, 87 (1889).

20. *Kendall v. Green,* 67 N.H. 557, 559, 42 Atl. 178 (1893).

21. See above 127–30.

22. *Edgerly v. Barker,* 66 N.H. 434, 447, 31 Atl. 900, 902 (1891).

23. Ibid. 472, 31 Atl. at 913.

24. *Stevens v. Underhill,* 67 N.H. 68, 72, 36 Atl. 370, 372 (1883) (dissenting opinion).

25. See discussions of *Green v. Gilbert* above 345 and *Androscoggin River* above 346–47.

26. Gray, "General and Particular Intent in Connection With the Rule Against Perpetuities," 9 *Harv. L. Rev.* 242, 243 (1895).

27. *State v. Pike,* 49 N.H. 399, 442 (1869).

Chapter Twenty-Nine. The Obscurity of Over-Elaboration: *Style and Influence*

1. For an extended discussion of the material in this chapter see Reid, "The Obscurity of Over-Elaboration: The Style and Influence of Mr. Justice Doe," 24 *Pitts. L. Rev.* 59 (1962) and Reid, "Almost a Hobby," 49 *Vir. L. Rev.* 58 (1963).

2. Jeremiah Smith, *Memoir of Hon. Charles Doe* 19–20 (1897); Smith, "Memoir of Charles Doe," 2 *Proc. So. N.H. Bar Ass'n* 125, 141–42 (1897); Letter from Jeremiah Smith, Jr., to William E. Chandler, Oct. 20, 1881, Chandler Coll., N.H. Hist. Soc'y.

3. Hening, "Charles Doe," in 8 *Great American Lawyers* 241, 243 (W. D. Lewis ed. 1909).

4. Letter From Charles Doe to John M. Shirley, April 29, 1876, in Doe Papers, N.H. Sup. Ct.

5. Jeremiah Smith, supra note 2 at 27; Smith, supra note 2 at 149; *Dow v. Northern R.R.,* 67 N.H. 1, 3 n. 1, 36 Atl. 510, 511 n. 1 (1886); I Edward Chase Kirkland, *Men, Cities and Transportation: A Study in New England History 1820-1900* 462–63 (1948); William E. Chandler, *The People's Interest in the Concord Railroad of New Hampshire* 9 (part 2) (1895).

6. 30 *Am. L. Rev.* 286 n. 1 (1896).

7. Letter From Charles Doe to Clark Bell, Jan. 10, 1889, in Bell, "Editorial: The Right and Wrong Test in Cases of Homicide by the Insane," 16 *Medico-Legal J.* 260, 266 (n.d.).

8. *Blaisdell v. Stone,* 60 N.H. 507 (1881); *Smith v. Marden,* 60 N.H. 509 (1881).

9. Leon Burr Richardson, *William E. Chandler: Republican* 446 (1940).

10. Letter From Charles Doe to William S. Ladd, Feb. 22, 1872, quoted in Hening, supra note 3, 259; *Fuller v. Bailey,* 58 N.H. 71 (1877).

11. Folder 579, Doe Papers, N.H. Sup. Ct.

12. See above 135.

13. Dover (N.H.) *Enquirer,* Dec. 19, 1890. See also Boston *Daily Globe,* Dec. 16, 1890; Boston *Journal,* Dec. 19, 1890; Letter From Isaac Sawtelle to his counsel, Dec. 26, 1890, in Dover (N.H.) *Enquirer,* Jan. 9, 1891.

14. *State v. Sawtelle,* 66 N.H. 488, 32 Atl. 831 (1891).

15. Eastman, "Chief-Justice Charles Doe," 9 *Green Bag* 245, 250–51 (1897).

16. Plymouth *Record,* Nov. 21, 1891; *Independent Statesman,* Dec. 3, 1891; Dover *Enquirer,* Dec. 4, 1891; But see Roberts, "Famous Murder Trial Conducted at Plymouth in 1891," Laconia *Evening Citizen,* May 27, 1961.

17. Hening, supra note 3, 263 n. 1.

18. Dover *Enquirer,* Nov. 27, 1891 and Oct. 2, 1891.

19. Concord *Evening Monitor,* Nov. 19, 1891.

20. Plymouth *Record,* Nov. 21, 1891; Concord *Evening Monitor,* Nov. 25, 1891; Portland *Press* quoted in Dover *Enquirer,* Nov. 27, 1891; Brooklyn *Standard Union* quoted in Concord *Evening Monitor,* Nov. 23, 1891.

21. Concord *Evening Monitor,* Nov. 19, 1891; Plymouth *Record,* Dec. 5, 1891; Hening, supra note 3, 262.

22. *Ball v. United States,* 140 U.S. 118, 129 & 131 (1891).

23. Concord *Evening Monitor,* Nov. 25, 1891.

24. *Independent Statesman,* Dec. 3, 1891; William E. Chandler, supra note 5, 48 (part 2).

25. See New York *Sun* for Nov. 21, 1891.

26. Quoted in Concord *Evening Monitor,* Dec. 3, 1891.

27. *Independent Statesman,* Dec. 3, 1891.

28. Concord *Evening Monitor,* Dec. 3, 1891.

29. Karl Llewellyn, *The Common Law Tradition: Deciding Appeals* 5–6 (1960).

30. Eastman, supra note 15, 246.

Chapter Thirty. Born to the Judgeship: *The Heritage*

1. See remarks in Cross, "Charles Doe," 2 *Proc. So. N.H. Bar Ass'n* 91, 94 (1896).

2. Reported in Boston *Morning Journal,* March 10, 1896.

3. Printed in Concord *Daily Monitor,* Feb. 20, 1896.

4. *The Dartmouth,* June 14, 1895, p. 333.

5. Reported in Boston *Daily Globe,* March 10, 1896.

6. See Dover *Republican,* March 2, 1896.

7. *Plessy v. Ferguson,* 163 U.S. 537 (1896).

8. Owen Wister, *The Virginian* 504 (1925 edition).

9. Jewett, "The Old Town of Berwick," 16 *N. Eng. Mag.* 597, 607 (1894).

10. Sarah O. Jewett, *Deephaven* 190 (1877).

11. Henry McFarland, *Sixty Years in Concord and Elsewhere: Personal Recollections* 17 (1899).

12. Letter From Charles Doe to John Henry Wigmore, Feb. 4, 1895, Wigmore Coll., Northwestern Univ. Law Lib.

13. File 582, Doe Papers, N.H. Sup. Ct.

14. Draft Letter From Charles Doe to Frank N. Parsons, Feb. 26, 1896, File 580, ibid.

15. Ibid.

16. Pike, "Memories of Judge Doe," 3 *N.H. Bar Ass'n Proc.* 463, 484 (1916).

17. Draft Letter, supra note 14.

18. Reported in Boston *Daily Globe*, March 10, 1896, and Boston *Morning Journal*, March 10, 1896.

19. *Strafford Inquirer* (Dover), March 11, 1828.

20. Aldrich, "Alonzo P. Carpenter," 2 *Proc. So. N.H. Bar Ass'n* 297, 326 (1899).

21. Letter From John Henry Wigmore to Robert G. Pike, March 27, 1916, in Pike, supra note 16, 477; Letter From Jeremiah Smith to John Henry Wigmore, March 20, 1896, Wigmore Coll., Northwestern Univ. Law Lib.

22. Aldrich, supra note 20, 326; Concord *Evening Monitor*, March 9, 1896.

23. Sarah Orne Jewett, *A Country Doctor* 38 (1884).

24. Boston *Daily Globe*, March 10, 1896.

25. Concord *Evening Monitor*, March 9, 1896.

26. Otis G. Hammond, *Some Things About New Hampshire* 54–57 (2d ed. 1930).

27. Book Review, 18 *Harv. L. Rev.* 478 (1905).

28. Pound, "The Place of Judge Story in the Making of American Law," 1 *Mass. L.Q.* 121, 134 (1916) (also 48 *Am. L. Rev.* 676).

29. Roscoe Pound, *Formative Era of American Law* 4, 30–31 n. 2 (1938).

30. Hurst, "Who is the Great Appellate Judge?" 24 *Ind. L.J.* 394, 397 (1949).

31. Burleigh, "Charles Doe," 2 *Proc. So. N.H. Bar Ass'n* 101 (1896).

32. Smith, Obituary Note, 9 *Harv. L. Rev.* 534, 535 (1896).

33. Allen, "Charles Doe, 1849," 13 *Dart. Alumni Mag.* 283, 284 (1921); Cross, "Charles Doe," 2 *Proc. So. N.H. Bar Ass'n* 91, 93 (1896).

INDEX